Christianity
and Creation

Christianity and Creation

*The Essence of the Christian Faith
and Its Future Among Religions*

A Systematic Theology

James P. Mackey

continuum

NEW YORK • LONDON

2006

The Continuum International Publishing Group Inc
80 Maiden Lane, New York, NY 10038

The Continuum International Publishing Group Ltd
The Tower Building, 11 York Road, London SE1 7NX

Printed in the United States of America

Library of Congress Cataloging-in-Publication Data

Mackey, James Patrick.
    Christianity and creation : the essence of the Christian faith and its future among religions / James P. Mackey.
        p.   cm.
    Includes bibliographical references.
    ISBN-13: 978-0-8264-1895-1 (hardcover : alk. paper)
    ISBN-10: 0-8264-1895-3 (hardcover : alk. paper)
    ISBN-13: 978-0-8264-1907-1 (pbk. : alk. paper)
    ISBN-10: 0-8264-1907-0 (pbk. : alk. paper)
    1. Christianity – Essence, genius, nature. 2. Christianity – Forecasting.
3. Christianity and other religions.   I. Title.
BT60.M28 2006
230 – dc22

                                                            2006016050

For the three principal graces,
God given, that for me changed
All of this ambivalent world
To grace, and to hope without end

Noelle
Ciara   James

Contents

Part Two
CHRISTIANITY:
THE RELIGION THAT DEVELOPED FROM
THE FAITH OF JESUS THE JEW

Preface

The body of this book is written for those who still maintain a thoughtful and preferably critical interest in religion, whether they still retain any allegiance to Christianity, or indeed to any other religion in a world in which all religions are increasingly thrown together, sometimes violently, or their interest lies rather in the decline of religions that they have personally left behind, some with a sense of loss or betrayal, others with a more positive intent to contribute to the loss to the world, again either of Christianity or of any and all religions. But the Prologue to this book is written for a more specialized group. For practitioners and students of the theological profession. For students and young professional theologians starting out upon an increasingly hazardous profession, and wanting some undemanding overview of the more recent background to the context, mood and prospects of contemporary Christian theology. And for older professional theologians who like me have worked and lived through the sequence of theological movements that featured during the last century and now constitute for better or worse that century's bequest to our theological posterity; and who would welcome a concise aide memoire. The Prologue therefore can be passed over unread by those who have broader interests in Christianity, or in a brief history of Christian thought since the time of the Founder, or who are more particularly interested in Christianity's present rather beleaguered status and its future among the religions and the religionless of the world.

But I make no bones about the fact that I would certainly like to persuade these latter, as also the former, that the Christian theology contained in the body of this work is a good and true Christian theology, merely summarized and relatively underdeveloped no doubt, but for all that quite useful for this liminal time and for the foreseeable future. And if I could so persuade people, then at the very least we professional Christian theologians should not seem to ourselves or to those who have the unenviable task of following us, to have spent significant parts of the last century stumbling about rather haphazardly from theological topic to theological topic, finishing none, and never even attempting to bring all of these topics together, if only to see if Christian theology as a whole was going any distance at all toward the goal of offering an acceptable theology for our time.

For I believe that despite all of our stop-start/change-the-subject tactics, we were groping our way through accumulated and entangled overgrowth, and finding and missing and finding again the true theological way for this new millennium. And we are now at the stage at which we can go back over the ground covered and, if only by following the directions evident from each piece of the path re-traveled, and joining them up across the ground missed, we can see the true path for theology from the recent past through a somewhat puzzled present and into the immediate future. In this way, if the Prologue's account be at all true, the theology of the last century of the last millennium will lend its own probative force to the theology which in the body of this work is nevertheless presented as a stand-alone or, at least, a standing-on-sacred-scriptures theology. A thoroughly scriptural theology that is yet verifiable and falsifiable on the self-same universal and ordinary terms by which we verify whatever we hold true and valuable and desirable. These terms being the terms of our experience of life and of the quality of life in this natural creation, to which all that is truly true and good and beautiful contributes.

Yet, even though the Prologue is written mainly for professional theologians or others who have spent some time in the study of theology, I have not provided it with the obligatory apparatus criticus of footnotes and references. I have instead added as an appendix a list of the main publications in which I (like many others of my theological generation) engaged with the main movements in theology, philosophy, and culture that covered the greater part of the last century. This should provide for those who feel they need such things plentiful sources of notes and references, together with more sustained accounts of protagonists and arguments, that should help the more professional scholarly reader to take a more critical view both of the very general judgments that make up the Prologue, and of the positions accordingly taken and maintained in the body of this book.

For I provide the main body of this work also with no apparatus criticus whatever, nothing but scripture references and the odd poem, or title of a book, or mention by name of some philosopher or theologian of note; just my way of acknowledging in general my indebtedness for a key image or idea in the ongoing argument. And this for a number of reasons. First, because it took me too long, far too long to register with appropriate dismay the fact that far too high a percentage of our study, teaching and writing of theology consisted in effect in the study, teaching and writing up of theologians. So that Christian theology for too long simply fed off its own initial substance. There can be few disciplines in the world that remain so tied to conceptual frameworks so old and otherwise obsolete. And then theology repeats ad nauseam the mutually hostile positions of its remotest past, positions ever narrowed by repeated and cumulative hostilities. With the end result that the Christian faith over the long centuries is increasingly narrowed in perception and expression of its substance, where both could otherwise be increasingly broadened and deepened by our evolving experience of the Creator Spirit working always in our common creation. By the time one comes to the trinity of sola's — *sola fide, sola gratia, sola scriptura;* by faith alone, grace alone, scripture alone — and with each sola defined as much by what it excluded as by what it contained, the narrowing has come to involve in significant ways a betrayal of the faith of the Founder.

Second, because as the *sola scriptura* slogan is meant to remind us, Christians from the earliest centuries have pretended to take their theology from, or to make their theology to accord with the normative, divinely inspired and sacred scriptures. Whereas in actual fact when Christians first decided they needed a theology, they did not in fact open their Bible and work a theology fresh from its pages. For one thing, when they began to theologize their faith, they did not have as yet anything like the finished canon of scripture we now have in our Bible. So instead, from the end of their second century these early Christians recognized in a prevailing Greek theology of the time a ready-made vehicle quickly and easily adapted to their purposes of expressing their Christian faith in a form that the educated elite of the Empire would find less contemptible. And they used this Platonic philosophical theology so widely and so persistently thereafter that questions can still be asked as to what was being adapted to what. No surprise then to find that the oldest and still standard method of the use of scripture in theology is the cut-and-paste method. First, set out your theological position in Platonic theological terms; then go to the Bible and seek out texts that support the stated position, and paste these into place as proof-texts. A classical example? Augustine's magisterial work *On the Trinity,* where he first offers a definition of the Trinity in terms borrowed from the prevailing philosophical theology, and then goes hunting through the Bible for texts to prove each part of it. And that is how Christian theology has been done ever since. Even the theologians of the Protestant Reformation of the sixteenth century chose their texts from the Bible, texts by which they then simultaneously interpret and judge the rest of the Bible. And they then "prove" by means of these selected texts a theological position toward which their efforts to bring a necessary and long overdue reformation to the church had nudged them in any case: salvation by faith alone, not at all by works.

It must be well-nigh impossible at this point of time to read the Bible without reading into it these distilled theologies known as Christian doctrines. Yet the effort can and must be made, and oddly enough it is most likely to succeed in the case of those who have been steeped in the theological tradition to the point of knowing both its substance and the whence of the borrowing of so much of that substance: the theology of the pre-Christian Greeks. Such explicit awareness is of the greatest help toward discounting indoctrinated theologies, or at least so circumventing them as to see what is truly in the Bible. This I have tried to do, and to present the results in the body of this book, which can then be read by anyone with nothing but a Bible in their hands, the experiences of life meditated quietly within them, and as few preconceptions as possible in their heads. The task will be made easiest of all for those who realize that the Bible contains virtually no theology, but is mostly made up of myth, that is to say, a means of expressing the worldview to which it wishes to be committed, in image, metaphor, poetry and above all story, rather than in the terms of abstract concept and logic from which theology, being a branch of philosophy, is formed.

The Bible may also be read, by writer and readers of this book alike, without the prior intervention of those later doctrines about it: doctrines of divine inspiration, or divine revelation, or inerrancy, and so on. For the aim of this reading is to come as close as possible to the shape and substance of the faith for which Jesus of Nazareth lived and died, and which his followers eventually — almost two centuries after his death — succeeded in establishing as a new religion. For the writings collected there and commonly called the New Testament, in collusion with writings already collected by Jesus's fellow Jews and commonly called by Christians the Old Testament, offer the earliest surviving evidence for the faith-movement that Jesus initiated in his life and sealed with his death. It is from these that one can reconstruct the worldview of Jesus which his life-commitment made into a faith, and which the life-experience of himself and his followers verified and goes on verifying in the ordinary ways in which all such things are verified. Verified, that is to say, by the outworking of that faith, that worldview in their lives, and the blessed outcomes of such outworking. Doctrines of divine inspiration and inerrancy are designed to assure people that this lived worldview, this faith is the true one. But that assurance-by-doctrines comes after finding out what the faith was. So that the assurance-by-doctrine may well prove superfluous, even if still welcome, for those who find the faith verified in the very processes of all our living and dying.

It turns out that when one takes the Bible as one's first and principal guide, the faith of Jesus, first and last, appears as a creation faith. That is to say, it is a faith wholly derived from the creation, from the continuous act and ongoing event of creation, a faith by which all set themselves in turn toward creating life for all for eternity. It turns out therefore that it was right for the early Christians to recognize the affinity of their faith with the developed theology of the Greeks, and to borrow and adapt that theology for their purposes, instead of beginning to theologize from scratch. For both would in any case be natural theologies (the Greeks coined that name for it: *theologia physikon*) derived from creation and set upon co-operation in creation. Yet it was not altogether right for Christians thereafter to impose that Greek theology and its doctrinal distillations for too many centuries on their own dominant church. And it was wrong of them also to pretend that the truth and grace so ably caught in that theology and which showed itself in its fullness in Jesus the man, was really therefore franchised to them alone, so that — partially excepting Judaism — all other religions, including the very Greek religion whose theology they had borrowed, were pagan, idolatrous, and in servitude to the perfidious Satan. A servitude, they then seemed to suggest, that had never significantly subverted that truth and grace during their long stewardship of their own religion.

But enough of saying how it turns out. It cannot be a good idea to give away the ending of the book before reader and writer walk the biblical way together. And just so much has been given away, really, in order to explain two further features of the body of the book: the regular intervention of reports on old Irish religion, pre-Christian and Christian, and the appearance of a titular quotation from Nietzsche at the head of each of the eight chapters.

In view of what has just been said it must be worthwhile to consider, however briefly and sketchily, the relationship between Christianity and some other natural religion. It was more than a matter of *pietas* for me to choose the pre-Christian religion of my own people for this purpose. It was a matter of acknowledging how much I had learned from predecessors who had seamlessly united so much of their ancient creation faith, *their* "old testament," into an incoming Christianity. Thereby having the new Christian faith endorsed by the same true God they had always worshiped in other *personae*. Just as the first followers of Jesus did with their original testament. It was a matter of acknowledging also how much I had learned especially from the greatest Irish theologian (after Pelagius, who was probably a West Briton anyway), John Scotus Eriugena. His magnum opus, a comprehensive Christian theology in its final form for his time, was entitled *Periphyseon, Concerning Nature.*

And Nietzsche? In *The Critique of Theological Reason* I argued that those in the modern world who are accounted the definitively dismissive critics of Christianity, from Feuerbach to Sartre, were in reality preserving some important truth about God the Creator that Christianity had lost from sight. Feuerbach was recovering the immanence of God, but not well enough for Marx, who saw Feuerbach's own substitute human-species-creator-of-world as being still too idealized in concept and still "squatting outside the world" in which all real creation continues to be carried on. Sartre talked of the *Dieu Fabricateur,* the immutable creator who turned out assembly-line products, the rules for use of which could be read off from their static natures. His resulting portrait of a God who created and governed the world from an infinite height above it was a perfectly accurate portrayal of the creator God of Christian doctrine. A picture of divine Creator and creation, whose transcendence diminished immanence almost to vanishing point, that was as rightly rejected by Sartre as it was by Marx and Feuerbach before him. And rejected precisely on the basis of their own empirical understanding of the continuous process of cosmic creation — now known more familiarly as evolution — and in particular of humanity's ever increasing role in this creative-evolutionary process. Nietzsche understands cosmic creation as no Christian theologian or preacher of the time did. In particular he understood the need for the creator of cosmos to "go down" in order to "go beyond," to be immanent for the sake of every moment of transcendence. Even to the point of experiencing death in order to give life to others, and in the process to continually transvalue all existing sets of values. One only needs to read his seminal work, *Thus Spoke Zarathustra,* in order to see how central to Nietszche's whole philosophy is this idea of creation and creator.

And yet it appears that these masters of suspicion, with the possible exception of Marx, could not quite see how the empirical human species, seen simply as the sum total of past and present members, could qualify credibly for the post of ultimate creator of cosmos. For Feuerbach talked instead of the "species-being," as creator, but never explained satisfactorily quite what kind of being that is; reason enough for Marx's complaint that it was nothing more than some kind of idealized being "squatting outside the world," and just as far outside the world as the more common figment of the Christian imagination seemed to be. So Nietzsche likewise pictured the creator of cosmos as somehow of the image of man, but as Super-Man (how super?), of whose coming (again?) Zarathustra is the prophet. In view of the sole franchise on God-talk claimed by the Christian establishment, it is perhaps easy to understand why Nietzsche could not call his ultimate creator of cosmos "God," and preferred to announce that (the Christian) God was dead.

It is not quite so easy to understand how the substitute creator, Super-Man, could still be described as "coming" if cosmic creation had always been in process. And yet, in spite of all that difficulty, Nietzsche preserves and restores a far fuller truth about the creator of universe, and about the nature and implications of that continuous process of cosmic creation. A fuller truth that is actually to be found in the Bible, and is indeed available from all our experience of living and dying as we play our own part in cosmic creation and destruction. A fuller truth that had been substantially betrayed by the main Christian tradition about creation as it had emerged by Nietzsche's time, but was preserved by those who could still see what was naturally revealed in and by the creation itself. For that I am more indebted to Nietzsche than to any of the other masters of suspicion, and I pay some of that debt by taking — mostly from his seminal work, *Thus Spoke Zarathustra* — the titular quotes for each chapter. Though I am never as indebted to any of them as much as I am to Hegel, the greatest Christian theologian of the modern era, whose rhythm of creation and being in its return to Spirit from which it came, is in the end but mimicked more simplistically in Nietzsche's borrowing and use of the *niedergang-übergang* form of the Hegelian dialectic. It is just that Hegel's original and superior form of that dialectic is so much more inaccessible and difficult to quote or even to paraphrase.

Feast of Brigid
Creator Goddess/Christian Saint
Imbolc/February 1, 2006

Appendix

Readers desirous of a full apparatus criticus for the historical argument of the Prologue to this book, or desirous of more extended critical accounts of the manner in which the main topics covered in this book arrived at the form and content that this book now presents as their true and proper destiny for our liminal time, or readers desirous of both, could consult the following writings previously published by this author as he was carried along over the last half-century — not uncritically, he dares to hope — by the series of philosophical and theological movements, the main examples of which are briefly outlined in the Prologue, and which could have converged both critically and constructively, but somehow never quite managed to do so.

Articles

A series of surveys of "New Thinking" in Christian theology published in *Herder Correspondence* (English language edition, Dublin), 1967–68: "New Thinking on Original Sin," "about Christ," "on Natural Law," "on Divorce," "on the Eucharist," "on Prayer," "on Revelation."

"Original Sin and Polygenism." *Irish Theological Quarterly* 34 (1967) 99–114. German trans. in *Theologie der Gegenwart* (Spring 1978).

A series of articles on the faith of the historical Jesus in *Horizons* (Journal of the College Theology Society, U.S.A), 1974–1975: "Jesus in the New Testament," "The Theology of Faith," "The Faith of the Historical Jesus."

Books

Life and Grace. Dublin: Gill, 1966. U.S. edition: *The Grace of God, the Response of Man.* New York: Magi 1967. *Vida y gracia.* Mexico City: Ediciones Paulinas, 1969.

Tradition and Change in the Church. Dublin and Sydney: Gill, 1968; Chicago: Pflaum, 1968. *Tradition et évolution de la foi.* Tours: Mame, 1969. *Tradycja I Zmiane W Kosciele,* Warsaw: Pax, 1974.

Morals, Law, and Authority. Dublin: Gill and Macmillan, 1969; Chicago: Pflaum, 1969. *Il Magistero morale: Compiti e limiti.* Bologna: Dehoniane, 1973.

The Problems of Religious Faith. Dublin: Helicon; Chicago: Herald, 1972.

Jesus the Man and the Myth. London: SCM, 1979 (repr. 1994); New York: Paulist 1979. *Jesus der Mensch und der Mythos.* Munich: Nymphenburger, 1981; Frankfurt/M: Ullstein Sachbuch, 1991.

Modern Theology: A Sense of Direction. Oxford University Press, 1987.

New Testament Theology in Dialogue (with J. D. G. Dunn). London: SPCK; Philadelphia: Westminster, 1987.

An Introduction to Celtic Christianity. Edinburgh: T. & T. Clark, 1989 (rev. ed. 1995).

Power and Christian Ethics. Cambridge University Press 2000 (repr. 2005).

The Critique of Theological Reason. Cambridge and New York: Cambridge University Press 2000 (eBook, 2001).

Christianity
and Creation

Prologue

The Lapses in Christian Theology
at the End of the Second Millennium

Any balanced, critical retrospective account of the main moves in Christian theology during the twentieth century could hardly fail to notice the gradual emergence of an interesting pattern. Each move set out in turn in the same direction as the one before it, and by so doing seemed to record some gains for Christian theology. Some greater cogency and clarity seemed to accrue, if only because of an increase in *aggiornamento*, as good Pope John put it in the course of calling for the Second Vatican Council. Some increasing openness and relevance to the cultures and conditions of the present and the impending future. But then each move in turn seemed to falter before its fullest promise could be redeemed, and some moves even seemed to take one step backward for each step forward. The following list and analysis of the main moves in twentieth-century theology is designed to illustrate the common direction that seems to have been taken, and the gains recorded and then largely lost in the course of successive lapses. This list has been compiled of course by one who has lived and worked through the Christian theology of the second half of the twentieth century, and who is well aware of the fact that the list of what are deemed to be main moves may seem somewhat arbitrary to others. Closeness can lend distortion to the view. Nevertheless, this list can serve to illustrate adequately enough the alleged lapsing, while leaving others free to add to or to subtract from both alleged lapses and alleged degrees of detriment sustained in the course of the theological enterprise of the twentieth century as a whole.

History and Faith

At the dawn of the twentieth century the quest for the historical Jesus was already over a hundred years old. During these years a number of

3

problems had been posed to the portrait of Jesus painted by the faith of his followers. Mainly this problem: historical research uncovered a portrait of a human being fully engaged, as is our common humanity, with the natural world, whatever beliefs about the supernatural he himself may have held. With the result that Jesus began to appear somewhat different from the all-knowing, all-powerful divine being whose claims to being divine and so to bring us the fullness of grace and truth were proved true by the miracle of his resurrection. The historical portrait seemed distinct, to say the least, from the dogmatic portrait painted by the faith of Jesus's followers. Proffered solutions to this problem then seemed to have settled on Kahler's formulaic distinction between the Jesus of history and the Christ of faith. It takes faith to come to know the divine Christ; mere historical research cannot reach so far. By mid-century this solution seemed to have solidified around Bultmann's peremptory pronouncement to the effect that Christian faith cannot be made to depend upon the historian's labors.

Now this kind of solution to the main problem raised during the long quest for the historical Jesus seemed to require — or was it to reinstate? — something of an unbridgeable chasm between human reason (historical investigation being one of reason's major learning modes), and a Christian faith correspondingly thought to be entirely dependent upon special, supernatural divine revelation. Yet the quest of the historical Jesus, the second quest, as it came to be called, was continued, not least by Bultmann's own best pupils, for all that the master could say or do. But then, like other movements in the Christian theology of the twentieth century, as we must see, this one also simply seemed to peter out. No final audit of the gains of this second quest produced or published. No assessment attempted of the kind or quantity of the contribution these gains could make to the next phase of academic production in this sector of the business, the theology of divine revelation.

Revelation and History

In the first decade of the second half of the twentieth century René Latourelle realized that something large and important was missing from systems of Christian theology: a theology of divine revelation had nowhere emerged. Christians had claimed from the beginning that they had their distinctive truth through special divine revelation. And down all the centuries all preaching, deployment, explanation and interpretation of this received truth was accompanied by the insistence that it was especially revealed by God. Yet, although theological expositions of every main element of that truth had been on offer since the third Christian century, no properly thought out theology of divine revelation itself had ever appeared. Latourelle's own effort to fill this longstanding lacuna proved to be the beginning of a move that over the next two decades drew many of the best minds in Christian theology to the construction of a theology of divine revelation. Briefly the move began with a rather concerted and adverse critique of the propositional model of divine revelation or, more bluntly put, the verbal dictation model of the revelation of Christian truth. Despite the support for such a model apparently offered by that synonym for divine revelation, "the word of God." And the move ended, or rather it petered out, with a model of divine revelation as history.

On this alternative model of revelation as history, God was thought to be revealed, and God revealed what God wished to reveal, in and through events of history. In the case of Christianity it was the historical person of Jesus of Nazareth, his life, death and destiny, that offered to all those who would follow him the full and final revelation of God and of God's ways with the world. The words of Jesus, his parables and other preachings and propositions of his, were of course part of this revelation. There was talk of them as "word event," but that very phrase in itself suggested that the words were subsidiary, pointing up the true significance of the actual events that were primarily charged with the divine revelation. It was therefore not essential that the actual words of Jesus, the *ipsissima verba*, be recorded and retained verbatim. Suitable suits of words could always be found to clothe, present and interpret, especially to people who used a different language and a different idiom, the true meaning and significance of the human origin and the human journey of the one in whom, as Christians claimed, the Word of God was incarnate.

But there is, and there remains, a problem about this view that divine revelation consists essentially of historical events. The problem is this: when theologians talk of historical events as the prime medium of divine revelation, do they have in mind a special series of special events, and not just a series of events of the kind that are commonly and currently reduplicated, and that make up the stuff of ordinary history? There had been much talk about "salvation history" in the years before, and that phrase continued in common use during this move to the theology of revelation as history. Was this salvation history made up of a special sub-set of exclusively miraculous events then, that is to say, events which allegedly bore the signature of a special divine intervention? Not altogether, for certainly some of the central stories in the Christian Bible's history of the Israelites are in the main concerned with events that are quite common in the all too ordinary history of our race. A subjugate people escaping servitude and by a military campaign finally winning for themselves the freedom of life in their own lands. Or the execution, even the wrongful execution of a man judged guilty of threatening the security of the state. Yet the latter event, and often these two events together, with the former in the role of prophetic sign of the latter, are seen as God saving the human race from sin. But surely, since they are instances of common or garden variety historical events, one has to ask how a divine revelation, a revelation of the divine, can be seen in just these Jewish examples, and in none of the myriad of other examples of escapes, conquests and crucifixions that litter the course of history? Or did God communicate to the mind of some prophet, or to the prophet Jesus, the message that what was really going on in that singular execution in Jerusalem long ago, was in fact God's saving of the whole human race from sin?

Some of the writers who seemed to have reached a view of divine revelation as history, still made room for such prophetic necessity. Which meant that they could not face up to the full implications of ordinary history as revelation of the divine. For did the actual divine revelation not now consist in some special divine communication conveyed to the prophet, and to others through the prophetic office, rather than in the historical event as such? And how far had these theologians really come after all from the older and much criticized propositional view of divine revelation? Once more a move in modern theology had petered out without finally tackling the final problem it itself had raised. Once more, as in the case of the quest for the historical Jesus, a theological move toward the search for God in natural history reintroduced an older chasm between a natural and a supernatural realm, between the events that took place in the one and those that took place in the other. While still limping forward, for a while, toward some acceptance and assessment of the new sense of the religious relevance of the natural and the ordinarily historical.

The Bible as Revelation, History, Literature

That move on the theology of revelation was paralleled by yet another move in twentieth-century theology, a move this time on the theological theories concerning the Christian scriptures. Mainline Christian churches, from Calvinist to Catholic, would have considered themselves under assault upon these scriptures from historical Jesus questers, from modernists and from other assorted attackers boasting a heightened critical sense of either history or literature, or both. So these churches at the outset of the twentieth century still stood staunchly and together by the following view of their divinely inspired scriptures. A divine inspiration reserved for the human authors of these scriptures had the effect that the words they used, all the words they used and without exception, conveyed the revealed truth, the whole of that truth, and nothing but that truth. It was sometimes stressed, as it was by Calvin himself, that this did not amount to divine dictation of the text, in which case the "sacred" authors would be no more than recording secretaries. This was not a theology of verbal, propositional revelation, it was stoutly maintained, for the inspired scriptures are not themselves, Qur'an-like, the actual revelation, the divinely revealed word of God. Rather did the doctrine of the divine inspiration of the scriptures amount to this: the inspiration in question simply saw to it that those scriptures formed an absolutely and entirely inerrant witness to a divine revelation which took final form in the incarnation of the Word of God in Jesus of Nazareth.

Despite such assertions, however, it is hard to see how this theology of scriptural inspiration differed in the least degree in its overall outcome from a theology of direct divine propositional revelation. And it is correspondingly easy to understand just how the most faithful followers of those churches to this day think and talk about these scriptures as if these subtle theological distinctions between divine inspiration and divine revelation did not exist. And yet, as far back as Galileo and as recently as the most recent findings of scientific cosmology, to take just one class of example, the assumptions and assertions of the Bible concerning the form and coming-to-be of the cosmos was brought so far into question by science as to qualify, to say the least, those other assumptions and assertions of the absolute, word-for-word inerrancy of the Bible. Gradually, as the twentieth century rolled on, qualifications of this kind were officially sanctioned. For example, in the Roman Catholic Church it became acceptable to say that only what was directly asserted in the sacred text of the scriptures was made inerrant by divine inspiration. *Obiter dicta*, assertions incidental to those primarily intended, did not enjoy such protection. So that the former, but not the latter, would lead us unerringly to the truth divinely revealed. So, for instance, at the very outset of the Bible it is directly intended to assert that God created the world out of

nothing. But the quaint ancient cosmology, a flat earth floating on an
ocean with a sky-canopy stretched over it, is merely incidental to the main
assertion. Because that ancient cosmology, as it happened, was the best
description of the created world that was available at the time to those
who proclaimed, truly, that God created the world.

The distinction between direct assertions and *obiter dicta*, however,
proved increasingly difficult to keep in line with any distinction between,
on the one hand, religious assertions (God created the world) that constituted the directly intended assertions of a sacred text like the Bible and,
on the other hand, those secular-type assertions concerning cosmology,
history and so on, that are included in the Bible only incidentally, and
by those less informed on such matters than we now are. When Jahweh,
the Lord of Hosts, that is to say, the commander-in-chief of the Israelite
armies also, commands them through prophets to engage in what can only
be described as total ethnic cleansing, the untruth entailed in such texts is
on the religious side of the religious/secular divide. It belongs firmly in
that "deposit of faith and morals" that Roman Catholics see as the yield
of special divine revelation. Some of the most religiously conservative of
Israeli Zionists provide an illustration of the contemporary currency of
this kind of understanding of biblical revelation of the will of God. Little
wonder then that Karl Barth, the greatest theologian of the twentieth century, insisted that errors in the Bible cannot be confined to secular matters,
but that errors in the domain of religion must be allowed there also. Yet
Barth too insisted that the Bible, despite its proneness to ignorance and
error, inevitable in view of the very humanity of its authors, can still bear
adequate and authoritative witness to the final revelation of God's Word
in the man, Jesus. Provided that the Spirit who inspired these authors to
achieve such written witness enlighten our hearts also as we are drawn to
seek the living God in the pages they left to us.

Once more, just as in the case of a theology of divine revelation, what
seemed to be a move toward a theory to the effect that this revelation
came in the public events of natural and human history, then seemed to
be reversed in favor of an older theory of private divine communication.
For now a set of scriptures, the very proneness of which to error and
ignorance of various kinds seemed to show them up as thoroughly human
in authorship, had their previous image as straightforward communication
of divine revelation severely qualified by the added necessity of an inner
divine communication to their readers to enable the latter to see only the
truth, and the whole truth that they contained.

Yet scholars have continued to study the Bible by increasing, if anything, the usage of all those tools and methods commonly in evidence in any and all attempts to uncover all the truth about the natural world and the human race that natural and human history has to offer. In pursuit of the recovery of the overall import of the Bible these scholars apply to it, as to any other book, the standard methods of literary criticism. In pursuit of the social, political and geographical background against which the history of the Israelites and especially of Jesus was played out and can be better understood, they apply the critical methods of the social, historical sciences, including human geography. In pursuit of the particularly religious affordances of the Bible they apply the critical methods of comparative philosophy and religion. And all of this has unquestionably contributed, and continues to contribute, to a clearer account of the faith that his followers believe comes to them from Jesus of Nazareth. It contributes also to a finer assessment of the ensuing Christian religion in which that faith of the historical Jesus came to be embodied. Including in that a finer assessment of the fidelities and betrayals incurred in the very course of that continually changing embodiment. In particular from the point at which the faith of Jesus the Jew became fully and finally embodied in a new religion called Christianity.

All of which confirms the character of the position in which we find ourselves at the beginning of a new millennium of the Christian era. The quest for the historical Jesus, and for the wider history of the times and places and peoples from which he emerged and of which he was such an integral part, or in which he and his movement engaged in mutuality of influence, continues at least in the normal course of biblical studies. And it continues, at least in that particular specialization of Christian theological studies, to let shine the light that this historical Jesus and the faith he fashioned from his own Jewish tradition of faith, throws upon the being of God and of God's ways with the world. Yet the theology, and especially the theology of divine revelation, that would underpin and correspond to this ever clearer vision of the truth that came with the historical Jesus, and that continues to result in its purification from subsequent religious, moral and political adulteration, still awaits adequate formulation. It seemed as if it might emerge from the quest for the historical Jesus, but it was blocked by the introduction of the dichotomy between the Jesus of history and the Christ of faith. Then the second quest for the historical Jesus, under that specific title, simply petered out. And although the second quest could be said to be continued anonymously as it were, in the general area of biblical studies, nothing specific is yet being done to remove the theological blockage of the dichotomy between the Jesus of history and the Christ of faith. It is just this kind of dichotomy between history and faith that continues to keep in place in most modern theologies of divine revelation the forms of the dichotomy between, on the one hand, reason and history and, on the other, special divine communication and a corresponding, unquestioning faith.

Sin and Salvation in Nature and History

There were other moves that dominated for a while the theological land-scape of the twentieth century, and that were also allowed to peter out before their best results could be established and recorded, and brought into contact with other theological moves of that century for the ad-vancement of the whole of a unified and consistent Christian theology for our times. There was, for example, the move on the traditional West-ern theology of original sin. This move came about almost accidentally. The developing sciences of evolution had been causing problems for some time for the traditional Christian understanding of its biblical account of creation. And then, suddenly, one angle of one of these scientific theories caught in the dominant traditional Christian account of original sin, and threatened to cause a large tear in it. The study of the origin of the species suggested that the species, *homo sapiens,* as such species tend to do, evolved from a population and not from a single member or a single couple. And if this was so, it made little sense to say that anything passed from one original member or couple to all the rest of that species without exception through the very process of procreation itself. Yet, whatever differences there may have been between the accounts of original sin offered in dif-ferent Christian churches and traditions, and whatever differences there may still be about the precise mechanism of such transmission, there is general agreement in the official teaching of the Christian churches of the West at least, that original sin is contracted by every member of the race by the very fact of being conceived and born into the race. And the central assumption behind this official teaching was that all contracted the sin by procreation from the first man, or first couple, who alone actually commit-ted the original sin. But it was precisely this account of original sin that saw a serious challenge arise from the science of evolution that regarded polygenism as the favored formula from all the evidence of the origins of species, with monogenism a scarcely conceivable alternative.

The responses of Christian theology to this challenge, as with the responses to evolution theory in general, varied in kind as much as in their power of conviction. From the utterly reactionary insistence that biblical propositions must ever be held higher than scientific hypotheses, to new and creative theological efforts at saying just what this original sin consisted in, and how it was transmitted from generation to generation. For example, one type of theological suggestion would have it that original sin consists in effect in a form of idolatry, more specifically a deifying of human self-interest, at the expense of other peoples or groups, and indeed of the whole of creation. The kind of thing one finds, for instance, in that worship of Mammon in which all of us at all times and to one degree or another engage, and which brings untold evils to the human race as well as to the natural world. A kind of endemic immorality that is transmitted culturally down all the sad centuries of human tenancy of this lean earth; but at all events certainly not transmitted at or through the simple process of the fertilization of women's ova.

This theological excursus also petered out before any generally agreed reformulation of the traditional Western theology of original sin, widely thought to have originated in Augustine's writings on the subject, could be developed. With the result that this Augustinian formula remained in the more official teachings of the churches, and thence in the minds of the great majority of church members. Now one does not need to delve any deeper at this point into the details of this fourth main theological move of the twentieth century before one realizes that it shares a certain characteristic with the other three. Just as theology seemed to be moving toward a position in which the substance of the Christian faith, or at the very least some central elements of that faith, appear to be accessible from the natural history of the natural world, the move peters out. And by doing so it fails to deliver the full potential outcome either for itself, or by linking up with the other moves in such a manner as to urge them forward also in a direction in which they already seemed to be going. That is to say toward what would most likely result in a combined position on the Christian faith, in which its content would seem more and more derivable from nature and history.

For whatever else might be said about this allegedly inherited sinfulness, in relation to a just God and so on, one thing is certain. Since this original sin is not, and not even a result of, a sin committed after Adam, it is now and in itself entirely undetectable on the stage of nature and history. Some theologians persist in saying that it is detectable through its symptom, concupiscence, disordered sensual desire. But concupiscence stands in no more need of an essentially undetected causal explanation for its occurrence than do the disorders of any other human faculty or habit. A plentiful supply of detectable causal explanations are available for all of these. And there is an interesting corollary to this utter undetectability of original sin. The cure is equally undetectable. For the cure is said to consist in divine grace, and in particular the grace that is poured into the infant's soul, as normal theological idiom would have it, on the occasion of the infant's baptism. So divine grace and its operation is also undetectable on the empirical stage of nature and history? Apparently so, indeed even more undetectable than original sin; for the common theological view among traditionalists in this matter is that concupiscence continues even after original sinfulness is washed away in the waters of baptism.

The upshot of all of this must be that all of this activity, the transmission of sin, the ensuing state of sinfulness in every human neonate, and the forgiveness or washing away of this original sin, all take place in some supernatural, supra-historical realm, in some kind of alternative world and history that is, during our natural life-time at least, invisible, inaudible, intangible to all earthlings. So that we certainly seem to have yet another example of a piece of modern theology that tried to talk of an element of the Christian faith that could be detected in natural history, but then let the matter drop, and allowed both original sin and God's grace in respect of it to recede once more into some realm of agents and activity above and beyond nature and history. To be known only through some special divine communication to a select few by or from whom it would then have to be communicated to others. And if the grace that washes away original sin is undetectable in this natural world by our own normal means of perception, does the same apply to all of God's grace of whatever sort and purpose, saving, auxiliary, sanctifying? The answer, again from an analysis of the teachings of the mainline Christian churches, would appear to be in the affirmative.

Nature and Grace

The textbooks of Roman Catholic theology that continued to be published well into the second half of the twentieth century provide in ample profusion the evidence for the view that divine grace does not belong with the natural world and is not therefore detectable through our natural modes of perception. Textbook evidence is particularly important, for textbooks provided the common sources for the training of the clergy of the Christian churches, and their preaching in turn formed the minds of the generality of Christian believers on this and all other relevant matters. In these textbooks what was found was what the few theologians who dared to criticize it called the superstructure model of divine grace. Divine grace in all its forms — sanctifying, saving, and enabling both generally and during particular bouts of moral activity — was modeled on the structures of human nature. That nature was then understood to consist of the human essence or substance itself, together with its faculties or powers, and the characteristic activities of the former. So divine grace in turn was thought of on this model as a created complex consisting of a new being or entity corresponding to the human essence or substance (sanctifying grace), new faculties or principles of operation (the supernatural virtues), and the activations of these that then made up the active life of the human being endowed with the grace of God (efficient graces).

A doppelgänger nature, in short, added to the natural nature, essence or substance of the human being and to its natural faculties and activities. That is to say, a supernatural entity in its entirety, by which the human being lived a supernatural life. A life lived by that person, but literally over and above (*super*) the natural life lived by the human nature we directly experience in ourselves and in others. As such "the supernatural life of grace" became a common phrase for a kind of superstructure raised above the structures that made natural life possible. For, as the matter was further explained, since the ultimate goal of human existence was in itself something supernatural, namely, the final union with God known as the beatific vision of God, the life of grace by which this goal beyond the grave could be reached, must of necessity be something equally supernatural and simply not accessible to natural powers of observation. And even though the imagery of this strictly supernatural model of divine grace sometimes included talk of "elevating" our human nature with its characteristic powers and activities to the point of enabling these to be accommodated to the beatific union with God, no real prospect of a natural detectability of divine grace ensued. The overall doppelgänger-supernatural structure of divine grace militated against such a possibility; and the beatific vision was, with the exception of occasional and very temporary divine favors for unique individuals, reserved for another life and another world. The history of this natural world, including the history of humanity, moved on a different and separate plane therefore from that of divine grace and its strictly super-natural ends. And so the superstructure model of divine grace emerged and colonized the common textbooks of Catholic theology.

As in the case of other elements of the Christian faith already analyzed above, there was a move in the case of the Christian theology of divine grace also, to bring it closer to, if not fully into, the natural world and its history, where its presence and power would be more accessible to all. For example, Karl Rahner, conscious perhaps that Henri de Lubac's *Surnaturel* had been placed on Rome's index of prohibited books for arguing for continuity between nature and grace, argued instead that nature was a "remainder concept." By this he meant that God had from the beginning of creation destined humanity for a supernatural destiny, a return to a union with God called the beatific vision, and for no other goal. This divine decision then sets up a "supernatural existential" as the inmost thing in concrete human existence in all of its concrete history. An existential structure consisting mainly in God's own immanent activity in humanity and its history and resulting first and foremost in all that we call divine grace — the life-structures, the principles of operation and the activities of these already mentioned. This inmost existential condition is then detectable to us in our concrete life and history in this world. In fact, it is so much a part of what we are and perceive in all of the actual and concrete conditions of our life in this natural creation, that it is only by revelation (a special revelation, presumably) that we can distinguish this supernatural existential from whatever in us and our history would without it remain as purely natural. In this sense then nature and natural are remainder concepts; the connotation of these concepts is complete in what is left over from our account of all that our nature and its history in this world tells us, once the supernatural existential, which we know from the same inspection of nature and history, but are told by special revelation *is* actually supernatural, has been subtracted.

This whole maneuver of Rahner's is little more than a fine example of sleight-of-hand, typical of Rahner when he wanted to introduce an idea he knew would be unacceptable to his ecclesiastical masters. In this case the idea that was unacceptable was that God's presence, power, light and grace was all of it detectable as an innermost existential in our history as part of the natural world. But Rahner still appeared to support the opposite, the authorities' professed idea, namely, that the supernatural existential was truly supernatural in that, although it could be detected in the course of our ordinary experience of our nature and history, we had special revelation to tell us that it was not part of the merely natural after all.

Of course, some would deem this critique of Rahner's move to be unfair. But it does at least point up a problem with the other theological efforts of that era to get away from that dichotomous distinction between nature and supernatural grace that was endemic to the superstructure model of divine grace. The problem is this: why, as these new theologians investigated the incidence and extent of supernatural divine grace in the world and its history, did they stop short of including in this the very creation and thereby God's free gift (*gratia*) of natural existence and natural life and all the abundance of sources for life and life ever more abundant for all?

Or, to put the problem in precisely parallel terms to the terminology of divine grace, to put it in the terminology of revelation: why, when it was admitted by all, including Calvin, that the one, true God was revealed in ordinary created nature and its ordinary, natural history, did theologians persist in driving a dichotomy between, on the one hand, special supernatural divine revelation accompanying the special creation and gift of the alleged grace-superstructure and, on the other hand, the natural knowledge of God's power and presence in the creation and gift of the natural structures of existence and life? When the problem is phrased in the terminology of divine revelation, the Calvinist answer is clear. The knowledge of God that is available from nature and history has always been sufficient in itself to light and empower our way to our eternal destiny in union with God. But then original sin entered upon that blissful natural world and so blinded us to the revelation of the life-giving God in the natural creation that a special supernatural revelation became necessary and was in fact vouchsafed. This special revelation, witnessed in divinely inspired scriptures, had essentially the same content as the original revelation in nature and history, except for the addition of a word concerning God's special arrangements for the forgiving of sin. The Roman Catholic answer, whether the problem is posed in the terminology of grace or of revelation, is less clear. But it does seem that a fear of reviving what was believed to be the heresy of Pelagius was the operative factor here.

This fear could then be outlined as follows: if the divine grace was thought to consist of God's free creative activity in giving existence and life and all the supports and affordances of life from time into eternity; and if the creation could then be seen correspondingly as sufficient revelation of this God and of God's power and presence, then surely the conclusion would somehow emerge that human beings can come to know God and to progress toward their destiny in eternal communion with God by, as it is sometimes put, pulling themselves along to this blissful goal of their whole existence by their own bootstraps. Nature itself and alone, and human nature in particular, enables the eternal God to be seen and reached, and that is thought to be the crowning error with which the good name of Pelagius has been besmirched to this day.

But that, as the necessary revisionism of modern historical theology has long proven, is not something that Pelagius's own thought either endorsed or entailed. For divine creation is now seen as it truly is. Not a one-off act that long ago put the world in existence, but rather a continuous divine activity that gives origin to forms of finiteness and creatively empowers these to create others in what eventually becomes a living and hence a continually evolving universe. Then the free initiative always remains with God in gifting all the life that stretches from time to eternity, and in concomitantly revealing God's self ever more fully to all those who possess powers of comprehension sufficiently developed to receive such revelation. Our activity, our living is therefore always a response to God's continuously creative initiative. Our knowledge of God and of our destiny with God a response to the self-revelation of God that is conveyed through that same continuous creativity that is pictured in the scriptures in the imagery of the Word of God by which the world is created. But this is to anticipate the argument of the book that is to follow. For the moment it is necessary only to observe that, in the case of the theology of grace there is yet another example of a twentieth-century move toward seeing an element of the Christian faith revealed in nature and its varied history; yet another move of this kind and this general direction that was then once again aborted. Or for one reason or another it petered out before it could be finally tested, at the very least by being driven, in the company of other moves in the same direction, to its logical conclusions.

Creation

So far it seems that the theology that the twentieth century bequeathed to the new millennium was comprised in effect of a series of start-stop movements, each of which began by reaching out to the natural world, and particularly perhaps to humanity, and the history of that world and the history of humanity within it, in the expectation and hope of finding there true traces of the presence and power of such a being as one might deem divine. Hoping to find the traces of that being's boundless grace for life and life forever more abundant, and of such blessed mutual knowledge and love of the gracious being as its infinite creative benevolence always initiates and correspondingly promises to fulfil. Yet each and every one of these theological movements, although each and all could boast some better insights into the content of the Christian faith, and some potential improvements in its social structures and communal practices, either ground to a halt or virtually reversed its direction. In either case, the kind of theology that was left in possession was a theology that located the substance, power and activity of God's grace, together with the source of our knowledge of this, in some supernatural realm. A realm which, even in its breaking into the realm of the natural world, remained quite distinct from it. No one seemed to think of following the clues provided by the very fact that all of these movements began to move in the same direction and recorded some striking insights into the Christian faith while moving in that direction. No one seemed to sense the promises that might be redeemed by bringing all of these movements together and then continuing in the same direction of a quest through the natural history of the world for God and for the highest of human prospects with God.

There was one other movement in the course of twentieth-century theology that might have accomplished such a task. It was in fact a movement that concerned itself specifically with the theology of creation. But that movement seemed satisfied in the end with a repositioning of the theology of creation within the overall prospectus of Christian theology. It did not attempt to pursue the whole of Christian theology as a theology of creation. That is to say, as a theology, a critical, investigative and analytic study of God and God's ways with the world, the results of which would be taken from and based upon the evidences afforded by the natural creation itself, its origin, continuous development, recurring destructions, savings from these, and ultimate prospects. Rather, the new theology of creation seemed to be happy to promote itself to priority over the theology of sin. Just as certain moves in the moral theology of the twentieth century sought to promote the priority of charity, or the priority of the scriptures, over the priority of law and obedience and the sinful oppositions to these. In the course of this push for priority, the priority of sin in Christian theology was not taken to suggest that the sin of the creature took place before the creation of this material universe, even if certain early Christian theologians flirted with that idea. Rather was the priority of sin taken to mean that, in general, and particularly in certain crucial parts of Christian theology, if the idea of God having to respond to sin were to be the foundational consideration, then in these central parts of Christian theology, what might be called a sin-driven theology would inevitably emerge. A sin-driven theology is one that would promote the image of God having always to respond to sin. And it would situate this image so as to make it logically prior to the image of an ever active and eternal God as benign creator.

For example Christology, which gives its distinctive character to the whole of any Christian theology, could be said to have been sin-driven in all the main churches of the West. The pivotal event in the earthly life of Jesus, his crucifixion, was read simply and solely as the redemption of the human race from sin. Correspondingly, in the dominant Anselmian theology of salvation, the incarnation itself, in which the Word of God became man, was said to be necessitated by that same requirement of paying the price for the sin of the race. Indeed the very theology of original sin that was derived from the Augustinian model in the West was itself seen to be a necessary presupposition of the theological model which saw Christ's crucifixion as the saving of all of mankind without exception from sin. Without a doctrine of original sin transmitted to all in the very process of procreation, how could we be sure the sin infected every member of the race, so that Jesus was the savior of all human beings without exception? This question was often asked without any apparent awareness of the kind of totally sin-driven theology that same question presupposed.

These sin-driven theologies derived from epochal interpretations of the Christian sources, such as those provided by Augustine and Luther. Theologians who were themselves obsessed with sin, at the very least in the sense that their assessment of themselves as persistent sinners persuaded them to describe all other members of the race — the *massa damnata*, as Augustine called it — in much the same terms. And so wholeheartedly as to quite smother at birth any balancing assessment of themselves and all other human being as equally persistent creators of good, and as naturally capable of that as they are of evil-doing. In just such ways sin takes priority over creation in most Christian theologies of the West. Sin drove and fashioned the whole of these Christian theologies through the dominant influence of soteriology in Christology, and thereby the theology of creation was relegated to the simple task of accounting for the existence of the stage and the actors on which and by whom this great cosmic drama of sin and redemption is played out.

Now any attempt to displace this priority of sin in Christian theology was welcome, and always is welcome, if only because these sin-driven theologies did spawn, and must always tend to spawn, extreme forms of exclusivism in the polity of the Christian religion. For the more exclusively Jesus is seen as the savior of the whole race, the more must all other religions be excluded. Baptism in the name of Jesus, or at the very least faith in Jesus, is both necessary and sufficient for human salvation. Not surprisingly then, those who in the course of the move just mentioned tried to reposition the Christian theology of creation in the pecking order of subject matters dealt with, were criticized on many counts. They were criticized on the count of prioritizing "natural theology" at the expense of "revealed theology," for instance. But principally on the count of demoting the "supernatural" revelation of God sending his only Son to save the world, with all that this was thought to entail in terms of universal sinfulness. In the end, with such criticism to contend with, this final twentieth-century theology of creation petered out also. And it left us, as did the similarly aborted movements already mentioned, with the dichotomies of history and revelation, and nature and grace. In short, it left us with the kind of superstructure model of Christianity in which both the divine givings and other actions designed to achieve our blessed destiny, together with the processes by which these are made known to us, take place in a kind of doppelgänger universe, above and beyond the natural world of which we are such integral parts and knowers. Both the dichotomies and the superstructure models are designed, in reality if not consciously, to alert us to, and more crucially to lead us to a world quite other than this one.

The Franchise Theology That the Lapses Left in Place and Some Tragic Consequences Thereof

Another way to sum up the Christian theology of the twentieth century is to say this. Together these aborted or petered-out theological moves began by holding out such prospects for an ever-necessary reforming of Christian theology that would keep it faithful alike to the faith of its founder and to a human race that had discovered first history and then evolution. But all ended, at best by default, by inviting back what can only be called a centuries-old franchise theology, with all of its limitations and potentially damaging outcomes.

The term *franchise theology* is hereby coined in order to name the kind of theology, and in particular the theology of church, the ecclesiology that characterizes the superstructure model of grace above and beyond nature, and of revelation above and beyond history. If the divine acts and their effects that constitute grace belong to a supernatural realm, then divine grace is not accessible in the natural world and by natural means. Neither in consequence is the knowledge of grace or of the God who gives that grace accessible by means of our natural powers of perception. Both the grace and the truth about all of this must then be conveyed either to each human being individually, or to some chosen individual or group in the first instance, who can then distribute both grace and truth to others across time and space. The fullness of grace and truth, according to the Bible, came with Jesus the Christ. And the churches that have followed Jesus generally claim that they, and perhaps principally some leadership groups within them, have had entrusted to them the privilege and responsibility to make this grace and truth known and available to all nations and all ages, down to the last limit of place and time. It is with such a scenario in mind that the Christian theologies that promote or assume the superstructure model of nature and grace, history and revelation, are called franchise theologies.

Now of course these theologies, and the Christian churches that define themselves on their terms are not, all of them, quite as crudely exclusivist as the term *sole franchise* might of itself suggest. For the sole franchise refers to the *fullness* of grace and truth that came into the world with Jesus of Nazareth. So a particular church could say that God had granted some grace and truth to other peoples and religions, to Judaism in particular. Or it might say that certain other Christian churches that had either broken away from it or strayed from fidelity to the fullness of Christ's grace and truth, had nevertheless retained some of that grace and truth. But in both cases such generous acknowledgments, as they are intended to be, could quickly be seen to imply that the partial possessions or remnants of divine grace and truth still detectable in other religions or churches, should have as their proper goal and essential *raison d'être* the divinely authorized impulse to drive their possessors toward the Christian fold, or back into the one, true church to which alone the fullness of grace and truth is solely franchised. On such an understanding of the franchise theology, the upshot is the same for non-Christian religions and for all but one of the Christian churches, whether that one, true Christian church currently exists, as the Vatican thinks it presently subsists in its church, or whether it will only exist in some future union of Christian churches. The upshot is that all other religions and Christian churches are in effect instances of the *praeparatio evangelica,* the divine providential preparation of human kind for the fullness of grace and truth, divinely intended from eternity to be embodied in one, true, catholic or universal church, one *ecclesia,* one calling-out or gathering-in of human kind. So that all of these other religions and churches really ought to disappear as such by merging into this one, true community of all people of the one, true God.

That is but one general illustration of the manner in which the failures of twentieth-century Christian theology to follow up on the recurrent directions and promises of so many of its start-up movements, left Christians without the ability or willingness to appreciate the permanent value and future prospects of other religions or other Christian churches. Instead, these failures had long provided Christians, even through the modified versions of exclusivism just outlined, with opportunities to denounce members of other religions and churches for their deficiencies of truth and goodness, shortcomings that are then described as forms of falsehood and sin. And as these opportunities were wholeheartedly taken on board, divisions that already existed on ethnic or political grounds, and which coincided with divisions between Christian populations of different church allegiance, or between Christians and peoples of other religions, the attribution to others of falsehood and sin could not but exaggerate the degrees of mutual suspicion, hostility and even violence that so often set such communities at each other's throats for more mundane motives. The world today is not short of tragic examples of religious or church rivalries contributing to wars both civil and international, as Christian-Muslim divisions in the world and Catholic-Protestant divisions in Northern Ireland only too luridly illustrate.

The Case for a Full-Blown Christian Theology of Creation

Such a critical survey of the main movements in Christian theology at the turn of the millennium surely suggests that some sustained attempt to follow to their full and combined conclusions the very similar directions detected in all of these movements, to find God's grace and truth in the natural history of the only world we know to exist, might very well result in a sketch of the whole of Christian theology that would at the very least avoid the lapses of twentieth-century theology, together with the tragic consequences of these as already in part exemplified. What is then at issue and in prospect is a Christian theology construed entirely and in all of its traditional constituent parts — Creation, Fall, Salvation in Christ, Trinity, Eschatology, Revelation, Faith, Grace — as a theology of creation.

By that term *creation* is meant both the activity of bringing into being all those entities that have come into being, do now come into being, and will come into being; both these and the universe that results from these entities in their interconnectedness and indeed interdependence. By theology is meant simply what that term has meant since its coining by the pre-Christian Greeks: a philosophy-type and eros(*philo*)-driven quest for the wisdom (*sophia*) that would result, not merely from an ever-deepening understanding of the entities, agencies and processes that constitute the world, but from any guidance that might be given in the course of this quest as to how to live with all of these for the best and most permanent outcome for all. This one and the same quest was called theology by the Greeks at that part and reach of it where it investigates what appear to be traces of an ultimate and most comprehensive creative source of all empirical reality. A source of the continuous emergence of all things into being, and correspondingly a source of guidance for their well-being. A source of such ultimacy and import that it attracted the epithet, *theios* (divine) or *theos* (god). Theology, from the early centuries of the origins of Greek philosophy, long before Christianity came upon the scene, was the name for a rational investigation and account (*logos*) of *theos,* and of the interaction of *theos* with the world (*theos-logos*).

A Christian theology of the creation can be taken then to envisage an interrogation of the history of our universe, with particular attention perhaps to the history of humanity and of humanity's prospects of in-creasingly pivotal significance within that universe. But if it is to pass muster as a Christian theology of creation it must envisage an interro-gation of nature and history that is conducted through the authoritative source documents of the Christian faith; first of all, the Bible, and then some secondary sources such as the creedal formulations of the faith that the Bible presents and promotes. For the Bible presents us with the earliest and most comprehensive account of the faith of Jesus, a perfecting, as it was seen by his earliest followers, of his own Jewish faith in his time. So it is the Bible, and the whole Bible that will yield the evidence that the faith of Jesus was a creation faith through and through. The case for Christian faith as in origin a creation faith could be made by starting somewhere else. For instance, a theology of creation could be first constituted by use of reason (yielding philosophy) or imagination (yielding myth) as happened with the Greeks. And then one could search through the Bible for texts that would confirm as much of this resulting theology as possible. But that would quite justifiably attract the objection that the old, discredited proof-texting, scissors-and-paste method was still in use — picking from the Bible an assorted selection of texts to prove that a creation theology of creation was in fact witnessed there. The result would surely be that the whole operation could be rightly suspect of eisegesis, rather than exegesis. Suspect, that is to say, of reading something into the Bible and not out of the Bible. So the task must be to go through the Bible itself in order to discover how much of God's grace and truth the Bible regards as being present and revealed in the natural universe and in its history, and particularly perhaps in the history of humanity within the universe.

As a brief initial indication of just how extensive in the Bible is the Christian truth that, it is suggested either explicitly or implicitly, stems from a revelation in the ongoing creation, one needs only to observe how the foundational idea and image of divine creation is used from beginning to end of the Bible. And it is used, not merely to describe the continual bringing to be of all things, but also to fill in the details of theological topics that theologians have treated in volumes additional to the one on *God the Creator*. For example, the matters treated under soteriology (God the redeemer), and eschatology (God the bringer of final fulfillment), are described in the Bible simply as new or renewed creating, giving rise to a new or renewed creation. In any event, it is only by setting the Bible as the primary and authoritative source for these claims concerning a necessary and sufficient theology of creation, otherwise known as a natural theology, that Christians will find in the least credible such claims to the effect that this creation theology fully coincides with all that is taught in the authoritative source. All the truth proposed in the Bible about God, about God's ways with the world, and about the prospects for us humans and for our world that are held out for our free choice in the normal course of the natural revelation of that truth.

The implications of all of that for our relationships as Christians with other Christian churches and with other religions, or indeed with those fellow humans who owe allegiance to no religion at all, must await the completion of a thoroughly biblical sketch of a Christian theology that is altogether a natural theology. As must the implications for human moralizing, for the ability of human beings everywhere to arrive at the highest and most compelling values for human living, values that yield the truest guidance toward life and life ever more abundant for all. And the implications, indeed, for organized religion as such, and the implications in this respect for the franchise theology that has been developed by different Christian churches on different bases, and that we Roman Catholics have had adopted by our hierarchical leaders, and never more imperiously than in the Decree on Ecumenism from the Second Vatican Council.

Yet it is worth ending this prologue by remarking that this is by no means the first time that a complete Christian theology has been presented as a creation or natural theology. An Irish predecessor, so anxious to ensure that his Irishness was never overlooked that he called himself John Scotus Eriugena, a name which translates as John the Irishman who was born in Ireland, achieved just such a result already in the ninth century. Eriugena, whose knowledge of Greek was well-nigh unique on the continent at this time, so that it prepared him for a major role in the Carolingian renaissance of learning that helped Europe out of the dark ages, called his magnum opus in Christian theology, simply, *Periphyseon (Concerning Nature)*, or in Latin, *De Divisione Naturae (Concerning the Divisions of Nature)*. In it he told the (hi)story of the creation in its journey from the Ultimate Source, the Uncreated Creator, through every genus and species of reality, to the final restoration of all of it in a union with the Uncreated and now no longer creating One, from whom it came and who was therefore at all times and places revealed in it and through it. In the telling of this story Eriugena explained the pivotal place of one species, *homo sapiens*, and within that species, the even more pivotal role of one man, the one in whom the creative Word of God became incarnate. So his story, told through a mixture of imagery and abstruse theological concepts, covered all the main areas of traditional Christian theology. *Periphyseon* is a thoroughly Christian theology, yet at the same time a thorough-going natural theology, a theology of *physis*, nature, as the title indicates.

And now memory gains momentum, and recalls another great Christian figure of some three centuries earlier than Eriugena, one who, like him, at a turn of the times, but now a turn for the worse and not for the better, wanted to translate the best of Greek wisdom to a Western empire that was rapidly losing the Greek language. This man was Boethius, and he had his understanding of his Christian faith focused as sharply as only impending death can sharpen one's focus on the most important things. He wrote his finest work, *The Consolation of Philosophy*, in his cell on deathrow. In this book he tells of being visited in his cell by a woman called Sophia (as in *philo-sophia*). We have little difficulty in identifying her with

Sophia, a woman we shall meet again in Proverbs 8, as the one through whom God creates the world. She leads Boethius to see all that is revealed in the natural world and its history, and in particular all that in his own sorry state epitomizes the problem of evil, of God and God's relationship to this world, its origin, course, salvation and destiny. (As Eriugena put it: *nemo intrat in coelum, nisi per philosophiam;* nobody enters heaven except through the love of Sophia-wisdom.)

Yet Boethius, unquestionably born a Christian, and a Christian who in fact has some fine works of Christian theology to his credit, never mentions Jesus the Christ by name during the whole course of the *Consolation*. This has puzzled most commentators, and might leave us permanently puzzled if memory did not interrupt once again to remind us of the fact that the Christians of the second century, just at the time when they were beginning to look like a new religion, decided that they needed a theology for their faith and way of life. They then borrowed for that purpose the theology that represented the very best of Greek philosophizing at the requisite theological level, and adopted it with only the occasional need for adaptation. This was a Stoicized Platonic philosophy of the *Logos*, or Word of God by whom all things were made; and they adapted it by claiming that this same divine Word had taken flesh in the man, Jesus of Nazareth. So total was the take-over of that Greek philosophical theology that Augustine felt he had to justify it by claiming of the Platonists: "change a few words and phrases, and they might as well be Christians." Once one considers that it is not the man, Jesus, as such, but the divine Word incarnate in him, that creates the world and finally saves those who fall foul of sin within it, it might begin to seem not quite so odd that Boethius could give an account of the faith in which he as a Christian found the final consolation and hope for life eternal, through the figure of Sophia, the feminine counterpart of the masculine Creator Word or Logos, without explicitly using the name of Jesus at all.

That can still seem very odd, of course, and it continues to pose a disturbing problem about the Christian faith of Boethius. Yet the point of interest for this prologue is not to solve that puzzle about Boethius, but to let memory bring to mind the extent to which Christian theology from the outset was, and can still be seen to coincide with, natural theology. Even the Christian theology of the Trinity directly borrowed its definitive logic and its distinctive terminology (one divine *ousia* in three *hypostaseis*), from non-Christian Platonists like Plotinus and Porphyry. So much for Aquinas insisting that, although God the creator is revealed in the natural world,

God's triune being is not. But enough reminiscence of past performance. There are some among the more evangelical and exclusivist of Christians who to this day would say that the extent of borrowing from the ancient Greeks is the extent of the pollution of the pure Christian water of life. And that any persistence in attempting to construe a Christian theology as a natural theology can promise little less than the end of the Christian faith. And, furthermore, that the only admirable parts of all these theological moves of the twentieth century, were the parts at which they faltered, petered out, or restored the clear distinction and total supremacy of the supernatural order of divine revelation and grace. To the point, preferably, at which nature and its detrimental history was entirely displaced as source of revelation and support of faith. And so, once again, the only way to meet this position on the matter is to pursue through the authoritative sources of the Christian faith recognized by all Christians, namely, the books of the Bible, the extent of any coincidence there in evidence of that Judeo-Christian faith with creation faith and the natural theology in which that latter is expressed. And only on that kind of study can further implications be assessed, for relationships of exclusivism or inclusivism, or of various degrees of these, as between different churches and religions and those of no church or religious allegiance at all.

Part One

THE ESSENCE OF THE FAITH
OF JESUS THE JEW

Chapter One

CREATION

One must have chaos in one, to give birth to a dancing star.
— Nietzsche, *Thus Spoke Zarathustra*

The Bible as the Foundation Myth of Christianity

The Christian Bible, made up of the Jewish scriptures that Christians now call the Old Testament, with the addition of a series of writings that Christians call the New Testament, is not as such, according to Christians, a divinely revealed text, as the *Qur'an,* for instance, is a divinely revealed text according to Muslims. Rather is the Bible a divinely inspired text, and as such it is for all Christian communities in the world the most authoritative witness to divine revelation in nature and history, and consummately of course the witness to the divine revelation that occurred in the life, death and destiny of Jesus of Nazareth. It is essential therefore that a one-volume Christian theology that purports to recover yet again the very essence of Christianity, be derived from beginning to end from the Bible, and be seen at every step to be honestly derived.

Begin then at a well-known beginning, with the creation myth that opens the Book of Genesis, and thereby opens the whole Bible. Remember only that myths are made of images. Images are those configurations through which reality first rewards the attentive, or more precisely the contemplative mind. The particular agency of the mind that deals in such revelations of reality is known as the imagination. Imagination works those configurative promptings by the real called images into suggested or seemingly possible interactions and movements, making a movie out of what might otherwise mistakenly seem a series of stills. And at the outer limits of this exercise the imagination eventually ends up by telling a cosmic story, resulting in nothing less than a cosmic myth. This is done through metaphors, for instance, the units of all poetry in particular. Metaphors bring the revealed and received images into at times quite surprising

29

interactions. So that each image in every such encounter is made pregnant with more meaning, or all are made pregnant with a broader and dynamic pattern of meaning that then seems to emerge from previously darker depths or hitherto impenetrable heights of the fabric of reality.

The lion is king of the forest; that juxtaposition of images allows a little more insight into the nature and behavior of lions, and of kings. The boy is father to the man; that imagined reversal of a normal sequence of these terms allows a more far reaching insight into the whole process of origin and growth. The distribution of prime numbers (the "atoms" of mathematics), though still impossible to predict by any mathematical formula as yet found for the purpose, seems to be mirrored by a subtle music that consists in combining sine waves of different frequencies (sine waves being those that come from the pure tone of a tuning fork). Until a certain configuration or image, this time an acoustic one, a configuration of "the music of the spheres," throws some light toward the mathematical configurations that might enable us to see yet further into the construction of reality itself. A musical mirror image that can shed light on the structuring of the physical universe. Reminiscent of Einstein's remark, "I think in music."

Therefore, the literal meaning and truth of metaphor in poetry or prose *is* the metaphorical meaning. That is to say, it is the meaning and especially the surplus of meaning that is released as it relieves the tension of images made to interact by the creative imagination of those well endowed with creative imagination. Those best endowed in this way are the seers or poets who are open to the images and their interactions offered by reality itself in the course of its self-revelation. From the beginning then of one's reading of the creation myth with which Genesis begins, and right through to the end of the Bible, it is essential to pay the closest attention to the imagery employed, and to the interweaving of that rich and concrete imagery. For otherwise the rich tapestry of truth that the Bible has to offer will not be recovered anew from a fabric that sometimes seems faded and frayed from the wear and tear of the ages.

The Christian Myth of Creation

Begin then with the first phrase of the Genesis myth and with its opening image which, as it happens, is an image of beginning: *Bereshith*, the first word of the Hebrew Bible, is translated "in the beginning." Now already this opening image is much richer in content than any simple temporal reference could exhaust. In fact, it need not really refer at all to the first day, the first moment in linear time of the existence of the universe. For it belongs to a family of image-terms that includes "once upon a time," *en arche, in principio*, "in origin" in the sense of "at source." As Eliade often remarked, the time of the cosmic myth is a time out of time; eternity, in fact. Though not eternity as an infinite length of linear time, but rather eternity in the sense in which Boethius defined it: the simultaneous and total possession of life without limit. So the myth that is governed by that first phrase is set to imagine the created order as it exists in and comes from the ultimate source at each and every moment of our linear inner-cosmic time. An act of creation and a created order then that is coincident with each moment of linear time. And continuous with all of them, immaterial whether their number in the end turns out to be infinite in either or both directions of past and future as we finite creatures see it. To imagine divine creation truly, that is to say, to imagine it as it is revealed at or from the ultimate source of all, is to imagine it happening now, at every now. From the world's-eye view of every creature immured in the cosmos it is continuous divine creation. But not an act of divine creation completed during the first day(s) of the world's history. Placing in existence a world that thereafter needed only to be sustained, whatever that might be taken to mean, or occasionally tweaked, whatever that might be taken to involve. Much the same can be said about mythic accounts that purport to portray the end of the world, and at first blush once again seem to do so in plain historical terms. These myths too are really accounts of the creation of the world as seen at the source, or from the source; and not as (to be) seen at some specifiable date in the future of linear time. Except that the imaginative strategy now is to show the creation returning to the source (eschatology), as it always does, rather than show it coming from the source (protology), as it always also does in creation myths of the "in the beginning" category.

Next, as one contemplates the creation at any given moment in its history, and sees as deeply into its at-source origins as its dynamic self-revealing structures allow and a finite human imagination can apprehend, questions begin to arise. What image of the divine act of creation seems most adequate to that which is so indirectly and dimly seen? The second word in the Genesis creation myth offers the biblical answer to that question. This is the Hebrew word, *bara*. It is always translated as "creates": but as this is myth and not a discourse in the logic of abstract ideas it must be asked: what image is implicated in this term? The answer is found by noticing that the root image in the term, *bara*, is the image of cutting; as in cutting out, shaping or forming. God the Creator creates by forming things, cutting or separating off, as the story continues and God is seen separating off light from darkness, waters above the sky-firmament from waters below it, dry land from the waters below. Such imagery of cutting out, separating and shaping — in short, forming — supplies the dominant imagery that offers human access to the primordial and ever-present activity of divine creation.

But cutting out of, forming out of what? That question seems to be suggested not only by the etymology of *bara* and the resulting image of forming, but by the very phrases in which, as the myth continues, some such question seems to be answered: "As God created (*bereshith bara elohim*) the heavens and the earth (that is, the whole world, the universe), the earth was without form (*tohu*) and void (*bohu*), and darkness was upon the face of the abyss." So far those who have taken up that question, "forming out of what?" and interpreted the answer are roughly divisible into two groups that in fact fall into opposing camps. One group takes this myth to imagine a kind of primeval soup, water and solids mingling in a material chaos, lying there in darkness, before God arrives with a will to make out of that chaos an ordered universe in which life could begin and blossom into eternity. As life could not even begin to do in the primeval chaos in and of itself. The other group resents this reading into the foundational text of their sacred scriptures what seems to them to be a crass form of dualism of God/spirit and chaos/matter, with its implication that God's creative activity is faced with a dark, utterly chaotic, life-hostile blob of matter independently in existence, that would forever of its very nature act as an adversarial force against God's purpose for life. Instead they propose a reading of the text in which a full stop is placed after the word "earth" ("In the beginning God created the heavens and the earth."), so that we are now to understand that God created the universe, all matter and spirit alike, but at first in chaotic form. And then, in a second move as it were, God brought order or form to this chaotic material soup so that life emerged from it. So read, this second group then insists, the text yields, or at the very least it prepares people for that abstruse philosophical theory known as creation out nothing.

Both interpretations misread the text. And although they are similar in the extent to which they fail to make due allowance for the fact that they deal with an imaginative apprehension and construction of what reality reveals of itself, they differ in what they get wrong as a result of this failure. The first group makes the mistake of taking the opening image of our myth, "in the beginning," to be a reference to linear time. So that it would make sense to say: before God began the activity of forming, this soupy lump of matter existed (and for how long?) The second group postulates an act of divine creation — together with a piece of punctuation of the text — for which there simply is no authorization in the text itself. An act of divine creation, this time, which must be imagined as something other than forming; an act — how imagined now ? — to be then followed by the divine act of forming a universe out of whatever it is that the first act of divine creation brought into existence.

Back then to the actual images as deployed in the text, in order to see if that importunate question — formed out of what? — needs to be reformulated, or how it can be answered. And first take into account the simultaneity of the effects of God's creative act, a simultaneity required by the realization that linear time, with its before and after has no place in the mythic image of the *bereshith*. For then it will be easy to see that the text imagines a fundamental feature of the world, namely, that chaos, however we later try to define the content of that image in concepts, comes into existence simultaneously with the forms that result from the creative act of forming. This feature is construed by a concurrence of images: the formless (*tohu*), the insubstantial or unreal (the root meaning of *bohu*), and the dark abyss in which there is not even light. What is conveyed by this mythic construction? What fundamental feature of creation comes into existence simultaneously with the forms continuously (from our worm's-eye point of view) created by God? Such a feature cannot in any case consist in another thing or kind of thing, for "thing" is a *form* of reality made by drawing lines (or cutting out along lines), drawing limits that define a thing or make it finite (from *finis*, the Latin term for limit). So this feature first characterized as formless (*tohu*) is a no-thing, a nothing, as all the contributory images in that context serve to clarify. *Bohu* connotes the insubstantial, the unreal; the dark void connotes the utter emptiness of any formed or formulatable content of any kind. And what the text then tells us is that an incursive no-thing-ness erupts into the cosmos simultaneously with the forming of finite things and of the entire universe that is continuously created from the interaction and interdependence of all finite things.

But how is this no-thing, this nothing, to be understood? In a purely static universe brought into existence, let us say, by an irresistible divine word of command, the "nothing" would probably have to be imagined as an actual "something," an empty receptacle, a great void that surrounds the boundaries of cosmic space. Into which the things that make up the universe, and indeed the whole universe, or the universe of universes might disappear forever, unless of course God kept them from falling in. But this is nonsense, strictly speaking. For we are now talking in terms of an empty space outside filled space, and that makes as little sense as talking of time before time. Space-time (the new name for the universe), in Stephen Hawking's felicitous phrase, is both finite in extent *and* without boundaries.

What then? Back once more to the terms of the myth. The divine act of creation is most adequately described as an act of forming. This creative act of forming is eternal, that is to say, from our point of view, continuous. And then, as further parts of the myth will shortly tell us, the God who forms the universe and everything in it does so in a manner that enables the creatures to co-operate in this creative forming. Therefore the universe was not completed in its content and structures a long time ago, thereafter needing only to be sustained and governed, and perhaps repaired every now and then. So that creatures are left with two, and only two, options: either to live in and with it as it is, or to damage it. The universe is a continuously created and creative entity through and through, created by a range of agencies, from the creator God down to the meanest thing that exists. In sum, the universe intrinsically and essentially and in all its parts is a truly evolving universe. And this means also, with implications to be drawn later, that what is so often referred to as sustaining and governing, or ruling the universe on God's part, is in reality nothing other than God's continuing creating of the evolving forms of reality. Continuously creating through the creative contributions of all creatures, down to the meanest thing that moves; creative abilities of which God is also the source and enabler.

For evolution is an activity that goes on, and not an account of a process that happened and happens by chance. It is an activity whereby God and creatures combine by God's creative initiative to bring about ever new forms of things, that is to say, transformations of things. Evolution is just a name for continuous creation. Aristotle recognized something of this fact when he defined nature (*physis*). Nature, he wrote, is a name for that which things of a certain species have in common: human nature, for instance. So Aristotle defined nature as a form (of reality) that has within itself the possibility of movement, change, development. And all of the ancient myths and legends of metamorphosis (*morphe* being the Greek term for form) bear witness to that same feature of our universe by which it is continuously transformed. The transformation takes place at the level of the individual thing; as when I want to die to, when I want to kill off, my old self and become a new person. It takes place between things and species of things because of that interaction and interdependence that makes (them) a universe. They invade each other and assimilate each other so that the lines of the forms that define each and everyone as things in their own right become malleable and permeable. The bodies I eat and defecate, the air I breathe in and out, the light and heat I absorb and reflect, the water I drink and exude — the four ancient elements: earth, air, fire and water — more than amply illustrate this permanently transformable and ultimately evolutionary character of reality. Although none of these ancient ones could describe that process as modern science can do.

So every transformation in the universal process of evolutionary creativity involves a death of existing forms or a de-formation. And since it is form that makes each thing and species of thing to be and to be what it is, the de-forming becomes the negative, nihilating force whereby one form of reality or thing is turned into another and thus itself made to cease to be what it was. This negative, nihilating, no-thinging force is then the inevitable negative pole of the positive force of creative evolution that forever brings new or renewed forms of being. It is a force of no-thing-ness, of un-thing-ing a previous form of existence. This force of nothingness is not something distinct from, or independent of creative power, and as such over against creative power, adversarial, satanic, as it is so often portrayed in crass dualist myths and philosophies. Although it can sometimes approach such satanic status in the case of agents who deliberately do evil, but that matter is dealt with later in the creation myth of Genesis. For the moment it is sufficient to notice that it is the same creative force that brings into play simultaneously both being and the incursive nothingness; the advancing forms of life and the accompanying deformation or, more strongly put, the death of previous forms.

Part of what has been observed in the course of the long and studious contemplation that gave rise to this book is that the great poet is the seer, the prophet, the visionary, who sees to* deeply into the fabric of reality that the ways of the Creator with creation are revealed in the ensuing poetry, and with a power and a clarity seldom equaled in other forms. For instance, in a poem by Dylan Thomas, the title of which is its first line: "The force that through the green fuse drives the flower," the same force that "drives my green age" is also the force that is "my destroyer." Likened

*Should ' so"@@?

by some commentators to the image of "chi" in Chinese Taoist philosophy and thence to the image of the creator spirit in Judaeo-Christian creation theology, this "force" in Thomas's poem clearly reveals its dual effect in creating ever-new life by destroying older forms of it. Or as the Bible puts it later (Isa. 45:7) in a chapter that has the Genesis myth much in mind: "forming light and creating darkness, making *shalom* and creating evil, I am the Lord who does all these things." (*Shalom*, peace means more than the absence of strife: it means well-being, prospering toward life full and undiminished.)

Here incidentally is an understandable meaning of that otherwise abstruse phrase, creation out of nothing. Every new creation comes from the de-formation, the no-thing-ing of the (form of) thing that went before. That is a process that can be witnessed in all the co-operative divine-creaturely creativity that continuously makes our everyday world to evolve. Of course, to refer to this process simply as creation out of nothing, and to say no more about it, would be tantamount to giving a very partial, not to say biased view of creation. That would be to see the process of creation solely from the perspective of the negative pole. In reality the process is governed throughout by the positive pole: a creative act takes a form of reality and makes of it something new or better, introducing a determinate incursive nothingness of previous form as a passing element on the way. And this would be better described as a transient nothingness that comes out of creation, before being described as a creation out of nothing (the nothing-ing of the previous form), as it also always is.

And yet there is a certain honesty in describing this process from our worm's eye point of view as first and foremost a continuous creation out of nothing. For creatures who are always inclined to cling to whatever comforts the present forms of their existence may bring (like Nietzsche's Ultimate Man), are generally fearful also of the unfamiliar. And yet more fearful of any talk of destroying, of dying, of any form of existence coming to nothing. When such fears bring the thought of dying in any shape or form to the forefront of minds contemplating creation, it is to that thought they have to steel themselves. And so they have to persuade themselves, as they try to raise the will to create, that it will be, and be worth being a creation out of an incursive nothingness. In any case, that is one way of reading the Genesis text as an endorsement of the idea of creation out of nothing. The act of creation faces both God and creatures with the simultaneous prospect of the darkness, the emptiness, the chaos through which they have to go in order to reach the fullest goal of all creation. That the whole of the continuous and progressive creation of this universe must be, from the beginning, a creation out of nothing-ing, out of a certain inevitable nothingness.

So nothingness must be experienced by God the creator as much as it is experienced by the co-creative creatures. In fact God must experience nothingness in a generic as well as a determinate sense. That is to say, as the ultimate source of all the finite reality that constitutes space-time, God experiences the nothingness that is brought into existence on the limits of that reality, like a darkness that comes naturally and inevitably into existence at the limits of light emitted. But God also experiences the incursive determinative nothingnesses that accompany the continuous transformation of each and every thing that makes up the space-time universe. And perhaps the generic experience of nothingness is simply the generalized impression of all the determinate nothingnesses that are continually brought to bear by the very divine act of creating from the beginning the auxiliary creators. The inevitable transformations of these that is forever simultaneously brought about by the God who forever brings them into being as co-creators.

In any case, it is this revelation of God as inevitable creator also of the incursive force of nothingness, that is captured for the imagination in the biblical images of the deep, the waters that always threaten to flood and obliterate once again the formed earth (as in flood stories). It is captured more specifically still, in the images of those mythical monsters of the deep, the *behemoth*, of which Moby Dick is one of the latest avatars, that also signify this incursive and destructive nothingness. For these are represented as creatures of God, certainly: "So God created the great sea monsters." But they are created in the sense in which God creates the darkness by creating the light; the incursive no-thing-ness that God must of necessity create; and that God cannot but create — "forming light and creating darkness . . . I am the Lord" (Isa. 45:7) And that darkness that always inevitably emerges at the limits of the light, that nothingness God can then constantly overcome only by continuous creation.

It is this feature of divine creation that Plato, in his story of divine creation in the *Timaeus*, so clearly captures when he portrays the creator making everything as good as is possible, faced as the creator is by a certain constraining necessity. It is the feature that Hegel had in mind when he wrote about the suffering God, and even of the death of God; for God knows the suffering of deformation and death in God's very being as creator. It is also the point of the idea of *zimsum* in a certain Jewish theology of creation: the notion of a contraction of God, a withdrawal, an incursion of nothingness into the very being of God as creator, in order that creatures should be and live and reach fulfillment in God. Even Plotinus, for all that is said about the utter immutability and invulnerability of a Platonist divinity, allowed that though God's being in itself does not change or suffer, God the continuous creator is ever immanent in the creation and as such experiences the change and the daily dying that characterizes creation. For, as Plotinus himself put it, "we must not think of ourselves as cut off from the Source of life; rather we breathe and consist in it, for it does not give itself to us and then withdraw itself, but ever lifts and bears us."

Nietzsche might well be our master in these matters of understanding the true nature and process of creation, for creation provides the key image and idea for his seminal work, *Thus Spoke Zarathustra*. Except of course that Nietzsche could not bring himself to include in his account of continuous creation the God he heard the Christians preach. As he heard the Christian message, this God had created everything long ago, had left us no room for further creation, had left humanity to accept the status quo, to accept the undemanding pleasures and achievements of the present, as if humanity had always already reached, in this earthly life, the status of the Ultimate Man. What would there be to create, he asks, if such a creator God existed? So Zarathustra, the prophet of the Superman (and candidate for the role) calls for co-creators, people who can take to heart this knowledge: "that the creation may exist, that itself requires suffering and much transformation." One must take chaos to one's heart, to give birth to a dancing star. The evolving Superman most of all must have the courage to "go down" (*untergang*), to see destroyed in himself first and then in others much that was good, much of the values of past and present forms of existence. But all in order to transcend (*übergang*) those to higher forms of existence, and the higher values of truth, goodness and beauty, ultimately indescribable in our present state, that will then be realized.

In this cosmic tale of constantly leaving off the affirmation of present forms, of serial dyings in order to transcend all of this toward life now unimaginable, Nietzsche is a true Hegelian. Except that Hegel's *Phenomenology of Spirit* — *his* seminal work and arguably the most accomplished work of Christian theology in the modern era — saw past the superficial picture of a God who created the world out of some indeterminate nothingness in a one-off act. Hegel saw in the Christian sources the Creator Spirit that forever "objectifies" itself in the creation. And since it is a *Creator* Spirit that is "objectified," that is revealed at work in every creature down to the lowest thing that exists, then, as Nietzsche put it: "all creatures hitherto have created something beyond themselves" — and Nietzsche said this in the context of his angry question to Ultimate Man, "do you want to be the ebb of this great tide?"

The Phenomenology of Spirit, like the masterpiece of that great Irish theologian, John Scotus Eriugena's *Periphyseon* before it, adopts once more for the portrayal of this continuous creation that ancient master symbol of exodus and return. The journey of created reality as it emerges from God, out to the limits of matter. And then, and it is on this that the *Phenomenology* concentrates, the return journey of all things, back to a most intimate union with the God from which they came. A return journey in which the human being proves pivotal. And this part of the itinerary is plotted as a repetition of the dialectic of being and becoming: the affirmative stage, still clinging to the status quo, then the other two stages of the negation and the negation of the negation. Together these two apparent negatives make up a positive: a transformation involving, first, going through the nothingness, the destruction, the death of the forms of the previous stage, and then the overcoming of the negativity of the second stage, thereby raising all that was best in the first stage to higher forms. The journey continues with the repetition of these three stages, until the reunion of finite spirits with the Creator Spirit is complete of its kind. A Hegelian dialectic of existence that had already found a more pithy expression in Jesus's statement to the effect that you must lose life to gain life.

But this is running far ahead of the reading of the Genesis myth so far, and in fact anticipating much that the myth still has to tell. So, back once more to the text, and to the next image that it introduces, the image of agencies in creation. (Agencies in creation is the most neutral term possible for these, before attempting a fuller explanation later on of all that may be at issue in this context.)

Images of Agencies Involved in the Creation of the World

The Genesis myth, as early as its second and third sentences, introduces what appear to be two agencies involved in the creation of the world. The first is introduced under the image of spirit: "the spirit of God hovered over (or brooded upon) the surface of the waters." Now this first, spirit-agency creation-image receives only minimal reference and development in the course of the Genesis myth itself. The root meaning of the Hebrew word for spirit, *ruach*, is moving air, wind, breath. And so the image is used when the myth describes the creation of human life in terms of God breathing "the breath of life" into the nostrils of the molded clay figurine of Adam (Gen. 2:7). There the image of the spirit of God depicts the creation of human life, but later in the Bible other ancillary images are used in order to stretch the connotation of the spirit-image further than the creation of humanity.

Later in the Bible there is the ancillary image of the dove, for instance, the form in which the spirit (of) God is depicted coming upon Jesus at John's baptism (Luke 3:22). The dove is the sign of *shalom*, the rest and peace of the possession of life fulfilled and undiminished, the end goal of all divine creation. That image of spirit also is anticipated here in the first sentence of this myth, in the imagery of hovering or brooding over the abyss. It resonates with other ancient images of the origin on the world as a giving birth to, a bringing forth and hatching out of the world, as it appears perfect and yet growing, from the God who creates it. Later in the Bible also there is the ancillary image of fire, the form in which the spirit (of) God is depicted coming upon the disciples of Jesus in the Pentecost scene, for example (Acts 2:2–3; see also Acts 10:44–45 for the "Pentecost of the Gentiles"), where the ancillary image of tongues of fire is added to that of the mighty wind. Fire in fact is without doubt the most ancient, universal and comprehensive image of continuous divine creativity. For just as the dove-symbol provides the image of the grand fulfillment of all divine creation; fire, the heat-and-light transformer that brings new forms of things into existence in the very process of destroying old forms, provides the most comprehensive image of the whole process of creation from beginning to end. And fire as the image par excellence of creation is inevitably instanced for us who live in the solar system primarily by the sun as symbol of the divine creator.

But then the creation myth of Genesis switches at the beginning of its second sentence to another image for what appears to be another agency in the divine creation of the world: the image of the word, "And God said." And this myth then leaves the image of the spirit, with its ancillary images, for later recall. At first blush the image of the creating word, as it enters so abruptly here, does seem to go against the image suggested by the verb, *bara*, and by its ancillary images of separating out, cutting out, and so shaping, forming. It certainly seems as if the image of the word is the image of a word of command: "And God said, 'let there be light,' and there was light." An order from the all-powerful; no argument; utter and complete compliance.

Many, probably most, Christian theologians and preachers take this image of irresistible command to be the dominant image of divine creation in the whole of this opening myth. Despite the fact that the text immediately goes on to speak of God cutting out, separating light from darkness. Despite the fact that all of the following words of God quoted in the myth convey a different image of word and words than does the image of word conveyed in this second sentence when taken altogether separately and all by itself. For all the other quoted words of the creator God convey the impression of God talking to herself, God outlining ideas, designs, plans by which to carry out the actual creation. And to carry it out, it is worth noting, *either* by God directly engaging in the separating out, cutting out, forming, *or* by God empowering already formed entities to then themselves form others, to bring others into being. As when God says, "let the earth put forth vegetation, plants yielding seed, and fruit trees bearing fruit in which is their seed, each according to its kind"; and "let the waters bring forth swarms of living creatures"; and "let the earth bring forth living creatures according to their kinds, cattle and creeping things and beasts"; and above all when God says, "let us make man in our image" — surely in this context meaning the image of a creator.

So there are two rather different images of word, both of which appear to be suggested in the myth. One, the image of word as an expletive, a command: present arms; light, present yourself. The other, the image of a formulation of ideas in the mind, a formula expressed in words or equivalent languages, like the language of mathematics for instance. A formulaic design or plan first conceived in an imaginative mind, by means of which the creation in question is then executed. This second image of word is best illustrated by reference to one Greek term for word, the term *logos*. This is the very term that is chosen in the opening sentence of the Fourth Gospel in order to repeat what is implied about an agency in creation at this point of the Genesis myth. "In the beginning was the Word (*Logos*) . . . all things were made through him." Now *Logos* connotes a rational, intelligible construction — a plan, a formula, a design — which in its verbalized form could run to anything from a sentence to a book; and in the language of mathematics could run from a succinct equation such as $E=mc^2$ to several pages of numbers, letters and other ciphers.

But any and all of which can in principle be read off from the resulting realized forms, designs, patterns, plans, observable in nature and in natural behavior. By extension *logos* can refer to reason, to the mind, the rational or intellectual principle that conceives the exemplar ideas that make up such rational, intelligible structures, in the process of executing them in reality.

It is interesting to note that scientists today sometimes think of DNA sequences, those determinative factors in the evolution of living species in this constantly creative and co-created universe, as sentences in which words or perhaps even letters repeatedly change or are changed. And it is interesting to note also that this *logos* image of word, when repeated in the Fourth Gospel, becomes personified. That is to say, it is then extended to become an image of a reason, an intellectual principle, a mind that contains the dynamic design and implements it in the activity of continuous creativity that is seen from the perspective of the intelligent creature as the process of evolution. The image of "word" has then become, by dint of its own natural possibilities of extension, the image of a thinking, willing, executing reason. An entity such as we would normally include in the category of person. "In the beginning was the *Logos* . . . all things were made through him."

But of course it was not necessary to wait for the addition of what Christians call the New Testament to what thereby became the Christian Bible in order to see this particular image of an agency in creation personified in this manner. For this was already done, and most thoroughly done in what then came to be called by Christians the Old Testament. Take for example the Book of Proverbs, if only because other books in which this personification is carried out are considered by some Jews and Christians to be apocryphal. The personified agency through which or rather, as it must now be phrased, through whom God creates the world, is named in Proverbs, in the Greek Septuagint text, as *Sophia*, Wisdom. Now the term *Sophia* is like a twin to *Logos* in that it connotes a rational construction of knowledge or truth that is then operative in the execution of the creative act. And yet, these are not quite identical twins. For there are two differences between the *Logos* image and the *Sophia* image that are relevant to the fuller understanding of the foundational Christian doctrine of divine creation as that is conveyed by myth. The first difference lies in the fact that, when this agency in creation is personified, the image of *Sophia* suggests that the personal agent through whom the world is created is of the feminine gender. Whereas the image of *Logos* suggests that this agent is of the masculine gender — this by sheer dint of the gender of the Greek words used. This may then seem quite accidental, yet it does have implications for discussions of the gender of God, and for some of the erstwhile effects of this discussion in social and political terms.

The second difference is more difficult to define, yet much more important for this analysis of the full meaning of the Christian myth of divine creation. Put it this way, perhaps: the *Logos* term for the mind and for the formulae it produces in the process of creating the world, suggests a rather theoretical structure of abstract concepts or ideas. Whereas the *Sophia* term, and the formulae it produces in the process of continuous creation by God and creatures, suggests rather a more pragmatic structure of images and ideas. For *Sophia* must be translated as "wisdom," and wisdom suggests, less a purely theoretical knowledge of the world than a practical knowledge of it that tells us how to live in and with it for the best outcome for all. From the point of view of the creature this latter term appears to be preferable if only because it is by engaging with the world that we learn all we will ever know about it and about all other agents that are operative with us within it. As a pragmatist epistemology would have it, knowing how is prior to knowing that, or knowing what things are comes from learning how to deal with them. So that *Sophia* refers to a learning of the truth by walking a way, by living a life. Just as Jesus is made to describe what he wished his followers to learn as a way and a life, and as such the truth about God and the world. But long before Jesus, at least as far back as Heraclitus, those whose profession it was to spread the love of wisdom (*philo-sophia*, philosophy), the philosophers, insisted that the acquisition of this wisdom consisted essentially in learning a way, in living a waking life, as Heraclitus himself put it, rather than the self-enclosed life of one walking about in a permanent day-dream.

From the point of view of the agency through which God creates the world then, the naming of this agency as *Sophia* suggests that this agency achieves the truth, goodness and beauty of created reality precisely by acting formatively and transformatively on and with each and every nature that constitutes reality. Creating them in such a way as to inform and empower these to form and transform themselves and each other. Thereby revealing *Sophia's* own presence and something of its own nature, simultaneously with the revelation of some broad lines at least of the way the creatures are to walk so that all reach fulfillment as their end. More briefly stated, the *Sophia* image for this agency in creation achieves far more substantial and consistent expression of its immanence in the evolving creation than does the twin image of *Logos*. For the latter can always leave lying about an impression of a mind full of more theoretical ideas existing before, or beyond an actual creation — however the terms, before and beyond, are then to be understood or explained. Whereas the image of *Sophia* gives more the impression of more practical knowledge, the knowledge characteristic of the creator in the act of creation, and shared then by derivative co-creators.

In the Book of Proverbs (8:22ff.) there is a myth that reprises so much of the imagery and events of the opening myth of Genesis that it can be seen as a retelling of the latter. It is a kind of commentary on Proverbs 3:19, "the Lord by wisdom founded the earth," and an anticipation of the Fourth Gospel's opening account of God creating all things through the Word. In this myth Wisdom herself speaks: "The Lord brought me forth at the beginning of his way...from eternity I was appointed...when there were no depths, I was given birth...before he made the earth...when he established the heavens, I was there...I was beside him like a master craftsman"; or, clearer still, at the beginning of Proverbs 9, where an ancient image is used, an image of the world as a house with the sky-roof held up by pillars: "Wisdom has built her house; she has hewn out its seven pillars."

The use of the image of wisdom for this agency in creation then adds to the use of the image of word, even in its *Logos* form, a clear impression of a knowledge, a truth that is initiated in envisaging something to be done or made, something to be created, a knowing how that then entails a knowing that. This is a knowledge that is then expressed and communicated most fully and efficiently in the course of the resultant doing or making in itself. And as a consequence, it is a knowledge and a truth that can best be partaken of by those who take part in the doing and making at first envisaged and simultaneously engaged in by the original agency. No wonder that the agency imagined as wisdom in the text is also personified so that the image expands to convey the connotation of the wise creator of the world. The image of *Sophia* is then an image of a divine woman; for the credentials of creating the world are the best indicators of divine status that we may have. Correspondingly, her most original, essential and comprehensive self-revelation consists in the continuous creation in which she is engaged, a continuous creation that gives existence and life and brings all to the perfection of *shalom*.

Further, the creatures who can come to know her do so by engaging with her in that same creative work, and learn as they do so to advance toward that same goal of all creation, the unthreatened perfection of limitless life. Recall the way in which the opening Genesis myth imagined creatures like the earth and the sea, various seed-bearing species, and above all the human species made in the image of the creator and hence husbandman of the creation, as procreators in the grand creative, evolutionary élan of all existence. Further still, seeing that it is by living among and with all things for the best outcome for all in the utter interdependence of all things that make up the universe, that we learn all we may ever know about ourselves and all the other interactive agencies we encounter, it follows that whatever knowledge of truth we gain is simultaneously a knowledge of right. In other words, just as the whole of creation is a moral enterprise, just so does the truth we acquire have the joint character of a truth of how things are and how they ought to be. Just so does the truth we acquire have as its source and inspiration the constant revelation of the ultimate creator at work and with that the revelation of the general lines of what is and will be for the best. As the much maligned medieval Scholastic metaphysics used to put it: *ens et verum convertunter* (being and truth are convertible), *ens et bonum convertunter* (being and goodness are convertible); so that truth and goodness are thereby convertible also. The whole relationship of religion and morality in the Judeo-Christian tradition is here implicated, but that must await a fuller analysis later.

Little wonder that the personified *Sophia* of Proverbs, having declared herself to be the agent-creator of the universe, then goes on to declare, "he who finds me finds life . . . all who hate me love death" (8:35–36); and even goes on to portray in terms of eating and drinking the necessary partaking of her (wisdom) by those who would be pro-creators: "come eat my bread, and drink the wine I have mixed" (9:5). That eating and drinking imagery for the partaking of creative wisdom, is put more strongly still in another piece of so-called wisdom literature, the apocryphal *Wisdom of Jesus ben Sira* (24:21), where *Sophia* now talks in terms of being eaten herself: "Those who eat me will hunger for more, and those who drink me will thirst for more" (perhaps another way of saying that they will never hunger or thirst for anything else). The imagery here echoes back to the "Fall" episode of the Genesis myth, and the eating of the tree of the knowledge of good and evil; an echo back that is authorized in Proverbs 3:18 which says of *Sophia*, "she is a tree of life to those who lay hold on her." The imagery also echoes forward to the eucharistic imagery and sacramental symbolism of the New Testament and in particular to the difficult eucharistic text of the Fourth Gospel (John 6:51–59) in which Jesus talks of his followers eating his flesh and drinking his blood, of being himself consumed by them. But these aspects of the wisdom imagery must be left for later analysis also when the Fall comes up for consideration and, later still, the Christian sacraments.

It is a little difficult to say if this arresting imagery of *Sophia* herself being eaten yields and confirms the theme enclosed in the idea of creation out of nothing: the theme, namely, that the creator experiences nothing-ing, suffering, death even, in the very course of continuous creation. And that these same experiences are inevitable and even more real for all creatures that procreate under the divine Creator's guidance and power. Or perhaps what should be said here is that it would be difficult to say this with certainty, with reference to the Wisdom material, if one stopped reading the Bible before reading what Christians call the New Testament. For in that latter collection it is made entirely obvious once again that the cooperation in creation to which human creatures in particular are called, in the image of the Creator, and as partakers of divine wisdom, entails their daily dying. And not least the dying to self, the de-forming of current forms of existence, as part of the evolving trans-formation that creation promises. For example, Jesus in all four Gospels talks about eating his flesh and drinking his blood, under the symbolism of the bread and wine, symbolizing Jesus giving his life on the cross for the coming of the new creation, in which the divine creator's way with the world will truly rule the world, as it did "in the beginning." For the kingdom of God arrives when the pro-creators who symbolically eat this self-sacrificing, flesh-and-blood incarnation of divine agency, Jesus, thereby commit themselves to their pro-creative responsibilities, through all the crucifixions encountered on the way to *shalom*. Paul puts all of that much more pithily, and just as clearly in the imagery of the Wisdom literature when he defines the cross of Jesus, that is to say, Christ crucified, as the wisdom of God, the paradigmatic event in which the power and presence of divine *Sophia* makes its appearance in the world. For that reason, Paul declares that he "decided to know nothing among you except Christ and him crucified." Here then is a major text of the wisdom literature of the Bible — and this none the less for the fact that Paul also writes at the opening of this text of "the word (*Logos*) of the cross" — in which the theme of creator and creatures suffering their own nothinging is at the very forefront of the ac-count of creation, and of creation's ultimate source and its final promise (1 Cor. 1:18–2:5).

Finally, in the Wisdom literature of the Bible, not only is *Sophia*-Wisdom twinned with Word-*Logos*, she is also linked with *Ruach*-Spirit in this same respect. Just as Word and Spirit were together as agencies in creation in the opening Genesis myth, a scenario briefly recalled in Psalm 33:6: "By the word of the Lord the heavens were made, and all their host by the breath of his mouth." And this same twinning and linking of Wisdom and Spirit is continued in a variety of forms in the Wisdom literature written before Christ. In the Wisdom of Solomon, Wisdom is described as spirit: "For she is a breath of the power of God" (7:25); and she is again twinned with the Word: "O God...who hast made all things by thy word, and by thy wisdom hast formed man." Or it is said of Wisdom, "the fashioner of all things" who thereby teaches all who desire wisdom that, "in her there is a spirit that is intelligent, holy...loving the good...beneficent...omnipotent...penetrating through all spirits that are intelligent and pure...she pervades and penetrates all things" (7:22–24). Creator Wisdom, Creator Word, Creator Spirit, the agencies — or do we still need the plural? Perhaps the singular would suffice? — the agency through which God creates all things and reveals all to all.

Paul, it is already noted, sees the power and presence par excellence of the Creator Wisdom in the cross of Jesus, the event in which Jesus accepts his own nothinging for the sake of a new creation, and a certain twinning with the Word of the cross was hinted there also. And that presence and power is affirmed in the life of Jesus from conception to redeeming death and beyond in the use of the image of Word becoming flesh in Jesus, deployed at the beginning of the Fourth Gospel, where it is specifically described as the Word by which the world is created. Is the Wisdom imagery used of Jesus's life also? In rare texts, yes, but then the use of the Word image is even more rare in respect of Jesus. During his public life Jesus justifies table-fellowship by saying that "wisdom is justified by her deeds" (Matt. 18:19), a particularly interesting passage in view of the symbolism of the meal invoked by Wisdom herself. And then there are the questions asked about Jesus in his home synagogue: "What is this wisdom given him? What mighty works are wrought by his hands?"

And the related imagery of Creator Spirit used with respect to Jesus? Well, that is simply everywhere in the New Testament, from his conception to his resurrection and beyond. "The Holy Spirit will come upon you...therefore the child to be born will be...the son of God," so the angel speaks to Mary at the conception of Jesus (Luke 1:35). And this imagery of his conception, now a Spirit imagery, is designed to secure what John's Word imagery secured for the same event, namely, a claim concerning the presence and power in Jesus of God's agency in creation. So powerful a presence as to allow Jesus to do just as God does through the agency of Spirit (as of Wisdom or Word), namely, to continuously create and re-create an ever new creation, and by so doing to earn the title *son of God*. So throughout the Bible the imagery of Word, Wisdom, and Spirit, separately or together, all equally images of agencies in creation, are used in order to present the claim that the world is continuously created and re-created. And this apparent interchangeability of the images of Word, Wisdom, and Spirit must add to the inevitable question of the metaphysical status of such agencies in divine creation the equally inevitable question: is it not one agency with three names, rather than three agencies, or more? But these further questions must await the section on Trinity.

For the moment it is useful only to rehearse in summary form the differences between envisaging the Willed Word or Logos/Sophia-like Spirit as a formula set in motion, a dynamic design enacted, rather than an expletive-like command issued by an irresistible power. First, it has been suggested already, on the former understanding of the Creative Word there is no difference between a continuously created and creative universe and an evolving universe. So that all of these tiresome and increasingly obtuse arguments between creationists (mainly religious) and evolutionists (mainly scientists) really do look like an increasingly irrelevant side-show. This matter will come up again in the last chapter. Meanwhile, one can only hope that the creationist-evolutionist debate, if not ended, can be confined to the more backward parts of the United States.

Second, the forming rather than the commanding image of the act of creation enables us to see that divine immanence and divine transcendence are co-ordinates rather than contraries. For the forming image envisages God always working in and with all the material of the universe, rather than shouting it into existence in some static form from some "infinite qualitative distance." So that God is even closer to us creatures than the sandals on our feet, and the double immanence in which the Bible deals then obtains in fact: we in the hands of God, and God ever working in and through us. And divine transcendence, like ours, consists in God ever moving and drawing us creatures beyond all current forms, while remaining in and among and with us.

Third, when it comes to understanding the relationship between Creator and creatures in the matter of morals, the image of the act of creation as a command issued by irresistible power is likely to spill over into a divine command theory of the origin of moral law. A theory of morals already and inevitably infected with the might-as-right virus that presages the death of all true morality. Whereas the wise-design-in-effect image of creation communicates to creatures the formula for being and for well-being, as it simultaneously invites creatures to take their own imaginative, creative and responsible parts in advancing that same evolving creation, with all the dignity of genuinely free partners in the grandest project of all.

And, last but not least, the image of creation by dynamic design invokes the idea of God, the Ultimate Artist. It invokes the image of creation as a work of art, and so it invokes the familiar adage in this context: *ars gratia artis*, the work of art as its own end and purpose, requiring no ulterior motive. This imagery at the very least forestalls an all too common picture of the divine Creator as some sort of egotistical megalomaniac who can never get enough of praise and glory, not in all eternity. This does not mean that we should not praise and thank, for indeed we should, and such a eucharistic attitude proves to be an important spur to our moral responsibility, as we must soon see. But it does mean that the purpose of divine creation is the goodness and beauty of what is created, no ulterior motive or purpose required, or even allowed, for Creator or creature.

A Borrowed Theology: The First Christian Theology of Creation

The biblical account of creation as seen here so far is predominantly, if not exclusively, mythic in form; it is contrived by means of image and story. Now early Christianity expanded into a Roman empire that still up to the end of the first century C.E. had koine Greek as its lingua franca, and that for much longer conducted its highest analytic and critical thinking as a continuation of a tradition of Greek philosophy which at the end of that century was already some seven hundred years old. And as Christianity expanded and preached its good news about God and the world, its proponents came under increasing mockery and expressions of contempt from the educated elite of that Greco-Roman world. After all, Greek philosophy had originated partly at least out of disillusion with myths and the kind of unedifying, not to say pernicious, nonsense the myths spread, about gods behaving even worse than the lowest classes in society. And here it was all back again! Or so it seemed, if one listened to these Messiah freaks (for that is what the nickname, Christian, conveyed) spreading some nonsense about an executed state criminal from some obscure part of the empire coming as son of God, no less, to save us all. Folly indeed to "the Greeks," as Paul admitted and, yes, as he also allowed, it was mostly the uneducated lower classes who embraced the new nonsense. So, toward the end of the second century C.E. some educated Christians decided to write apologias for Christianity that they hoped would obviate the demoralizing contempt of this educated elite and facilitate instead the spread of their faith. And the shared strategy for doing this seemed to be to prove to "the Greeks" that the Christian scriptures and preaching were saying nothing different, if perhaps something more, than what was said in the philosophy of their cultured despisers. Most particularly at the level of their philosophical investigation into the ultimate creative sources of the world, its ways and its final prospects, the level of philosophy known then as now as natural theology (*theologia physikon*).

Now this strategy clearly involved a borrowing of Greek natural theology, the theology with which the philosophers of Greece had furnished indigenous Greek religion. And, as it happened, so successful was the strategy that educated Christians thereafter continued to borrow the same theology right down to the time when Christianity became the established religion of the empire and Christendom was born. By the fifth century C.E. virtually the whole of the Christian story of God and the fate of the world — even the image of the triune God — was converted into the terms of the natural theology of "the Greeks." The implications of this fact — and it is a demonstrable fact — are far reaching indeed. The implication that most interests the argument of this present work is this: the Greek natural theology borrowed for these apologetic and thereafter missionary purposes must have contained a very great deal of the truth about God and the world, for otherwise it could not have served so well for presenting the substance of the Christian myth. This is the implication that was acknowledged so handsomely by Augustine when he said of the dominant Neo-Platonists of his time, "change a few words and phrases and they might be Christians." So it is necessary to outline on its own terms and as briefly as possible this philosophy of a rival religion, if only to assess the rate of survival of our biblical faith in this its latest embodiment so far, and to understand the reasons for such rate of survival as may be recognized.

Even the briefest description of Greek natural theology — the theology of those whom the Greeks themselves called the *physiologoi* (the rational investigators of nature) — must go back, however briefly, to Stoicism.

This was a school of philosophy founded by Zeno some three centuries before Christ. Zeno said that the world derived from two principles, an active and a passive, which he named respectively as *logos* and *hyle*, word and matter. *Logos* is the intellectual principle, reason, and it is the truly creative principle that actively forms the universe. It is described as a *spermatikos logos* in that it contains the *spermatikoi logoi*, the exemplar or seminal (seed-like) forms by which all the dynamic things that then form the universe are themselves formed. Further, from the point of view of this first principle of the universe those creatures called human beings, creatures themselves formed in such a manner as to be endowed with reason, can also be called subordinate or derivative *spermatikoi logoi*. For they can consciously co-operate in the continuous creation that is the hallmark of the Source-Logos, or not co-operate, as they have the ability, the freedom and the dignity to choose.

Because of this element of continuous creativity the ultimate fashioning *Logos* is called a *pur technikon*, a craftsman-like fire. And by association with this image, it is also called *pneuma, ruach*, spirit, as air is linked with fire — and earth with water — in the ancient ranking of the elements. The oldest symbol of a creator of the universe is thereby evoked, and a clear and distinct echo heard of Heraclitus's divine Logos-creator of a world in constant evolution. This *Logos* — the initial capital letter for deity is now unavoidable — is then also called Zeus, an indication of the fact that Greek philosophers did not take themselves to be providing some abstruse rational alternative to the religion that people practiced. Rather did they take themselves to be providing a truer and more inspiring account of that religion's worldview and consequent praxis than myths had managed to achieve. No surprise then to find Cleanthes, the second head of this school of philosophy, composing a hymn to Zeus that has survived to this day.

Finally, the creator *Logos* was also called *physis* or Nature. And because the Stoics set out as one of the prime objectives of their old-new system of philosophy to get rid of what they thought to be the endemic and increasing dualism of mind and matter so characteristic of the dominant Platonism of the time, the early Stoics insisted that calling God *physis* meant that God was indeed, like everything that existed, a body, or at least an embodied entity. Their line of argument toward this conclusion is easily observed. Aristotle had defined *physis*, nature, as a kinetic form, that is to say, a form of reality that was a source of development. To Aristotle had also been attributed the achievement of bringing down to earth Plato's

Forms, those perfect exemplar ideas for all imperfect material things. The Stoics did not welcome the results of believing that such Forms, or indeed the Mind whose Ideas they were, floated detached, like pure spirit, above and beyond the only world we know. Only to be thereafter too easily appealed to by certain elites for convenient explanations of things or events, explanations that were not available to other observant inhabitants of this lean earth. Hence the insistence of the Stoics that everything that truly exists and makes a difference to other existing things, must be an embodied entity in one way or another.

As a result of this their opponents to this day call the Stoics materialists and atheists; hymns to Zeus, "proofs" of God's existence, constant insistence that God was ever interested and active in achieving the best for human destiny, all of this to the contrary notwithstanding. Christians in particular have engaged in this Stoic-bashing to this day, despite the fact that they unashamedly borrowed so much of their early theology from these same Stoics, together with their main traditional method of moralizing (natural law morality). But, then, Christians have always been adept at quickly ignoring, if not actually biting, the hands that fed them, in their anxiety to assure themselves that theirs is inherently superior to any other theology. One notices, for example, how badly our current crop of Christian ecologists, faced with criticisms of their creation myth seeming to allow humanity to simply dominate the earth, so desperately need the idea of the world as God's body. And then, incidentally, one also notices as if for the first time, that in point of fact Christians had always proclaimed that God has "become flesh" in one Jesus of Nazareth. God has a body then? And how far does that take us beyond Zeno, the ancient Eleatic?

The fact of the matter is, and remains now as it was then, that it is philosophers and theologians who act on an assumption of mind-matter dualism, who then mean by the epithet "materialist" something entirely mindless, and therefore in cosmic terms, in comments on philosophies in which gods are thought to manifest themselves as minds, something entirely godless also. Much the same can be said of modern scientists when they declare themselves materialists, allegedly because that is how science sees the universe. Think of Bertrand Russell attributing to "omnipotent matter rolling on its relentless way" the origin of all the evolving species and all the events of coming to be and passing away that constitute this entire universe from beginning to end. These scientists then assert that mind is nothing other than the human brain and nervous system and their whole electro-chemical carry-on. Or, if they feel that such reductionism is a bit much to stomach in view of everyman's experience of consciousness, they then describe the episodes of consciousness, its various thoughts and imaginings, desires and decisions, as mere epiphenomena of the said brain. And then, when it is pointed out to them that calling something an epiphenomenon simply means to say that it occurs around or about something else, as if thrown off by that thing, and tells us nothing whatever of *what* it is, they moan about the difficulty of discovering how a material (i.e., in this dualist assumption, mindless) brain can toss off what people are accustomed to relate to mind, and John Searle sighs for another Newton to solve for us this apparently insoluble problem concerning experienced consciousness.

The Stoic philosophers however, were professedly *not* acting on an assumption of mind-matter dualism. Quite to the contrary, they set out deliberately to erase such dualism once and for all from philosophical discourse. So what then did this Stoic denial of dualism leave us as an alternative? For after all, even though they said that everything was body, they still talked in terms of reason or mind, as well as talking in terms of matter. The alternative seems to be this: that mind and matter are co-relates in our accounting for reality; not names for dichotomously distinct substances, as in the familiar if falsely attributed "Cartesian dualism," in which they must appear as some kind of contraries. The alternative suggestion might be that there is always something of mind in all matter as we experience it, and something of matter in all mind as it manifests itself. In the case of God, that God the Creator is, by definition, embodied in that ever-emerging creation, that the material creation as a consequence bodies forth the Creator God, that there is no time or place or circumstance in which God the Creator is not so bodied forth and embodied, that God the Creator is so from eternity, that is to say, at source.

All of this becomes much clearer when the second principle from which the world emerges, according to the Stoics, is analyzed. This principle is referred to simply as matter, and it is said to be purely passive, that is to say, (as yet) untouched by any *spermatikos logos*, by any of these active, dynamic forms that continually form and transform reality as we know it. These are forms of which we ourselves become acutely conscious as we participate in that cosmic evolutionary dynamic, dynamic evolving forms that come from the ultimate source, the divine *Logos* through whom is made everything that is made. Now matter unformed immediately calls to mind Aristotle's prime matter, for this is the idea of matter that the Stoics borrowed. Being (as yet) unformed, prime matter is not a thing, not anything; it is a no-thing, for things are entities (already) formed, cut out, shaped, and thereby having length and breadth and duration, that is to say, being spread out over a limited section (cutting off again) of space and time, or space-time. Prime matter comes into existence and can only come into existence simultaneously with the creation of form, with the originating creative activity of forming. Although from our creaturely, worm's-eye point of view, already embedded as we are in a material world, it looks as if forms emerge from, are cut out of matter, rather than matter emerge out of the perpetual forming engaged in by creators original and derivative.

Just here in this philosophical context there comes into play a meaning for the phrase "creation out of prime matter," that is just like the meaning that can be given to the phrase "creation out of nothing," for matter as yet unformed is (as yet) a no-thing. Einstein, as it happens, in his own epoch-making speculations about space-time, offered an analogy by which we can understand a little more clearly this aspect of the account of divine creation, in which matter comes about through creative forming, as an outcome of the dynamic activity of such forms rather than their static predecessor. First, Einstein pointed out that the image/idea of field had replaced the concept of matter as the irreducible element, that is, the foundational image in the physicist's apprehension of reality; just as space-time had by then become the preferred name for what is still otherwise referred to as the material universe, or referred to as just Matter, as Russell called it. But with this essential proviso, that space-time can no longer be conceived as some always already-made receptacle into which material bodies are placed, so that if there were fewer of the latter there might then be spaces empty of things, and times empty of events. Rather is space-time itself a structural quality of a field, in short, a consequential function of fields rather than their precedent. Now a field (of force or energy) is a form, hence formulatable (mathematically), and as such much more aligned with mind, which produces forms as its natural *modus operandi*. And it is with the formation of fields that space-time is simultaneously brought into being. It is better to imagine fields as undulating, wave-like entities within which material points or particles emerge, the universal ensemble of which makes up what might be called the gross, visible, touchable matter of the universe.

Yet, once again, looked at from the worm's-eye point of view of observers immersed themselves in space-time, it must seem as if the emergence of particles, as quantum physics describes this very random occurrence, is an emergence in or out of, like things cut out of, a sub-strate. But that is not the case in reality. In reality it is the materiality of the universe that is the epiphenomenon, or at very least materiality in the sense of the "hard" matter in atomic form that one can touch and taste. And it is the mind-like functions of formulating, forming that throws up materiality. Materiality is then better explained as the outcome of a cre-ative mind. Trying to explain mind as an out-cropping of materiality is a foolish enterprise, likely to be engaged in only by those who hold to a crude and dogmatic mind-matter dualism, and a philosophy that is then materialist in these terms. The true approach to such problems is more likely to start from the non-dualist perspective of the Stoics, that sees matter always shot through with mind, and all mind in the only universe we know always manifested in matter. In theological terms this preferable approach results in an idea of a totally immanent divinity, forming things from within rather than shouting (at) them into existence from without, yet at the same time a totally transcendent divinity as one that ultimately sources all this carrying-beyond of all current forms, until some ultimate and infinite state is reached by all, if by each presumably after its own kind, as a state of final and perfect "double" immanence in which God will be all in all (1 Cor. 15:18), and all will be once more "in" or in perfect union with God from whom the take their origin.

It must already be clear from this account of Stoic theology how hap-pily these early Christians saw in it the very substance of their own biblical myth of God the creator, and hence the possibility of an adequate vehi-cle for their apologia. For they saw in it a creator divinity called Father, *Logos/Sophia*, Spirit. A God who formed all things through a dynamic forming that would bring all to undiminished perfection of life, and who thereby in-formed creatures in such a way that they could cooperate in this continuous creation. A God who in-formed some creatures to the point of making them rational, capable of being reflectively conscious of this self-revelation of God through world. So that these rational animals could acquire a wisdom rather than a mere theory, a means of valuing and trans-valuing, and they could correspondingly acquire the dignity of co-operating with full creativity, rather than reacting in accordance with received or instinctive patterns of behavior. For the Genesis myth had talked of God's agency in creation, using images of word and spirit. These images had been developed in those deliberate retellings of that myth in the wisdom literature, in which Word is now Wisdom, a knowing-how to be creatively engaged with creation for the final good of all. And the

Genesis myth had pictured some entities in God's creation (the land, the sea) bringing forth others, and had used the imagery of the seed with much the same outcome.

And finally, of course, the myth had pictured *homo sapiens* in particular as a creative species in the very image of its divine creator, *Sophia*, herself the image of God the ultimate creator. An aspect of the myth developed further in the Wisdom literature when *Sophia* is said to have delivered Adam from his transgression and thereby enabled him to rule all things (Wisd. of Solomon 10:1–2). Or as Psalm 8 has it: "you have made him a little less than God . . . have given him dominion over all the works of your hands"; or in *The Book of the Secrets of Enoch*, "I created man . . . I placed him on earth, a second angel . . . to rule the earth and have my wisdom." (For it must be remembered that God governs, rules or reigns simply by continually creating; so to say God commissions humanity to rule likewise by creating is to say simply what is said already by saying that humanity is created in the image of the Creator.)

However, by the time these early Christians came along to benefit from this Stoic philosophy much had changed, for these early Christian apologists lived in an era in the history of philosophy now known as the era of Middle-Platonism. It was an era characterized by scholasticism and eclecticism, in which Platonists continued to dominate, partly by absorbing much that was best in other schools of philosophy. While the latter counteracted such take-overs by claiming that they had anticipated the key ideas of this new Platonism in the first place. Hence the Stoic *Logos* was by now presented as the Mind of God in which the Platonic Forms existed as his exemplar ideas. The *spermatikoi logoi* first existed as these forms in the mind (of the) Logos, and by these the world was first envisaged and subsequently made. So that this Mind, this *Logos*, was now in Middle-Platonism commonly presented as a second (dimension of) divinity; the first (dimension of) divinity being characterized by Plato's descriptive phrase, *epekeina tes ousias*, beyond all being, substance, nature; inconceivable and unimaginable, and named simply, the One. The creative activity of this One, which Plato in the *Timaeus* had imagined as an act of overflowing goodness that resulted in our empirical universe, was then pictured as the One creating the world through or by the divine Mind, the second (dimension of) divinity, through whom therefore, it could then be said, was made all things that were made. No longer was the *Logos* the name for creative divinity as such.

And there were other ways in which an always-dominant and all-absorbing Platonism changed the original ethos of the original Stoicism. For one thing, an increasingly Platonized Stoicism concentrated almost exclusively on the *Logos* name for the creator God. Ignoring as it did so other images of that same creator that were the equal, in classical Stoicism, of its Logos image: the images of fire, of spirit, of nature, in the Aristotelian sense, and of seed in its creative rather than its merely reproductive sense. All images of divinity that suggested a continuous creation of derivative creators, thereby securing the self-revelation of the universe as a continuous creation, an inherently evolutionary entity. Correspondingly, the *Logos* creator changed subtly but surely in Platonized Stoicism into a divine mind filled with exemplar ideas, immutable like itself, according to which all things were made, and the creator therefore of a rather static universe.

There was a feature of Middle-Platonism that could have counteracted this deleterious effect upon original Stoicism, and it was this. The highest (dimension of) divinity known as the One was seen in Middle-Platonism as the source of Mind, or Intellectual Principle, with its Ideas/Forms. The One was then the source of the (dimension of) divinity that the Stoics called *Logos*. And since the One was not itself a formed entity, it was not itself a mind with its immutable forms, and so potentially limited. So that, as long as the One was thought of as the source creator, it could then be perceived as indeed a continuously, eternally and infinitely creative divine creator. And although the One still created through its derivative (dimension of) formed mind, that mind need not then be seen to be limited to a static, immutable content. But then a concourse of influences conspired to counteract the image and idea of the One as source-creator acting always and creatively through its own mind-like (dimension of) divinity. And a contrary impression emerged. This was the impression of the divine mind full of immutable exemplar ideas for a universe, standing between the One and the world created according to these ideas, and rather obscuring both the view of the One beyond it, and the Spirit (at this stage within it).

Christians themselves contributed to this impression of a *Logos,* a mind-like (dimension of) divinity, containing immutable ideas or forms, and tending to obscure the dimension and creative presence of the One, and of Spirit. (Not everything that went astray in the theology of creation and the Creator can be blamed on the Greeks.) It seems to have happened like this: Christians claimed that the *Logos* through which God creates the world was made flesh, as John's Gospel put it, in the founder of their faith, Jesus of Nazareth. They naturally assumed therefore that they had inherited the definitive revelation of God. So that they and only they knew the one, true God fully and without falsehood. And they knew all there was to know about God's ways with the world, and about the world's way to God. Furthermore, they knew all of this in scriptural and creedal expressions of all of that truth that were inerrant and immutable. So in the excitement of this exclusivist superbia, with its accompanying franchise theology, Christians rather too easily slipped into the habit of saying, not that the *Logos* was incarnate in Jesus, but that God was incarnate in Jesus. Or, more crudely still, that Jesus was God. And this common manner of speaking served only to further obscure both the (dimension of) the divine One, and the (dimension of) Spirit. And left us with the impression once more of an immutable Mind-like divinity squatting outside a very mutable world indeed, between us and the One.

That having been said, however, it is worth adding that the fault of the reigning Platonism in this matter, especially at a more popular and less sophisticated level, is deeper and more insidious still. In this way, Platonism, from the start of its existence as a school, centered in the Academy at Athens, had always been tempted toward a dualism of mind and matter of the so-called "Cartesian" kind. Mind and matter as separate kinds of substance. With matter seen as the source of all that was unwanted: change and the inevitable de-forming of things, suffering, obsolescence, death, and all of the destructive fears that accompany the anticipation of such experiences. So that the instinct of the less sophisticated Platonist philosopher is to distance the creator God, who is wholly good, as far as possible from direct involvement with matter. Including prime matter that, it must be allowed, God does inevitably create. In this climate of thought, and pushed along by this logic, the main agencies in creation tended to be seen as distinct divine intermediaries, operating between the One and the world, and thereby keeping the One as distant as possible from direct involvement with the hands-on business of creating world. At this point the by-now no doubt tiring repetition of the phrase in parentheses whenever an agency in creation was being described as a second (*(dimension of)*) divinity can finally be dropped. And that is why some Platonists in the Middle-Platonic period, and even Philo whom we must now meet, talked of the divine, creative Mind/Word as a second god.

For anyone who wishes now to see in some detail just how this Platonized Stoicism was used in order to express to the educated elite of the

Roman empire the substance of the biblical myth of creation, it is both interesting and highly instructive to look first, not to any of the early Christian apologists who borrowed this theology for their purposes, but to a Jewish apologist for this same biblical faith in God the Creator, one Philo of Alexandria. He shared the same century with Jesus and Paul, and shared the same borrowing strategy with the first Christian theologians. Indeed since it was not fellow Jews who in the main took up this theology of Philo in the centuries after the latter's death, it could well be that Christian use of the strategy involved a following of Philo rather than a simple coincidence.

Philo's Jewish faith in the God who could not be imagined, or defined, and should not even be named, translated easily into the Greek One, similarly beyond all human knowledge and language. Yet, Philo insisted, though God in God's inner essence could not be comprehended, God as active on the world in God's powers (*dynameis*) and their works (*energeiai*) could be apprehended. The two major powers of God Philo named Creator and Lord, for in the works of God's creating and thus ruling the creation we can see and know something of God. The term that Philo borrowed to connote the (dimension of) divinity that is manifest in God's creative deeds of power in the world is *Logos*. For his own scriptures authorized him to say that God created the world through the agency of his Word. This divine *Logos*, Philo then went on to say, is the idea of ideas, the pattern and mediator of creation, the archetype of human reason. He also calls the *Logos* the first begotten Son of the uncreated Father, and even the second god. And finally, as his way of securing for Moses the role of founder of his Jewish faith, Philo said that the divine *Logos* dwelt in Moses, to a degree that made of Moses a *theios aner*, a divine man.

However the relationship between Philo and the early Christian apologists and theologians is to be construed, that account of the result of Philo's borrowing of the dominant Greek theology of the time provides a fair copy of the theology produced by early Christians with motivations quite similar to Philo's. God, the One, about whom no other descriptions can be offered, the ultimate source of all creatures (apprehended by the image of Father), creates all through the agency of his *Logos/Sophia* (apprehended under the image of son/daughter). In this Word/Wisdom, and in its immediate, hands-on and continuous creative work all creatures then participate, and none more so than the species *homo sapiens* that is created especially in the image of that divine creator.

Then some three centuries after Philo wrote, and almost two centuries into the early Christians' task of borrowing a Platonized Stoicism for purposes of giving an elite theological expression to the faith they believed they inherited from Jesus of Nazareth, a second agency-in-creation was added to Word/Wisdom as a permanent, constitutive element in the account of divine creation. This was the agency of Soul, in Greek terms, or its counterpart in Christian terms, Spirit. Now these images had been around all along, the first in Greek theology and the second, as we have seen, in Judeo-Christian scriptures. But up to the end of the Middle-Platonic period of Greek theology and up to the (suspiciously coincident) end of the third century of the so-called Christian era, Soul and Word, like Spirit and Word, were rather interchangeable images, as indeed we have seen them so in the creation myths of the Bible. So that, in both camps, the impressions conveyed of God the creator, despite the occasional presence of Trinitarian formulae, were more generally binitarian. That is to say, there was one agency under the One, in the process of sourcing the world, not two. The decision of the Christian Council of Nicea in 325 C.E. concerned the relationship of the Father to his Word; though soon after that the Spirit was formally added in such a way as to construct a fully fledged Trinitarian theology of God the creator.

Before this happened in the development of Christian thought, Plotinus with his disciples had so renewed a Platonic tradition of philosophy now three-quarters of a millennium old, that the period of Platonism Plotinus inaugurated is called Neo-Platonism to this day. And it is from Plotinus's system that we first find the kind of truly Trinitarian theology of divine creation that Christian theologians then borrowed. In Plotinus's system the One gave origin to all things through the two agencies of, first Mind and then Soul. Mind being the Intellectual Principle in which were conceived the exemplar ideas of the creation, Soul the craftsman-like principle that then fashioned the material universe according to these seminal ideas. This system yielded an account of God the Creator as one divine *ousia* (being or substance — although in reality beyond being and substance, as Plato put it), in three *hypostaseis* (a term difficult to define, but for which Latin-speaking Christian theologians substituted the term *persons*). It was this Trinitarian formula, one divine *ousia* in three *hypostaseis*, that Greek-speaking Christian theologians borrowed from their counterparts, Greek philosopher-theologians like Plotinus and his followers, for a fully Trinitarian Christian theology of God the Creator. And it is these Greek-speaking Christian theologians, men like the so-called Cappadocian

Fathers, who are still credited to this day with the most successful version of a Christian theology of the Trinity.

It is worth noting that when Christians got round to borrowing this now definitively Trinitarian theology from Plotinus and his immediate followers, they failed significantly to notice and to avail themselves of Plotinus's highly sophisticated Platonic understanding of the relationship between mind or spirit, on the one hand, and matter on the other. Plotinus's renewed version of Platonism, like Stoicism in this, treated mind and matter as co-ordinates rather than contrary substances. Prime matter was no substance in itself, but an outcome of mind. Just as darkness is an outcome of the shining of light inevitably occurring at the limits of that shining. Correspondingly, the deforming, nothinging force of prime matter was seen by Plotinus as an integral part of continuous creation of life ever more abundant. Christian borrowers should have been alerted to this feature of Neo-Platonic theology, at least when they read the part of Plotinus's *Enneads* where he condemns in the strongest terms the crudely dualist Gnostics. Especially where Plotinus insists that matter which is formed, the only matter that can be said to actively exist, is always to that extent good. But most Christian borrowers of Neo-Platonic theology got that theology, as Augustine did, very much at second hand. So that they imitated still and retained the instinct of the less sophisticated Platonists, namely, the instinct to distance the One as far as possible from direct involvement with matter. And to see the agencies in creation as distinct divine beings of some kind, intervening to keep the world and the One at arm's length from each other.

This impression of distinction as separateness, despite the intimacy of their inter-relationship through being birthed or breathed by the One/Source — as the mythic expression of this matter would have it — is hardened by the Christian use of the term *persons* for the three. For no matter how sophisticated the redefinition of the term *person* by Christian theologians of the Trinity may turn out to have been — and it is sophisticated to a point of extreme abstrusity — the use of the term *persons* for the Three leaves most Christians, both preachers and hearers of the gospel of God the Creator, with the impression of three distinct and in that sense separate divine, well, *persons,* the latter two positively intervening between the first One and the material world. The term *transcendence* is then almost automatically characterized by a dominant spatial imagery. The One is beyond the material universe, that is to say, separated from it; all the

more so by being a person fully distinct from the divine creative intermediaries who are themselves distinct persons with respect to each other.
This kind of theology of creation cannot but be helped when the idea of
the Three as three distinct persons is rendered crude to the last degree in
the currently dominant social model of the Trinity recently made popular
by Moltmann.

The upshot of this peculiar confluence of different influences in keeping
the agencies in creation so distinct from each other, placing two of them
between the One and the material world, and so focusing attention on one
of the two, *Logos*, as to obscure our vision of the third, Spirit, almost as
much as the One is already obscured, is now obvious. The divine Creator
comes to be seen as an eternal Mind, already made up, having formed and
being formed by eternal, hence immutable ideas. Creation then consists
in rather mechanically reproducing these ideas in matter, where they cease
to be immutable of course. But only because material, space-time condi-
tioned copies of them are subject to decay and death and the consequent
need to have them keep on reproducing themselves. It is this kind of
image of divine Creator and creation that causes and fuels a war between
self-styled creationists and their opponent evolutionists, a war carried on
by Christians in face of overwhelming evidence for evolution, particularly
in more backward parts of the United States. It is this kind of concept
of divine Creation that results also in a natural law morality that consists
in a reading-off from created nature allegedly immutable moral rules for
the ways in which we humans are to act in and with the natural universe,
thus entirely inhibiting our responsible creativity under God.

The Christian Theology of Creation in the Modern Era

But more seriously still, it is this idea of a divine Creator that has caused
the most persistent attack upon Christian theology by so many of the
best philosophers of the modern era. For theirs is in essence an attack
upon a divinity that in Heidegger's phrase, echoing Marx, squats outside
the world, in the form of a mind containing from eternity the final plan
for the universe, and therefore the fully formulated truth of all that ever
was, is or will be. A total travesty of the reality, as we know it to be. We
who in all of our living and dying, responsibly or irresponsibly, creatively
or destructively participate in its continuous creation. It is this Christian
doctrine of a divine Creator that Nietzsche so roundly rejects, for a Creator who created everything as it is to be, in a one-off act of creation

coincident with the first moment of time thus also created, is a Creator who thereby robs us humans of that creativity that is both our birthright and our highest calling. Such a divine Creator, in Nietzsche's inimitable imagery, is an "eternal reason-spider" who weaves a spider's web of rules in us that confines our knowledge and realization of good and evil to what is currently the case, and prevents us from envisaging and working toward an ever greater good. A continuously creative role, forbidden by this Creator God, would involve us in breaking (through) currently conceived values and concomitantly causing the evil that is the destruction of their current forms ("I offer myself to love, and my neighbor as myself"). As is ever inevitable during a creative ascent to a perfection of life as yet unimaginable. So, for Nietzsche, the Creator God for so long now pictured and presented by Christianity had to be declared dead. So small a god could allow no room for a quintessentially creative humanity. And since this was the only God that Nietzsche and his contemporaries knew from God's self-designated representatives on earth, the death of god pure and simple was the message to be preached by the prophet of the Superman. Atheism was the word, and as Nietzsche and other philosophers of the West in the modern period show, atheism is, like religion, always culture-specific. We are dealing here with Christian atheists.

It is Feuerbach, to whom Marx attributed the final critique of religion, whose replacement of this Christian God with mere humanity managed to spread this case most widely and effectively in modern times. He argued that the attributes of God — reason, will, love and their inherent creativity — were really human attributes, and all that they enabled human beings to create was in consequence a human achievement. The world is humanity's creation in humanity's image: "There is no well so deep that a man on looking into it does not see his own face." Yet, since humanity took some time to come into full possession and realization of its creative powers — and indeed there is still some considerable way to go beyond our present limitations — we have long formed the habit of wishful-thinking into existence a god that could do for us all we could not yet do. And we then quite naturally imagined that this god really did everything for everyone anyway. In short, as Marx so pithily summed up the matter, *die Religion ist eben die Anerkennung des Menschens auf einem Umweg;* religion is actually humanity's recognition of itself by a roundabout route. So that religion, as Marx added, is the *vis inertiae*, the great force for inertia in human history. Everything having already been decided and made as it is by God. Leaving us now with no option but to replace this little god with humanity. Something that Christianity, without realizing this, had already foreseen, as Feuerbach pointed out, when its central doctrine proclaimed that God became man. Something that, in consequence of this central doctrine of the Christian religion, permitted Feuerbach to entitle his most influential work *The Essence of Christianity*.

As a last and most recent example of this by now conventional criticism of Christianity in the modern era, take Sartre. Sartre rejects outright the little god he describes as the *Dieu Fabricateur*, the god of the factory production line who machines his various product-lines according to previously chosen designs. Designs that then function both to define permanently the nature of each and every product, and to be read as the set of instructions for their operation and use. Sartre rejects this recognizably Christian-promoted divinity, once again, in favor of humanity. And more specifically, in favor of the freedom of the human being. But with this intriguing twist: he does not feel he has to deny the very existence of a creator divinity who put this universe in place. He needs only to assert the utter and entire irrelevance to us and to our world of such a divine creator. For Sartre in denying that humanity has a preset nature opens our eyes to the fact that we make ourselves and simultaneously make our world through our own visions of what to be and what to do, and by our unencumbered will so to do and to be. For that full creative responsibility, in which our authentic humanity consists, and to which Sartre says we are thereby condemned, alone and without excuse, is what Sartre calls freedom. Not some pale substitute that consists merely in the choice of obeying or not obeying some so-called law of nature. And that is why Sartre does not need to pose as an atheist. All he needs to point out is that even if this God that the Christians preach did exist, that would change nothing. Or as he puts it in a line in *The Flies,* "once freedom has exploded in the heart of a human being, the gods can no longer wield any power over that one." We simply carry on creating regardless, and taking full responsibility for the world we create for ourselves, because our freedom makes it so.

So far then the case for Christian atheism seems to be rather well made. Until, that is, the investigation of the theme of cosmic creation begins to notice the finer detail of the fuller descriptions offered by those modern philosopher-theologians (for any form of atheism that is the result of philosophical reasoning is a theology), as they secure a place for a replacement creator of our world, a creator of whom Marx also declared the world to be its extended body. Sartre named this free creative agent as the

Pour-soi, the For-itself, and described it by analyzing human consciousness. He pointed out quite rightly that as we are conscious of anything, we are conscious of being conscious of that thing, and in general of the world of things he named the *En-soi*, the In-itself. We are thus conscious of consciousness itself; we are self-conscious, conscious of a self, conscious of something of which one can say that in and of itself it is nothing but consciousness. That is to say, it has in itself no particular form or forms to define or limit it, and for that reason it can be conscious of any and all forms. It can transcend any current content of forms toward an envisioning of other or different forms, or alterations or combinations of current forms, *ad infinitum*. There is something unlimited, infinite about it, and for that very reason it is an inherently creative entity, so that human beings can be said to truly create themselves, and if only incidentally, create their world also.

Sartre then says of this For-itself that it constitutes a dichotomously distinct realm of reality, distinct from the realm of all formed entities that make up the In-itself. It is not just a second dimension of even consciously apprehended, formed reality; and he in fact calls it an absolute. Echoes already of the old theological discussion of a formless divine being, seemingly replaced in the course of Christian theology by what was originally a second (dimension of) divinity named *Logos*, and now recalled for a reverse replacement?

Feuerbach also argues for a replacement creator characterized by limitlessness, infinity. His opening argument in *The Essence of Christianity* is as follows: humanity is the only species that has religion, an awareness of God as creator and ruler of the world. It is also the only species that is conscious of its own nature, which already suggests that religious consciousness is awareness of humanity's own nature. But religious consciousness encounters a limitless, infinite being, does it not? Yes, and that poses no objection to the argument for (as Sartre also pointed out) a human being is aware of a level of transcendence that reaches infinity as a feature of its own mind, or consciousness-in-action. Therefore in its religious awareness humanity is conscious of its own, not limited but infinite nature. And in any case, he adds for good measure, a truly limited being cannot have any awareness of its own limitations, if only because it cannot see beyond these. So once again, humanity has the quality of infinity that qualifies it for the role of creator of a world. And yet according to Feuerbach — and it is important to note this — the infinity in question, as a feature not merely of human consciousness as such but of operative human creativity, characterizes neither any individual human being, nor any number of these at any time operative in and on the world. For each of these, and all of them together suffer the limitations of their existence in their time and place. What then, according to Feuerbach, does the infinity of the true creator characterize? It characterizes the "species being," the human-species-being. And what precisely is that? Difficult to say, really; but it seems to be some idealized entity that comprises all human beings through all stages of their evolution, past, present and future.

Something similar happens when one questions Nietzsche more closely on the precise details of his replacement creator. Nietzsche's true creator is not just man, but Superman, a creator preceded by the prophet, and as such yet to come. Which raises the same inevitable question as that raised by Feuerbach's creation scenario: who then is there, who now has the requisite stature to be creating the world as we speak? Indeed there is a further and equally inevitable dimension to that question. As hinted by the child who, when asked the first question in the old penny catechism, "who made the world?" replied, not unreasonably, "I don't know; it was here when I got here": if anything is obvious to us human beings it is that a world fitted somehow to our existential requirements was already created for us before our species-being evolved. So if we are now truly creators with increasingly cosmic influence — even if that seems at this time to be obvious more in our destructive than our constructive capabilities — and if it is obvious from evolution that we did not create ourselves, who then created and continues to create the world? And that same question could be asked, if they were able to ask questions, by every species of things that preceded us humans and that are still evolving in intimate interdependence with us. For as Nietzsche himself pointed out, "all creatures hitherto have created something beyond themselves."

It is difficult indeed to avoid the impression that what these modern atheistic humanist philosopher-theologians are really doing is this: they are trying to envisage a creator of the world. They cannot attribute this role to the human race as hitherto and currently constituted, with all of its obvious limitations and depredations. So they suggest in different ways that the role is reserved for some being or entity that is in the image of humanity, that is to say, a being that, like the conscious entities we humans are and know, boasts of the character of infinity, limitlessness, formlessness in its innermost self. The character necessary for true creativity; the character that then manifests the ability to conceive of dynamic forms, to desire, to love these, to the point of the power to give them existence as co-creators. And to suffer with them the inevitable pain and loss of their consequent co-creative enterprise, that will bring them to the fullness of life and being. That, or something very like that, really seems to be what Nietzsche seeks to envisage in his *Übermensch*, Feuerbach in his human-species-being, and Sartre in his For-itself; something (a little?) more than humanity in its empirical existence, yet in line with the image of humanity as we now know it. And then one finds oneself asking the question: why should Christians object to these philosophers of our era doing this, and in just this manner? After all, the Christian creation myth tells of humanity being created in the image of its creator, and of its then being like an angel of God, only a little less that God. And if that account of the divine creator being imaged in particular in humanity carries the mind from God to humanity, why cannot the questing mind travel in the opposite direction from the image to its source? The direction is given, and the "little less" measures the distance to travel as accurately as the "little more." Therefore, it is true to say, that the best of our modern philosophers retained those parts of the truth of creation and the Creator that Christians had come to overlook. And that in turn suggests, surely, that the revelation of God the Creator is in and from the creation, and the full and most basic truth about God and God's ways with the world is not therefore franchised solely to Christians.

Those modern philosopher-theologians, both when they reject the deformation of divinity that occurs by defining it solely in terms of a *logos* eternally squatting outside the world, even if it does interfere now and then, and when they then (re)introduce the other element of an infinite, higher dimension of self, are really enabling us once more to envisage a true, ultimate Creator of the continuously created and creative universe that we actually experience. That original, recovered Judeo-Christian theology of creation can then be summarized as follows:

The Creator of the universe is in essence an infinite, limitless, formless entity that cannot be directly conceived or imagined nor, therefore, defined or properly named. But it becomes manifest as something of the order of self as it forms a universe by means of dynamic forms. For the forms that make things, that make finite entities that, in turn and *ensemble,* in their inter-relationships and interdependence, make up the universe of space-time, are intelligible to us in their structures and behavior. And so they resemble ideas and images in a mind somewhat like ours, though incomprehensibly greater. While the dynamic nature of these forms, which enables them to reproduce and develop, to produce other forms, to transform themselves and others — that is also analogous to our own experienced fire of desire, of love, in short our own operative will to make real the ever-new, ever renewed, ever better and more beautiful.

These manifestations of a divinity, as in its creative outgoing it comes within range of our finite understanding, are named *Logos/Sophia* and Soul/Spirit. So far they have been referred to, as the myth seems to imagine them, as agencies in creation. What further may be said of them, whether they can be called persons or personifications of divine attributes, or second and third divinities, or whether they must be named in some altogether different manner, that must be decided later in a section specifically devoted to Christian (Greek) Trinitarian theology. But whatever is decided then — and this must be our guide in all such decisions — what cannot be gainsaid is that the divinity creates by forming all things with permanently dynamic forms, fashioning them in their innermost natures and being, so that creative divinity is ever at work within the world. "My Father works until now, and I work," so said the Word Incarnate, according to the Fourth Gospel. And divine transcendence accordingly can never be captured in any spatially dominated symbol of the beyond that separates creator from creation. Transcendence must instead be construed entirely in terms of the continuous transformation of the creation in which stage after stage is transcended from within, toward some final *shalom* when all things are brought back to a union with the divinity from which they came. For that is what the biblical myth imagines. And all the suffering of the deformation and death of current forms of existence that is an essential part of transformation — Plato too regarded the pursuit of philosophy, the active love made real in walking in the way of *Sophia*, as a training to die — will in that union simply cease, death having no more dominion. "Endgame," as Beckett put it in his play of that title, "old endgame, lost of old; play and lose, and have done with losing."

Chapter Two

FALL

... there is no eternal reason-spider and spider's web in you —
A little wisdom is no doubt possible;
A *little* reason, to be sure, a seed of wisdom scattered from star to
    star —   — Nietzsche, *Thus Spoke Zarathustra*

The Myth of the Fall

At the very heart of the creation myth that opens the Bible is the much smaller, but for all that not much less significant, myth of the Fall. Sufficient advertisement surely for the fact that at the heart of the creation process itself from beginning to end lurks, not just humanity, but a fallen humanity. From beginning to end? Yes, because the smaller myth shares with the larger myth that contains it the defining character of all cosmic myths. It has as the time of the action of the myth, not a moment or similar measure of linear, inner cosmic time, but rather a time out of time, a time coincident with every and all moments of linear time. So that the story is as much about the last humans on earth, if there are to be last humans on earth, as it is about a first man and woman on earth, if the monogenistic thesis is true and the human species evolved from a single pair rather than a population. And so it is a story about every man and woman, a story about the position and the role of humanity in ongoing creation.

Stories of eschatons, like stories of origins, are both stories of the world *sub specie aeternitatis*, from a viewpoint of eternity; and this is therefore true of the Fall myth also. This would certainly come clear to any reader who had managed to make her way from the beginning of the Bible to its very end. For in the apocalyptic scenes painted in the Gospels and other writings toward the end of the Bible the same cast of characters appears that appeared at the beginning of the Bible. The satanic tempter who leads

69

people astray so that they destroy rather than co-create. The most intimate relationships of mutual love and support torn apart by a turning to hostility and hatred; family member turning against family member. The creation itself groaning under servitude to a humanity turned destructive. Until the very order and harmony of natural agencies is threatened and brought back to the very point where darkness overcomes the light . . . but the creative forces in the end always prevail, in a victory initiated, as always, by God. Until, as the last chapter of the Book of Revelation, the last chapter of the Bible, has it, the garden of paradise is restored, with its "river of the water of life," and access open to "the tree of life," the way to which from the beginning is guarded by the angels of God, the cherubim with their flaming swords.

This Fall myth then is a story of a continuous titanic struggle between creation and destruction, between life and death. But the creation myth itself is just such a story. Continuous creation constantly involves the destruction, the death of existing forms of things, the intrusion of original chaos that has then to be constantly overcome by the same creative élan that causes it. So that there must be some new facet of this titanic struggle between life and death that requires the interlacing within the general myth of creation of an additional myth of a fall. There is, and the new facet consists in this: *homo sapiens* who, being made in the image of the creator, has an especial part to play in continuous creation, also proves to have always its own special contribution to make to ever-threatening destruction and death. It is for this reason that the creation myth requires an insertion within it that offers a fuller account of humanity's role in the life and death struggle. And that gives an added resonance to Beckett's lines, "old endgame, lost of old; play and lose and have done with losing."

Notice next that this myth-within-a-myth in Genesis (2:9, 16–17; 3:1–24) is a piece of the Wisdom literature in the Bible, as it is called. That is to say, the dominant image of creator and creation is *Sophia*, Wisdom herself. Therefore, the further exposition of the Fall myth in other documents that belong to the genre of Wisdom literature is likely to provide its best initial exegesis. First to be noticed then in that further exposition is this, that the tree of the knowledge of good and evil in the fall myth is the Wisdom Tree. The phrase "good and evil" is one of those Hebrew phrases meant to indicate totality by putting together two mutually distinct but in combination comprehensive terms. Just as heaven and earth, seen and unseen, connote all things, the universe; so good and evil connote all knowledge in the form of know-how, how to create all and make life ever more abundant for all, all-wisdom. As the woman of Tekoa put it when flattering king David in the hope of a favorable verdict in her case, "My Lord has wisdom like the wisdom of an angel of God to know all things that are on the earth"; "my lord the king is like the angel of God to discern good and evil" — there is never any harm done by repeating a piece of flattery (2 Sam. 14:17–20). And there is no need to be confused, much less frustrated by the fact that Proverbs 3:18 imagines *Sophia* as "a tree of life," and that there appear to be two separate trees in the Genesis garden: the tree of life and the tree of the knowledge of good and evil. It is true that in the two-tree version, the question does arise: if *Sophia* is the tree of life, how can she be the tree of wisdom?

But look at it this way. The tree of life is the mythic symbol for the source of all existence and life, and it is in its continuous creative gift of all life and existence that that same creative source reveals both itself and the "way" by which continually evolving creation is achieved, wisdom. The know-how, the practical wisdom from which all knowledge of what then is, was or will be derives, comes in and through God's continuous act of creation. Looked at from the worm's-eye point of view, it is by partaking of that life and even more so by participating in the continuous creation of it that creatures endowed with imagination and intelligence can both live it and know-how to advance it within their own measure. In effect then it would not matter whether the myth has two trees — Revelation 22:1–2 has its tree of life "on either side" of the "river of the water of life" — or just one. For wisdom is a way of living, so that the source of living and its know-how is one and the same, and can be symbolized by one and the same tree. The central point of the myth could then be gained by picturing humans aiming at excessive access to, and possession of the life-tree, which simultaneously conferred life and life-wisdom; an access so excessive that it would mean their wanting to be God's equal in creation. But the same point could be put, perhaps more clearly and forcibly, by having two trees in the story, a tree of wisdom and a tree of life. Then the story pictures humans wishing to gain access to divine wisdom independently of that creaturely, ever-limited partaking of God-given life that is their lot. Gaining this access independently of their partaking of the tree of life, as if they could have an independent access to divine wisdom that would once again make them equal to God.

Sophia herself declares, "he who finds me finds life, and obtains favors from the Lord; but he who misses me injures himself, all who hate me love death" (Proverbs 8:35–36). Creation in itself is the battle of evolving being with adduced and incursive nothingness. But this Fall myth inserted within the myth of creation endeavors to portray a further dimension of destruction and death deliberately contributed by one made in the Creator's image. A further level of nothing-ing arriving almost simultaneously with the co-creative activities of the human race. The myth in its entirety, as it is developed throughout the whole Bible, tries to offer an explanation as to how this additional level of destructive agency comes about and how it then persists through the whole course of the continuous creation of the world, and how also it can be overcome. This cosmic myth of human being, this Genesis story of humanity's place and role in creation, is then both simple and profound. It tells of humanity tempted to think it can appropriate to itself that total divine wisdom by which the world is continuously created, thereby making it the equal of God the Creator. Humanity tempted to think of itself as the one, true creator of the world, its world, and of whatever prospects for life and life ever more abundant, prospects that seem at first sight limitless, that this world might then hold.

The serpent in the story that tempts man and woman to appropriate the fruit of the wisdom tree is an ancient symbol of wisdom and immortality. Wisdom and immortality go together in this symbolism, because of the assumption that someone has the know-how, not just to create life, but to create unending life. The serpent, often the fire-breathing serpent or dragon — fire being the supreme symbol of the act of creation — is also an ancient symbol of healing. For the one who has the wisdom to create all life and existence must have the ability and know-how to save or salve the death-dealing wounds that derive from all destructive forces. The one who possesses such wisdom is by convention called God, ultimate creator-source and healer-savior who can hold out the prospect of limitless life. So another way to explain this shared serpent symbolism in the mythology in the ancient Near East is to say that the talking serpent represents the personification of that supreme attribute of divinity, infinite wisdom. And then to say that one is tempted by the talking serpent is a mythic way of picturing humanity ever tempted by the exalted status of the derivative, co-creative role of one made in the very image of God the Creator. The Ultimate Creative Source creates humanity with such high intelligence, such access to the divine wisdom ever evident in the ongoing creation — a little less than the gods, the *elohim*, as the Bible puts it — that humanity is thereby tempted to claim and appropriate all-wisdom; to become, as the current myth has God put it, "like one of us." Tempted to appropriate to itself the totality of divine wisdom, so to secure for itself and by itself life without limit. So that, as another version of the Fall myth puts it, humanity by its own efforts could build its world up to the status of heaven (Gen. 11, the myth of the tower of Babel). And now one can scarcely avoid memories of Nietzsche, Feuerbach, Marx, and even Sartre.

Then the story turns sinister and insists that yielding to this temptation can bring to humanity, not life and more life, but hardship and suffering, harbingers of a harder death that people must then die. As nature herself makes production and reproduction subject to further destructive forces, hazardous and life-defeating:

> ... in pain you shall bring forth children. ...
> cursed is the ground because of you;
> in toil you shall eat of it all the days of your life;
> thorns and thistles it shall bring forth to you;
> and you shall eat the plants of the field.
> By the sweat of your face you shall eat bread
> until you return to the ground,
> for ... you are dust,
> and to dust you shall return. (Gen 3:16–18)

Humanity acting like the divine creator then brings to this world destruction, pain and suffering, all harbingers of a more horrific death. And so much is made of this in the rest of the Bible that a reader quickly begins to see that the kind of death and destruction so introduced to the heart of reality greatly outruns the nothing-ing of forms of things that is an integral part of the very process of continuous creation. As the Genesis story of the first human beings continues the reader meets another creation myth that tells this time of the sheer scale of the destructiveness of the fall of humanity grown so grievous. God, according to this fall myth, allows the co-creative process of creation to reach the point at which destruction and death initiated by fallen humanity overwhelms and virtually reverses the transience of the nothing-ing that is a normal part of continuing creation. According to this myth the chaos, the utterly unformed and insubstantial, the primeval deep, floods and obliterates the creation. So that the whole formed and furnished world has to be made to emerge from the chaos once more. And the human race is made to begin again from another innocent couple, as God gives a solemn and signed promise that creation is forever, and will never be allowed to fall back or to be violently forced into permanent nothingness (Gen. 6–9, the myth of the flood and Noah's ark; flood stories are creation myths, and some of them can contain the requisite fall myth also).

Much later in the Bible, in his Letter to the Romans, having recorded the evil-doing, "without excuse," of all generations from Adam to Paul's own contemporaries, Paul summed it all up in the sentence: "sin came into the world through one man and death through sin, and so death spread to all men because all men sinned" (5:12). And he referred a little later to the whole of creation waiting with us to "be set free from its bondage to decay," waiting for "the redemption of our bodies" (8:19–23). Such sheer impressions of the magnitude of the death and destruction caused by human beings are commensurate perhaps with the magnitude of humanity's creative powers in the image of the divine creator. So much so that it is incumbent upon us to ask how a yielding to the temptation to appropriate a divine know-how results in such excessive destruction and death, and what all is entailed in that destruction and the death in which it culminates. There are a number of different answers provided to this double-barrel question in biblical (including what some churches regard as apocryphal/pseudepigraphical) sources, answers that have then been expressed and handed on in various theological traditions.

According to the Wisdom of Solomon, "God created man for incorruption, and made him in the image of his own eternity, but through the devil's envy death entered the world, and those who belong to his party experience it" (2:23–24). Some have taken the writer of that sentence to see the garden of the Genesis myth as Paradise, where humanity was destined to live forever in the company of God the Creator. But when Adam yielded to temptation and disobeyed the Lord, when Adam sinned, God put him and his wife out of Paradise, thereby passing a sentence of death upon these first parents and upon all their progeny. It is not then Adam's sin that is somehow transmitted to all of Adam's progeny, but a penal mortality is transmitted to them by the very fact of their becoming members of the human race. A similar interpretation has been offered for a similar sentence of Paul's, already quoted: "sin came into the world through one man and death through sin, and so death spread to all men because all have sinned." Except that, with respect to Paul's sentence, a certain class of commentator understands the sentence to say that both Adam's sin and his consequent death sentence are transmitted to all of Adam's progeny by their very generation as members of the human race. Now it is important to realize that neither of these sentences envisages the transmission of either sin or a consequent death penalty to the whole of human kind, by virtue presumably of a divine decree, and by the simple process of each one's conception and birth into the human family.

That should be obvious to any reader who reflects for a moment on the last phrase in each of these quotations in turn. Nor does any other biblical text or context contain such an inherently questionable concept as that of the transmission of sin or penalty by the very process of generation, and that presumably by divine decree. The Wisdom of Solomon in describing in detail how the Creator, *Sophia*, continues to create and to re-create the world (after a cosmic flood, for instance), has this to say of her work through Adam: "Wisdom protected the first-formed father of the world, when he alone had been created; she delivered him from his transgression, and gave him strength to rule all things" (10:1–2). So that Adam could hardly pass on by breeding that of which he himself had been shriven.

Clearly what the author of The Wisdom of Solomon has in mind is this: God intended humans to be immortal, but they sinned, each (but not every?) one of them in imitation of Adam. And so to each and every case of human sinfulness God then applied the penalty of mortality, which their conduct deserved: "God did not make death, and he does not de-light in the death of the living... but ungodly men by their words and deeds summoned death" (1:13). And our author clearly does envisage some members of the race who do not sin, who remain righteous, for he is puzzled by the fact that the righteous also die. His solution to that apparent problem is simple: the death that the righteous die is not really death at all; well, hardly worth referring to as death. It is rather a transi-tion from a limited life-time in this world to a place or state in which the righteous will live with God forever, a reentry to paradise for those for whom the sting of death, which consists, after all, in its utter destructive-ness, has been drawn. Death, as Paul later asks, where is now your sting? So, "the souls of the righteous are in the hands of God.... In the eyes of the foolish they seemed to have died, and their departure was thought to be an affliction, and their going from us to be their destruction; but they are at peace (*shalom*)" (Wisd. 3:1–4). The wicked, on the contrary, will come to realize that their death is a final disappearance into that dev-astating darkness into which shadows pass: "For our allotted time is the passing of a shadow, and there is no return from our death" (Wisd. 2:5).

Before passing from this particular class of construction of the meaning of the Fall and of its consequences, two further features of it are worth noticing. First, those who believe that all human flesh, and not only the righteous, actually pass through bodily death, adjust accordingly the sense in which we should understand "death" as the divinely ordained wages of sin. Sinners now do pass over death understood as the dissolution of bodily life in its present form, but they are really passing over into a divine tribunal that condemns them to a "death" of eternal damnation, perhaps in a "fire." Here "fire" is no longer the symbol of transformative creation in which deformation is merely a transient, if essential episode; but the symbol, rather, of an eternal deformation, infinitely painful and punitive. The death-as-the-wages-of-sin understanding of the Fall then simply helps itself to the kind of picture of the Great Judgment that Jesus seems to paint in the words of Matthew 25:31–46.

A second feature of this class of story of the Fall and its consequences provides a paradoxical account of death as at once the wages of evil-doing and at the same time, in a way, the cause of that evil-doing. That is, the people who do evil are pictured as mesmerized by the apparently utter destructiveness of human death; so much so that they cannot be persuaded to see beyond it. And so they adopt a *carpe diem* kind of philosophy for their inevitably short lives. Eat drink and be merry; no limits observed; even if this utterly unrestrained self-indulgence is to prove, as it usually does, to be at the expense of others, and mostly of the most vulnerable in society. "Let us oppress the righteous poor man; let us not spare the widow nor regard the grey hairs of the aged. But let our might be our law of right, for what is weak proves itself to be useless" (Wisd. 2:10–11). So now the very death which is the divinely decreed punishment for sin proves itself to be a major incitement to a sinful life that will in turn deserve a punishing death; either in the sense of death as annihilation or as a gateway to an eternal death in a wraith-like existence, or by roasting.

There is no doubt a further version of this theme, to the effect that a certain state of feeling mesmerized by death can actually turn us from God. This is a version that harps, not on the prospect of that death that ends our current bodily life, but rather on the possibility of a bad result from our judgment by God, and on the ensuing "death" of our being plunged into eternal flames. Christian ministers who attend the death-beds of their parishioners occasionally encounter the disconcerting impression that they are not welcome. Not because the dying person has simply ceased, for want of convincing evidence, to believe that there is any life beyond, but because she does not want to believe that there is. And she does not want to believe, either because she finds the ordeal of a tribunal that might damn her too awful to contemplate — who could ever be quite sure that all their sins are remitted? — or she finds the judge who appears to be so uncharacteristically vengeful to be thereby unworthy of her belief and trust, or both. Long before the death-bed scene takes place, sentiments such as these can spur on the *carpe diem* option, by tempting people to simply choose to believe, or at the very least to hope that death is indeed the end of them forever.

Now there can be no doubt about the fact that this class of construction of the biblical account of the Fall contains profound insights into the origin and nature of that human engagement in evil-doing that, because it is always adversarial, satanic toward the continuous work of the Creator, is also called sin. And these profound insights must be carried forward into any analysis of human sinfulness that aspires to the least degree of adequacy. Nevertheless, two things must immediately be noted about this death-as-the-wages-of-sin construction of the Fall. First, that the main harvest of perennial instructive insight must be gleaned from that area of this construction that requires to be entitled not "death as the wages of sin," but rather, "sin as the wages of death." Second, that this class of construction of death-as-the-wages-of-sin is well out of kilter with the Genesis myth of the Fall, in two respects in particular. The Genesis myth talks about death in the normal, natural sense of the no-breathing, heart-stopping, brain-dead ending of this bodily life. And it does not at all seem to regard this death as a punishment for the fall of Adam (that is to say, of mankind, humanity, for the Hebrew *adam* can be so translated in the Genesis text, even though the mythic form allows it to be used simultaneously as a proper name). Instead, the punishment is described as one that consists in various forms of life-threatening hardships to be suffered "until you return to the ground." A phrase then followed by a kind of reminder that can be paraphrased, "for, by the way, in case you have forgotten this, you did come from the ground; you are not immortal; you are dust, and to dust you will return."

The fact that human death is natural in the original myth and not a punishment for sin is acknowledged in other pieces of Wisdom literature in the Bible. In Psalm 49:10, for instance, when the psalmist asks himself why he should fear the rich man intent on increasing in riches, presumably at his expense. For (the rich man) "shall see that even the wise die, the fool and the stupid alike must perish." It may also be acknowledged obliquely in the present class of (re)construction of the original myth, when death is no longer regarded as the annihilation that constitutes the final punishment of sinners, but rather as the crossing-over of both the just and the sinners. So that the sinners can be punished by the "death" of a dark shadow-land, or, less frequently and more controversially imagined, a torture by eternal fire.

Further then, God's reminder at the end of the Genesis myth that human beings must all die, points to another area in which the death-as-the-wages-of-sin construction of the Fall myth seems to be out of kilter with the original. In the latter construction it does not seem to matter much in what precisely the sin consists. Witness to this is the fact that to this very day the "original" sin is described most commonly simply as an act of disobedience. And that is further understood as an act of breaking some specific divine rule, any specific divine rule. The specific rule in the Genesis myth happened to be a rule forbidding the taking and eating of the fruit of a certain tree. A tree thereafter named the tree of the knowledge of good and evil probably, according to this type of interpretation, because by eating its fruit humans first knew evil. The nature of morality assumed in all of this is fundamentally a morality of law, and divinely made and promulgated law at that; but that is an issue for later analysis. For the moment it is necessary only to note that the Genesis myth does actually specify the sin as consisting of something rather different from a disobeying of a seemingly arbitrary divine prohibition. The original sin in the Genesis myth — and it is quite specific about this — consists in the human attempt to appropriate to themselves the absolute wisdom that the immortal One, the Creator, alone can possess. Humanity can possess only that measure of divine wisdom that comes through the existence and life that is continuously created for it. It comes in and as the creation, as human beings know that creation by both benefiting from it and acting creatively in their turn in and with it. It comes as "a seed of wisdom scattered from star to star," a seed that can grow and grow with the growth of life itself toward *shalom*, but which must always with humans be derivative and participatory. The pretension to the appropriation of divine wisdom itself, as if humans had some independent access to it, that is the supreme sin of self-deification, of idolatry, of acting like God. And upon the commission of that sin, as sure as night follows day, will follow all the hardship and death-dealing destruction that are then the natural punishments of the sin. A sin original in the sense that it is the father and mother of all other opposition to the continuous divine creation of life.

But can one explain how such a catastrophic fall occurs? This is just a version of the old question asked in the course of some older constructions of Adam's fall: how could the wise Adam, protected by *Sophia* herself, have been so foolish as to fall like that and to place the whole future of himself and the human race in such extreme jeopardy? There is an explanation, or at least a partial explanation, following on the understanding of creation out of nothing already adopted, and along the lines of the sin-as-the-wages-of-death option offered above. Human beings looking down the vast vistas of creative possibilities in this continuously created world, see first and foremost the sequence of nothing-ings of current forms, at least as far as the final dismembering of our current bodily form that we call death. We feel simultaneously the *angst* engendered both by these waves upon waves of nothing-ing coming toward us from the horizon to our vision that is our death, and the dizzying depths of the freedom and responsibility that we bear as co-creators with the Creator God of the future that lies deep below that horizon of death. And a vertigo invades our very mind and soul. So that instead of soaring in faith over seventy thousand fathoms, we fall. And we grasp at finiteness to sustain ourselves (a phrase, like the rest of this description of the Fall, taken from one of Kierkegaard's more striking accounts of it). And this grasping at finite resources to sustain myself at whatever the cost to others, then causes the deprivation of the lives and livelihoods of others. . . .

To say now that the explanation of the Fall that seems to fit best with the Genesis myth goes beyond this explanation is not to deny this a permanent contribution to the explanation sought. But remember that it was divine wisdom, personified by the talking serpent, that the same serpent tempted humanity to consume and make their own, so that they would be God's equals. The very structure and imagery of the opening Genesis myth suggest then that it is the very position of humanity as image of the divine creator, it is humanity's god-like power and wisdom, that explains the Fall. It is this high status of humanity in the created and creative order that constitutes the temptation for humanity to act as the sole creator of human life and of what is then seen as humanity's world. Other explanations convey little more than an account of conditions, sufficient but never altogether necessary, under which the proclivity to fall for this temptation kicks in, to the point of being well-nigh irresistible. The Fall is a sin of pride as much as, if not more than, a sin committed in cowardice before nothing-ings or from existential angst. Pride seems to be the explanation of the Fall that fits best with the original Genesis myth. And it also seems to have become more rather than less generally applicable as humanity evolved to what we now like to think of as its coming of age — remember again Feuerbach and Marx, and Nietzsche, and the Age of Heroic Materialism, the dawn of which the former two announced.

The Genesis myth says especially of humanity that it is made in God the Creator's own image, and this is glossed later in the Bible as humanity being created a little less than God. So, if it is but a little way from God to humanity, it might seem also to humanity to be but a little way to divinity; to the absolute wisdom that can create eternal life, or at least all the life that can ever be created. The sin is a sin of idolatry, in the specific form of making humanity the idol, the equal of the one that other people worship as the one, true God. The imagery of the original Genesis myth, then, makes it more clear than do other developed versions and explanations of the Fall, that the sin consists in humanity's making an idol of itself. Chapter 17 of the Wisdom of Solomon, from which Paul borrowed so much of his account of human sinfulness, actually says that idolatry is quite understandable — although no less inexcusable for that — because of the awesome beauty of so many of the things that are made, and none so awesome in the eyes of humanity as humanity itself. But the point now is this, that idolatry is so often treated in the Bible, again down to Paul, as the fertile ground from which grows most other kinds of serious sin. It is in that further sense an original sin, originating as it does all that further excess of destruction and death that humanity, in grasping at finiteness in order to sustain and secure its existence, brings upon its world.

The "how" question of the Fall itself is then followed naturally by a question as to how in particular that first idolatrous sin comes to be at the origin of such excessive destruction and death in God's good world that the Noah flood story actually envisages the utter destruction of that world. The answer is multi-layered. First, there is the all-influencing self-centeredness, and its potentially cosmic effects. Plotinus, in his account of the Fall, pictured humanity, living on the very edge of the creative outreach of spirit and light, on the very edge of darkness and matter. Daunted in this twilight existence at the onerous prospect of looking upward over the long and arduous ascent to the One, humanity looked downward instead to the material world it could immediately control, thus constituting itself the highest self by whom and for whom the world would continue to be made. And we know from our experience ever since that such self-centeredness, such selfishness most naturally then occurs quite simultaneously in individual, social and indeed race-wide forms.

In race-wide forms humanity on the whole treats itself as the whole and exclusive raison d'être for the very existence of this earth. So the earth can be plundered without constraint for the needs of human living, for food and drink, energy, shelter. No matter the damage done to the earth in the process. In individual and social forms of the same self-centeredness, the same plunder is also at the expense of the necessary life-supports of other human beings. If the ecology crisis today illustrates the former, the world-wide deprivations, the hunger and death by starvation of millions in a world that has the capacity to feed the whole of humanity, amply illustrate the latter.

The fact is that the developed world, facing obesity as one of it major life-threats, creates just its kind of world at the direct expense of the so-called developing world. And does this by quite deliberate strategies, such as lending the developing peoples large sums of money that then result in repayment debts that prove increasingly crippling. Or subsidizing their own producers, thereby creating effective trade barriers against the poor countries, and preventing them from earning the money to pay off their debts. Or having their so-called multi-national companies exploit the mineral, oil and other wealth of poor countries, or their labor force, in such a way as to expatriate most of the profit, becoming ever richer at the expense of the poor. It is unfortunately only too easy to illustrate how the most successful world-creators today aggrandize themselves and their lives, grasp at finiteness to oversustain themselves, and do so in such a way as to increase to quite appalling extent the suffering and death of humankind, and the deprivation of the patient earth that is material mother to us all. The wielding of economic power in the modern world is the new formula for that self-idolatrous death-dealing toward others hitherto achieved by the waging of wars. But of course wars are still waged today, civil and international wars, commonly and often. And hundreds of thousands of innocents, mainly women and children, are massacred; often quite deliberately, as in Hiroshima, Nagasaki, Dresden . . . and the lives of ten times as many others are stunted and their livelihoods destroyed. In all of these ways the amount of destruction and death visited by humankind on the world increases exponentially with the increase of humanity's creative powers over its world. To the point at which it threatens to turn the transitory nothing-ing that is part of continuous creation into permanent annihilation — at least with respect to life on earth, the very scenario anticipated by the myth of Noah's flood.

One of the best biblical illustrations of this understanding of humanity's original sin and of the enormous increase of unacceptable death-dealing hardship and suffering that it brings, is to be found in the words of the prophet Ezekiel, delivering the Creator's judgment on the King of Tyre: "Thus says the Lord God: Because your heart is proud, and you have said, 'I am a god'...yet you are but a man, and no god, though you consider yourself as wise as a god...by your wisdom and your understanding you have gotten wealth for yourself...by your great wisdom in trade you have increased your wealth...because you consider yourself wise as a god, therefore, behold, I will bring strangers upon you, the most terrible of the nations; and they shall draw their swords against the beauty of your wisdom and defile your splendor...you shall die the death of the uncircumcised by the hands of foreigners; for I have spoken, says the Lord God" (Ezek. 28:1–10).

The second half of this chapter in Ezekiel is a lamentation for the King of Tyre as if the judgment were already executed, and the lamentation is cast in the imagery of the Genesis creation myth with its fall in the garden: "Thus says the Lord God...You were the very model of perfection, full of wisdom and perfect in beauty. You were in Eden, the garden of God...You were anointed as a guardian cherub, for so I ordained...You were blameless in your ways from the day you were created, till wickedness was found in you. Through your widespread trade you were filled with violence, and you sinned; so I drove you away in disgrace...and I expelled you, O guardian cherub...all the nations who knew you are appalled at you; you have come to a horrible end" (Ezek. 28:11–19). The implication here, as one could gather in any case from the nature of cosmic myth, is that Adam stands for humanity, so that the Fall happens at all points of linear time. With the further implication, of course, that paradise is created at every point of linear time — in our terms. The creation as it comes from eternity is always good, in fact perfect with respect to each stage of the evolution of existence and life. Heaven is here, until we make it hell. As God through Ezekiel said to Tyre: "You were in Eden...till wickedness was found in you."

Note in particular in these texts the threat to bring strangers upon the king, to put him to the sword; for violence breeds violence or, as Jesus put it, those who live by the sword, die by the sword. If for no other reason than this, that the ones deprived by violence, armed or economic, are often driven to the last resort, to violent protection of life and livelihood, and evil increases exponentially for all. There being no real winners in war, either in trade wars or in military wars. "A victory" cried a gushing lady to the Duke of Wellington, "must be the most exhilarating thing in the world." "A victory, madam," the Duke replied rather coldly, "is the most tragic thing in the world, saving only a defeat." And in such tragic circumstances evil increases, not only for humans, but for the very earth itself ravaged in the process. And God who sustains and enlivens all, the good and the wicked alike, takes responsibility also for this destructive punishment: "*I* will bring upon you the most terrible of the nations": "bringing *shalom* and creating evil, I am the Lord who does all these things." As indeed it is at least implied in the creation myth at the opening of Genesis that God takes responsibility for tempting humanity to fall in the first place. In that it is the serpent, the personification of the divine attributes of wisdom and immortality that does the tempting. A mythic manner of saying that it was by creating us with such high and self-conscious wisdom for our role in co-creating the world that God has God's own share in the responsibility for our temptation.

Note also that the other side of the coin of idolatry is infidelity, that is to say, failure to take Kierkegaard's leap of faith toward the infinity of possibility held out by cooperation with the true Creator, failure to keep faith with the true Creator. Put in terms of the creation theology already developed from the Bible, the choice of human individuals or groups to appoint themselves as the only creators of a world that can support and secure human life, can bring only an excess of suffering and death to all living things. Such a choice is the very opposite, adversarial, that is to say, satanic with respect to the choice of entrusting oneself to the true Creator and playing one's derivative but genuinely creative role in a process of continuous divine creation. So the Fall and its effects, in addition to being termed idolatry, can equally be called Satanism. And in so far as it is all in the self-centered service of humanity thus satanized, it can be seen as the service of Satan. Idolators whose father is Satan; so will the Bible down to Jesus and Paul and beyond describe those who still remain within the ethos of the original sin of the race.

Note finally and consequently, that infidelity, the lack of faith in the divine source of existence and life, is no mere mental attitude, no mere failure to give mental assent to some proposition, such as "Jesus is Lord." It is rather a failure in practice, in the way one lives; a failure to co-operate as image of the Creator in the Creator's own creative work. A failure to love one's neighbor as oneself, to give to others life and the supports of life, and to receive from others life and the supports of life. So that in such mutual love and its creative giving in imitation of the divine, there may always be life and life ever more abundant for all. For that is the law of the creation as it comes from the hands of the limitlessly bountiful and loving Creator. That is therefore the essence of righteousness, so that faith and righteousness coincide.

To keep faith with Creator and creation is to act morally; to replace the Creator with an idol is inevitably to act as a satanic force against the limitless life-giving propensities of the creation, and to act immorally. That closest of coincidence between keeping faith with the one, true Creator and achieving righteousness and its limitless rewards is found in so many parts of the wisdom literature of the Bible. For example, when kings were considered cosmic figures, sons of God, lords, christs (three biblical titles for King David and his line), they were correspondingly considered to be made especially in the image of God precisely by receiving from the Creator the necessary share in divine wisdom. They were therefore especially ordained, anointed to keep the garden of creation fair and free from the depredations of the wicked — as Ezekiel's words confirm, when he likens the King of Tyre before his fall to the guardian cherubim who were set to guard the garden in the Genesis creation myth. As *Sophia* herself put it, "By me kings reign, and rulers decree what is just"; and Psalm 72 spells out the expected results of rulers being ruled by their participation in that creative wisdom: peace and prosperity in the kingdom (for it is now really under the reign of God; it is the kingdom of God), a prosperity that characterizes the earth itself, "abundance of grain in the land; on the tops of the mountains may it wave"; a total *shalom* that will see this kingdom expand universally and endure as long as the sun.

It is essential for anyone who wants to understand adequately and accurately the teaching, life and fate of Jesus of Nazareth, to appreciate this biblical account of the seeds of divine wisdom scattered in the course of the continuous activity of divine creation "from star to star," and so entering the minds of human beings, in particular those who would rule others and rule the earth itself. It is essential to understand faith as practical, entrusting commitment, and to come to realize that those who prioritize the gaining of life by themselves and for themselves will lose life for themselves and destroy it for others. But since Jesus is, perhaps unfortunately, predominantly understood as Savior, this claim for continuity of biblical creation imagery into the substance of the New Testament is best secured in the course of a chapter on Salvation. Meanwhile, if only to secure the conviction that the true God and God's true ways with the world are revealed in the creation, together with the fall that is a continuing feature of that same continuous creation, it is worth pausing to take a short trip through some areas of comparative religion.

First, those who study the mythology of an ancient Celtic people called the Goidels or Gaels, a Gaelic-speaking people (mainly the Irish and their old cultural colony, the Scots), and who enjoy some command of theology or religious studies, will find a pre-Christian myth of creation and fall that is remarkably similar to the biblical myths and at least as ancient. This myth tells of the continuously creative God/ess, of many names and alternating gender, who fashions the formed world out of watery chaos (floods), and engenders the human being many ancient princely genealogies go back to a named divinity, just as in Luke's genealogy of Jesus, "the son of Joseph, the son of Heli...the son of Seth, the son of Adam, the son of God." This God/ess then also appoints kings who will rule the earth according to the *fir flathemon*, the truth, right, justice (for it is a practical wisdom, not a pure theory), that comes from the divine realm. So that the true and righteous ruler, according to one of the myths of Irish kingship that survived centuries of Christianization, is deemed to be married to a divine woman, wisdom personified. A kind of scene hinted at in Solomon's prayer to the Lord, "send me the Wisdom that sits by your throne" (Wisd. of Solomon 9:4). And this is then the same Creator Woman who, as soon as the king lets loose in the land injustice, will turn into a death-dealing hag, abandon the land and people to destruction and waste, and bring about the death of the king himself.

And there are of course a great many other ancient myths from peoples far separated in time and place from the people of the Bible, that are of comparable import. David Turner, a Canadian anthropologist who, unlike so many of his fellows is quite literate in theology and religious studies, has written a remarkable account of the myths and practices of the Australian Aborigines of Groote Eylandt in Australia in *Genesis Regained* and other books. Suffice it to say here that at the heart of the fundamental attitude to the whole of reality exhibited by these Groote Eylandters is a powerful image of Renunciation which means — far too crudely put, even for purposes of brevity — that all material reality is to be given away to whomsoever needs it. A philosophy of life merely approximated by the adage in 2 Cor. 8:15, "he who gathered much had nothing over, and he who gathered little had no lack." A way of life resulting in the experience that, when everything is given up, "someNothing" continues to exist, a transcendent being in which all then participate.

Suffice it to add that the good Christian Europeans who discovered Australia in their turn decided that these Aborigines were too primitive to have even a law of property and a recognizable God to confirm such laws. And since the apparent absence of a law of property suggested that nobody owned the land, since the land was a *terra nullius*, these good Christians felt quite entitled to take it for themselves. So they drove to the worst deprivation those "primitive, a-moral creatures" that they had not already shot dead in the process. Who then was living out something very like the biblical theology of divine creation, and who was committing something very, very like the biblical original sin, aggrandizing themselves and spreading destruction, hardship, suffering and death in the process? The despised Aborigines were doing the first; the self-styled Christians the second. The end-result of such excursions as these into the area of comparative religion must surely be the gradual dawning of the realization that the foundational knowledge of what constitutes justice and injustice, right and wrong, wisdom and folly, good and evil derives, like and with the knowledge of the one, true God, from the experience of God the Creator ever present and active in the creation.

A further example, this time an example of committing original sin by the idolatry of cutting God down to the size of one's people. This in turn can be done in a number of ways. It can be done in the manner in which certain people speak of God as their kinsman, for instance, massively more powerful than any other kinsman, but kinsman nonetheless. And as such faithfully reflecting the interests of the group in whose image God is now cast. A god who supports their desires for control of land and for all the other resources that they deem necessary for the security and enrichment of their lives, no matter the cost to others or the destruction and death that must be visited upon them. "*You* are my people, and I am *your God*," the Creator cut down to size is then required to announce. But this can be achieved through other civic and public processes also.

The execution of Socrates is a case in point. Socrates stands in the long line of Greek philosopher-theologians that eventually offered to both Jews and Christians the precise theology they needed in order to express the knowledge of God the Creator revealed in the creation and hitherto communicated through the category of myth. Socrates, therefore, as far as we can see into his mind through the lenses of Plato's dialogues, glimpsed the one, true God to the extent that humanity's frail vision can do so.

He caught sight of God the Creator, and he understood that the rule of human life was, as Plato put it, the *homoiosis theou:* to live in the likeness of God the Creator; a formula for morality quite similar in fact to Jesus's summing up of his sermon on the mount: "you therefore must be perfect, as your heavenly Father is perfect" (Matt. 5:47). The rulers of Athens, however, saw in this theology nothing less than a threat to the gods worshiped by the city state of Athens. Hence the specifics of the capital charge against Socrates, that he was undermining the religious piety of the people and in particular the piety of that part of the people so crucial to the future of Athens, the aristocratic youth of Athens.

And what piety was that? It was a practical faith in the gods of Athens, gods on behalf of whom the Athenians could confess: *we* are your people, and you are *our* gods. It was a practical faith in gods that could be counted upon to know whose side to be on when Athens needed to aggrandize itself further, in whatever conflicts might then arise between itself and other city states or peoples. As simple as that; and for that, and for the true Creator God that he saw and wished to serve, Socrates went willingly to his death, in order to bear for others such final witness to that truth that the giving of one's life to it, and then for it, can alone bear.

The Greeks, by the time of Socrates, had already classified theology into three categories: *theologia mythikon*, the account of God in God's world in the form of imagery and story; *theologia physikon*, the same account in the form of conceptual analysis and synthesis; and *theologia politikon*, the account given by the establishments of states (and presumably also of churches designed like states, or even like empires). And it looks as if the last of these categories, containing accounts of establishment gods, is always liable to give an account of a god made in the establishment's own image, mirroring its own self-aggrandizing aims, and eventually creating the hardship, destruction and death-dealing that such self-centeredness inevitably entails. But one does not have to look to the Greeks of the ancient world or to Christian *conquistadors* in the new world in order to find examples of this particular kind of idolatry. As the kinsman language can easily remind us, the Bible itself bears witness to the manner in which a people from its very opening pages witnessed to a practical faith in God, the infinitely benevolent creator of all. But then, later in that same Bible, in the course of a very different kind of practical faith, in the course of an incursive idolatry in fact, they reduced that Creator to the role of commander-in-chief of their armies, the Lord of (their) Hosts, the old ethnic-cleansing Jahweh of 1 Samuel 15.

The story goes that King Agag of the Amalekites opposed the Israelites coming out of Egypt and seeking to settle in lands they claimed God had given them. So Yahweh, according to the prophet, Samuel, ordered Saul and his Israelite army to "go and smite Amalek, and utterly destroy all that they have; do not spare them, but kill both man and woman, infant and suckling, ox and sheep, camel and ass." In the event, the victorious Israelites saw no point in slaughtering good livestock, and Saul even spared his fellow, if opposing king, Agag. *Noblesse oblige*, as the saying goes. All of which brought the prophet Samuel back to the camp in a divinely incited rage at this open disobedience to the express command of the Lord of Hosts. Having informed Saul of the due punishment for his disobedience, Samuel then said, "'Bring here to me Agag the king of the Amalekites.' And Agag came to him cheerfully. Agag said, 'surely the bitterness of death is past.' And Samuel said, 'as your sword has made women childless, so shall your mother be childless among women.' And Samuel hewed Agag in pieces before the Lord in Gilgal. . . . And the Lord repented that he had made Saul king over Israel." So much for this prophet of the Lord; so much for the lord imagined by such a prophet, and by those who listened to him, or who wrote down such words for his lips.

The Fall in the Christian Theological Tradition

Just as in the case of the inclusive biblical myth of divine creation, the myth-within-a-myth of the Fall also was turned into a piece of theology. Using the same predominantly Platonic philosophical theology that was available for the purpose at the time of the origins of Christianity as a distinct religion. And unfortunately, in the latter case as in the former, a certain temptation in Platonism, which only the highest form of Platonism, in the works of Plotinus for example, altogether resisted, did a good deal of damage to the resulting Christian-Platonic theology. This intrusive temptation in Platonism to this day consists in reading the mind-spirit-soul/physical body-matter dualism in its metaphysical form as a dualism of two separate substances. Such that, in its moral form, the physical, sensual, material body, with its "lower soul" and its characteristic complement of functions and tendencies, is seen as the substance that pulls the "higher soul" aside from its connatural path to spiritual union with the good and utterly spiritual God.

Now the only generalization permissible to anyone who looks back to these remote origins of this Christian theology of the Fall is that it gradually lost the best of its biblical bearings, until it finally lost the plot altogether in that feature of the Fall that is traceable to Augustine and solemnly defined by the Roman Catholic Council of Trent in the sixteenth century. The feature, namely, that sees the original sin transmitted to every member of the human race, through the very process of their generation into that same human race. And the only subsidiary generalization that can be added is this: that the most obvious cause of this losing of bearings and of the catastrophic mess in which the theology of original sin found itself right down to modern times, is mainly, although no doubt not quite solely, the intrusion of this so-called "Cartesian" kind of dualism, in both metaphysical and moral forms, into the Christian theology borrowed from Platonism.

The trend is set in a sense by the Jewish philosopher-theologian Philo of Alexandria. The opening theme that is to become standard in Christian Platonism is already stated by Philo: it is the soul in humans, and the higher soul at that, the *nous;* it is this that is made in the image of God, the image in particular of the divine *Logos.* Yet, Philo allows, the earthly Adam was at first perfect in wisdom and grace. Until, that is, he engaged sexually with Eve, and thus brought on the pains of childbirth for her, toil and labor for himself, and the acrid taste of his own mortality. Sex and procreation, multiplying and providing, pain and hardship and the very sight of one's prospective replacements: all of these are harbingers of bodily mortality. *Eros* and *thanatos*, as in Freud (although he seemed to be much more engrossed with the former), the twin instinctive forces that are deepest in the human psyche. And then, for Philo, the resulting obsession with such bodily functions and processes that bury the soul and keep it out of paradise; for paradise is not a place but a state of the soul in its journey to the divine.

Yet the earlier Christian theologians, or apologists as they are called, do not seem to have been unduly influenced by this corrupt form of Platonic dualism. They seem happy to explain the apparently permanent sinfulness of the race by the persistence of satanic temptation from the beginning, without going into much further detail about the nature of the sinning. As Justin Martyr put it in his *Dialogue with Trypho*, "since the sin of Adam, the human race has fallen under the serpent's power of death and error." We are born, he allows, with wayward inclinations. But the fact that he also seems to accept that we are each responsible for our own sins, means that he is taking the inclination to evil-doing, the biblical *yeser ha ra*, in its true and full biblical sense. It is not a stand-alone proclivity to sin that works through our sensual bodily parts and their lower soul, in order to deprive us of freedom and responsibility. This is not therefore a biblical endorsement of that concept of concupiscence that later theologians of original sin, as must shortly appear, take over with the intrusive dualism of the kind of Platonism just noted. The true and full biblical view of this matter can be gleaned from a few texts: "he who created man in the beginning . . . left him in the power of his own inclination, *yeser*, and *yeser* here means something like will. For the quotation goes on immediately to say, "if you will, you can keep the commandments" (Sir. 15:14–15). And there are other biblical texts that talk of a *yeser* to good, not evil: "Thou dost keep him in perfect *shalom* whose *yeser* is steadfastly set on thee" (Isa. 26:3). So inclination is will, and will toward either good or evil is free will, and that is part and parcel of human nature, an endowment of all human beings as they come from the Creator. It cannot then explain how humanity falls rather than not fall. Tertullian too stresses Adam's freedom in his fall before temptation, and though he does talk of the irascible and concupiscible elements in our lower soul being "by second nature" inclined to sin after the Fall, he continues to stress also our sinning in imitation of Adam, and so encountering trial, trouble and death.

Similarly with Tatian and Theophilus, except that they think that humans are created neither mortal nor immortal, that their fate in this respect depends on their behavior. And Athenagoras simply adds an angelic fall, in order to explain the satanic temptation and the havoc it causes for humanity. Irenaeus above all, obsessed as he is with Gnostics, and seeing in their characteristic kind of metaphysical-moral dualism the seed-ground of most, if not all of the heresies of the age, insists that Adam fell freely. Although he does break with the tradition of Adam created perfect, insisting instead that Adam was child-like in comparison with humanity later come of age. And insisting also that Adam was immediately called to repentance and, unlike Cain in this, answered that call, and was saved from his sin. Adam's sin did point his progeny to the wrong path, but God who created Adam with a view to growth toward that perfection much later realized in Jesus of Nazareth, correspondingly continued to save people from sin in anticipation of Jesus the Christ's superabundant grace.

It is with Origen then and other Alexandrians, those highly Platonized theologians, that the variations on Philo's themes really emerge, and the cautions of Irenaeus against the dualist Fall theology of the Gnostics appear to be overlooked. Not so much with Clement of Alexandria perhaps. For although he does echo Philo's account of a fall coincident with the sexual awakening of Adam and Eve, he nevertheless insists always that human beings retain their free potential for good and evil. Origen however, believing that human souls preexist their individual incarnation, and seeing these souls as images of *Logos/ Sophia*, who is in turn the image of the One, actually envisages a precorporeal fall of human souls on a similar model to that of the fall of the angels, a sin of pride leading to rebellion. And the fall of Adam, and with him of all human beings, now consists essentially in the temporal embodiment on earth of these human souls. This earthly body being itself a source of defilement. Although Origen does sow some confusion in this matter by seeming to distinguish defilement from sin properly so called.

There is another famous grouping of early Fathers of the Church, as these great early theologians came to be called, a grouping referred to as the Cappadocian Fathers. Among these Basil, ever conscious of heretical dualists, constantly stresses the freedom of the fall of angels, of Adam, and of the rest of Adam's race. In fact he often uses "Adam" as a cipher for humanity. It is Gregory of Nyssa who shows the clear influence of Philo and Origen. For Gregory humankind is so much in the image of God, so exalted in spirit, that we surpass our own ability to understand ourselves. And if we could come to know ourselves adequately, we could see the Archetype in whose image we are made. That, however, is true only for Humanity the Exemplar created in the first creation, and not yet gender-differentiated for marrying and giving in marriage. But that Human Being fell, being induced to rebel by an angel already jealous of its high estate, and the result was a fall into bodily existence, by means of the second creation. A fall into the experience of sex, concupiscence, pain and struggle, multiplication, replacement, death: all the ills to which human flesh is heir.

And so to Augustine, who had this kind of highly Platonized Christian theology largely second hand, through his mentor, Ambrose, and people like the Latin-speaking Neo-Platonist and convert to Christianity, Marius Victorinus. Augustine somehow managed to construct from all of this the most disastrous doctrine of the Fall and original sin in the whole history of Christianity down to the present day. For Augustine also the image of God in humanity is found in the soul, which is by nature spiritual and immortal. The theme of the two creations is discretely present, but it is the embodied Adam, and not some noetic version of Adam, that falls. And falls, not by a sin of sexual concupiscence, but by a sin of pride. Yet that first sin causes concupiscence, the common name for all the evil tendencies of the lower, sensual soul, to be set loose. And that concupiscence, because of the disordered sexual act involved in all procreation, infects every new soul. That much is clear from Augustine. And one other thing is clear, if only from the statement of the Council of Carthage of 418 C.E., in the course of its condemnation of Pelagius, largely engineered by Augustine: "even little infants, who could not as yet commit any personal fault are, in all truth, baptized for the remission of sin, so that regeneration may cleanse in them that which they have contracted by generation." It is perfectly clear at this point that Adam's own original sin is held to be contracted by all of his progeny through the very process of their generation.

After that, not very much more is clear, and in particular it is not clear just *how* sin is transmitted in the very process of human generation. Followers of Pelagius, like the extremely sharp and competent Julian, tried to get Augustine to admit to a belief that the soul of the newborn was, as well as the body, derived from the parents, so that sinful souls might hand on to their children sinful souls. But Augustine refused to be tied to this theory of the origin of individual souls. As distinct, say, from the theory of a new creation of each individual soul by God. And so it remains unclear as to whether the concupiscence that is transmitted is itself original sin, or whether it is just a sign that original sin is in fact being transmitted. Those who take the trouble to read the lengthy and complex debate between Augustine and those followers of Pelagius who produced increasingly sophisticated arguments against what Pelagius considered to be a piece of pernicious nonsense, may never all agree on the clarification of this matter of Augustinian exegesis. Yet Augustine's insistence that the sin of the individual, Adam, is transmitted through human generation, not by imitation, to all of human kind, remains intact down to the Roman Catholic Council of Trent and beyond; and it is therefore an undeniable feature of this doctrine of original sin.

The Western tradition of Christian theology did attempt to answer the question of the "how" of the alleged transmission of Adam's sin through the natural process of generation. This was done through one dominant manner of analysis and argument that in fact reveals the deepest Platonic dualist source of this most distorted version of the theme of the Fall. It was done by taking one central feature of myth in general and of the Genesis creation myth in particular, and then giving it a sense supplied by the suspect dualism of lesser Platonism. The central feature? Cosmic myth speaks of and to every time and every place; so it speaks of everyman in speaking of one (original) human being, as a result of which *adam* can be and is translated according to context, either as the name of an individual, or as a noun for humanity. Now transpose this into the idiom of our suspect Platonic dualism and it reads as follows: Human nature is a Platonic entity, best illustrated in the picture of a preexistent Human Exemplar, and in essence identified with the soul. Ambrose of Milan, who first showed Augustine the promise of a Platonized theology for Christianity, used to insist that the soul is I, I *am* the soul, I *have* a body. It then becomes very easy indeed to speak of all human beings participating in that Original Humanity. Even if one wishes to eschew any idea of Original Humanity's temporal preexistence, and to assert instead that it makes its first existential appearance in the body of the Original Man. It is then easy to speak of all of us being in Adam, easy to speak of us sinning in Adam. And, cobbled together with the view that the soul is the *real* human being, it becomes fatally easy on these Platonic principles to convey the impression that sinning inevitably involved the concupiscence of the body. While remaining somewhat vague on the hen-or-egg issues that then begin to appear.

Something like this is what seems to be behind the efforts of major theologians of the Western church as they persist with the doctrine of an original sin transmitted through generation to all. Anselm, who finalized the still dominant salvation theology of the West, concluded that since human nature was fully realized in the historical Adam, all subsequent humans were also in a very real sense "in Adam." So when Adam sinned, all can therefore be said to have always already sinned in Adam. Aquinas, who refers to this original sin as a taint or defilement, while insisting that it did not actually consist in the concupiscence that was also transmitted and not wiped out by baptism, expressed the same view as Anselm. But he expressed it more stylishly in one of his comparison-in-contrast constructions: whereas in Adam the person by sinning tainted the nature, in all our cases the nature taints the person with real sin. And so this daft doctrine reached the Council of Trent, which in more than one context translated Paul's 1 Corinthians 5:12: "wherefore as by one man sin entered the world, and by sin death; so also death passed to all men, *in whom* all sinned." The very grammatical awkwardness of this translation, in trying to refer the "whom" all the way back to the "one man," might have alerted these learned men to the fact that they were misconstruing the meaning of Paul. And in that process they misrepresented nothing less than the whole biblical witness to the Fall, which never anywhere or by any manner of means teaches the transmission of sin simply through the process of generation.

The more one thinks of this whole tradition of theology of the Fall, the more one gets the distinct impression that it is a theory made up to support and defend something else that one feels one has to say anyway, for quite different reasons. Even if the supporting theory makes little or no sense in itself, and begins on closer inspection to look like plain nonsense, or at best pure mystification. In this case the thing that Christian theologians wanted to say anyway, and increasingly as the centuries pass, was that Jesus redeems the whole of humankind from sin, every human being, past, present and to come. And the only way to make sure that every human being is, was, and will be in need of redemption from sin, is to deny the central assertion of Pelagius in this matter. This is the assertion that every newborn that comes from the continuous creation of the infinitely benevolent God is, like everything else created, good, as the Genesis myth repeatedly insists. The newborn babe is good, not already mired in evil and sin; and furthermore, every little neonate is graced by God with a creative will for good and for more good for all, and with the freedom and dignity of that responsibility. Even if that further dignity can allow the child as it grows to give in to the temptations ever present in its own exalted state, and ever almost overwhelmingly present in the world around it, namely, the temptations to turn and to destroy in itself and for others the promise of life ever more abundant which is forever contained in the very creation of which it has now become so co-operative a part.

Pelagius had to be condemned, then, and the doctrine of the transmission of real sin through the natural process of human generation had to be defined as dogma; and even Baptism had to be seen primarily, not as the sacrament of the transmission of life, but as a sacrament of the cleansing of sin, particularly in neonates. What can one say of a doctrine of the salvation of all by Jesus, the Word incarnate, that is thought to require the support of this Augustinian doctrine of original sin and, in addition, this understanding of the primary symbolism of the sacrament of Baptism? Only that the doctrine of salvation involved, and the doctrine of the sacrament of Baptism entailed, are as likely to have somehow become as damaged as the doctrine of original sin which is thought to be the necessary support for the one and the necessary context for the other. So that, in the overall scenario, as much damage is present in the theology of baptism and in the theology of salvation as is then present in the whole of Christian theology, as the symptomatic presence of this mystifying doctrine of transmitted sin indicates. And what damage to the whole of theology is that, then? The image of a Creator who would condemn to some eternal limbo an infant that dies before baptism, provides perhaps the single most apt illustration in Augustinian terms, of the nature and extent of the damage; for that is the image of a gruesome divinity, as gruesome as Moloch or any Aztec divinity allegedly thirsty for the blood of children. Then there is the damage done to the moral fabric of humanity, and to the freedom and dignity of their creative role in the creation, and the damage (already?) done to the theology of salvation, and the theology of grace, and the theology of the sacraments, and the theology of church.... The list can be long, but there is little point in expanding on it here. Time enough to do so when these further areas of theology come up for analysis.

For the moment it is necessary only to conclude that the whole history of the Christian theology of the Fall, in particular as it develops in the Western Christian church in the wake of Augustine, carries little enough of the rich biblical offerings and insights. Little is carried forward of the nature and of the effects of the sin in which the Fall in essence consists. The frequent acknowledgment that it is a sin of pride might have helped people remember the true nature and origin of the temptation in the very stature of human beings as co-creators. And in this way to understand the persistence of the temptation through all generations of humanity, and the consequent universality of the yielding to such temptation, helped further and forward by the power of example and its transmission as culture. And finally to understand the excess of suffering and death, of destruction in lieu of continuous creation that is ever its natural result and endemic penalty. Instead, the reference to a sin of pride is taken to indicate some unspecified act of disobedience to a specific divine command to Adam. So that the penalty also will seem, not a natural outcome of such a fall, but an additional divine decision, this time in the form of a penal ruling that is arbitrarily at the choosing of the judge.

The Biblical Account of the Fall and Original Sin in Summary

The species-specific and endemic temptation of humanity, due entirely to humanity's innate creative role, unequalled among known creatures in this universe, is this: to think itself the sole supreme creator of the world; though in truth it is itself created in the image of the true supreme

Creator, who, needing nothing, continually creates this universe out of overflowing goodness for the purpose of making all things as good as they can be or, to put the matter in other words, in order to bring all creatures, each in its own manner and measure, home again to its share in the Creator's own superabundant life, the life from which it first took origin. The one, true divine Creator creates all creatures so as to be co-creators with God and with and of the others. The earth is created to bring forth and support living creatures, and they in turn bring forth and support others, each primarily after its own kind, but all eventually co-involved in the continuous creation of the universe as it journeys on its way to its share in the final peace and prosperity, the *shalom* of God. And each therefore having to suffer the deformations inevitably involved in the transformations achieved by the adaptations of themselves and to each other that their interdependence on the evolutionary way of the world toward life most abundant for all requires.

This temptation of the human being is so innate that it might be pictured as something transmitted at birth to each one, more especially when falling to the temptation becomes a very culture that is also transmitted through the very education of successive generations, as Pelagius so well explained. This innate temptation is triggered to well-nigh invincible strength by both the negative and the positive features of this co-creative stature. Looking down the infinite range of possibility that creativity opens up brings simultaneously a dizzying vista of the deformations to be undergone, culminating as it seems in the complete dissolution of this bodily existence, as part and parcel of the creative pursuit of the currently unimaginable abundance of life that may finally be experienced. Faith is called for here, faith in the infinite promise held out by the Source-Creator of all that is always already given, the promise of life and existence, limitless and for all. But there is also called up a deep, deep anxiety before the range of the consecutive loss of familiar forms, the daily deaths culminating in the dissolution of the present bodily form, and an anxiety before the awesome responsibility of one's own creative role. To the point at which one's awareness of the very status of that human creative role in the world — a little less than God — can tip the balance and make one opt for a role of sole supreme creator of a world that could possibly relieve one of the daily dying, support one's current forms of life in all their positive affordances and enjoyments, and postpone — perhaps indefinitely? — the death that dissolves this current form of earthly existence, the only form we can adequately know.

To yield to this most insidious of temptations is to be guilty of idolatry, and idolatry indeed in the specific form of making a god of humanity. However much we may try to disguise this idolatry from ourselves by making gods to worship that are not in our own image, but are really within our control. Or, better still, by taking the true God so truly revealed in the creation and subtly reshaping that God into one of our own, into the image of just another one of us, but so much bigger and stronger. For the practical goal of idolatry, however we seek to disguise it in these ways, is to serve and secure the best of life as we now know it, for ourselves. It is a quintessentially self-serving form of faith. For faith, of course, is still required; it is required as much in atheistic humanism as it is in true religion. Faith and trust in humanity alone to amass such supports of life as will keep all daily dying at bay, and at least postpone the dissolution of the body — a dissolution which in this form of faith must appear final — for as long as possible.

Yet such idolatry inevitably proves to be a truth, a life, a way that increasing destruction, suffering, death-dealing and despair, rather than increase creation and limitless hope. For if it is practiced by the whole race, the quintessential self-centeredness of it threatens to rape and plunder the very earth that supports this earthly life. If it is practiced by individuals or groups, the self-same self-centeredness threatens the supports of life and the life itself of other human beings. And as for the death we all have to die, Fall or no Fall: for the idolators among us it is a death stripped of all hope, for they place their faith in themselves. And for those they deprive and kill it is a cruel death, a destruction before their time carried to them by those who should be their fellow creators of an ever better life for all.

That, or something not unlike it, is the best biblical account of the Fall and original sin, and of its penalty, paid in an excess of destruction, suffering and death-dealing. The punishment for our fall and original sin, it seems, consists in nothing more than the excess of destruction, death and despair that the race that continually falls into such original wickedness visits upon itself. If paradise is in this world, in the form of this world as it comes continually created from the hands of God — *chomh friseailte le haran, chomh fionnuar le fíon*, as one of our poets put it, as fresh as new-baked daily bread, as refreshing as a draught of cool wine — then so is hell also in this world, in every here and now.

Chapter Three

SALVATION

[Jesus's good news] does not prove itself, either by miracles or rewards and promises ... it is every moment its own miracle, its own reward, its own proof, its own kingdom of God.
— Nietzsche, *The Anti-Christ*

I taught them to create the future, and to redeem by creating all that *was past*. ... For I want to go to man once more: I want to go under *among them*. I want to give them, dying, my richest gift.
— Nietzsche, *Thus Spoke Zarathustra*

The Biblical Story of Salvation

Salvation/Healing; Deliverance/Liberation; Recapitulation/Restoration; Victory, Final and Irreversible; Reconciliation; Redemption/ Ransom; Satisfaction/ Expiation.

Myth is noted for the profusion of images it uses, as well as for the different ways in which the same image may be used, even in a single context. Much of that profusion seems to serve only to elicit responses of confusion, bewilderment, and perhaps instant dismissal. Such responses stem from neat logical minds that prove impatient, if not intolerant of any suggestion to the effect that tolerance and patience may yield the richest harvest of insight in any and every matter touched upon by myth. The opening list of images noted above, even though it is probably not exhaustive, offers nevertheless a fair impression of the profusion of imagery with which the Bible treats the matter that is of concern in this chapter. So that, given such profusion, it is probably best to begin the investigation of the biblical data with the images that are the least metaphorically deployed.

For just as concepts, together with their linguistic expressions, can be used either univocally or analogically across a range of references, depending on whether they carry the same content of meaning (John and Paul are both persons), or a content of meaning that is at once similar and different (John and God can both be described as personal beings); so imagery too can be used univocally (God and the doctor, or the faith healer, both heal people), or metaphorically (God is the true monarch of the United Kingdom of Great Britain and Northern Ireland; Elizabeth II, the *eikon basilike*, is the true monarch of Great Britain). It is best then to start with the image that is used most univocally in the Bible for that which in subsequent theologizing is as frequently but more metaphorically termed *redemption*. It is best to begin the investigation of the current topic with the image of salvation. Salvation, *salvum facere*, means to make well or to make whole, as in the case of the woman with the hemorrhage who was healed by Jesus merely by having touched the hem of his outer garment, and then told by him "your faith has made you well" (Mark 5:34). And in any case, since the focus of this study is centered upon Christianity, and therefore centered upon Jesus, it is more than apposite to observe that the Hebrew name, Jesus or Joshua, itself means "he will save." As the angel said to Joseph on the occasion of Jesus's conception: "You will call his name Jesus, for he will save his people" (Matt. 2:21). As Savior is the first title of Jesus of Nazareth then, salvation/healing must be the first image, used in a primarily univocal sense, for that which he, or at least the Word incarnate in him, or the Spirit through him, accomplished in God's good but compromised creation.

Yet it is also important to note at the outset that the naming of the man from Nazareth as Jesus, "he will save," cannot of itself be taken to imply either that Jesus alone saves, where the God he calls "Father" is content with creating, or that God saves only through Jesus. Only if one went solely by the names and by nothing else said in the Bible about them, could one conclude that Father and Son Jesus differ in that the Father creates and Jesus redeems. It is true that the Israelite name for God was YHWH, probably pronounced Jahweh; the etymology of which is given (in Exod. 4:13–15) when Moses asks for God's name. A form of the verb "to be," *hayah*, YHWH is in the third person and most probably must be translated, "He causes to be." And Jesus in its Hebrew form, it has already been remarked, means "He will save." Creator, then, and Savior naming different roles for different persons? No, for one cannot read further in either what Christians call the Old Testament or in what they then call the New Testament, without realizing that Yahweh, the Father God of Israel, is also Savior; and that Jesus, "He will save," is eventually called the Son of God who also creates the world. For just as the serpent was simultaneously the symbol of wise creator and healer-savior so, as far as the Father is concerned, the very context in which He reveals His name to Moses, "He causes to be/Creator," is also the context in which he promises to be the savior of Moses and his people from their oppression in Egypt: "I promise that I will bring you up out of the affliction of Egypt to . . . a land flowing with milk and honey" (Exod. 3:17; probably the nearest Hebrew term for saving is *ga'al*, used in the human context of vindication or pledge-keeping by a kinsman).

It is worth noting also that in many contexts in what Christians call the Old Testament, God is imagined to save, heal, deliver; for these terms can be seen as a cluster of images of like connotation. And it is through God's Word or Wisdom that salvation is effected for human kind. Psalm 107 is a good example. Picturing people wandering in a desert, hungry and thirsty, prisoners of affliction, bowed down with hard labor, the Psalm says that He sent forth His Word and healed them, and delivered them from the destruction of their lives. Whereas Wisdom, the doppelgänger of Word, has her role as God's master craftsworker in creation made clear in Proverbs 8. In the Wisdom of Solomon 10 She is heard to say how She saved the earth from the flood, delivered the people from a nation of oppressors, rewarded them with the benefits of righteousness, and so on. God the creator is the savior of the world. God's Word/Wisdom saves the world before any biblical mention is made of Jesus of Nazareth.

Correspondingly, Jesus the savior-figure is also presented as Creator of the world. This is clear from the Prologue to the Fourth Gospel which identifies him as the one in whom was enfleshed the Word through whom God made the world, and without whom nothing is made that was made. And then, quite intriguingly, in a further series of texts it is made clear that the work that he accomplishes in his role as savior is itself counted as creation. For example, what Jesus accomplished on the cross is called "a new creation" (Gal. 6:14–15); and anyone who can be said to be "in Christ" is "a new creation" (2 Cor. 5:17). These are but parts of a total mythic pattern which imagines God creating the universe with his messiah, Jesus, already in mind; creating, that is to say, with Jesus in mind as the operating center of the ideal universe God wants to create from the beginning. Furthermore, as the myth continues to imagine divine creation, it is in Jesus that the perfect universe as God made and makes it —

"My Father is working still, and I am working" (John 5:17) — is "brought to a head," fully restored from the destructive episodes both natural and wilfully adversarial that intervene in the course of its evolution and history. As the Letter to the Ephesians sums it up in the opening blessing of God, the Father of our Lord, Jesus Christ, "He chose us in him before the foundation of the world. . . . For He has made known to us in all wisdom and insight the mystery of his will, according to his purpose which he set forth in Christ as a plan for the fullness of time, to recapitulate [*anakephalaiosis*] all things in him, things in heaven and things on earth" (1:4–12).

The impression is everywhere then that it is God the Creator who is God the Savior, and that this God effects creation/salvation through the agency of Word/Wisdom — Paul calls Christ crucified "the power of God and the wisdom of God" (1 Cor. 1:24). But does this mean, as some texts already analyzed seem to suggest, that the divine work of creating the universe is itself, without further ado, the work of saving also: "I taught them to create the future, and to redeem by creating — all that *was past?*" Is it the case that all God ever does through Word/Wisdom is to carry on creating? That it is we who call the divine activity continuous creation when it overcomes the destructive deformations that are simply part and parcel of every transformation in a world that is not created in mechanical stasis, but rather created to co-create, to evolve? Whereas it is we who decide to use the term *salvation* and its equivalents or supplementaries when we see the divine activity overcome that wilful intensification of destruction and death that constitutes the original sin of the race? Yet from the point of view of God's own agency, in so far as we can adopt that point of view from our experience of the end result of that agency in our world, it all still fits under the heading of creation? The best means of answering that one question in its many forms is to go once more to the Bible and to ask one further question: what kind of things is God depicted as actually doing through Word/Wisdom when God is called either Creator or Savior or both?

The paradigmatic act of saving, paradigmatic for the whole of the Bible, is the exodus from Egypt, celebrated each year in the Jewish festival and meal of Passover, for which the Christian meal called eucharist is sometimes thought to have been substituted. Now the exodus from Egypt was an act of deliverance. It was a deliverance from the slavish oppression of the Israelites by the Egyptians, and from the life-diminishing, death-dealing conditions of hard labor, cruel deprivation and other forms of violence visited upon the Israelites during their captivity in Egypt. It was a deliverance to a land flowing with milk and honey, to free and equal access to all the supports and enrichments of human life that God provides for all in the good world that God created for all. Deliverance to the peace and prosperity in which the fullest realization of human life and dignity can be experienced as humans live up to their calling in the image of God, to be co-creators of life and ever better life for each and every human being and indeed for the whole created world of which we humans are God's stewards.

Of course, the God who saves in this way is the God who condemned his people to these life-diminishing, death-dealing conditions of oppression and deprivation in the first place. In the Prophetic literature the exile in Egypt is often combined with the Babylonian exile as examples of the punishment that God brings upon those people turned idolatrous and unrighteousness. So that the eschatological oracle in, for example, Isaiah 27:12–13 makes use of the imagery of the people being delivered from these two exiles, to the service of the one, true God, in God's good creation. And that great tragic scene of man's enduring inhumanity to man, its life-diminishing, death-dealing inevitabilities, and the corresponding and seemingly permanent need for salvation is still played out to this day on the international stage of exile and return, or of the oppression of peoples and nations. It is even more persistently played out at the more local and micro levels of relationships between individuals and families. As evidenced also in the Prophetic literature, but now more particularly in the Psalms. The poor man fears the rich, with a smoldering fear that is often fanned into flame by the recurring experience that the rich never seem to be rich enough, but are always driven to aggrandize themselves further and further. And always, inevitably again, at the expense of the very livelihood of the already poor. Until the fear burns with the intensity of the prayer from the Psalmist's pen that the Lord, the Creator would save the poor from such deprivation of life; and with the intensity of the promise of the same Lord, also from the Psalmist's pen, that the rich will die a death of the hopeless destruction of the possession of all they depend upon as guarantor of life. How difficult it is for the rich to enter into the kingdom of God; whereas the poor man, even if he never becomes rich but only keeps faith with the Creator who continues to pour out life and life's increasing enrichments quite indiscriminately to all, need never lose hope in the God of the living, even in the face of death itself.

Confirmation in all of this literature, then, that divine salvation always consists in restoring the original relationships between Creator and creature, in which God pours out life and all the supports of life to all eternally, in profligate abundance, beyond measure, limitlessly. Despite the fact that human beings, dignified in the act of creation itself with the rule and responsibility of creatively advancing that life, regularly attempt instead to play God, control the supports of life for the selfish promotion and security of their own lives, and thereby bring death-dealing to others and ultimately to themselves. And God, the ultimate source and sustainer of all human life and action sustains also all of humanity's self-inflicted punishment, while continuing to pour out to all, life without limit. Everywhere one looks in what Christians call the Old Testament, and particularly in the Psalms and the Prophets, it is life, and especially the life of the human being that is being saved, healed, delivered from death-dealing to life-enhancing conditions, and liberated for its limitless possibilities under God the continuous creator. And all of this is being done before, during and after all those perennial episodes of the Fall, in which human beings persist in attempting to provide and promote their own lives all by themselves. So that they only have to turn back to the original creative source of life for all in order to end the punishing destruction that their own self-idolatry inevitably entails; and in order to enjoy once more the limitless hope that life, so prodigally poured out and forever healed of its self-inflicted wounds, holds constantly in view of any who care to contemplate this good creation.

Salvation by Jesus

So much for what Christians call the Old Testament, and the God who is at once creator and savior, healer, deliverer, liberator; the God who is savior simply by continuing to be creator and sustainer. But what, according to what Christians call the New Testament, does Jesus of Nazareth, the one named "he will save," what does this one actually *do* in fulfillment of the promise contained in his very name? Not, what does he say about it, for talk is cheap. But what does Jesus actually do to save us? It is only by answering that very specific question that we will know what precisely is conveyed under the image of salvation, and then know more surely what precisely is conveyed by all of the other images that accompany this one in the biblical description of Jesus's work in the world.

The simplest way to answer that question is to take an overview of any of the Gospels. Take the Gospel According to Matthew, for example. Before Matthew tells what Jesus actually did, he tells of something that was done to Jesus both by God and by the devil. From his very conception the Holy Spirit has come upon or into this man, Jesus of Nazareth, so that people can be saved through this man, and this man, as a consequence, can be named both Jesus, "he saves," and Emmanuel, "God with us." The point of the coming of the Spirit, therefore, is the work that Jesus will do. Paul's phrase about Jesus as "life-giving spirit" (1 Cor. 15:45), gives the clue as to what work Jesus actually does, as does the imagery of dove and fire for the coming of the Spirit on Jesus in the baptismal scenes in the Gospels. Spirit that both by its etymology as breath and its attributes of brooding bird and fire connotes the Creator Spirit, the breath that makes things live, the fire that continually transforms all and so re-creates creation until the final *shalom*, symbolized by the dove, is accomplished. So Jesus must reveal in his works more than in his words, in the practices of his life more than in his teaching and preaching and parable-telling, the reign of a God who remains king of creation simply by continuing to create and to recreate. And simply by doing this, and by inspiring and empowering the rest of his kind in particular to co-create God's good world and theirs. For the Holy Spirit is recognized primarily as the creator, not just in the Bible, but in the prayers and hymns for the feast of Pentecost, for example, the festival day for the Holy Spirit:

> *Veni Sancte Spiritus,*
> *Et emitte caelitus*
> *Lucis tuae radium.*

(Echoing the opening creation myth of Genesis: Come, Holy Spirit, and send from above a ray of your light.)

> *Veni Creator Spiritus,*
> *Mentes tuorum visita;*
> *Imple superna gratia*
> *Quae tu creasti pectora.*

(Come Creator Spirit, into the minds of your faithful people; and fill with your supernal favor the hearts that you create in them.)

Yes, yes, that is all very well in general, but can it be verified in particular by the Bible's description of what it is precisely that Jesus *does* during his earthly sojourn? Time to put this question to Matthew indeed; but not, in deference to Matthew himself, before letting Matthew tell us first what the devil tried to make Jesus do, and with which Jesus refused to have anything to do. Briefly, the Adversary suggests that Jesus, weak and hungry from fasting in the desert, yet enjoying the status of son of God, should simply turn stones into bread, the staff of life. Then Satan suggests that Jesus should throw himself from the roof of the Temple and trust in God for his safety. And finally, he (in the absence of any feminist move to insist that Satan also is female, we may continue with the conceit that he is male) offers Jesus all the kingdoms of the world, which he seems to believe are his fiefdom, if Jesus will but worship him openly. It is of course possible, but it must nevertheless be rare for the alert and biblically tutored reader to ruminate on that story for any length of time without noticing features of the original fall myth of Genesis, and subsequent reprisals of it.

Like Mark and Luke, Matthew insists that it was the Creator Spirit who led Jesus into this temptation in the wilderness. Seen in the light of the fact that in the original temptation story, the original temptation for all people comes from the very status of wise co-creator originally conferred upon humanity by the Source-Creator, that first part of story of the temptation of Jesus in the Gospels makes perfect sense. And then the details of the temptation. The more one dwells on them, the more they seem to coincide with the details of the original Fall as these continue to be developed in the Bible. Thinking that the necessities of life can be in one's complete control and command (turning the very stones into bread, the staff and symbol of life), so that one can guarantee one's own life. Making a god of oneself, either by oneself acting the equal of god, or by invoking a god made in one's own image, a god who has one's interests entirely at heart, and is thereby at one's beck and call (a commandable failsafe for the most risky of one's leaps, even from the pinnacle of the Temple). So that limitless possession of all the earth (all the kingdoms of the earth) and its life-giving riches for one's own security and aggrandizement is the only final horizon one can really contemplate, all at whatever cost to other individuals and groups. All the hallmarks are here in the details of this temptation story; all the features of the original Fall to which everyman is tempted, and to which everyman — with the exception of Jesus, according to Matthew — succumbs in one way or another.

Then Matthew begins to tell what precisely Jesus did to spread the true reign of the one, true Creator God among those to whom he felt he was sent. Having moved from his home town, Nazareth, to Galilee on hearing of the arrest of John the Baptist, with whom he seems to have been associated, Jesus settled in Capernaum. He called for a change of heart and mind from those who would acknowledge the reign of God among them; and he called two sets of brothers, Peter and Andrew, James and John, to follow him and to accompany him on his mission to make followers of others. "And he went about all Galilee, teaching in their synagogues and preaching the good news of the reign and (here, finally, is what he *did,* and did not just talk about) healing every disease and every infirmity among the people . . . and they brought to him all the sick, those afflicted with various diseases and pains, demoniacs, epileptics, and paralytics, and he *healed* them" (Matt. 4:23–24). *Salvum facere,* to make whole, to salve or save.

Later Matthew has Jesus commission those he called to participate in his own mission, now grown in number to twelve (symbolic of the new twelve-tribe Israel), to go only to Israel to preach the kingdom, yes, but to see it spread by obeying his directions to "heal the sick, raise the dead, cleanse lepers, cast out demons" (Matt. 10:8). Later still, when John sends from prison to know if Jesus is "he who is to come," Jesus tells John's disciples simply to report what they saw: "the blind receive their sight and the lame walk, lepers are cleansed and the deaf hear, and the dead are raised up, and the poor have the good news preached to them" (Matt. 11:2–5). And, finally, in Jesus's own description of the Great Judgment, those who will "inherit the kingdom prepared for you from the foundation of the world" (the creation) will be those who fed the hungry, gave drink to the thirsty, gave hospitality to the stranger, clothed the naked, and visited those sick and in prison, whereas those who did not do these things will face the "eternal fire" (Matt. 25:31–46).

Now most of the material in all four Gospels, when they are telling their story of what Jesus did rather than what he said and what must be made of it all, tells of Jesus doing all of these things. With the possible exception of feeding the hungry, a project to which he seems to show a certain personal indifference, if not a dismissive attitude. Particularly in John's anointing scene at Bethany when Judas complains that the money spent on the precious ointment could have gone to the poor (John 12:7). There are, of course, the stories of the feeding of the four thousand and the five thousand. But these are not really feeding the poor stories. Undoubtedly there were some genuinely poor people among those fed from a few loaves and fishes; people, that is to say, who were deprived of the basic means of livelihood to a life-diminishing degree. But most were more likely above the poverty line, and had simply forgotten to bring their sandwiches. They perhaps had not expected the preacher to go on and on for quite so long about whatever he was on about. No, these are eucharistic scenes and, as will appear in the course of their examination in that context, the service they would inspire to all whose lives are diminished by those who are in the service of another master, Mammon, would provide their due benefit to the poor and hungry also. Paul makes quite a din about Corinthian followers of Jesus who profane the eucharist by the rich ones regularly getting drunk at the table of the Lord while others go hungry (1 Cor. 11:18–32). But the hungry poor are not the particular focus of the eucharist in general. Similarly, when Jesus does appear to have had his own table in Capernaum to which to invite people, the Pharisees are concerned that it is sinners he invites to it, "tax collectors and (other) sinners," and tax collectors to this day are seldom either poor or hungry.

So perhaps it is simply that Jesus, on the road and living the life of poverty he enjoined upon his closest companions in mission, was in no position to feed the hungry? But then, someone may say, he appears to have performed miracles to save people from all kinds of other life-diminishing conditions; why could be not have miraculously fed the poor in particular? That is a good question, if only because it raises the issue of the miraculous nature of the performance of the deeds in which the reign of God is now said to consist.

From time immemorial the community of Jesus's followers in the world have treated his saving, his making well or making whole activities, as miracles, in the sense of deeds beyond all natural powers, if not indeed against all natural laws. Despite the fact that the most common term in the Bible for these activities is *dynameis*, deeds of power. The deeds, in short, of "the kingdom, the power, and the glory" of God coming into effect in and as creation. Despite the fact that to take them otherwise, to take them as proof-miracles designed to prove true some claim of Jesus himself, serves only to shift our gaze from these literally saving deeds to some other achievement of Jesus in which the real substance and arrival of the reign of God will then be thought to consist. And despite the fact that to take these deeds as proof-miracles and signs in that sense reveals an attitude to Jesus and to his deeds that Jesus himself explicitly rejected. For he specifically attributed that attitude to an "adulterous generation" — adultery in this context meaning a relationship with false gods, idolatry. Jesus, according to Matthew, tells these "adulterous" scribes and Pharisees that there is only one sign on offer for them, the sign of Jonah; and that

sign consists — not so much in the similarity between the three days that
Jonah spent in the whale and Jesus in the tomb, and their respective ex-
its — but in the sheer and simple fact that Jonah in his mission to Nineveh
brought about the requisite change of mind and heart (Matt. 12:38–41).
Paul too referred to the Jews who "demand signs," and tells them bluntly
that he preaches to them no more, but also no less than "Christ crucified
(not even raised), a stumbling block to Jews" (1 Cor. 1:23) — but the
examination of that consummate deed of Jesus must wait a little longer.

The miraculous, in the sense of some act or event beyond, if not contrary to, natural powers and their rules of procedure is simply not the
point here. Perhaps Jesus, in some instances of his saving activity, did cir-
cumvent the laws of nature as we know them, or go beyond their normal
means of operation, as people's current understanding of these things go.
Perhaps other healers, saviors of life from death-dealing forces, had done
so before him, and have done so since. But the point is that the Creator
Spirit who came and dwelt in Jesus reigns by saving, by making well and
making whole, by supporting and sustaining and advancing life through
all adversity, and that all who would follow Jesus can and indeed must —
remember the judgment scene — participate in such saving activities, by
whatever means they find at their disposal.

There was an Irish theologian in early medieval times who took this
kind of view of so-called miracles in the Bible. He was named Augustine, presumably after the more famous bishop of Hippo; yet he wished,
by calling himself *Augustinus Hibernicus*, the Irish Augustine, to prevent
any possible confusion of identity with the sin-obsessed North African.
As would any self-respecting Irish theologian of such "Pelagian" persua-
sion as to believe that all created and re-created nature was all good in
every place and time as it came from the hands of the Creator Spirit;
and that all creation and new creation therefore constituted both the life-
enhancing favor of God into eternity, and the revelation of the one, true
God. Our Irish Augustine argued that each "miracle" recorded in the Bible
was really a work of nature, that God brought it about, as God brings
about everything that happens in this world and into the next, through
created agencies themselves. So that what we actually witness in the case
of these so-called miracles is merely a divine speeding-up of natural processes, or something of that kind in any case. The Irish Augustine then
goes through the Bible and miracle after miracle in detail in order to argue
his case. There is no doubt about the fact that the resulting exegesis often
seems suspect to our sophisticated scientific minds. But there can be no

doubt either about the fact that my ancient countryman got the essential issue exactly right. It is the Creator Spirit who came into Jesus, who continues to create through the created and creative agencies that make up the world; except that on these select occasions that invite talk of miracle, the ever-identical creative work of that Spirit is now really a re-creation, a making well and whole again of deficiencies in human well-being, whether these are due to natural causes or to wilful adversarial forces that injure or neglect. And it is our Augustine who, perhaps alone among the theologians of the West, fully illustrates the real point of the miracle aspect of the healing or saving stories taken ensemble: namely, that the import of the miraculous element is the demonstration in mythic manner of the fact that Jesus accomplishes his main work of making human beings whole again, through the power and the presence of the one, true God who is Creator-Savior working in and through him. And that Jesus is therefore in the image of God, and so son of God, as Luke said Adam, created in God's image, was son of God (Luke 3:38).

It may be no more than an implication of our Augustine's work that the miraculous element in these making-whole stories is not the point; an implication drawn from the fact, as our Augustine argues, that all of these "miracles" can be shown to be brought about through and by natural agencies. But that simply points up the main implication of the miraculous element in the stories, one that is crucially important for the reader of this major element in the mission of Jesus. People came to see that Jesus of Nazareth did seem to exhibit in his life and dealings the ways of God with the world, and the way of the world to God, the way God ruled the world, the reign of God in the world that Jesus said he was bringing to light among them. People then became convinced of a special presence of this God in Jesus. So that keeping faith with the eternal God who continuously creates, heals and transforms life, by their own cooperation in creating life continuously for all in accordance with their abilities, meant to them keeping faith with the creative persona, the Word/Wisdom/Spirit of God-in-Jesus. Irrespective of the fact that the historical Jesus as such might or might not have had some supra-normal healing or restorative powers. The miraculous element in these mythic stories functions in such a way as to focus attention on the fact that it is God's Word/Wisdom/Spirit-in-Jesus that is the inviting object of our trust and faith. It is the continuous Creator-Savior who sees all alike through the healings, restorations, transformations that make up our lives, and especially through that final transformation that coincides with the dissolution of our current bodily form that we call death. It is this One whose power and presence is always at work in all the world, who now appears especially present in the whole life and principal work of Jesus. So the stories picture God doing all of this through Jesus, by means of the miraculous element, however that is further defined. The true function of this miraculous element, then, is not to prove anything, thereby to relieve us of the need for faith commitment. Because faith commitment, properly understood, is entrusting life to, and so keeping faith with the Source-Creator of all, precisely as that eternal Creator is seen to create, heal, restore through faithful creatures. A view that is of the essence of these saving stories, their point and purpose.

And that is why faith plays such a prominent part in these stories of making life whole again. According to Matthew, Jesus noticed the faith of the paralytic and his friends who brought him for healing (9:1–8). He told the hemorrhaging woman, "your faith has made you well" (9:22). He conceded to the persisting Canaanite woman, whom he at first sought to repel with the most racist of snubs, "great is your faith" (15:21–28).He asked the two blind men, "do you believe I can do this?" (9:28–29). He admired the centurion for having a level of faith not found in Israel (8:5–10). He told his closest disciples, when they failed to make some people whole, that the failure was due to their lack of faith. In fact the instances of such contexts in which faith is said to be essential to the advent, recovery or advance of well-being, increases greatly in number once one realizes that to have faith in something or someone is equivalently described as worshiping, serving, being a son of, some person or power. To worship, as all hero-worshipers know, is to want both to serve and to imitate as children by nature imitate parents. So, too, the full meaning of having faith in such powers goes far beyond believing some alleged truths about them, and entails action, life-style, entrusting oneself to these as co-operative imitators of their way, their life, in the hope of approaching something of their status: be perfect as your heavenly Father is perfect. It is the Creator Spirit that can give life and, as in the instances now under examination, restore it from the ravages of nature and of adversarial forces. Just as it is the same Spirit that can sustain and enhance life without limit. Therefore one must have faith in that same Creator Spirit, keep faith with the Spirit that in these instances works in and through Jesus. These are the conditions for the possibility of hope without limits. Not just hope for life without the limitations imposed upon it by the present and particular destructive forces that these saving stories enumerate, but hope for life that is limitless *tout court,* for life eternal, as the Bible calls it.

According to these saving stories, one must have faith in the Creator Spirit who saves simply by carrying on creating at each and every incidence of the incursion of life-diminishing forces. The Creator Spirit does this through created agencies, and does it to a degree that limitlessly exceeds the mere restoration of life diminished by each act or event of diminishment. But someone might then ask, well, what alternative human option does the Bible have in mind? That the one who is told to believe in the one, true Creator Spirit to the point of cooperating with that Spirit, might simply not believe at all, in any god whatever? No; such pure and simple atheism is never really an issue in the Bible. And indeed, where the sustenance and enhancement of life is the issue, such sole and entire lack of faith in some power that might at least appear as a replacement for divinity is simply not practical. That is not to say that we do not encounter people who have plumbed such loss of faith in life as to have fallen into total despair, and are then at times carried on the currents of despair to premature death by suicide. But, given the life-force that surges through all living things and arouses in them a very instinct for survival, the particular alternative to true faith that consists in complete despair is much more likely to be a result of, rather than a further alternative to, the common and realistic alternative which the Bible has in mind.

This real alternative to keeping faith with the Creator Spirit is the alternative already so often referred to under the image of the Fall and original sin. Driven by the life-force itself to have faith in someone or something for the sustenance and enhancement of life, humans are tempted to have faith in themselves. Or more precisely expressed: since they are required to have faith in themselves also by the true Creator Spirit who equips and inspires them to be co-creators of their world, what they are really tempted to do is to have faith in themselves alone, as the sole supreme creators of the life and the world they want. In this way human beings divinize themselves in one or more of the ways already suggested. Either by simply advertising humanity as self and world creator — Feuerbach, Marx, Nietzsche, Sartre; or by creating something which, although it is their own creature, they will have faith in. The Bible gives as examples of such created gods portable idols carved in the image of humans and other creatures or, more persuasively, money. For money, as Marx remarked, is a spiritual power (a *daimon,* in the old Greek sense of the word); for money is not only the coins, notes or credit cards in your wallet, but rather the power to buy and sell the supports of life and indeed life itself, a power that is embodied in coins, notes and credit cards. It is when people place their faith in such powers, and only in such powers, that the final despair unto death may overtake them. And who among us is not guilty of doing so for some, and perhaps at certain periods, for all of the time? In any case, that is what the saving stories in the Bible envisage as the alternative to the faith in the true Creator Spirit that Jesus knows to be working through his mortal body. As Jesus put it in the course of Matthew's composition known as the Sermon on the Mount: "you cannot serve God and mammon."

Salvation from Sin

The connection between these salvation or making whole stories and a saving from sin is a further feature of this central element of the mission of Jesus. The connection occurs constantly throughout the stories about Jesus, "Savior," and so it needs a thorough understanding if this central theme of salvation by Jesus is ever to be fully and properly understood. The connection culminates, perhaps, in the story of those who accuse Jesus of serving satanic idols in his ministry of making whole, and as a consequence are accused by Jesus in turn of the unforgivable sin against the Holy Spirit (Matt. 12:22–32). And it is highlighted already in the story told at the outset of Jesus's ministry, in almost identical terms in Matthew, Mark and Luke, about the healing of the paralytic. The salient points of that story for present purposes are these: Jesus saw "their faith," that is to say, the faith of the paralytic and of those who brought him with great difficulty into the presence of Jesus; and he said to the paralytic, "my son, your sins are forgiven." At this point some of the same learned leaders who in the story above were accused by Jesus of sinning against the Spirit that dwelt in him, seriously question Jesus's declaration of forgiveness, and accuse him of blasphemy. To which Jesus responds with a question to them: "which is easier to say to the paralytic, 'your sins are forgiven,' or to say 'rise, take up your pallet and walk?' But that you may know that the Son of man has authority on earth to forgive sins," — he then tells the paralytic to arise and walk, and the man did so (Mark 2:1–12).

Put these two stories together like that; the story of the learned leaders being accused of blasphemy when they say that Jesus saved people, made them well, by the power of the demon; and the story of Jesus being accused of blasphemy because he conflates such healing with the sin of the sick man being forgiven. Then the fully attentive gospel reader will almost certainly call to mind the passage from the Gospel of John (chap. 8) that itemizes a long altercation between Jesus and such leaders, in which Jesus accuses them of being sons of the devil, servants of a satanic god, who will "die in their sins," and they in turn insist that it is Jesus who is possessed by a demon in all that he does, and he is not therefore the son of the Father both parties claim to serve). Add to this the general view from the Fall stories to the effect that the transiently palliative results of the Fall for some are quickly overtaken by life-diminishing, death-dealing results for all, and that both the sin of the Fall and the suffering that results from it are bonded together under the image of the servitude of, or the possession by an idol or a satanic spirit, and the full context in which the forgiveness of sin theme in the saving stories may be adequately and accurately understood, is most probably in position.

Against the background of such an account of a sin that spreads like an infection that triggers a genetic weakness, all of the above mentioned inter-related themes become transparent. The sin against the Holy Spirit consists in the service of another creator of life and world, and as long as it continues it cannot be remitted. ("Remitted" is probably a better translation of the Greek, *apheontai*, and more obviously of the Latin, *remittuntur*, than is "forgiven," a term that is too much associated with a more calculating, bargaining type of theology of sin and of our salving from it, a theology that must shortly come under consideration.) Only a *metanoia*, often translated as a repentance, but more literally and intelligibly translated as a change of heart and mind, the very thing that Jesus called for in the very first move of his public ministry — "change your hearts and minds, for the reign of God is at hand" — only this can send original sin, the mother and father of all sin, into remission. And the change of heart consists essentially in a change of faith, trust and service to the one, true Creator Spirit, who invites such trust by eternally creating life without measure for all at all times and places, and who does this particularly through the healing ministry of Jesus.

Therefore when Jesus sees in the very conduct of the paralytic and his friends that they are accepting this perennial and now particularized invitation to a life of true faith, trust and service, he can tell them that their sin is already sent into remission, as a cancer might be sent into remission with the prospect that it might stay that way. Jesus can also correlate the making whole of the shattered life of the paralytic with the change to the true and living faith — "which is easier to say, 'your sins are remitted,' or to say, 'take up your pallet and walk' " — precisely because it is the faithful co-operation of humanity in particular with the God who is eternal source of life without measure that ensures the making whole of life beyond all transient and sin-occasioned depletions, "in this age and in the age to come." It is Luke perhaps who portrays with greatest clarity this correlation between sin in remission and life healed, when he has Jesus say, "your sins are remitted ... your faith has saved you ... go in *shalom*;" go now toward the peace and prosperity that is the goal of the whole of divine creation.

Against this background also it becomes understandable, albeit inexcusable, that the religious leaders of his own people should accuse Jesus of the same original sin, the same idolatry/blasphemy of which he accuses them in turn. For as they in effect confine access to the one, true divine Creator to a path that leads through their own religious establishment, they in effect also reduce the Creator to something approaching their own interests and stature, and that is just another form of the self-idolatry that the Fall in essence brings into play. Yet, as we must shortly see Jesus observe in greater detail, these religious leaders do persist in such self-centeredness, particularly in their assessment and use of their own religious creations, mainly Torah and Temple. Instead of using these to point to the true God who is universally creative, and as such revealed to all as the One who invites all without condition to the true, life-serving faith, they take the view that the limitless benefits of life are available only to those who come to recognize them and their religious establishment. So as long as they persist in this point of view, they are bound to think that they have little option except to suspect that it is Jesus who is serving a false god, tailored to his own seemingly anti-establishment program and ambitions. They are bound to suspect him of doing this for the sake of the transient life-enhancement of himself and of others foolish enough to follow and support him. And as long as they remain bound to their false presumption of domesticated divine presence and its ensuing prejudice, they are also bound in the end to seek to rid their nation and their religion of his increasingly challenging presence. In the end, as Jesus himself sadly concludes, they must kill this prophet of the true God, as their establishment predecessors had killed the prophets who were sent before him.

Finally, it helps toward a clearer understanding of these related themes if warning signs are already posted against two common kinds of misinterpretation. First, there is the misinterpretation already referred to, that consists in favoring the miraculous as the key feature of the saving stories.

When this happens in the context of the conversations that took place at the healing of the paralytic, the exegete will too easily conclude that the healing of the paralytic was not in itself the saving from sin, not a *dynamis*, a deed constitutive of the power of the reign of the true God in action — as Luke puts it: "power came forth from him and healed all" (Luke 6:19). But that it was instead a proof miracle designed, like all miracles, to prove that Jesus was divine, and therefore that he could forgive the sins of human kind. So, no, the healing is not so separate from the forgiveness; as Jesus most probably hints when he asks, which is easier to say, "your sins are forgiven," or to say, "you are healed?" The healing is the reversal of the deformations suffered as part of life's élan, and where someone's original sin has caused the injury, it is an intrinsic part of the eradication, or rather the reversal of the consequences of that sin.

But, second, this very correlation between healing and the remission of sin, constantly tempts people to think that each one's suffering must be already fitted by divine justice to each one's crime or at least, in terms of ancient tribal cultures, to the crimes of one's extended family. Once again if, as the Bible rightly does, one looks at all sin as part and parcel of original sin — that is why exorcisms of a satanic spirit are included in seamless sequence and without more ado with all other healings — then one sees easily that the punishment for sin is a self-inflicted punishment by humanity on humanity. A self-inflicted punishment, moreover, that shows no respect for any fitting of the punishment to levels of guilt among the sufferers of it. The contrary is in fact the case in many, if not most, instances of suffering inflicted. For example, in all those cases called war, in which misguided men go to kill their fellow men or be killed in the attempt, it is always the relatively innocent women and the innocent children who suffer the most punishment. So Jesus on more than one occasion deliberately breaks any straightforward connection between any person's sin and that person's suffering. As Luke has Jesus say about the people killed by Pilate in the course of one of his occasional massacres, or the eighteen people killed by a falling tower at Solo'am, "these victims were not worse sinners than any others" (Luke 13:1–5). Therefore, Jesus must go beyond the healing of a particular illness, life-crippling defect or suffering, if he is to send into remission the mother and father of all sin that causes so much indiscriminate suffering. And he does this by using any particular healing to invite the people concerned to see in it the work of the eternal Creator Spirit who heals life for all in the continuous creation of life equally for all. He invites people in all his healings to keep faith in their own lives with such a Creator Spirit, or he recognizes that they already are keeping that faith with God in their approach to him as a man of God, of the one, true God. And so it is that complex of conditions and effects that sends all sin into remission, and that interprets Jesus's image of the equivalence of healing and the forgiveness of sin, when he asks which is easier to say, "your sins are forgiven," or "you are healed?"

That still does leave hanging in the air a still very pressing and very practical question, especially for those who feel that their suffering in life, particularly at the hands of their fellow human despoilers and oppressors, far outweighs their own original guilt: how can such people handle such excruciating failures in distributive (in)justice? That issue must come back again when issues such as morality, justice and divine judgment take their turn. In the current context it must suffice to pursue the inquiry into what Jesus did, in the course of saving the world and, skipping over some things he did that can be reprised later in other contexts, to come now to that action of his that stands at the very center of Christianity to the present day, the act on which he based his chief request to his followers that they take up their crosses daily if they were truly to follow him: he died . . . for our sins?

But before coming to the cross of Jesus it might be well to sum up the few findings of this section on salvation from sin, in the following words. The Fall is intrinsic to the very process of continuous creation in that it is the Creator's endowment of humanity with such co-creative wisdom and power that it tempts human beings to take to themselves the prerogative of creating their own worlds for themselves. All human experience testifies to the universal force of that temptation and to the ensuing excess of destruction, despair and death that follows on falling for it, and then committing the mother and father of all sin. (It is astonishing — though perhaps it should not be — to see Ezekiel so long, long ago, in delivering judgment on the king of Tyre, offering as the main example of this insidious evil, what he detects as the violence of trade that enhances the lives of some people at the cost of a dreadful depletion of life for others — today numbered in their millions.) And what does God do about this recurring Fall and the avalanche of evil that it sends down the slopes of history? What God does not do is to assign a special penalty to each evil-doer. So people can simply stop trying to point to some human suffering as a divinely contrived penalty for some particular piece of human evil-doing. As John has Jesus say, when asked whether it was the blind man or his parents who had sinned, "It was not that this man sinned, or his parents, but that the works of God might be made manifest in him" (John 9:1–3).

There is no punishment for the evils of original sinning — and that covers all sinning — other than the suffering that we original sinners inflict upon ourselves. As the Book of Wisdom puts it, "that they might learn that one is punished by the very things by which he sins" (11:16). That can be deemed divine punishment also of course, in that it is God who enlightens and empowers in the course of continuous creation all of our original evil-doing and its consequences. And God takes responsibility for all of that, as God's words through the mouth of Ezekiel to the king of Tyre proclaim. But God neither adds nor subtracts punishment in order to make it fit individual crimes. What God does is simply to carry on creating, pouring out, supporting and exponentially enhancing existence and life for all; thereby also healing, restoring and bringing to *shalom*, through creative creatures also, who are invited by the eternal largesse to keep faith with its processes and aims, the whole of creation, and thereby sending all sin into remission. The forgiveness of sin is therefore already contained in the eternal act of what appears to us as continuous creation. It is a creative forgiveness in God's case, and ours in imitation, consisting in doing good to all, even those who do evil, healing and restoring life through its natural and wilful deformations, as the story of the paralytic illustrates. And advancing life with no threat of future reprisals; merely the warning, which Luke's text adds to Jesus's judgment about the victims of Pilate and the falling tower: unless you have a change of heart — keeping faith with the true Creator rather than setting yourselves up in God's place — you will continue to suffer the same excess of death, deprivation and despair. You will all perish in the same despairing fashion. Is this the understanding of the matter of sin and salvation that the paradigmatic deed of Jesus reveals, when he sets his face for Jerusalem and his certain death?

Salvation on the Cross: The Way to the Cross — the Challenge of Jesus to Torah and Temple

Of the profusion of images for the work of Jesus introduced at the outset of this chapter most, it would appear, could be subsumed under the image of salvation taken univocally as the creation or re-creation of the wholeness, the well-being of life. The following images at least could then be subsumed under that of salvation and in that univocal sense, as images of parts of the process or of results achieved, all of which could be and are covered comprehensively by the master-image of salvation. So, healing refers to the riddance of the wounds and deformities, mental or physical or both, and of the resultant suffering that comes either from natural causes or from the violence entailed in human beings making gods of themselves. Deliverance or liberation refers to freeing people from their enslavement to the very tempting personified powers that cause such ill-being whenever these are exercised in human history. Restoration or recapitulation refers to the wholeness that has always been and always will be the original goal of all divine creation of life and of all creaturely co-creation. As does also the image of victory, final and irreversible, over all adversarial forces that emerge in the very course of continuous creation itself. And all of this is comprehensively covered in the image of salvation: making well, making whole, the fullness of life, eternal peace and prosperity, *shalom*. Even the image of reconciliation can be subsumed under this comprehensive image of salvation, for it really refers to the resumption by those who have made gods of or for themselves, of their original relationships with the Creator Spirit who made them co-creators of life for all, and not dependent destroyers of life, first for others and then inevitably for themselves also.

But consider now the two final pairings of images listed above: redemption/ransom and satisfaction/expiation, to which might be added, atonement. For although that last image can be given a number of connotations, involving elements of reconciliation (at-one-ment), for example, it is most usually used in this context to denote some detectable elements of a price to be paid, or a suffering to be undergone in the course of the achievement of the desired result, thereby uniting in itself connotational elements that are also characteristic of redemption/ransom and satisfaction/expiation. Now the very first general observation that can be offered concerning that last cluster of images is surely this: that metaphorical usage has now begun to grace these texts of the Bible once more. Adding perhaps that failure to detect the shift to metaphor here can, as in the case of all such failure, result in much misapprehension and misinterpretation of what the Bible has to say.

What then does the Bible have to say about what Jesus did next? What is the overall biblical view of Jesus going to his death in the course of promoting his cause, of Jesus setting his face for Jerusalem, the city he himself is said to have described as the persistent killer of God's prophets (Matt. 23:37)? Well, first and foremost it is essential to observe that the New Testament understands the death of Jesus to have been the result of his being found guilty of a capital charge. A charge that is brought by the Jewish tribunal of the High Priest as the charge of blasphemy. And that is brought before the Roman tribunal of Pontius Pilate as the charge of pretension to messianic status when the Jewish authorities wanted Jesus crucified by the Romans rather than being stoned to death by themselves. It is not necessary to pause here to inquire further into the reasons why the Temple priesthood wanted Jesus condemned and executed by Pilate. The answer probably lies in that fragile and, no doubt, mutually resented but politically necessary collusion between the indigenous authority of the priestly leadership and the secular Roman overlordship. Particularly in an atmosphere that prevailed at least since Herod's ostentatious temple-building served, as did other such monumental building, the aggrandizement of ruling power, secular and attendant sacred alike. Something like that may explain why the priestly authorities wanted Pilate to participate in the condemnation of Jesus, the leader of the new religious movement, when they would later be satisfied with stoning Stephen on finding him guilty of a charge that coincided in part at least with the charges brought against Jesus, namely, the charge of speaking against their Temple. But it is the detail and nature of the substance of the charges, rather than the reason for the double judicial hazard to which Jesus was subjected, that may tell us what we most need to know at this point.

The capital charge against Jesus brought before the tribunal of the High Priest is fully intelligible in light of what has already been said about these repetitive and reciprocal accusations of demonic possession, satan-serving, idolatry, hence blasphemous conduct that seem to have characterized the encounters between Jesus and the leaders of the Jewish religion throughout the public ministry of Jesus. A paradigmatic evocation of this charge is given in John's Gospel (John 8); and note the number of times in John's Gospel that "the Jews" try to stone Jesus. The God to whom Jesus gives unconditioned access to all is plainly opposed to the God of whom these Jewish leaders think and say that He is *their* God, the God to whom *they* as his people have privileged access. For Jesus to prefer his God to theirs is to these established leaders of the Jewish religion plain blasphemy, and blasphemy is punishable by death.

Yet this capital charge, put in these terms of blasphemy and idolatry, would have mattered little to Pilate, who presumably could care less what Jews thought to be the truth about God, or about those who disagreed with them on the subject. Just as long as they stayed quiet and paid their

taxes. However, if the same charge concerning a blasphemous misrepre-
sentation of God were to be put in terms of Jesus claiming to be the
messiah of such an idol — and that in itself might seem a legitimate thing
to do, in light of the gospel evidence to the effect that many who had
experience of Jesus's ministry, as well as some of his closest disciples,
apparently accepted Jesus in terms of the fulfillment of messianic expectations — then Pilate might well be expected to sit up and take notice.
For "messiah" meant "anointed one"; kings were anointed; and the one
sent to restore the Israelite nation and religion to its proper place and
freedom under God, if named the messiah, could well conjure up images
of a liberator like King David. And Pilate would then take a very keen
judicial interest indeed in the matter at hand, for the matter is now one
of politics as much as theology. It is interesting to note the part of this
biblical story that tells of Pilate failing to find any substance in the charge
so formulated, even though he thought it more prudent, politically, to
have the fellow hanged anyway. That is interesting, and informative, in
view of the gospel evidence, particularly in Mark's Gospel, to the effect
that Jesus himself sought to prevent people from proclaiming him the
Messiah. The reign of God, as Jesus understood and (re)inaugurated it,
seemed to have had as little use for kingly styled rulers like Pilate and his
emperor as, it must shortly be observed, it had for priests: the two very
types that colluded in condemning Jesus to death.

It is worth pressing a little further this questioning about the charges
brought against Jesus, if only in order to understand as fully as possible
what Jesus died for when executed on this charge of blasphemy, this
charge of the allegedly false messianism involved in seeking to restore
an allegedly false ideal of the chosen people of God and their religion.
We might then understand more fully what Jesus achieved, according to
the Bible, in accepting the bitter chalice of his execution for the cause he
had been chosen to promote, under the inspiration of the Creator Spirit
that, as he and his followers believed, dwelt in him. It is worth pressing
this question a little further in this direction, by asking what precisely was
it about the truth, the way and the life that Jesus lived that the priests
thought blasphemous? And, vice versa, what precisely did Jesus in turn
think to be blasphemous about the truth, the way and the life of the religious Jew at the time, as lived and taught by priests, scribes and those most
meticulous promoters of the Torah, the Pharisees? The answer does not
lie in his admitting to being son of God. For in the context of that time

that is not a claim to divine status that would support a charge of blasphemy. Israel or its king were called sons of God; the title meant simply that they were like God in carrying out God's reign or will on earth.

The clues to the true answer to these latter questions are found then, first, in a series of disputes between Jesus and Jewish leaders on the subject of Sabbath observance; then, in certain encounters in and about the Temple; and after that, in certain other scattered references and incidents. The many details of disputes on the subject of Sabbath observance need not delay this inquiry. Suffice it to say that Jesus heals, that is to say, saves on the Sabbath, and his followers pluck ears of corn on the Sabbath to assuage their hunger, and so on. And these and many other things were forbidden in the Torah as part of the obligation to keep sacred to God's acknowledgment and worship, this one day in seven. But it is the principle which Jesus announces as the principle that governs all issues of what one can do and not do on the Sabbath; it is this that furnishes the answer to our pressing question, rather than the specific details of the laws or their breaking. For there are other occasions also on which Jesus and the leaders of his early followers object to obligatory laws, whether of the ethical kind or of the kind composed of ritual rules laid down for those who wished to have access to God's grace and salvation.

Jesus himself is depicted in the Gospels, in the course of his many diatribes against the learned leaders of Israel, condemning them for laying so many burdensome rules on people's backs in the name of their national religion, while not lifting a finger to ease the burdens imposed. And the Pauline correspondence offers striking evidence of a dispute about the ritual rule of circumcision. This was a dispute which divided those who felt that the rule need not apply to Gentiles who wished to avail of the access that Jesus revealed to God the Creator and Savior, from others who felt that the rule of circumcision did in fact continue to apply to any who would like to be numbered among the people of God. This dispute resulted, apparently, in some of the leaders of the nascent community of Jesus-followers continuing to confine their mission — as Jesus confined the mission of the close disciples he first sent out as part of his own mission (Matt. 10:5–6) — to the card-carrying, circumcised members of "the house of Israel." While these same leaders agreed that others, and Paul in particular, should invite the Gentiles to follow Jesus, without undergoing this circumcision ritual for becoming Jews (Gal. 2:1–10). But it is still the principle which Jesus stated with respect to the laws governing Sabbath observance; it is this rather than a trawl through individual rules of the

Jewish religion, whether ritual or ethical, that will answer the question as to what lies at the heart of the accusation of blasphemy brought by Jesus against the leaders of the Jewish religion, and at the heart of the corresponding charge against Jesus brought by these leaders

The principle in question is stated in its most radical form in the course of Mark's account of a confrontation concerning Sabbath observance, after which the Pharisees took counsel as to how to kill Jesus (Mark 2:23–3:6). The principle, perhaps the most radical religious principle ever formulated, is this: "The Sabbath was made for man, not man for the Sabbath." The implicit reference contained in the term *egeneto* was made, or came into being, is to the creation myth that opens Genesis, according to which God created for six days and rested on the seventh day from the work of creation. This latter element of the myth is traditionally and rightly regarded as the divine establishment of the Sabbath ritual. And since it is an integral part of a creation myth, then, like all other parts of the same myth, it has to do with a correct understanding of, a living, active state of being true to, the creation of the world, in itself a continuing process. Briefly, the purpose of the divine indication of rest on one day of the week, the seventh, and of calling that the Lord's day, is to ensure that we humans, creators also in the image of the divine creator, acknowledge that the prime creator is the divine Creator Spirit. Or, more precisely put perhaps, it is to ensure that we entrust ourselves and our future to the divine Creator who continues to give existence and life ever more abundantly to all. It is to ensure that we so acknowledge and entrust ourselves as to see ourselves therefore as derivative, co-operative creators within this grand divine enterprise, guided by both the fact that the creative enterprise is equally for the benefit of all creatures, and by the created and creative designs already inscribed in all creatures according to their kind, as much as in ourselves. And the simplest way in which we can symbolize such acknowledgment and trust is this: for one day in seven, we simply and as far as humanly possible, keep our grubby little paws off the thing altogether. Thereby relieving ourselves of the most destructive illusion, namely, the simultaneously idolatrous (with respect to us) and blasphemous (with respect to the one, true God) illusion that we are the sole creators of our world. Thereby also pointing ourselves toward the acknowledgment of, and faith in the true and eternal supreme source of existence and life for all, and toward our responsible role and dignity as its derivative co-creators.

To say that the Sabbath, so understood as part of the creation myth, was made for man, is simply to reflect the fact that it is by such active acknowledgment and lived faith in God the continuous creator of all that human kind can co-operate to achieve the fullness of life and the hope of eternity. Sabbath observance is a sacrament of creation — a sacrament being a sign that effects what it signifies. For it symbolizes and puts into effect that lived faith in the Creator Spirit with respect to whom we find our proper place as co-operative creators. The Sabbath meal is an important part of that same sacrament, for it enacts the enclosed myth of being fed with food we did not (during that sacred time) procure or prepare for ourselves. For the meal adds the element of feast, festival, joyful and thankful celebration of life given to us in such abundance and always before we do anything of ourselves to provide and enhance it. Sabbath is the human celebration of the gift and promise of life without limit, that shows us how to take it and help make it. Sabbath comes into being, therefore, so the Genesis myth suggests, as a revelation of the true ways of God with the world, and of Adam's progeny with God; ways that ensure eternal life with God. The Sabbath was made for man.

"Not man for the Sabbath." What contrary position is suggested by these words? What contrary views of the ways of God and humans are then accused by Jesus of nothing less than blasphemy? The most obvious meaning of that contrary phrase is found from those instances in which the Sabbath observance is said to forbid the making-well of human lives. Despite the fact that the Sabbath was designed in the process of creation itself to remind people that entrusting themselves in active co-operation with the eternal source of all well-being is the way, the only way to ensure their well-being in this age or the next. For now human co-operation in God's continuous creative/salvific work has to be sacrificed to Sabbath observance. Human well-being is sacrificed to Sabbath observance; man is made for Sabbath observance, not the Sabbath for man. Which raised the further question: what kind of God is now honored by keeping the Sabbath sacred? Not the God revealed in the whole of creation as eternal source of life, but rather a god opposed to life without limit, a satanic figure, an idol and a blasphemy to the one, true God.

The same kind of thing can happen, as hinted already, with any kind of law or rule, not merely ritual but also ethical, that any religion seeks to impose in the name of the God it purports to represent. When a Roman Catholic pope forbade the use of "artificial" contraceptives and it was pointed out how much damage this could do to the lives of Catholic families, and even more so to AIDS-infested populations thereby denied the use of condoms, a common response from Catholic clerical leaders was: if it was up to us we might be able to do something about such suffering, but this is God's law, not ours; so it is God who asks these sacrifices of your lives. And once again God is portrayed as a satanic figure, who intensifies our suffering unto death instead of saving us. Religions after all are groupings and institutions created by human beings coming together for purposes of responding to the furthest prospects and the deepest problems faced by humanity. And they naturally assume that what they can see and express of the deepest source of life in nature and history, and of the ways of this God with the world, represents nothing less than the wholeness of truth and favor as it comes from the Source itself. Yet religions, no less than any other grouping or institution of human beings, are subject to the pandemic temptation of human kind to make gods of themselves, to make idols that remain within their control, to whittle down to their own relative size and service the one, true Creator God always and everywhere active and revealed in the creation in favor of all. And when religions fall for this pandemic temptation, the resulting intensification of suffering and death-dealing to others and to themselves is always the same.

Forget the context of continuous and hence evolving divine-human creativity then and two things happen simultaneously in the case of legal systems fostered by religions. First, the law and its observance becomes a badge of identity for the members of a particular religion. And, second and simultaneously, the law is absolutized in some form frozen in time and place, and its prescriptions hardened and no longer malleable, on the grounds presumably that it is after all simply a legal version of a way, a truth and a life that comes from the Absolute. And the upshot of these simultaneous happenings is that God is presented as the God of this group and institution, so that they are God's people, and any other person who wishes to become one of God's people must come to them, if not become one of them, and adopt their laws, whatever the cost to his or her social, psychological or physical well-being. This is the larger scenario that is implicitly condemned by Jesus when he insists that man was not made for the Sabbath, and when he takes the Sabbath observance as the paradigm of law issued in the name of religion and of a god blasphemously, demonically, idolatrously (terms used by Jesus himself) reduced to being the god of a particular religion, serving first the interests of that religion. For this is the scenario identified already as original sin, now operative in and as organized religion. And upon the commission of this sin, in this form also, come the deprivation, suffering and death of others not only in the burning of heretics, the fatwahs, the stoning of God's prophets who speak out for the true creator who gives life without measure equally for all, and even the forceful conversion of, or holy wars against peoples of other faiths; but in the justification of customs, laws and practices that bring suffering and damage, destruction and death to people, by attributing these laws to the absolute will of God.

Jesus, using the paradigmatic case of Sabbath observance was, in effect, trying to recall the leaders of his religion to their original faith in the God revealed to Moses well before Moses issued the Torah, as the Creator ("He causes to be") of all and, consequently, as the Savior of all from the ravages wreaked by the adversarial forces that emerge in the course of creation itself. For it is by such faith, lived out in co-creative service to the true God, that they were then, and for all time will be, saved from life's adversities, and not by allegiance to any absolutized legal system. And Jesus was the first to recognize the fact that in the exercise of that prophetic role to which he felt called by that same Creator Spirit, he would threaten that religious establishment in all the power and dignity of its exclusivist claims. To the point at which his own life, like that of other prophets before him, would be forfeit. The same kind of scenario can be painted by contemplating the second element of the charge brought against Jesus under the umbrellas of blasphemy and false messianism, namely, that he spoke against the Temple and, if only by implication, against the priesthood that served the Temple.

However one may reconcile and interpret the various versions of Jesus's recorded words about the Temple, his actions against some practices conducted within its precincts, and words of his that seem to suggest its replacement, one thing at least is clear. His attack upon the Temple did not stop short with his attempt to cleanse it of the element of money-making, the service of Mammon. He went further, much further, to the point of predicting the destruction of the Temple, and its replacement by some body somehow related to himself in some form or other. Now the Jerusalem Temple was, according to the Jewish religion of Jesus's time, the place where the presence of the Lord, the Shekinah or Glory of God was particularly located. Direct access to that Presence was the prerogative of the cultic priesthood, offering sacrifices and carrying the prayers of the people, and so on. And most particularly, it was the prerogative of the High Priest who could enter into the inner sanctuary within which, one might say, the immediate Presence was domesticated. It is of this whole establishment that Jesus is reputed to have said that, either if it is destroyed or when it is destroyed, he would replace it. In other words, it is not necessary to have this temple establishment in order that the creative and saving presence of the Lord be active and accessible in the world.

According to Matthew, Jesus not only turned on the money men in the Temple; he also carried on his own creative saving work there. As in the case of his healing on the Sabbath, he healed in the Temple under the very noses of the Temple priests, and to the great indignation and hostility of these leaders of the Jewish religion also (Matt. 21:14). The Acts of the Apostles 6:8–7:60 then tells the story of the stoning of Stephen, one of those who preached Jesus and performed in his name the deeds of power that characterized the reign of the Creator Spirit, that Jesus called the kingdom of God. Now the specific charge against Stephen was that he "never ceases to speak words against this holy place (the Temple) and the law (the Torah)," claiming to follow Jesus in these respects also. In his defense against this charge, Stephen simply returns the charge with interest. It is these Temple priests, he claims, who try to confine the Creator Spirit to their Temple, and are guilty of domesticating the divine Spirit there. For this is a domestication of God about which God had explicitly warned through the prophet Isaiah, saying through that prophet, "Heaven is my throne, and earth my footstool." In short, the world that God created, heaven and earth, is thereby the house in which God dwells. Correspondingly, Stephen continues, it is these priests who stand accused of a satanic resistance to the true Creator Spirit, the One that came upon and spoke and worked through Jesus, one who was just an ordinary man and no priest. And it was these priests that carried that resistance to the Creator Spirit to the point of murdering that man, Jesus, as they had murdered God's previous prophets, and were now intent on murdering Stephen also. The establishment, therefore, had been taken over by a power adversarial to the true Creator God who lived and worked in all the world; the alternative lay in access to the true God that dwelt and worked in Jesus, and was accessible to all.

All of this is made much clearer in John's interpretation of Jesus's reported words against the Temple — destroy it, and I will rebuild it in three days — "he spoke of the temple of his body" (John 2:21). This Johannine interpretation of the words of Jesus are almost certain to remind the Bible reader of other scattered sentiments, such as: "God was in Christ reconciling the world to himself"; "for in him all the fullness of the deity dwelt bodily"; "for it pleased God that in him (the Son) all the fullness of deity should dwell, and through him to reconcile himself to all things" (Col. 1:19; 2:9). And more, much more revealingly, the whole context of Paul's 1 Cor. 12–15, in which this life-giving Spirit who dwells in Jesus and through him breathes life eternally through all the world, dwells also and breathes in and through the followers of Jesus who, like Stephen, entrust themselves actively to the true divine Creator, so that all who so entrust themselves and allow this Spirit to breathe in and through them also become thereby part of the body of Christ, part of the true Creator's true cosmic temple. At this point of the contemplation of the early community of Jesus-followers quite grand vistas of divine salvation and divine revelation begin to open up once more. Vistas that had been closed out by exclusivist and absolutist, and indeed idolatrous/blasphemous attitudes to the Temple. And once again, as in the case of words and acts against the Torah, Jesus and his followers are not rejecting these basic elements of organized religion as such. There is no evidence at all to suggest that Jesus or any of his followers thought it necessary to found another religion. Quite to the contrary, Jesus and Stephen are simply trying to recall their Jewish religious structures to their role of truly embodying and reflecting the truth, the way, the life originally revealed to them in a ray of divine light vouchsafed to Moses in particular and now — as Matthew portrays him in his sermon from the mountain — to Jesus, the new Moses, so that this light should shine through these and their people into the dark places of the world. Albeit this is also a light, as John is also careful to remind his readers, "that enlightens everyman" in any case (John 1:9).

Some insightful readers of the Bible have suggested that Jesus himself did not quite see from the outset the full universalist implications of that special vocational service to the divine Creator for which he was invited, quite literally as it turned out, to give his life. He had apparently to learn this, these readers point out, in the course of certain encounters. Such as the encounter with Canaanite woman, whose request for salvation he at first rudely refused, and with the Roman centurion whose faith Jesus saw more quickly. And there perhaps lies another clue to Jesus's reference to Jonah as the only kind of sign that would be made available to the adulterous generation. For in addition to the fact that formed the main substance of this sign, the fact, namely, that Jonah preached to the people of Nineveh and actually succeeded in changing their hearts and minds, there is also the fact that Jonah did everything to avoid going to the Ninevites in the first place, for they were Gentiles. Until he was punished by three days in the whale's belly. And even when he did then go where God sent him and was successful, his stubbornly residual Jewish exclusivism still made him regret having done so. A regret so strong that it made him want to die, and if he was not to die soon, then to send him into a sulk for the rest of his life. Prophets too seem to have to learn as they go along, and to learn above all that God's special choice of their bodies and lives does nothing to imply that God's creating and saving ways are not always already accessible to all the world. That Jesus learned that lesson faster than Jonah and more thoroughly, is hinted by Matthew when he has Jesus say, having seen the faith of the centurion, "many will come from the east and the west and sit at table with Abraham, Isaac and Jacob in the kingdom of heaven, while the sons of the kingdom will be consigned to the outer darkness" (Matt. 8:11–12).

So then, having passed such judgment in both word and deed on Torah and Temple, the same judgment must now be passed on Jesus himself as was passed on Socrates for a similar critique of his established religion, the same judgment from the politician as from the priest: he must be killed. Because Pontius Pilate, even if he sent Jesus to his death only because of being threatened with blackmail by "the Jews" — and we cannot be certain about this, if only because of the suspicion that Bible writers may not be altogether objective in apportioning the blame for the killing of Jesus — Pilate, too, if he had thought about the matter a little more deeply, would have seen in Jesus at least as much of a threat to the imperial institution he represented in Jerusalem, as Jesus was to the Jewish religion and its establishment. He would certainly have seen in Jesus a far greater threat than Barabbas. And perhaps, if we had a more objective account of the part played by Pilate, he did see just such a threat in Jesus. Faced with the two "sons of God" (*bar-abbas* translates as son of "abba," the Father) Pilate, on reflection, would surely have thought the Jesus version of son or servant of God a far greater threat to his imperial power and self-aggrandizement, than the other version of son of God who was brought before him on that fateful day. For the other version, the freedom-fighter or brigand (depending on your political allegiance and point of view) called Barabbas, wanted only to be allowed to replace Pilate's person and institution in his country with quite similar Jewish ones, and so he would be quite satisfied if Pilate and his crew simply went home. The son of God named Jesus, however, wanted nothing less than the replacement of all such self-aggrandizing institutions with ones in which those who would be leaders would be the servants of all. So Jesus's challenge to either or both of these institutions, in the name of the eternal Creator of life without measure intended equally for all, could only result in the ultimate violence to his person, the death-penalty. And the only question that remained for Jesus — and it was a real question for him, for he sweated blood in the Garden of Gethsemane, and asked God to take the chalice of final suffering from him — was what he was to do about such a verdict, in continuing fidelity to the reign of the infinitely beneficent Creator Spirit that breathed in and through all of his life.

The answer, again according to Matthew, had already been formulated by Jesus as the new Moses giving the law from the holy mount: "Do not resist one who is evil. But if anyone strikes you on the right cheek, turn to him the other also; and if anyone would sue you and take your coat, let him have your cloak as well; and if anyone forces you to go one mile, go with him two miles. . . . Love your enemies and pray for those who persecute you, so that you may be the sons of your Father who is in heaven, for he makes his sun to rise on the evil and the good, and sends rain on the just and on the unjust" (Matt 5:39–45). Jesus must die rather than resist the ones who would kill him, especially since, as Barabbas could patiently explain to him, his only other option would be to kill them first.

Now this must sound to your ordinary reasonable, calculating man, it must be admitted, like a recipe for exponentially increasing disaster. For suffering and disaster, it seems from common experience, fall more upon the innocent in any case. And if one followed the rules laid down by Jesus, that would simply seem to encourage the original sinners to deprive others of even more than they otherwise would. Surely a more reasonable set of rules for the spread of the kingdom of God would read something like this: if anyone robs you, make him pay back the same amount; and if anyone comes to kill you, get your retaliation in first and kill him (as the new foreign policy of Christian leaders of two Christian countries, the USA and Great Britain, and of the broader coalition of the willingly bribed and the unwillingly bullied, has exemplified it in the current war in Iraq). And then, when a level playing field has been achieved, as it were, then we can allow in the reign of God, and have all equally and co-operatively access the sources of life for all.

But, of course, by taking that apparently reasonable route, you are merely co-operating with the original sinners, and enabling them now by opting to share in their death-dealing violence, to bear away into captivity even such small seeds of the reign of the God of steadfast love that may already have begun to take root on human soil. You cannot send original sin into remission by co-operating in its patented projects, and serving the satanic spirit therein embodied. Now these last two sentences actually contain the gist of the answer to one final question concerning the cross of Jesus. If we have now seen a full and adequate account of the manner in which, with an unusual and yet compelling inevitability, the execution of Jesus came about, can we now find in that account an explanation of the way in which both the Bible and the bulk of Christian tradition regard the cross as *the* "moment" of the salvation of human kind? A brief meditation on some words of Jesus himself, which the phrase about sinners and their death-dealing violence above would bring to mind could well help us to that final explanation.

"From the days of John the Baptist until now the kingdom of heaven has suffered violence, and men of violence take it by force" (Matt. 11:12). Jesus could just as well have said, "from the beginning"; but he was talking to a crowd that had just witnessed disciples coming from John the Baptist's prison cell to ask if Jesus was restoring the reign of God as John had tried to do (Matt. 3:1–2; 11:18), so Jesus prefaced his remarks about violence and the kingdom on this occasion with the phrase "from the days of John." And contemporary readers of the Bible can update that "until now" to their own place on the calendar of history. For if there was anything that Jesus left unclear about the way of the Creator and the creation, the reign of God, he certainly left nothing unclear about the role that violence has to play in it. "I have come that they may have life without measure; (yet) I have come to bring, not peace but the sword; so that all who would follow me must take up their cross, daily."

It must be clear by now, from all that has been said concerning both creation itself and the original and apparently permanent sinfulness of the race, that violence is continuously brought to bear upon the reign of God, that is to say, upon those who live it, promote it and preach it. That violence, it must be clear also by now, is many-layered. There is the violence involved in the deformation of forms of life in the continuous process of transformation to ever higher forms of life. For example, the violence done to the delicate body of a woman in the act of giving birth to new life, matched by the violence to the child in expelling it so forcefully from the womb, the only safe haven it has so far known. There is the general violence suffered by all at the hands of those who pursue, like little gods, their own security in life through self-aggrandizement. There is even a violence to oneself that is involved in attempts to wean oneself away from sinful ways and one's strong inclinations toward these. Such violence is well illustrated in the penitential practices of early Irish monks, who had a definitive influence on the penitential practice and sacrament of the Western Christian church. It is illustrated in such punitive practices as those in which my gluttony and drunkenness is corrected by fasting and abstinence. My use of the tongue to lie, deceive, coerce, and put down others, is corrected by elected silence. My inordinate pride in general is corrected by submitting my very will to the will of someone I believe knows the true way. It is illustrated also in the asceticism that characterized the work of John the Baptist in his efforts to promote the reign of God.

But there is a further level of violence that may be expected by those who try to live out and to promote the reign of the true Creator God in God's good world. This violence is reserved for those in whose living and preaching the presence of the rule of the everlastingly beneficent Creator Spirit proves to be so powerful, inspiring and influential, that it poses a particular threat to the whole life-style of the idolators and to the self-made gods they serve. A threat that can be so great as to have it regarded as a threat to the very structures and ethos of a whole society that lives by such an ethos. And therefore sufficient reason for the raising of a capital charge against the one who poses that threat. Now if the general violence visited on their fellows by fallen human beings, especially on those who are trying their best to live by the rule of God, succeeds in inciting the latter into a violent and destructive reaction, the result can reasonably be described as taking into captivity whatever extent of that kingdom humans have already managed to cooperate in establishing. And how much more apposite then is the image of captivity of the kingdom of God if the one who is most influential and inspiring in spreading that divine rule, when threatened by death for so doing by the same fallen men of violence, is thereby provoked into trying to rid the world first of these would-be executioners? Or trying to avoid execution by confirming the would-be executioners in their service of a false god, Mammon, by offering them a huge bribe? On either option the reign of God is being allowed to be "taken by force," as Jesus put it, by the failure of the courage (to which Jesus was tempted in the garden) to refuse to meet with violence those who would apply the ultimate violence under the rules of the civic or religious establishment they presided over. So Jesus, like Socrates, had no option but to die as a final act of keeping faith with the Creator God whose reign in this world he served throughout all of his life.

Nietzsche showed how fully he understood all of this when he has Zarathustra insist that he is the first among men who must go down into death itself, the great *niedergang*, if he is to accomplish his mission as the prophet and forerunner of the ultimate life still at the continuously created and evolving stage. Just like Jesus has to descend into *she'ol*, as the Gospels say he does at his death; another way of saying that his death was a truly human death, and not just a retiral for a time previously calculated and known to him to a place or state to be occupied before the revitalization of his corpse took place. Or as Nietzsche puts the matter also, Zarathustra, prophet and precursor of the superlife, realizes that he must offer himself as a supreme sacrifice to love — for love is the spur in all of this — before he can thereby inspire others to offer themselves to love likewise. "I offer myself to love, *and my neighbor as myself* — that is the language of all creators. All creators, however, are hard."

Correspondingly, far more powerful and inspiring is the act of such a one in dying in fidelity to the reign of God, rather than killing to avoid such injustice, than is the general disposal to which all of us are urged, to meet the general violence done to us in life with nothing but forgiveness and beneficence toward those who do us the harm. And that is why the Christian Bible and the Christian tradition settles upon the "moment" of the crucifixion of Jesus, as *the* "moment" at which Jesus sends into remission the original sin of the race, and the saving of them that thereby results.

The Fourth Gospel, which has the deepest insights into all that Jesus did, is most persuasive in highlighting that "moment." John, under the imagery of the pouring out of the water of eternal life (that is to say, the Spirit), through Jesus and his followers, links the full pouring or giving of the Spirit through Jesus to the glorification of Jesus on the cross (John 7:38–39). Now the glory, the *shekinah*, is the image of the presence of God, and it is clearly conveyed to John's readers that it is in Jesus's finest hour, the hour of his trial, passion and death, that God-in-Jesus will appear in his fullest glory: "'I have come to this hour...' 'Father, glorify thy name...' 'I have glorified it and I will glorify it again...' 'Now is the judgment of this world; now shall the rulers of this world be cast out; and I, when I am raised up from the earth, will draw all men to myself.' He said this to show by what death he was to die" (John 12:27–33). Then, as Judas leaves the company to betray him and hand him over to the priests, Jesus says, "Now is the Son of man glorified, and in him God is glorified." And, finally, at the moment of his death he cried: "'It is consummated'; and he bowed his head and handed on his Spirit" (John 19:30). "Handed on" is the translation here preferred to "gave up," partly because it fits both the Greek, *paradosis*, and the Latin, *traditio*, but mostly because it fits better the full context in which the fullest and most effective presence or glory of God in the world is realized, and as spirit breathed out into the world, according to John, on the cross of Jesus of Nazareth.

In order to appreciate the fullest import of this fuller context in John's Gospel, and to understand fully the consummate role of the cross of Jesus in the salvific breathing of the Creator Spirit into this world, take up for a moment the theme of the resurrection of Jesus. It is necessary to anticipate here something that can only emerge more persuasively later under the heading of "Incarnation," namely, that in the Bible the resurrection of Jesus is consistently and properly understood to imply much, much more than the reviving of a dead man, such as is said to have happened, for instance, in the raising of Lazarus from the dead. God's raising of Jesus from the dead is nothing less than his exaltation to the status of life-giving Spirit, as Paul puts it in his chapter on resurrection (1 Cor. 15:45). Or as Paul puts it at the opening of his Epistle to the Romans when he talks of Jesus being manifest and installed in his true status as "Son of God in power according to the Holy Spirit by his resurrection from the dead, Jesus Christ our Lord." The resurrection of Jesus is his raising to the status of Son of God and Lord, exalted to that status by the Holy Spirit that possessed Jesus and was fully present in the body of Jesus.

John had Jesus say during a visit to Jerusalem for Passover near the outset of his mission, and in the context of declaring that all needed to be baptized or born again of the Spirit, "as Moses raised up the serpent in the desert (to heal all who would look upon it), so must the Son of man be raised up, that whoever believes in him may have eternal life" (John 3:14–15). And now, in the imagery in which John perceives and presents the significance of the cross, he writes about Jesus being raised up (*exaltatus*, in Latin) from the earth (*ek tes ges*, in Greek, out of the earth) on his instrument of execution, the cross. So that the moment of his death is then described by John as the moment par excellence of his being manifest and installed as life-giving Spirit, the moment of resurrection understood in that same sense of exaltation to the status of Spirit. Nor is this vision of the execution of Jesus as his raising out of a land ruled by death to the stature of life-giving Spirit, necessarily, a Johannine idiosyncrasy. Notice that Matthew has people raised from the dead at the moment of Jesus emitting his spirit/breath (Matt. 27:50–52). And is the same vision not at the very least implied in Luke's story of the brigand crucified with Jesus asking to be remembered when Jesus came into his kingdom, to be told, "*today* you will be with me in paradise" (Luke 23:39–43)? Just as John had also described Jesus's hour as the place and occasion of the consummate glory of God, the glorification, the effective presence of God, Creator-Savior in the world, unconfined to any Temple, in Jerusalem or on Mount Gerizim, or to any other of the establishments of these or of any other religions, their laws or their cults.

Mount Gerizim comes into it because of the context of Jesus's conversation with a woman of Samaria; for the Samaritan temple was on Mount Gerizim, and the woman wanted to know how her temple rated with reference to the Jerusalem temple, only too be told that, "the hour is coming when neither on this mountain nor in Jerusalem will you worship the Father." For although "salvation is of the Jews ... the hour is coming and now is, when the true worshipers will worship the Father in spirit and truth ... God is spirit, and those who worship him must worship in spirit and in truth" (John 4:21–24). And the connection with the crucifixion of Jesus remains central to the development of this universalist theme also. For the Gospels record that at the moment of Jesus's death on the cross, the veil of the Temple was rent from top to bottom; an arresting image of God's Glory, God's particular power and presence escaping from confinement within the Jerusalem Temple and diffused in all the world where, as always, it is exuded by the faithful Jesus, an ordinary man and no functionary of any religious establishment, and by all ordinary people who like him keep faith with the Creator God he called Father.

The Images of Salvation through the Cross

It is in this context, therefore, and with some such attempt at a full and accurate understanding of the matter in hand, that the remaining images for salvation — ransom/redemption, satisfaction (sacrifice)/expiation — can be properly interpreted and applied. And the first step toward this end is to take it that, unlike the image of salvation itself and its equivalents listed above, the literal sense of this new set of images for salvation in the Bible must be seen to be their metaphorical sense.

So then Jesus is said to have paid the highest price of all for putting original sin into remission. And in this paradigmatic case also, and indeed in this paradigmatic case in particular, it is necessary to keep in mind the fact that price-paying is to be understood strictly and always in a metaphorical sense. "Jesus paid the price for the sin of the race," and "John paid the price demanded by the pawn-broker for the release of his antique pocket-watch"; these two sentences do not use the image of price-paying univocally. And that is true of all deployment of price-paying imagery across the whole use of imagery of ransom and redemption. The same is true of the imagery that derives from the institution of slavery, where a price is paid to liberate a slave or to buy back her freedom, imagery that is then deployed of salvation on the heels of the deployment of the imagery of slavery for humanity's role with regard to original sin, as John says: "everyone who commits sin is a slave to sin" (John 8:34). In this deployment, the price-paying imagery of ransom or redemption (literally, buying back) is used metaphorically: nobody is actually paying a price for anything to anybody. (A sampling of Bible texts on enslavement and ransom/redemption may be found in Gal. 4:1–9; Rom. 8:18–23; 3:9; Mark 10–45.)

The imagery of satisfaction might be taken into account in connection with the imagery of ransom and redemption, if only because it occurs very prominently in theology to the present day. The image was widely operative both in ancient legal systems that think of the satisfaction for the deprivation and destruction of person and property primarily in terms of actual price paid, and in other systems that think of the satisfaction in terms of punishment meted out; in serious cases, capital punishment. So for example, in the old, pre-Christian Irish system of brehon law (that is, the case law developed by the profession of the *breitheamh*, or judge), the price to be paid to someone injured in the commission of a crime was reckoned according to the status or dignity of the person injured, and was known as the face price or honor price (*eiric*). So a price was actually paid for something to someone, and quite commonly that price would consist in a number of cattle given over to the person deprived or injured or to the person's family, in recompense for the loss sustained. Where the imagery of satisfaction is deployed in accordance with its usage in such a legal system, all that need be said here is that it must be deployed strictly metaphorically, and not univocally, as is the case with the imagery of ransom and redemption in general, when it is used of the death of Jesus.

There is another type of legal system, however, in which the imagery of satisfaction is deployed. This is really not applicable at all to the suffering of Jesus and of his followers who live out their faith in God the Creator in the face of the threat of death. Not even metaphorically may it be applied. For in this second type of traditional legal system satisfaction is achieved, in broad terms, by means of the *lex talionis*, eye for eye and tooth for tooth. Modified forms of such a legal system merely exacerbate its savagery: a mere insult to a personage of very high status might warrant capital punishment, otherwise warranted only by the unlawful killing of someone of lower status. This system of so-called justice in which direct violence to life is punished with direct violence to life is precisely the kind of rough justice explicitly condemned by Jesus as he urged us to do good to those who injured us, for the sake of the coming of the reign of God. It is therefore entirely unsuitable even as a metaphor for the price to be paid when those serving the Creator Spirit have to deal with original sin and the suffering it inflicts indiscriminately on innocent and guilty alike.

Indeed, as may appear shortly in reference to theologies of salvation, the embargo upon using the satisfaction image even metaphorically for the suffering and death of Jesus and of those who follow him, may be extended beyond its use in that second, penal model of satisfaction. The embargo might well be extended also to the first more literal price-paying model of satisfaction given, if only because it may not be clear from the mention of satisfaction on its own which model is in operation. And, furthermore, the fact that the death of Jesus took the form of an actual execution works against a metaphorical understanding of that same satisfaction imagery, for it too easily lends itself to the impression conveyed, that the death of Jesus was quite literally demanded by God as a satisfaction for whatever insult or injury to God, the ultimate aristocrat, sinful opposition to his will or rule was thought to cause.

Finally, the imagery of expiation, together with its subsidiary imagery of cultic sacrifice, appears in the Bible as a metaphor for the suffering and death of Jesus that formed an inevitable part of the process of (a price to be paid for) the replacement of the reign of satanic, life-destroying forces with the power of the reign of God. This imagery appears, for example, in Paul's references to "Christ Jesus, whom God put forward as an expiation by his blood"; and to "God...sending his Son in the likeness of our sinful flesh and as a sin offering" (Romans 3:25; 8:3). Now this clearly is metaphorical use of language, for Jesus was not a priest, nor were there any practicing priests among his followers as far as one can see from what Christians call the New Testament and the whole period covered by its various writers. The Epistle to the Hebrews, in which the language of priesthood and cultic sacrifice is deployed in a major move in its argument about Jesus's life and death, offers also the clearest evidence of the metaphorical status of that language. Hebrews invokes the priesthood of Melchisedech as a model for what Jesus achieved, and this was a priesthood outside the designated priestly succession that alone, in Jewish eyes, served in the cult of the one, true God. And in this way also the point was confirmed, the point, namely, that Jesus and his "sacrifice" did not belong to that cult. So that the effect of Jesus's life and death was to put an end to the necessity of such cultic priesthood and sacrifice, either for the purpose of ensuring God's effective creative and saving power and presence, or for ensuring human access to the same. Precisely the point that was made in Jesus's reported words about the Jerusalem temple, the temple on Mount Gerizim, and by logical extension about any other designated sacred building made by human hands, within which people might attempt to domesticate the infinite and eternal Creator of life, and offer cultic sacrifice through a designated cultic priesthood.

So it is then that in the Bible context the literal sense of this second set of images for what Jesus did and still does in life and death — ransom, redemption (satisfaction), sacrificial expiation — is the metaphorical sense. The first set of terms for the images of what Jesus did — salvation/healing, deliverance/liberation, recapitulation/restoration, victory final and irreversible, reconciliation — are not used metaphorically; for they are images of what actually is done and happens in Jesus's living and dying, and by all who live and die by the Spirit that breathed in and through him. Life is made well, healed and made whole again, restored and transformed, passed through victories over all adversarial, destructive powers, until life is consummated in a final and irreversible victory over such powers. In the deployment of all of this imagery the meaning of the terms is univocal with their meaning in the primary contexts of each and all. Salvation, making well, has the same connotation in the religious context as it has in the surgeon's operating theater, or in the health and fitness clinic, or on the psychiatrist's couch, or in the outreach of charitable organizations all over the world to bring food and medicine to the sick and starving millions in a world of plenty, and so on, and so on.

However, in the second set of images a metaphorical usage comes into play, precisely in order to stretch our understanding of all that is happening in the course of the processes actually described in the first set of images. If only because of the circumstances in which that process actually takes place, circumstances in which a powerful temptation endemic to humanity's high estate constantly and universally turns into satanic, death-dealing forces the very creatures who inherit in every generation the co-creative responsibilities to bring all of life to its consummate goal for all. This set of images and the terms in which they are cast is designed to stretch our understanding of the process of salvation of life to the point of realizing that — and here the metaphors begin already — a

high price will be paid, and severe sacrifice required of those who wish
to serve as co-saviors of life in face of these perennial satanic forces that
constitute the enemy within. But that the willingness to pay such prices
and to offer such sacrifice in one's own flesh, rather than return the direct
violence done to life by those possessed of the satanic spirit, will itself
prove to be the most powerful demonstration of keeping faith with the
eternal Creator of life, and the most effective inspiration to all to walk in
the way of the love of all living things. Rather than continue to march
on the well-trodden highway to dark, destructive, and hopeless death.

Having looked closely then at the little group of metaphors —
ransom/redemption, satisfaction, sacrifice/expiation — that have traditionally clothed the meaning of Calvary, is it still possible to say that God
punishes human beings with no punishment additional to the punishment that the said human beings inflict upon each other in the course of
falling for the age-old temptation? Yes, it is, and only the failure to take
as the literal meaning of these images in the biblical text their metaphorical meaning could make the matter seem otherwise. For to say that talk
of expiation made by the execution of Jesus on the cross is to be taken
strictly metaphorically, is to deny that there is here, as there is in the ancient and cruel religious rituals of cultic sacrifices, no killing of a victim,
willing or otherwise, thought to be demanded by God and offered by
human priests, as a punitive penalty for human sin that is additional to
any other punishments their sinning may bring upon each other. There is
no punishment evident on the cross of Jesus other than the pain and punishment we humans inflict so universally and persistently on each other in
the course of our self-divinizing quest for the security and enhancement
of life. There was no cultic sacrifice, no cultic priest or cultic victim present
on Calvary on that dark day of Jesus's death, just the servants of the civic
and religious establishments executing a man who had threatened their
whole power and ethos. So to say that Jesus died for (salvation from our)
sins, is to say these two things and no more: first, that it was our ancient
and continuing "original" fallenness that brought him to his execution,
like so many others that stood for the true God and the truth of God's
ways in the world. And it is an idle exercise to seek to place more of the
blame on Jews or Romans over the other. And second, that death was
the culmination and the consummation — as he said on the cross, "it is
consummated" — of his life's work of sending that original sin, with all
of its self-destructive entailments, into remission. For to die for keeping

faith with the steadfast love of God is the consummate means of inspiring others to join in sending original sin into remission.

The same is true of the price-paying descriptions of what happened on that cross on a Friday so long ago. Once again, these are metaphors. So that there was literally no actual price paid in pain or in any other currency, especially required by God and paid on behalf of humanity by Jesus. There was only, once again, the pain and death inflicted by one group of human beings on another, as part and parcel simply of the former's wayward will to have life as they want it at whatever expense to any who would want it otherwise. Therefore, the formula holds: God does not add or require any penalty of punishment for sin over and above the punishment that the sinful race quite commonly, freely, persistently and liberally doles out to itself.

The Traditional Theology of Salvation

The most generous overview of the history of Christian theology would find it difficult to deny that in the case of the doctrine of salvation, traditional theology from the beginning has distorted as much as it clarified this most crucial range in the whole spectrum of divine-human relationships. From the very beginning of Christian theology the terminology of buying, paying for, buying back, as found in the images of ransom, redemption and their cognates, was taken univocally across the enormous gap that separates commercial transactions of the (slave) market from transactions that separate and unite God and humanity. At its worst this failure to recognize metaphor resulted in quite bizarre scenarios in which Jesus paid Satan with his life-blood for the release of Satan's human slaves. But even as recognition of this egregious nonsense mercifully began to dawn on marginally more sensible theologians, things did not improve all that much. For at first more nonsense was added with stories of Satan being cheated of the payment due to him, because he did not realize that the one who earned the price of his slaves was the Son of God from whom no payment could be extracted by a mere creature.

After that, the story was changed to a version in which Jesus, by his death in particular, earned "merit," and this was then paid to God for the remission of all our sins and of the penalties they incurred. This version had the advantage of reducing the satanic spirit to its proper place in the scheme of things, but only at the cost of setting God and Jesus at opposite ends of a bargaining process for our eternal lives. A cost — metaphorically speaking, of course — not easily offset by the insistence of the tellers of this version of the story, to the effect that it was the Father's own love of us and corresponding wish to save us that sent his Son, Jesus, to the cross to earn this merit in the first place. That finally revised version of the price-paying story, still innocent of metaphorical intent, has done little to convince the doubters of any age that the divine attribute of love prevailed over the strict conditions of the allegedly equally divine attribute of strict distributive justice. For the intended result of the Father's act of love exhibited in sending his Son to the cross was to make sure that God got his pound of flesh from humanity one way or another. And that can hardly represent the true gospel meaning of the proclamation that God so loved the world that he sent his uniquely beloved Son to save us.

These early centuries of the Christian theology of salvation did see more acceptable use of other imagery. The image of the Christ as the victor over the satanic powers involved in humanity's original sin provides one of the better examples. And, better still, there was Irenaeus again, the theologian who, after Pelagius perhaps, offered the best theology of original sin as a human rebellion against the Good Creator that waxed rather than waned with humanity's growth from original infancy to its coming of age. A rebellion continually countered by the steadfast love of the Creator, until in Jesus the final victory of life-giving over death-dealing was both initiated and anticipated. A grand vista of the whole sweep of the history of the world assembled round the theme, "where sin abounded, grace did more abound." Unfortunately, however, it was not these less flawed and more promising theologies of salvation that dominated the great theological output of the high Middle Ages, and then went on to dominate the Christian theology of salvation to the present day. It was instead a theology of salvation still centered upon an image of price-paying, but presented in a terminology of price-paying that can be seen to be used univocally, rather than metaphorically and analogically across the enormous gap that separates the earthly marketplace from the demesne of divine-human commerce.

The paradigm for this most dominant model of salvation in more recent history is Anselm's satisfaction theology of salvation as contained in his *Cur Deus Homo?* For, although the term *satisfaction* as such need not imply actual price-paying, it is clear from what has been said about one version of its deployment already that it does coincide with the price-paying models of salvation found in the biblical imagery of redemption and ransom. As a consequence it must be subjected to close critical scrutiny

in order to ascertain whether or not it is using this imagery and terminology metaphorically or univocally. And the answer in the case of the
Anselmian theology of salvation as satisfaction, unfortunately, must be
that it is using the price-paying version of satisfaction-imagery, and using
it univocally. For, having ostentatiously set about the rejection of the old
idea of a price paid to the devil, Anselm immediately invokes the feudal
image of the honor or face price (the *eiric* of old Irish law) and then proceeds to the calculation that the price to be paid for injury done or offense
offered must match the dignity of the one injured or offended.

So, according to this ancient exercise in distributive justice, humanity's
offense to its Maker already offered in the Garden of Eden, calls for infinite
recompense. For God's aristocratic honor-status is of infinite dimensions.
But humanity, already owing to God all it has and is, all of which is finite
in any case, could never satisfy such stringent demands of justice. And
for God to simply cancel the debt unilaterally in one magnanimous act of
mercy, would amount in effect to a divine dismissal of distributive justice,
so necessary for the order and well-being of the whole created universe.
The only possible solution to this devastating problem in divine-human
relationships is that some human being give all, but that this human being
enjoy the status of divinity. In this way humanity pays the price it owes
the offended divinity, and the worth of the price paid is infinite. By such
means divine justice is satisfied, yet divine love too is fully in evidence
for as it happens, God sends his uniquely beloved divine Son to death
on the cross in order to save us from an otherwise inevitable and eternal
punishment for an infinite debt unpaid. It is this precise calculation of
debt owed and price paid that must convince any reader that price-paying
terminology is used univocally here, when it should never be used other
than metaphorically.

Most adverse criticism of this, as of others of Anselm's theological exercises, has concentrated on his allegedly rationalizing tendencies, trying
to prove by reason what should be accepted in faith. Most defenses of
Anselm have consisted accordingly in replies in kind, in terms of a better
understanding of the relationships of faith and reason. These defenses
have indeed improved understanding of faith and reason, but the fact remains that the worst mistake in Anselm's theology is thereby overlooked:
the univocal use of the imagery of price-paying, and the consequent image
of God extracting from the innocent Jesus the full price of an offense
committed by the guilty. And, as said already, the facts that the innocent
Jesus has been raised by God to the status of his uniquely beloved Son,

and as such has been sacrificed by God, and has himself gone willingly to his death in obedience to his Father's plan — none of this really softens the resulting image of a deity intent upon its pound of flesh. With the exception of Abelard and a few other theologians of some significance, such crucial shortcomings in Anselm's theology of salvation were overlooked in subsequent Western Christian theology, and so its dominant position has remained largely undisturbed to this day.

What did happen instead was that this satisfaction model of salvation metamorphosed at times from the first version of that model noted already, the price-paying version that Anselm adopted, to the second version mentioned above, the *lex talionis* version of a life for a life, where the life forfeit may be the life of the one who has killed one of the clan thus injured or, if that is not feasible, the life of some other member of the clan or family of the killer. In these latter circumstances, that second version of the satisfaction model becomes known as the penal substitution version. This version Anselm wished to avoid, yet it was taken up later in the course of Christian theology. It certainly seems to be present in the language of Session 22 of the Council of Trent, when the Mass, clearly a cultic sacrifice in the view of the Council, is defined as the re-presentation of the sacrifice that Jesus as a real cultic priest offered on the cross, and of which he was himself the sin-offering on Calvary, in place of the rest of human kind.

Finally then, as an embargo must be placed upon the penal substitution version of the satisfaction model in the Christian theology of salvation, an even stronger embargo must be posted against the use of the terms and imagery of cultic sacrifice for the execution of Jesus. More especially if there is any suspicion whatever that the terms are used univocally of these cases, cases covering both the death of Jesus and the sin-offerings of the Jewish or of any other religion. For then there could be no denying the fact that at the heart of Christianity is an instance of cultic human sacrifice. It was, after all, the man Jesus who died. So that the monstrous nature of the divinity involved in transactions of penal substitution is then enhanced by the impressions of monstrosity always evoked by instances of the religious practice of human sacrifice.

In sum, there is just so much historical evidence to the effect that the satisfaction terminology of salvation in its distributive justice version involved univocal use of that terminology across medieval inter-human and divine-human relationships, broken and restored. There is just as much historical evidence to the effect that that univocity continued when the satisfaction version metamorphosed into the penal substitution version and then annexed the imagery of cultic sacrifice. These transformations increased exponentially the monstrous image of divinity, so that nothing now remains except to return to the exceptional instances of better theologies of salvation. Or better still, to return to the biblical material already surveyed, and, by-passing all the eisegesis that has been passed off as exegesis in the centuries between, to base a theology of salvation on the clear lines of the story of salvation told in the Bible from beginning to end.

The outlines of such a true theology are easily drawn from biblical data properly read and attentively meditated: salvation means making life whole, and doing this without the restraint of measure. It means overcoming all the deaths of all the forms of existence and life that must occur in transit, in the course of creating forms of life ever higher than the ones that are continually transformed. As life evolves the point is reached at which all creatures share in the status and life of the source-creator, as far as ever their natures allow. And it means also, and most particularly, being willing to surrender one's life, back into the hands of the One who is the eternal giver, supporter and promoter of life, rather than killing the ones who come to kill those who live out the ethos of the Creator Spirit in the world. So then, the healing and making whole that is the substance of what is called salving, saving, salvation, coincides with the restoration and enhancement of life that continually takes life beyond its inevitable reversals, both natural and malicious, that is called continuous creation. So we do not need two different words at all? Creation would suffice as a term for all of it? God the Creator is God the Savior, creating through faithful creatures, and God does nothing more in face of persistent human sinfulness and its apparently unending destructiveness, than to carry on creating, as a creative act of ever anticipatory forgiveness? Yes, the language of creation could cover all of this, and often, in the Bible it does so. But it is possibly useful to add the term *salvation* if only to highlight the additional amount of creation that is made necessary by the sheer historical down-dragging, down-pressing weight of human adversarial will and deed. Our race is so highly endowed with divinely originated and exponentially increasing know-how, wisdom and the corresponding power to create, that its capacity for destruction is correspondingly awesome — a little less than the gods — and the need for "additional" continuous creativity in order to keep on making life whole again, and to keep it advancing toward the predestined *shalom*, does need the use of a second term in order to keep the whole picture before our minds. The whole enormity of cosmic risk and responsibility, and of the ever-corresponding superabundance of life eternally on offer.

Chapter Four

GOD

They call themselves the good and the just . . . they call themselves the faithful of the true faith. . . . Behold the good and the just! Behold the faithful of all faiths! Whom do they hate the most? Him who smashes their table of values, the breaker, the law breaker — but he is the creator.

—Nietzsche, *Thus Spoke Zarathustra*

At the beginning of God's creating the heavens and the earth, the earth was without form and void, and darkness was upon the face of the deep; and the spirit of God hovered over the waters. And God said, "let there be light," and there was light.   —Genesis

In the beginning was the Word, and the Word was with God, and the Word was God. He was in the beginning with God; all things were made through him, and without him was not made anything that was made. In him was life, and the life was the light of men. . . .

The true light that enlightens everyman was coming into the world. . . . And the Word became flesh and dwelt among us, full of grace and truth . . . (and we have seen his glory, glory as of the only son from the Father) . . . grace and truth came through Jesus Christ . . . that whoever believes in him may have eternal life.

—*The Gospel According to John*

If there is one central insight that develops from the investigation of the three foregoing themes — creation, fall, salvation — it is this: that all empirical life and existence derives from an eternal creative source, that is to say, a source that continually forms creative creatures, and none more creative, as far as we know just here and now, than the species, *homo sapiens*. This eternal creative source sustains life through all deformations, both those that are a natural and inevitable part of life's ever advancing

144

transformations, and those that result in the self-inflicted detriment of derivative creative forces turned satanic. This continuous creation provides both a light for the feet of those who want to walk in the way of the progressive creation of life, rather than walk in the way of the destruction of life. And it thereby furnishes those who do so with a concrete hope of the ultimate reward of a life of peace without strife and a prospering without measure, *shalom*. Finally it has been hinted that the fullness of this Creator-deity, mainly in the image of Creator Spirit, dwelt bodily in the man, Jesus of Nazareth, and still dwells in that spiritual body of his, as Paul calls it, to which all human beings are called who live on this earth, and into the fulfilled form of which they are transformed at (or by?) death. Such in summary is the central insight one gains from a combination of the two most foundational, powerful and insightful books of the Bible, Genesis and the Gospel According to John.

It is also already evident that it was from this clear, if complex insight, that early Christians, under the tutelage of the classical Greek philosopher-theologians, developed their further insight into the triune structure of the godhead, and they then duly presented this both as a myth and as a theology of the Trinity. For just as all essentially limited human insight into Divine Being is as enabled as it is constricted by our awareness of the traces of God's power and presence in the world, so Christians looked to the founder of their faith, Jesus of Nazareth, for the embodiment par excellence of that divine power and presence from origin to eschaton. And the image and idea that they came to use for their central claim to the effect that Jesus furnished them with a special revelation of that general revelation of the divine in nature and history, and to use almost exclusively as time went on, was the image of incarnation. And the phrase that they point to, once again almost exclusively as time went on, as biblical warrant for this image and idea of incarnation, was John's phrase, *kai ho logos sarx egeneto*, "and the Word became flesh"(John 1:14).

Now the image of incarnation can be unpacked in its general usage as an image of something indwelling, of being embodied in another, and bodied forth by that other. So, for instance, Philo claimed that the divine Creator Word operated par excellence in and through the man, Moses. And, to the extent that he was victim of an insidious Platonic dualism, he envisaged the Word taking on the form of the psyche of Moses, rather than his flesh. Nevertheless this is an instance of incarnation, for the psyche of Moses is in turn embodied in, and bodied forth through, well, his body, to which in such dualist contexts the term *flesh* applied. All the more so, in the traditionally non-dualist Jewish usage of the term *flesh,* where it means the human being itself, vulnerable and mortal in its current bodily form, the image of the incarnation, the enfleshment of the divine Creator Word, is the full equivalent of the image of taking human form. As Paul put it in that hymn in his letter to the Philippians, itself the most comprehensive incarnation text in the whole of what Christians call the New Testament, "to be found in human form" (Phil. 2:8).

Much then is promised to anyone who would investigate a little further in these two books and further afield in the Bible, asking questions such as, what then is the relationship between Jesus and God? For John requires of his readers not just a bare but crucial entrusting of one's essential and active life-project to the Creator, he asks for a similar faith in Jesus also. Or, to put the matter perhaps more precisely: in other scattered gospel contexts Jesus himself seems to ask for a share in the faith in the Creator that is required of all who would be saved. He acknowledges such faith in him also, when it is implicit in some people's actions, or very explicit indeed in the terms of their petitions to him to heal, salve, save. And then, another question which might be asked: what do these texts that refer to the Word or Wisdom of God, or to the Spirit of God — those images already referred to as images of agencies in creation — what do these texts add, if anything, to our understanding of God's nature and being, over and above what is contained in the simple confession that God is the Creator of all? The two questions, it would appear from the headline texts for this chapter, must be connected, as the faith in Jesus that is asked for is connected with the Creative Word incarnate in him. It probably does not matter which of these questions is taken first. So, since it is the Christian faith that is the prime concern of the current investigation, it is best to begin with what one can learn about God the Creator from the biblical description of God's relationship to Jesus. For in actual historical fact, it was from what the Bible had to say about that relationship that early Christians then derived their fullest account of the divinely revealed nature of the one, true God.

The Full, Flowing Biblical Myth of Divine Incarnation

Incarnation is here understood in the sense of indwelling-embodiment and consequent bodying-forth into the world (a complex piece of imagery that may be represented henceforth, for the sake of convenience, simply as indwelling-embodiment), and in all the modes of presence-in-action that the complementary imagery that accompanies the master imagery of incarnation as indwelling-embodiment can both uncover and communicate. Then, just as in the Bible it is through the agency of the Creator's Word-Wisdom-Spirit that the whole of created-creative reality comes into being, so it is that the indwelling-embodiment of God the Creator is from the beginning envisaged as the indwelling-embodiment of God's Word-Wisdom-Spirit, and indeed in otherwise named "agencies in creation," that may be added to these three.

The first, fullest and final (God all-in-all) indwelling of God the Creator consists of God indwelling the entire evolving universe that the Creator continually forms and transforms. This cosmogenic process is then accurately imagined in terms of an infinite God, through dynamic intelligent design, breathing into the world life of correspondingly infinite prospect. And this divine breathing of life can be imagined as occurring from within the world, from whence it carries the world successively and limitlessly beyond all current forms: transcendence from within. The universe as the house of God, or the universe as the body of God, makes the same kind of metaphysical sense as that in which we might be called members of the body of Christ. As the same Spirit that breathed through Jesus's life, death and destiny, breathed the same life into us, so the universe into which God breathes existence and life is thereby the body of God, indwelling-embodiment.

Next and compared to the universe as a whole, Wisdom-Word-Spirit is said to be more especially indwelling, embodied in Adam, meaning humanity, made in the very image of God the Creator. God breathed into humanity the breath of life. For humanity is endowed with reflective consciousness, and so it can reflectively contemplate the Creator at work in the world and in the depths of its own spirit, as it co-operates in creation. Of the first and paradigmatic human being, declared in Psalm 8 to be "a little less than God," *Sophia* declares that she delivered him from his transgression and gave him strength to rule all things (Wisd. 10:1–2). *The Book of the Secrets of Enoch* puts the matter even more succinctly: "I created man . . . I placed him on earth, a second angel . . . to rule the earth and have my wisdom." So *Sophia*, as Creator, Word and Spirit, is especially present and active in the busy mind and body of humanity; incarnate, then, more especially in the human race.

More especially still, in ancient cultures and civilizations, the king is a cosmic figure as head and as it were the sum of the human community he provides for, protects and saves, a father figure, analogous to Adam, the father of the race. As such the king's person was sacred (*nemed* in old Irish), divine even, and so the king bore the divine titles of Lord and Son of God (Ps. 110:1; 2:7). Also, since kings were anointed, the third of the main trio of titles applied to Jesus was accorded to them, the Messiah, the Anointed One. The king was then a *theios aner*, a divine man. Because of the active presence of *Sophia*, Creator Word and Spirit, with and indeed in him. Isaiah says of the messiah to come, "the Spirit of the Lord shall rest upon him...the Spirit of Wisdom." And *Sophia* herself says, "by me kings reign and rulers decree what is just; by me princes rule and nobles govern the earth" (Isa. 11:2; Prov. 8:14–15).

Simultaneously — if only because it is very difficult to put these instances of more or less specialized incarnations of Creator Spirit, Word or Wisdom, in any strict chronological order — the Creator Spirit, it is claimed is especially present and active in God's chosen people. Israel is God's uniquely beloved son, before and after monarchy, from the patriarchs to the Roman colonization and beyond. So *Sophia* continues her description of how, having created the world as her house, having begun her creative task of saving human kind in Adam himself; and having seen the collusion of the nations in wickedness, she chose Abraham and his progeny. She showed Jacob "the reign of God and gave him the knowledge of angels"; "she entered the soul of a servant of the Lord (Moses)," saved him and his people from Egyptian tyranny, and brought them to their own land (Wisd. 10). All of which is summarized in imagery reminiscent of the marriage of Divine Wisdom to the king: "Our God...gave her to Jacob his servant and to Israel whom he loved" (Baruch 3:35–36). And for the imagery of dwelling among people, the very imagery with which John glosses his statement about the Word becoming flesh in Jesus, "and dwelt among us," see this text: "the Creator of all things gave me a commandment...and assigned a place for my tent. And he said, 'make your dwelling in Jacob, and in Israel receive your inheritance.'...So I took root in an honored people, in the portion of the Lord, his inheritance" (Sir. 24:8–12).

Within that special area of the indwelling of the agency through whom God created the world, there is a smaller special area of that self-same kind of indwelling. Because Israel did not always body-forth the creator Wisdom that indwelt its whole history, it really was Israel-faithful-to-the-Torah that could be said to make the reign of the Creator effective and palpable in the world. So that Creator Wisdom is more surely said to indwell and to be bodied forth by Torah-in-practice. So both Baruch and

Jesus ben Sira conclude their accounts of the special indwelling of *Sophia* in Israel's march through geography and history with similar sentiments. "She is the book of the commandments of God, and the law that endures forever. All who hold her fast will live, and those who forsake her will die" (Baruch 4:1). "All this is the book of the covenant of the Most High God, the law which Moses commanded us as an inheritance for the congregation of Jacob. It fills men with wisdom, like the Pishon, and like the Tigris at the time of first fruits. It makes them full of understanding like the Euphrates, and like the Jordan at harvest time." All the imagery, in short, of the garden of Eden made fertile by four rivers. An incarnation in Torah-in-practice pictured restoring the creation to its pristine perfection, bringing the incarnations of the divine Creator full circle to a state of the whole creation in which God is "all in all." Paradise regained (Sir. 24:23–26).

Finally, take the hint from Baruch's phrase describing the Torah as "the law which Moses commanded." Add the much subtler hint from the statement in the Wisdom of Solomon to the effect that *Sophia* "entered the soul of the servant of the Lord (Moses)." And the figure of the prophet par excellence of Israel can be added to that of cosmos, humanity, kings and a people. The prophet of Israel is now, as prophet, a special locus of the indwelling-embodiment of the power and presence of the Creator-Savior. He is an incarnation of the Creator Word by his words (*pro pheta*, to speak for, to be the mouthpiece of the Word of God). But even more so by the mighty deeds that God wrought through him in the desert days, saving God's people from servitude to death in Egypt, and leading them to the land of milk and honey. And, yes, punishing them whenever they turned idolatrous and satanic. Moses was the very embodiment of the law, the reign of God, transmitted once again in this particular instance and mode to a world within which it was always and everywhere embodied, and always and everywhere resisted by those who were free to comply creatively or to resist destructively. *Sophia* entered the very soul of Moses. She thereby indwelt and was bodied forth in his life as chosen and sent leader of a chosen people; incarnation.

When now we follow the telling of this biblical myth of the incarnations of the Creator Sophia/Word/Spirit into the documents that Christians added to the Jewish Bible, we immediately begin to see clues to the correctness of challenging a common assumption to the effect that John's "and the Word was made flesh (in Jesus)," is *the*, if not indeed the only, incarnation text in the Bible. And we see consequently the need to look to a wide variety of biblical texts, in addition to those that feature the Word or Logos, in order to gain as full and accurate an understanding as we can gain, of the connotation of that term *incarnation*. Texts, for instance, that feature the Shekinah, the Glory of God as the image of God's creative indwelling-embodiment in creation, just as Philo used the images of Creator and Lord, in addition to the image of Word, for that purpose.

The first clue is contained in the fact that John's text has the image of the Word set in a structural meaning-context that is identical with other texts that use the image of Spirit instead of Word. The structured context is this: Word comes into, was made flesh in, Jesus; and as a result we see (the glory of) the son of God (John 1:14). Precisely the same structure of meaning is discovered again and again as we trawl through the later documents of the Bible; only on these occasions, the talk is of the Spirit coming on, remaining with Jesus. And with the same result: Jesus is now the son of God. In Luke's infancy narrative the Spirit comes at the origin of Jesus's mortal life in the womb of Mary, and therefore that which is born of her is the son of God. "The Holy Spirit will come upon you," Mary is told, "and the power of the Most High will overshadow you; therefore the child to be born will be called holy, the son of God" (Luke 1:35). Then as we look further we meet the texts that we have noticed already in another context in the chapters on creation and salvation: first the texts that describe the baptism of Jesus. Matthew, like Luke and Mark, has the Holy Spirit descend upon Jesus on the occasion of his baptism by John the Baptist, whereupon a heavenly voice declares Jesus to be God's beloved son (Matt. 3:13–17). And John, who carefully avoids mentioning the fact that his namesake actually baptized Jesus — well, it must have been something of an embarrassment to his followers that Jesus was baptized by the other John, in a baptism of repentance for the forgiveness of sin — recorded instead that John the Baptist bore witness: "I saw the Spirit descend from heaven . . . and I have seen and have borne witness that this is the Son of God." And then he adds that John also said that the Spirit remained on in Jesus, so that Jesus can then baptize people not just with water, but with the Holy Spirit, so often symbolized by fire, tongues of flame, for example (John 2:29–34). The parallels are clear and precise. As the incarnation text in John says that the Word was made flesh in Jesus and so dwelt among us that we see the glory of this unique son of God, so the birth and baptism texts say that the Spirit came upon and remained in Jesus, and we therefore see in him the son of God.

The clues continue as we meet much later a similar structure of meaning: when Paul writes that Jesus Christ was "designated son of God in power — power, as in the birth text above being a cipher for the presence of God as Spirit — according to the Spirit of holiness through his resurrection from the dead" (Rom. 1:4). And Jesus, as well as being recognized as son of God, is then said to be recognized also as Lord, one of Philo's three images. It is possible to derive from this text the insight that the raising of Jesus to the status of true son of God as a result of the coming into him of the Spirit was achieved if not solely, then par excellence on Calvary. This would seem to be confirmed in another passage from Paul's letters. The passage begins by talking of the Word of the cross, continues by describing Christ crucified as "the power of God and the Wisdom of God," and the one who saves. And he concludes, "He [God] is the source of your life in Christ Jesus, whom God has made our wisdom, our righteousness and sanctification and redemption" (1 Cor. 1:30). And as Paul also there refers to Jesus crucified as the "Lord of Glory," he reminds us even more of other texts we have met already, this time in the chapter on salvation, in which the act of saving, of sending sin into remission, the act that gave Jesus his name, is accomplished principally on the cross. Thereby suggesting again that images other than a coming and indwelling-embodied Word are used to justify Jesus's title, son of God, and to explain what that title means.

John, one remembers, situates the glory of God's creating and saving presence in the hour and on the cross of Jesus, in the very body of the crucified and dying son of God. Just as Mark and Matthew at the moment of Jesus's death have the veil of the temple torn in two from top to bottom, releasing the Shekinah, the glory of God that had been domesticated behind that veil, and a centurion acknowledges Jesus as son of God (Mark 15:37–39). Luke's description of the same event has the centurion confess simply, "this man was innocent." But then Luke makes up for this by having the Shekinah come down at the birth of Jesus, witnessed by shepherds to whom an angel explains that the one on whom it comes is Lord and Savior. And all three synoptic Gospels have the Shekinah come upon Jesus, with the prophets Moses and Elijah, at the so-called transfiguration scene, at which it is said that Peter, James, and John "saw his glory," and a heavenly voice declares Jesus to be "my son, the chosen one" (Mark 9:2–8 and parallels).

Given then the equivalence of the images for that of God which is incarnate in Jesus — Word, Spirit, Wisdom, Glory, Lordship, and so on —

across all of this array of biblical incarnation texts, two questions may be asked. First, what precisely is the point of having stories of the event of the indwelling, embodiment and bodying forth of this divine entity spread over various points in the life of Jesus, from conception to death? The answer would appear to be twofold. Looked at from the point of view of the eternal God, just as the act of God the creator is equally contemporaneous with every point of space-time, so the contributory act of God, infusing into Jesus the divinely originated attributes and powers of the Creator, to the full measure of Jesus's finite nature, must also be an act equally contemporaneous with every moment in the lifetime of this mortal man. That is the import of biblical statements to the effect that God chose Jesus for his creative-saving role "before" the foundation of the world. On the other hand, looking at the matter from the worm's eye point of view of the man Jesus and of all poor mortal beings, and keeping in mind the phrase for incarnation, "being found in human form," it must occur to us that achieving the full form of a human being is not something that can be accomplished at the moment of conception, or of birth, or of coming of age. In fact, however paradoxical it may sound, the full achievement of the human form is not achieved until death, and beyond. Therefore, the most comprehensive and revealing incarnation text in what Christians call the New Testament is that hymn-like text that Paul either composed or quoted in his correspondence with the Philippians.

"Have this mind among yourselves which you have in Christ Jesus, who, though he was in the form of God, did not count equality with God a thing to be grasped, but emptied himself, taking the form of a slave, being born in the likeness of men. And being found in human form he humbled himself and became obedient unto death, even death on a cross. Therefore God has highly exalted him and bestowed on him the name which is above every name, that in the name of Jesus every knee should bow, in heaven and earth and under the earth, and every tongue confess that Jesus Christ is Lord, to the glory of God the Father" (Phil. 2:6–11). One would choose this text because, in a condensed but clear and concise passage of imagery Paul surveys the life, death and destiny of Jesus, from conception to exaltation, in the course of putting forward the same claim that is made in the Spirit-possessing-ergo-son-of-God texts as much as in the Word-enfleshed-ergo-son-of-the-Father text that provides a once-off alternative formulation of that same claim; as well as all the other texts that use fully equivalent images of divine creative attributes and powers coming to indwell and be bodied forth as a living and dying human being, at any or all points of that one's life.

It is true that the term *Spirit* does not appear in that Philippians hymn, if that is what it is. Nor does any equivalent term appear, in order to account for the title conferred on Jesus at the end. Only reference to a "mind" that was in Christ Jesus. But in the sentences that precede it, it is made clear that having this "mind" among us is the complete equivalent of the "participation in the Spirit," that he there mentions. A participation in the Creator Spirit that Paul elsewhere says makes us members of the body of Christ, whom God exalted to the status of life-giving spirit. It is also made clear in the preceding sentences that the "mind" in question consists in a practical wisdom, encapsulated in Paul's edict about having the same love as Christ Jesus and, even more concretely put: "let each of you look not only to his own interests, but also to the interests of others." And that edict leads directly into the hymn and clarifies its context. For the passage of imagery in the hymn then acquires a familiar ring to it: here is one who was created and born in the form (equivalently, image) of God, as Adam/humankind is. Yet he did not grasp at equality with God, as Adam/humankind has done from the beginning. Rather did he overcome the ancient and original temptation to do so, and thereby avoided the fate of those who end up in the exclusive service of idols that are a mere substitute for an idolized self. Instead he lived for the service of others, channeling to them God's healing and salving power, to the point of dying for this service to the life of all, rather than kill those who would kill him. In a macabre kind of fittingness, he died by the form of execution reserved for the unfree, the death of a slave, the cruel death of crucifixion. And in that very act of supreme self-giving, he channeled to a consummate degree the glory of the power and presence of the creating and saving God, and was himself thereby exalted to the status of Lord. Jesus, whom the creating and saving power and presence of God indwelt, and who breathed and bodied it forth, unhindered and full in all of his life in this world, and through death itself.

The Christian Incarnation Myth and the Confession of the Divinity of Jesus

The second question concerns the meaning we are to find in such titles as "son of God" and "Lord," as these are conferred on Jesus on the strength of the sentence structure: the Word/ Spirit/ Power of the Most High, and so on, indwelt Jesus's humanity and was bodied forth by him; therefore he is to be called son of God, Lord, and so on. For depending on the meaning we give to these titles, will depend also the meaning we are to give to that otherwise rather vague phrase, the divinity of Jesus. Now there is no point in proceeding immediately and on the basis of all that has just been said above about all of that varied incarnation imagery, and the varied expressions of its implications for the status of Jesus. Because there has been in existence in Christian myth and theology, from virtually the beginning of Christianity's existence as a distinct religion, an answer to the question posed. It is an answer that has prevailed down the centuries of Christian teaching and preaching, to the extent that it cannot be ignored. Not even momentarily, for the purpose of going back again to the biblical data in order to see what answer is really reached on the authority of the Bible.

The ancient traditional answer to the question as to the divine status of Jesus as a result of the incarnation in him of God's Word, seems to have made two assumptions from the start. First was the assumption that there really was but one clear claim to divine incarnation in the Bible, and that was contained clearly in John's statement to the effect that the Word became flesh in Jesus of Nazareth. So that the only true instance of incarnation Christians can acknowledge is an incarnation of the divine being in the founder of Christianity. And, second, was the assumption that the story of Jesus's conception at the beginning of Luke's Gospel, with some help from a similar story in Matthew's Gospel, is a clear and unmistakable account of that utterly singular event called incarnation. In Luke's terms, remember, the angel of God declares to Mary: "The Holy Spirit will come upon you, and the power of the Most High will overshadow you...*therefore* the child to be born will be called holy, the son of God." To which Matthew adds his own similar terms when he has the angel of God inform Joseph that Mary is "with child of the Holy Spirit," so that, "that which is conceived of her is of the Holy Spirit." These are then the very kind of biblical terms for the conception of Jesus by Mary that are then summed up so succinctly in the ancient Roman Creed, when it declared Jesus to be "born of the Holy Spirit and of the virgin Mary."

So the reader must now ask, what precisely is conveyed by this story, composed as it is from these biblical texts, one from John, the others from Luke and Matthew? Perhaps this: the Most High God conceived and gave birth to the Word, also called the Son, and simultaneously brought about the human conception of the man, Jesus, in the womb of the virgin Mary. (It is best to keep to the phrase "the Most High God" in the current retelling of this story; for the image of the Holy Spirit conceiving and giving birth to the Word-Son can cause its own problems for the Christian Trinitarian myth, in which the Word would then be the son of the Holy Spirit, and the Holy Spirit would then be the Father of the Word-Son.) Therefore, the one born of Mary would be called the son of God.

There is no problem here about the Most High God bringing about simultaneously, if presumably by very different processes, the birth of the eternal Word-Son and the birth of the very mortal Jesus. For eternal acts of God are contemporaneous with all events in the temporal order of space-time. And there is no problem about the virginal conception of Jesus that seems to be here suggested, for presumably God can miraculously form a human being in Mary's womb without the normal contribution that would be expected in this case from Joseph. But there is a problem for our understanding of the manner in which this double-barreled process could also bring about anything that could reasonably be called incarnation. And, it does no harm to observe at this point, this problem would remain exactly the same whether the man, Jesus, was conceived miraculously in a virginal conception, or was conceived in the normal manner through intercourse with Joseph. The problem is this: the picture of these two being conceived and birthed simultaneously, particularly since they both seem to be understood to be persons in some univocal sense of that term, does nothing at all to enable us to imagine how one of them indwells the other to the point of being embodied in the other, and thereafter bodied forth in the course of the other's normal human life. On the contrary, the story contrived from this combination of texts would leave the reader with the impression of two persons, one divine and the other human, or two sons, together somehow in the womb of Mary, and after the birth of Jesus together somehow also in that little piece of space-time taken up by the very human Jesus. To the point at which, it must shortly appear, the problem as to whether there were one or two of them, one or two sons or persons, plagued the theology of incarnation for centuries. It brought about successive solutions, each of which in turn had to be declared heretical, and some would say it is a problem that has seen no satisfactory solution to the present day.

But there is another way of approaching this allegedly incarnational story, so contrived from this combination of texts; irrespective of whether it is true, or not true that this story, so told and understood, causes problems for the theology of incarnation that have not really been solved to this day. The clue to this other way is found in one feature of the story itself. Notice the overtly sexual content of the imagery in which the Most High is depicted as conceiving and birthing both the eternal Word-Son and the man, Jesus. "Will come upon you . . . will overshadow you": the imagery is the same as that used by breeders of thoroughbred racehorses: the stallion covers the mare; how many successful covers did this stallion achieve this year? Even the phrase in the old Roman Creed, "born of the Holy Spirit and of the virgin Mary," is reminiscent of phrases like, "by Great Whistler out of Sharp Invite." And then, immediately attention is drawn to a univocal sense of this language of intercourse, as between the Most High and a human "stallion," the cry goes up: this is *not* to be understood univocally, it is metaphor. Well of course it is, but then so is every other part and feature of the story that is built on these two biblical contexts. (John's piece of the story assembled here, incidentally, says nothing at all about incarnation taking place and completed at the conception of Jesus.) We are dealing in and with myth. Then what, so understood, does this story say? The answer must be: it says the same as all the other stories of incarnation that we have surveyed in the Bible.

It says that God's Word or Wisdom that ever forms and transforms by continuous creation, and the God of Love's abiding in-spiration to so create until the final *shalom* is reached, so entered the soul and the very sinews of this Jesus, and was thereby so embodied in him, and so bodied and breathed forth in the whole of his life, and consummately in his death, that he must be accorded the title of the very son of God. The forming wisdom, and the loving and empowering breathing-into that God engenders in God's self in God's eternal process of creation, entered and fashioned this man in the image of God. And it is that living likeness to God that earns for Jesus the title, son of God, in a metaphorical mode that can have no truck with early disputes as to whether Jesus, incarnated, indwelt by God in this way, is a natural or an adopted son of God. It is this phrasing of the matter also that gives their proper contents of meaning to such other biblical claims concerning Jesus, such as the claim that "God was in Jesus reconciling the world to himself," or "the fullness of the godhead dwelt bodily in Jesus." For God's wisdom and spirit of love are not persons in any sense univocal with the sense in which Jesus is a human person; nor are any of the other attributes of God that are ever active in creating the world, such as God's lordship, or glory.

John it is who illustrates best this metaphorical usage of the title *son of God*. He does this most clearly in his accounts of the verbal clashes between Jesus and the leaders of "the Jews" (John 8, for instance). Each side accuses the other of having as their father Satan, and not the one, true God. "We have one father, even God," claim the Jews. "You," retorts Jesus, "are of your father, the devil, and your will is to do your father's desires; He was a murderer from the beginning." It is their death-dealing ways that make them sons of Satan, in what is clearly the metaphorical deployment of the image. Correspondingly, it is Jesus's creative, life-giving activities, healing and making whole, that makes him the son of the true God the Father, which constitutes his counter-claim. The functions and operations, the "works" of Jesus are those of the eternal Father, creating and saving life. "I am come that they may have life, and have it without measure."

The sexual imagery of the story cobbled together by the use of a text from John, then Luke and Matthew, can now be seen simply as a graphic and memorable extension of the metaphor contained in Jesus's title, son of God. Just as the miraculous element in this story of Jesus's sonship, its virgin birth element, is just an additional and useful manner, but by no means a necessary method, of emphasizing that it is God's Word/Spirit that is working through all of Jesus's life and death, that God is thus the primordial and principal source of this man's being and life. (Virgin birth stories are often told of founders of distinctive religious traditions; like Plato, for instance, and the Buddha.) Just as the miraculous elements in some healing stories are a useful, if strictly unnecessary manner of highlighting the fact that God is the prime source, through an inscape of divinely originated wisdom and spirit, of Jesus's salvific activity.

It is perhaps worth a short trawl through other titles conferred on Jesus in the Bible, if only in order to see if the meaning conveyed is similar to that conveyed in the metaphorical title *son of God*. By far the most frequent titles conferred upon Jesus belong to that trinity of titles associated with the kings of Israel: *son of God, christ,* and *lord*. Christ, meaning anointed one, if it does anything more than point to a ceremony designed to ordain a person as king, may signify strengthening the elect king with the power or spirit of the Lord God. And since God exercises lordship of the universe precisely by continuously creating and re-creating everything, then Jesus's title of lordship is earned by his doing likewise. As he stresses himself when he insists that he, like those who would follow him, can be lord and master only by serving the life-needs of others.

The other two major titles for Jesus in the Bible, *son of man* and *prophet,* confirm that crucial point. Son of man is used of Jesus and indeed placed on his own lips in the Gospels, and that includes the Gospel of John. Now son of man, found as a self-description on the lips of a human being, is normally used univocally across the range of its primary references, namely, in reference to a human being. Its first and most obvious connotation in such a context, therefore, coincides with the phrase "this man here." It expresses the fact that the speaker is a full and card-carrying member of the human race, no more and no less. Yet the phrase *son of man* could also remind Jesus's hearers of the apocalyptic figure in the Book of Daniel:

> I saw in the night visions,
> And behold, with the clouds of heaven
> There came one like a son of man,
> And he came to the Ancient of Days
> And was presented before him.
> And to him was given dominion
> And glory and kingdom,
> That all peoples, nations and languages
> Should serve him;
> His dominion is an everlasting dominion,
> Which shall not pass away,
> And his kingdom one
> That shall not be destroyed. (Dan. 7:13–14)

But this is simply the vision, cast now in the context of an apocalypse, of the messiah-king, by God's decree and God's power coming through him, bringing to completion in all the world the reign of the Creator of all the world. The use of the title *son of man* at one and the same time indicates the humanity of God's son and promises the final accomplishment of his role in the cosmic history of salvation. Apt on both counts for the description of what Jesus was and was engaged in accomplishing: bringing the reign of God to full fruition.

Finally then — for although there are other titles for Jesus, like good shepherd, high priest, and so on, they add nothing of substance to the present selection — take the case of the title *prophet.* This is the title of a class of divinely chosen and endowed agents to whom God's Word or Spirit comes, and through whom God's Word is both spoken and operative in bringing about the healing and creating of life. The title of prophet is a title with which Jesus in all four Gospels is certainly comfortable, as he applies it to himself without hesitation or qualification. But there are two particular occasions on which he accepts and applies the title to himself. Both are occasions on which he faces what would certainly look to others to be a threatened failure of his mission and his life's work. So both are occasions on which he must himself accept and explain the prospective taking of his life rather as the consummation of his work and mission. That he could accomplish such acceptance and explanation under the title and image of prophet, offers its own implication for the sole sufficiency of that title for all he was and is in God's plan to bring the world to its final *shalom*.

The two occasions on which Jesus himself seems to choose the title of prophet as his primary title of preference are as follows. First, when Jesus brings the reign of God to his home town, and not only is he rejected but they try to kill him (Luke 4:16–30). And the second, when he carries his co-operation in the reign of God to the epicenter of his nation and religion, and sets his face for Jerusalem, where he will be killed: "no prophet is acceptable in his own country"; "O Jerusalem, Jerusalem, killing the prophets and stoning those who are sent to you." John who, characteristically, sees the deeper and more universal implications of such occasions, gathers these two into one, and has Jesus use the saying about the prophet refused honor, on the occasion of Jesus leaving Judea, to get away from "the Jews" who sought to get rid of him (John 4:44).

It has been common in Christianity nevertheless, practically from the very outset and particularly in relationships with Jews and Muslims, to regard the title *prophet* as an inferior title for Jesus. For it was a title that was thought to point quite accurately and successfully to some of the things Jesus did, such as transmitting some words of God to human kind. But of course, on this view of what is meant by prophecy, if it were to be considered to be the only, or even the principal title for Jesus, it would fail miserably to express all that Jesus was and did. In the event there is no need for this placing of stories of Jesus as the incarnation of God's Word/Spirit above stories of Jesus as prophet, and for the consequent downgrading of Jews or Muslims. And none of this need ever have happened if Christians had read their Bible, or if they had paid closer attention to the traditions about Jesus that finally resulted in their Bible, and most particularly to the tradition of Jesus as a prophet of even greater stature than that of Moses himself.

For Moses did more than transmit words of God and knowledge of God's doings and plans, in the form of prophetic speeches. Like other prophets, Moses did his deeds of power, deeds characteristic of the power of the eternal creator and salver of life who worked in and through Moses. Moses fed and watered and healed his people in the desert. Creation imagery is here: God giving and sustaining life, through Moses, in or out of the chaos of the wilderness. The very insight that is captured in the imagery of God's Glory coming upon Moses in the holy mountain, so that Moses's face had to be veiled from the people on his descent (Exod. 35:29–34); or the equivalent imagery in Wisdom 10 of Wisdom entering the soul of Moses, or Philo's language of God's Word or Son becoming *empsychos*, ensouled in Moses, so that he is a *theios aner*, a divine man.

Prophet imagery and incarnation imagery are therefore not different at all in the range or depth of their possible connotation. Something that John, with his characteristically deeper vision of what is actually going on in the case of Jesus, intimates most effectively when, instead of putting the formulaic words indicating the presence of a prophet, "thus says the Lord," on the lips of Jesus, he has God speak directly through Jesus, "before Abraham was, I am." In reality then, in biblical usage, prophetic imagery and incarnation imagery coincide more or less precisely in their extensive range of connotation.

So the other main titles of Jesus all tell the same story as do the stories of incarnation. They tell the story of how he gave life to members of a human race that daily experience its lessening and loss, both self-inflicted and natural. He continued to do this even when it meant that he was a law-breaker, a smasher of the tables of values, especially in the case of those laws that actually forbade on days of religious observance the work of making life whole. These laws were imposed by the self-proclaimed faithful and righteous people who at the same time tried to confine the power and presence of God, and therefore access to *their* God, to *their* temples and to *their* religious observances. And when these good, just and faithful leaders of the true faith came to kill him in the name of their God, he went to his death rather than take life for self-protection, in an act of consummate witness to the power and presence in his very soul and sinew of the One that possessed him. The One who possessed Jesus to the point of being said to be incarnate in him is none other than the eternal source of all existence and life, the One who pours out life without measure and through all of life's set-backs, death included, equally to all — "but he is the Creator." It is God in the mode of the Creator Spirit that is embodied and bodied forth in the life, death and destiny of Jesus of Nazareth.

The Theology of the Incarnate One: Christology

Christology, a reasoned account of the relationship to God of the person of the Christ, together with an ancillary soteriology, a reasoned account of the function of the Christ in God's project of salving or making life whole proved, naturally enough, to be the main concern of Christian theology, right from the start.

Yet, central as it was, Christology proves to have been deeply and consistently flawed down to the present day. And the persistent flaws are in the end all attributable to one basic fault and failure. Theologians ancient and modern failed to realize that the attribution of personhood to various agent-attributes of the divinity were all of them cases of personification of these "agencies in creation," as they were called in earlier chapters. Personification is a strategy used by myth in order to point to a being, or a "beyond-being," that is a personal being, but is so in a manner that exceeds our comprehension. Since our comprehension of personhood is pretty well limited to our own form of personhood. For my idea of a person is of some agent endowed with such faculties as, for example, intelligence (an intellectual principle or mind), and an operative faculty of energizing desire or will. So the myth's way of pointing to some beyond-being that is most likely personal, albeit in some manner and degree incomprehensible to us, is to talk of Intellectual Principle (Logos/Word, Wisdom, Mind, Soul, Spirit) as if they were persons through whom this incomprehensible One creates the world, as we create our world through our intellects and wills and to our very limited creative abilities. As the notes to Proverbs 8 in the RSV Bible puts it, Wisdom/Sophia is "but an aspect or activity of God metaphorically endowed with speech," that is to say, metaphorically personified.

Failure to recognize the metaphorical nature of such discourse leaves one open to thinking that the divine Word, for instance, really is being described as a person in some sense univocal with human personhood. And then *the* problem in Christology turns out to be the problem of having two persons, one divine and one human, incarnated and jostling for *lebensraum* within the restricted confines of the skin of Jesus of Nazareth. The history of Christology can then be seen as in a way what it is: a series of efforts, first to get rid of one of these "persons" in Jesus. Then, when that was decreed heretical, being driven to diminish one "person," the human one, by having the other, the divine one, take over its characteristic aspects and abilities. Then, when that was seen as just a surreptitious ruse for getting rid of one of the "persons" once again, returning to the unwanted opening impression of having two "persons," as that term is normally understood. And finally trying to escape from the first predicament by defining the term *person* in such an abstruse fashion as to persuade those who are capable of such extreme abstrusity, that there really were not two "persons" in that utterly abstruse sense, in Jesus after all. Leaving the rest, who have never been instructed in that abstruse meaning of personhood or are incapable of mastering it, to use the normal meaning of the term, and to endure still as best they can the opening predicament. Or else, as these ordinary people usually do, to revert to previously declared heretical positions, and to picture Jesus as if he were a divine person, and therefore was not, or was not fully, a human person at all.

So the earliest Adoptionists, as they were called, insisted that Jesus was a fully, thoroughly human being, adopted as such by God for certain revelatory and salvific purposes. At the opposite pole from this, Ebionites argued that the human body of Jesus was nothing much more than a phantom body, such as one in which a ghost might materialize for purposes of appearing and communicating with us. At both of these extremes there was no real room at all for an image or idea of the incarnation of a personal God in a human person. A much less extreme theology under the name of Apollinarius gained much more currency, in both its original form and in subsequent formulations. Indeed, there are some who see in this area of theology for many, many centuries afterward, signs of an increasingly sophisticated and refined Apollinarianism. Apollinarius's solution to the prevalent difficulties was simply to accept that the human soul of Jesus, or at least its most personal parts and functions at the rational, self-determining center of the human spirit, had to be replaced by the divine Word. A divine person was present in Jesus, but no human person. Apollinarius's Christology was challenged almost from its inception. On the basis of a principle derived from conjoined areas of soteriology, namely, that what is not assumed is not saved. That is to say, if any part of humanity is not "assumed" into the Word in the process of that Word becoming flesh, then it cannot be counted within the range of humanity that the Word enfleshed succeeded in saving. This principle then required that the human being, Jesus, share in the full and unqualified humanity which all humans share. And that included personhood in particular.

And yet, despite the robust assuredness of Apollinarius's orthodox attackers, it has to be said that forms or elements of the Apollinarian solution not only returned during succeeding centuries to challenge the self-styled orthodox, but one of these in a highly esoteric form has survived in orthodox Christologies itself to the present day. Take some examples of return games between orthodox and Apollinarians. Well into the sixth century of the Christian era theologians emerged to suggest that Jesus did not have a human will, in addition to his divine will — a view of the matter that could not have made much sense of Jesus's own much proclaimed obedience to the will of the Father. Or that he did not have a determinate center of human action, an *energeia*. Both formulae were declared heterodox during the third General Council of Constantinople of 680 C.E., and denounced with as much force as met the first Apollinarian formula. Jesus the Christ, the Council declared, had two wills, one human and one divine, and similarly two principles of action. Nobody seemed to realize that someone overhearing these learned debates, and without knowing the context, would naturally conclude that what was being discussed was some kind of freak-show: the man with no soul of his own, no will of his own; the man with two wills. . . .

The highly esoteric form of Apollinarianism that, it can be quite reasonably claimed, survived to the present day, began to emerge just as the term *nature,* or *physis,* took center stage in the theological account of the man, Jesus, in whom the Word of God took flesh. Nature, *physis,* names a dynamic form of reality, a form of reality that has within itself the source of its own movement of change, growth, development, decline. To refer to the nature of something, therefore, is to draw attention to the characteristic fashion in which it functions. And what is characteristic of the functioning of human nature is its rationality, or at least the level of its rationality. Human nature is comprised of a body and a behavior formed by a rational soul, a rational will, a rational determinative principle of creative (free) behavior. Just these elements of its form that make this nature in and of itself a person, and just these features of human nature that Apollinarius denied existed in human form in the man, Jesus of Nazareth. So now it is easy to see how, once the term *nature* took center stage in Christology, the difficulty of conceiving of the Word being enfleshed in Jesus without diminishing his humanity, became well-nigh insurmountable.

For by now the term *person* was established, particularly in the Western church, as the term to describe the Word: the second person of the

Trinity. Clearly then, when the Word was enfleshed in Mary's womb at the conception of Jesus, two persons were united. One a human person born of Mary, the other a divine person eternally generated by God. That was what Nestorius and his followers were taken to imply. And that was declared heretical, for Mary could not then be called *theotokos*, God-bearer, as the Council of Ephesus of 431 C.E. had insisted. She would have to be called mother only of the human person, Jesus (even Mariology in these early centuries is mostly extended Christology). And yet all previous Apollinarian-type suggestions, which might seem to have avoided the conclusions about two different persons united in some inexplicable manner, had hitherto been rejected also. So there seemed to be no answer to the question: if a divine and a human nature is to be described as being united in one person or *hypostasis*, as the Council of Chalcedon in 451 C.E. insisted against Nestorius, then how could anyone still say that Jesus was fully a human person, and not just a divine person with some elements of human nature tagged on, an unfeathered biped?

The mess was cleared up — if it ever really was cleared up — and the difficulty of talking about the Word enfleshed in the human Jesus but without diminishing his humanity was resolved — if it ever really was resolved — by a Mad-Hatter-like decision that the masters in any dispute use words to mean what *they* want them to mean, irrespective of what the same words mean in all ordinary human discourse. So, to make a long, incredibly complex, unbelievably intricate and excruciatingly boring story as short as any surviving remnant of fairness to these ancient protagonists could require: a definition of person produced by that Christian philosopher-theologian already encountered above, Boethius, was finally fixed upon, "the individual substance of a rational nature." "Substance" was then taken in the meaning of "subsistence," for to subsist is to exist with the continuity of a substantial rather than an accidental entity. Then, instead of seeing in the character of the rational features of the nature concerned — its reason, its rational will, and so on — the distinctive characteristics that define a nature as a person, as Apollinarius and everybody else before and since has done, these theologians fastened upon the nature's individual subsistence, its subsistence over against or in relation to other equally subsistent natures, and took this to be the defining characteristic of a person, a personal nature. They could then say that the Word, the second person of the Trinity, that is to say, the second subsistence or subsistent relation in the divine nature, on becoming enfleshed in the human nature of Jesus of Nazareth, provided the subsistence of that human nature. So that the human nature of Jesus does not exist by its own subsistence, and in these abstruse terms, did not have its own personal dimension. In other words, on this Mad Hatter definition of person, as an individual subsistence, the rational nature of Jesus existed by, or subsisted in the Second Person of the Trinity, and so did not constitute a human person in addition to that divine person. Further, and once again on this restricted definition of that in which the personal character of a nature consisted, it would be possible to say that the enfleshing of the Word in Jesus obviated the two-person view of Jesus that was not quite accurately attributed to Nestorius — for he operated with somewhat different definitions of nature and person — but that it yet left the human nature of Jesus full and undiminished, replete with its own soul, reason, rational will and so on, the very features of its nature that are most commonly and always taken to constitute a human person.

This Christology, so elaborated in terms of nature and person and these esoteric definitions, it could then be claimed, was fully in the line of meaning of the terms of the Council of Chalcedon of 451 C.E.: "One and the same Christ, Son, Lord, only-begotten (was) made known in two natures without confusion, without change, without division, without separation; the differences of the natures having been in no way taken away by reason of their union, but rather the properties of each nature being preserved, and both concurring in one person (*prosopon*) and one *hypostasis*."

So there it is then. Two natures, one human and one divine, each replete in itself and unchanged by virtue of the union with the other, united by the subsistence of the divine nature extended to the human nature, which has no subsistence of its own. And since the connotation of the word *person* consists in the concept of subsistence and not, as every ordinary person using language assumes, in features of the nature such as mind, reason, will, rational determinative center of free, creative, moral behavior, Jesus has (is) a divine person and not a human person. Now this odd, if not perverse Mad-Hatter-like approach to the meaning of one of the commonest words in any language had inevitably the following result: Unless the preacher, discoursing about the Second Person of the Trinity, or the about the divinity of Jesus, prepared the way by a lesson in the abstract metaphysics of subsistence, the hearers would simply assume that the Second Person of the Trinity was the only person to be encountered in Jesus. They would take it without further ado that Jesus did not have a human and so a fallible mind and will. Which is why most Christians to this day are happy, if unwitting Apollinarians.

The only real and lasting solution to this persistent theological confusion is to take the term *person* out of the Christian theology of incarnation altogether. And to put it back into the mythic account of creation, and then of incarnation, where it rightly belongs. For there it functions in a metaphorical sense for that of God — God's Word/Wisdom/Spirit — that is incarnate in Jesus, as it is in other creaturely agencies in creation. And since the term functions in the myth in a metaphorical sense, and not at all in a sense univocal with human personhood, it causes no problem whatever for the perception to which history bears witness. Namely, the perception of Jesus of Nazareth as fully and entirely a human person, of the common or garden type variety encountered in the whole of human kind. Except, as Paul once put it, that he had no truck with the original sinfulness of that same human nature and race. For he was entirely indwelt and possessed by that same Word/Wisdom/Spirit of God the Creator.

The Christian Myth of Trinity

The Christian myth of a triune divinity came about through certain refinements and developments of the Christian myth of incarnation. Just as one might expect of people who accepted as fact that all they truly knew about God, and indeed all that any creature could possibly know about God, came to them through the teachings of Jesus of Nazareth. As these teachings were lived out, clearly, comprehensively and convincingly in all the living and dying of a man who proved to hold such power over people well beyond his death. The imagery is the same in both myths, and its source is the same. It is the imagery of Creator/Wisdom/Word/Spirit, fitted out further with the imagery involved in personification: the image of a Father, a natural image for the source-provider of all for all, begetting a Son/Word or Daughter/Wisdom, and breathing forth a Spirit. And the source of that imagery, as always, is our experience of acting as fallible, indeed utterly unreliable co-creators in the processes and results of divine creation.

There are just two things that need to be noticed, however, in addition to what has already been said both in the chapter on creation, and in the discussion of incarnation. The first, odd as it might seem, is this: the processes of either imagination or abstract thought involved in giving the kind of account of the being of God that is here in Trinitarian form, could equally manage the matter at hand if it resulted in a Binity, or a Quaternity, or a Polyentity. It is quite easy to illustrate this feature of the matter from the biblical material as a whole. For of course one can take Word as Intellectual Principle, and personify it as Son; take Spirit as Operative Principle (will as love, enabler, enlivener) and personify it as, well, Spirit; and take Creator, and personify that as Father, because he is provider of existence and life, and of all the supports and enhancements of life for all. As he is also source of Word and Spirit, and it is through these as "agents" or agencies that he is source of all creation: and that yields trinity. But one could just as well take Wisdom to imagine and connote practical knowledge personified, an attribute that includes both reason- and spirit-attributes, as summed up in the term *philo-sophia* (love-wisdom, through which Eriugena said we reached heaven). And then say simply that the Father-Creator creates through this one: and that yields binity. It was this binitarian structure that dominated Christian myth and theology for the first three centuries, despite the occasional presence of Trinitarian formulae, such as Matthew's baptismal formula, in the name of the Father, the Son and the Holy Spirit. Or one could go beyond this duo or trio and add the image of the Shekinah personified, in a further attempt to imagine the bodying forth of the power and presence of the unnameable One: and that would yield quaternity. And the upshot of such observations is this: where one finds a predilection for Trinitarian forms of myth or theology, one may have to find reasons for the predilection, other than the claim that none of these other forms could do the job.

The second thing that one needs to notice comes into view when one focuses on the fact that it is our experience of the Creator as known from the creation that yields myths of trinities, as well as of other pluriformities. And then one focuses further on the fact that these binities, trinities, quaternities...emerge by means of a process of the personification of divine attributes or activities imagined as agents in creation. And then what emerges, rather bluntly put, is this: polytheistic myths, as we so often call them when we meet them in other religions, need be no more antithetical to monotheism than is the Christian myth of the Trinity. And the same would be true, if they had theologies attached, to the theologies attached to such polytheistic myths in other religions. Now that might seem to be a complicated statement and one, moreover, that would be quite unwelcome, certainly to Christians. But it is, happily enough, quite easily illustrated.

In the history of Christianity itself there is a well advertised instance of a different form of personification than the one we have just seen, but which just as successfully arrives at the Trinitarian formula that Christians consider orthodox, the formula that sums up the Christian myth of trinity in the expression, "three divine persons in one divine substance or nature." In this instance, the ongoing process of creation is divided into phases, and the production of these successive phases is then "personified" as the work of, consecutively, Father, Son and Spirit. Like this: the Father creates, that is to say, gives ultimate origin to everything that is; the Son saves, that is to say, creatively reverses all the adversarial elements in creation, whether natural or malicious; and the Spirit sanctifies, that is to say, brings the whole process to its consummation in the holy power and presence of God all-in-all.

A fine example of arriving at a Trinitarian myth by focusing on phases of the ongoing processes of creation, and personifying the divinity accordingly, is found in fact in the pre-Christian Irish religion mentioned already in the chapter on creation. Like many another so-called primal religion, and for the very good reason that it is true, the pre-Christian Irish religion regarded the process of divine creation as a continuous process. And it expressed this insight by having four seasonal creation festivals, each one dedicated to a phase of creation, and all making up the round of each year, and year after year, after year. . . . The first festival, *Samhain*, is celebrated in early November, and its imagery is set in stone at the great passage tomb at Newgrange where on the morning of the winter solstice a ray of the rising sun penetrates the long dark passage and lights up its innermost chamber (like the Genesis myth of the first creation, light, pushing back the darkness). *Samhain,* then, celebrates the ultimate origin of the existing and living world in the darkness and chaos, and attributes this to all the gods, that is to say to the one divinity within or behind the personae of named gods. The next seasonal festival is *Imbolc* at the beginning of February, celebrating in the name of the creator goddess, Brigid, the first shoots of life emerging from the dead, dark earth. Brigid, whose attributes include both all-wisdom and healing. The third is *Beltine*, at the beginning of May, celebrating the waxing of the sun with the imagery of fire, the creator spirit that works to bring all life to its final fruitfulness (possibly personified in a god called Bel, though that is not certain). And finally, there is the festival of *Lugnasa*, early in August, celebrating the final ripening and fullness, all the supports and enhancements of life that promise life and life ever more abundant, even through the hard times ahead. The god personified in this feast is *Lug*, a Jahweh-like divinity, who saves his people from all adversarial forces, and now presides over their lives in a land of milk and honey.

It is easy to see there a trinity of personifications of divine being as creator, corresponding to the phases of the continuous creation itself. (Every Irish schoolchild hears the story of Saint Patrick, who is wrongly accredited with bringing Christianity to all of Ireland, having to resort to a three-leaved shamrock in order to acquaint the Irish with the image of a triune God. When in actual fact Irish religion at the time, as is the case with most religions of the world, had more divine trinities than you could shake a stick at. There were, for example, three Goddess-Brigids-in-One.) It is easy to see, further, the similarities between this kind of myth-making and the kinds of myth-making found both in the biblical sources that are recognized by Jews, Christians and Muslims, and in further developments of these in these religions, and also in other religions, both primal and "world" religions. So that it should be very difficult indeed for the adherents to any of these religions — and particularly for Christians, if they understood their own myth-making for what it is — to see polytheism as a position essentially opposed to monotheism. And then to mount an automatic attack on any other religion as an abomination, as the Bible would put it, before the face of the one, true God. For, particularly in the case of Christians and Jews, it must be obvious that there is nothing whatever in what Christians call the New Testament that goes into the making of their version of the divine Trinity, that is not also available in what they then call the Old Testament. It behooves the devotees of each religion to come to an understanding of the processes of personification that are used in most, if not all religions as a strategy for seeing the one true divinity as a personal being, but personal in a manner quite incomprehensible to finite minds. And, in addition, to notice also the variety of strategies usually in use in religions, strategies designed to prevent the idea that there really is a plurality of divinities. Such as the strategy of personifying a particular attribute, like Wisdom, as one named divinity, say, Brigid, patroness of poets, the transmitters of divine Wisdom to humankind. Then calling Lug *samildanach*, that is to say, the master of all practical knowledge, all the creative arts and crafts, the all-wise. It behooves all, finally, to stop talking of abominations in other religions, at least before looking more thoroughly at what is and has been going on in one's own.

In the event, one might well look one more time at this scenario of the One God known and worshiped through its persona as creator, and then through its further personae dramatis as active sources of the various parts or specialities into which the process of creating a world may

be broken down. Only to wonder, this time, if it is not a positive appreciation of such a scenario that Paul has in mind when he arrived at the
Areopagus in Athens to present and, as it happened, to defend the faith
of Jesus. For the scene, as painted in the Acts of the Apostles 17:6–34,
sees his audience first understanding him to be preaching under the name
of Jesus a very localized and, worse, a foreign god. Worse still, this god
that Paul preached seemed to have the attribute, as they would see it, of
reviving dead people in something like their current bodily form. (This
idea of resurrection went very much against the more popular Platonism
of the time. And even if there were Stoics or Epicureans in the audience,
they would still not be aware, presumably, of Paul's Corinthian correspondence, and would therefore be unaware that he said that no one would be
raised in a physical body, but in a spiritual one (1 Cor. 15:44), a distinction that the Stoics in the audience would certainly want to hear about, as
the Areopagus story says some wanted to hear him again.) Paul's response
to the difficulties of his Athenian audience is to praise them for being
very religious people. On the grounds that they had erected in their city
statues to named and personified divine powers involved in and with the
world, with its everyday making, salving, protecting, and so forth. And
in addition, they had erected a statue to the unknown God. So from this
well chosen point of an argumentative engagement foisted upon him in
these terms, Paul says that the God he preaches in the name of Jesus, is
no local divinity, but rather "the God who made the world and everything in it," as their own poets had put it, "in whom we live and move
and have our being." In short, he was suggesting in this elegant fashion
that the unknown God to whom the statue was erected was none other
than the One God who appeared to all in the persona of the Creator of
all, and who appeared especially in the Jesus Paul preached. A God who
remains ultimately unknown and incomprehensible behind the attributes
and personifications by which all people seek to find God and to entrust
their lives to that ultimate Source and Destiny.

The Christian experience of God as Trinity then, uncovered and communicated in the form of myth, finds its formulation in the following
manner. Attributes of God, such as God's wisdom, intelligence and life-
giving power, or activities or phases of divine activity, such as forming
by means of dynamic and intelligible formulae, or stirring the "seeds" of
things, or waxing their growth, or bringing them to full fruition, any or all
of these, are personified. That is to say, the image of a person is applied to
them, but metaphorically (as in "metaphorically endowed with speech,"

in the RSV Bible note on Proverbs 8). And these metaphors then work as metaphor always does: in the tension engendered by attaching the image of a person to divine attributes or activities that are not in themselves, in our experience, persons (though intellect and will and their attributes and activities are defining characteristics of human persons), there is opened up an extension of meaning by which we can faintly envisage the One that is source of all, while infinitely beyond the human capacity to comprehend, as One that is at the summit of the range of the personal, rather than outside or beneath that range. Just as the lion lies somewhere on the range of ruling entities, a range that also includes kings. With this difference that, in the latter case, the human mind and imagination can calculate the similarities and the differences that obtain between the "rule" of lions and of kings. In the former case, such calculation exceeds our mental powers, and only the evidence of some ultimate Agent-Source that operates through intelligible forms (called evolving natures) can assure us that the range of the personal extends to that One also.

The Christian Theology of Trinity

Come now to the Christian experience of God as Trinity, uncovered and communicated now in the form of theology rather than myth; expressed, that is to say, by means of abstract concepts, such as *hypostasis* or subsistence, and their logical connections. Something of a consensus seems to have been reached by historians of theology, to the effect that the Trinitarian formula proposed by the theologians of the still Greek-speaking Eastern Church, and in particular by the so-called Cappadocian Fathers, Basil of Caesarea and the two Gregory's, Nazianzen and of Nyssa, represents the highest and best achievement of the long and tortuous theologizing of the Trinity in those early ages. This formula, borrowed from the first Neo-Platonists, selected as its key terms, first, *ousia*, which can be translated as either "substance," or "being," and for which the term *physis* or nature was sometimes substituted, and, second, the term *hypostasis*, the meaning of which is much more difficult to pin down, if only because any good lexicon is likely to give it meanings that range from an equivalent of the Latin *substantia*, substance, literally a standing under, to an overnight camping site. For the moment let the suggestion stand that the best single word with which to translate *hypostasis* is *subsistence*; and this not least because, as it happens an overnight camping site can have something to do with the subsistence of someone on a journey, a journey to the North Pole, for instance, or to the summit of Everest. For by an odd coincidence, the image of a journey, an outward and return journey, is among the oldest images for divine creation as a journey of all created things, and particularly of humankind, emanating outward from God as a result of God's creative agency, and the return journey that seeks a blessed union with God for eternity. This journey image is the beating heart at the center of all Greek theology, both pre-Christian and Christianized, to the point at which its influence on all the other imagery already in evidence above would be difficult to exaggerate.

In the theology of the by-now Latin-speaking Western empire, the corresponding terms of their theological Trinitarian formula were for the One *substantia* or substance, for which *natura*, nature, or even *essentia*, essence, were sometimes substituted. And then for each of the Three the term *persona* or person, the very term that has just been seen to have been at the center, if not the source of virtually all of the problems that occurred in an emerging Christology. That fact in itself might have been expected to alert theologians of the Trinity to the suggestion that they could perhaps do worse than drop that troublesome term altogether as they moved deeper into the being of God. Barth in his magisterial *Church Dogmatics* did decide that the term should be dropped, and that theologians should confine themselves to talking about three "ways of being," or "modes of subsistence," *Seinsweise*, of the One God. But nobody made that suggestion in the Western church of the patristic era, not even the great Augustine who, in his magisterial work, *De Trinitate*, gave as the last-stand reason for retaining the term *person* for the Three, the claim that it seemed to be the best of a bad lot. That is to say, it was bad indeed, and a member of a bad lot, but it was the best of these.

But enough has been said already in the chapter on creation of the damage that was done to the Christian theology of the Trinity by the use of the term *person*, imported as it was from the Christian theology of incarnation. A degree of damage that culminated in recent times in the utterly uncritical adoption of Moltmann's so-called social model of the Trinity by virtually every Christian theologian who wrote on the Trinity. And yet some puzzlement might arise for the reader at this point. The term *subsistence* taken as the meaning of the term *hypostasis* is now, as we deal with Trinitarian theology, about to be put forward in order to save us from the much advertised problems that occur with the use of the term *person*. Yet in the theology of incarnation, of which the theology of Trinity is said to be an extension and development, the use of that same term *subsistence* for the term *person* was said to aggravate rather than solve the self-same problems. The resolution of this puzzle lies in recognizing the different deployments of the term *subsistence* in its relationship with the term *person*.

In the case of incarnation theology the term *subsistence* was derived from Boethius's definition of person, and thereafter used as itself a definition of personhood while dropping from view the other elements of Boethius's definition, elements of a rational nature, the ones that define person for all ordinary usage of that term. Whereas in the case of the theology of Trinity the term *subsistence* or *hypostasis* is used in place of the term *person* and is therefore a means of avoiding the latter term altogether. This is not to deny the fact that Greek speaking Christian theologians used both terms, *hypostasis* and *prosopon* (Latin, *persona*) in formulating their incarnational and Trinitarian theologies; or that Augustine, when using the term *persona* acknowledged with some caution what he thought to be the Greek equivalent in the term *hypostasis*. But that kind of thing comes from the natural desire of the two parties to be seen to be saying the same thing in their theologies. It did nothing to obliterate the distinction between the damage that could be done by the term *person* when used indiscriminately in both the theology and the myth of trinity, and the good that could be done by the other term *hypostasis* if used in the theology of trinity so as to replace the term *person*.

There remains then only to give the briefest account possible of this Greek Trinitarian formula: one divine being and a threefold subsistence. The One; no further names, nouns or adjectives can be used in order to say what this One is in and of itself. For it is not a form or a collage of forms, no matter how many or how majestic. It is instead, and from this perspective, the no-thing, without the limits (*fines*) of form. It is infinite and so, nameless. The one way in which it can be positively described is as the fullness of being, but that phrase is not properly comprehensible to a finite mind. Although one may touch the outer hem of its garment if one meditatively makes one's way to the outer (or inner) limits of the perennially transcendent feature of one's own consciousness, as Buddhists do in meditation. At this point, the naming or, rather, not naming of the One, there is as yet no question of a *hypostasis*.

Then (and in this word as in the previous "as yet" there is no implication of a time-sequence, only what might be called a matter of metaphysical priority), the One moves into a creative mode of being, It gives origin to forms, to formed, finite entities, things, that are themselves dynamic.

Endowed with the *dynameis*, the creative powers, the energy, the force to evolve as ever transformed, mutually transforming things. Operating always according to a pattern or a series of inter-related patterns that result in an evolving universe. This universe passes through the temporal stages of prelife preparatory for life, and through all stages of life toward infinite prospects, as it would appear. This creative mode of being into which the One moves can be further specified by imagining it as having the dual character of an intelligent, rational, mind-like mode of being, for the resulting creatures have intelligible dynamic forms that transform in intelligible ways. Simultaneously this creative mode of being is imagined as having the character of an energizing, enlivening mode of being, empowering forms to be, to live, to transform. And all three modes of being are interconnected therefore in the most intimate manner. The mode of being of Creator entails simultaneously the mode of being of empowering a form to live (the mode of being of power or spirit), and the mode of being of mentally visualizing that same dynamic form of a species of thing or of the broader pattern by which things transform (into) a universe (the mode of being of mind or intellectual principle). Just as this whole creative process, together with the mode of being of the One as Creator, is mentally perceptible to intelligent creatures in and through the very process by which they themselves engage with all other creative forms and patterns. The very process in which they exercise to a unique degree their power, privilege, and responsibility to be co-creators, transforming and being transformed and knowing themselves thereby to be created in the image of the Source-Creator.

Needless to say, these modes of being are real modes of being of the One. They are as real as the creation that takes its ultimate origin from the One, and finds its ultimate goal in its most intimate relationship with the One in whom, as Paul puts it, we live and move and have our being. In fact, the One who exists in these modes of being is infinitely more real than the creation, for it is the One existing in these modes of being that keeps for the creation the difference between it and nothingness. Forms that transform are essentially transient, passing in and out of their own nothingness. These transient forms forever advertise the unreality that is their lot, if left without the ever-active power and intelligence of the creative Spirit, the creator Word. Hence the meaning of *hypostaseis*, hypostases, as the name for the Three. Taking the term *subsistence* as the best English word by which to translate *hypostasis*, it makes sense to make a sentence to the effect that the indefinable divinity takes on the mode of being of Reason, Intellectual Principle, *Logos*, in the course of designing a co-creative creation. And then to copy the truth of that sentence in another sentence: the indefinable divinity grounds, stands under, upholds and thereby subsists in the form(s) of the operative and intelligible design of a dynamic universe. Or, to copy that first sentence in yet another sentence: this operative intelligible principle, this *Logos*, subsists by or in the essentially indefinable divinity. The immanence imagery, as it has been noted already with respect to biblical usage, is a double-adaptor: God subsisting in us creatures, we creatures subsisting in God. The same sentence-substitution process will yield a second *hypostasis,* a second subsistence in or of the divine: indefinable divinity subsists in the enlivening, empowering force named spirit.

But that, the anxious believer in the Christian Trinity might already urge at this point, yields but two hypostases, not three. And that is true, and one can see both from the variety of Trinitarian formulations and indeed from the presence of binities in the course of these early centuries of tortuous and mostly ill-tempered debate in both the Christian and the Neo-Platonist camps, and between these, that this issue was already at least implicitly present in those early days. The simplest means of resolving the issue would seem to be to include the One as the third hypostasis. But there were and are problems about that. The One named God is the Incomprehensible, not ever to be thought to be comprehended in any set or number of creaturely ideas or images. True, the subsistences of the One in or as the enlivening and designing features of the act of creation allowed a certain analogical knowledge of God as Word and Spirit. But then to suggest that the One, as the One, is in addition a subsistence, a hypostasis in the very being of the universe, since our idea of being is used univocally of all that exists, would almost certainly tempt us to think that we know God as a being. That we then apply the term *a being* to God and apply it univocally in the selfsame sense as all other beings are, each one, a being beside and in addition to others. And since we can then think of God purely and simply as "a being," albeit a pure infinite, formless, limitless being, we really can give ourselves the impression that we can really comprehend God by means of one common concept after all. This is the kind of mistake that is only too easily made, for example, by all those people who have busied themselves down the ages with proving God's existence.

Some Neo-Platonists at this point of history, remembering perhaps Plato's description of the divinity, under the cipher of "the Good," as *epekeina tes ousias*, beyond being, reserved the name *One* for divinity in itself. As it was, "as yet," without reference to its hypostasis as Creator of all finite beings, and without reference to the twin attributes of a Creator, intelligence and will. Some Christian theologians followed in this direction also; most notably John Scotus Eriugena, believing that in this he was following Gregory of Nyssa, the member of the Cappadocian Fathers, incidentally, who was the most accomplished in Greek philosophy. Eriugena said that the One God subsisted in three real modes of being, that of Father (in mythic terms) or Source-Creator, that of Word or Son (in mythic terms), and that of Spirit(in mythic terms) or life-giving force; so that something of God could be known by certain creatures, by analogy from these three hypostases of the divinity, while it still remained true that the inner being of God's self remained incomprehensible to all creatures.

Now this Greek formula for a Triune God, one divine *ousia* (or better, hyperousia) in three hypostases, borrowed by Christian theologians from New-Platonists, is without doubt the most successful, and perhaps indeed the only successful form of Trinitarian theology ever issued. And it is so, paradoxically as it might seem, precisely because a theology centered upon the idea of hypostasis, in-subsisting and subsisting-in, could be made to work if these were said to amount to only two divine hypostases, or only one. (The issue of the number of divine hypostases here is similar to the same issue with respect to the number of personifications in the mythic form of the matter.) Consider this: the addition of the hypostasis of Word would not be necessary if the Spirit were considered to be an intelligent Spirit, a Spirit of Wisdom; which is presumably why in the Bible, it is the Spirit that is mostly said to be enfleshed, indwelling in the human life, death and destiny of Jesus, and only twice is the term *Word* used for that which is said to be operative in Jesus. Further, neither *Word* nor *Spirit* need be added once one understands that subsistence in or of an active Creator in continuous creation as we know it in our daily life and world entails automatically the attributes of intelligence and enlivening power.

All of which means that, just as in the case of the myth of Trinity, there is in this metaphysical schema no problem of reconciling unity with multiplicity in the divinity, a problem that certainly arises whenever talk about three persons in God forms part of that same metaphysical schema. For then we meet that mixture of myth and metaphysics that always causes confusion, at best. In fact worse than confusion results when the mix is so thorough as to be undetectable, when the myth's image of a person is redefined by the note of individual subsistence over against other individual subsistences. For with the latter terminology there is the additional intractable problem of explaining how only the Second "Person" can be said to be enfleshed in Jesus, when the "persons" are each and all inseparable from the divine substance, and the divine substance must be enfleshed together with the "Second Person." It is interesting to note how the Irish profession of hereditary poets, repositories of all wisdom due to the heavenly fire that gave them access to divine wisdom, when they embraced Christianity, talked regularly about the Christian Trinity in ways that brought severe censure from the orthodox Christian clergy. "God is Three and Two"; "Thou art One, and Two, and Three," said one of them rather peremptorily. "The death of the Father, Lord and Judge of the world, caused his children's salvation," declared another, although he sees no problem in saying later, "man's salvation came from the death of the Son of the King of Kings," and "the wounding of the Three in the person of One ended the trouble of Adam's race." And a third, praying to Mary in particular: "O Trinity, O gentle Mary, every glory but yours is passing; listen to my poem, O four Persons: your Son and your Husband were together on your knee." Although he adds, a propos of her Husband (the Holy Spirit), "the Lord made Mary's son without lying with you." The "Four Persons," a phrase that includes Mary in the very company of the original Three, one might admit, is more than somewhat suspect. Although on the other hand it makes little sense to deny some attribution of divine status to Mary, who is solemnly defined by the church as *theotokos*, God-bearer, an even more suggestive title than that of Mother of God, which might refer only to foster-motherhood.

But to condemn the rest of what these by now Christian poets have to say concerning unity, binity, trinity and even quaternity, is surely a case of true seers being attacked by the terminally confused. For even in the case of the apparent divinization of Mary, some justification can be offered, other than the reference to the title *God-bearer* and its implications. There is no doubt about the fact that to speak of Mary in such a way enabled people, and still enables people to this day to overcome those crude and harmful patriarchal impressions of God as utterly male. Especially people who are unfamiliar with the image of *Sophia*/ Wisdom as being of the feminine gender. Indeed as one can see from their prayer-lives, very many Irish people today follow their traditional poets in this at least, that their operative Trinity consists of the Father, the Mother Mary and the Son,

Jesus. One of the commoner prayers still in circulation fascinatingly co-opts the Holy Spirit under the name of the original addressee, Mary. And one recent Latin American theologian, conscious no doubt of the fact that Mary in the Christian faith of the indigenous people occupies the place of the Pachamama, the Great Mother Goddess (is it purely accidental that it was at Ephesus, a stone's throw from the shrine of the Great Mother Goddess, Diana, that the *theotokos* was declared defined dogma?) has argued that Luke's tale of the Holy Spirit coming upon Mary so that Jesus should be son of God, is as much an incarnation of God in Mary, as the Word coming into the flesh of Jesus is an incarnation of God in him. So that the resulting talk of a divine woman need have no more heterodox implications than the corresponding talk of a divine man

This understanding and these implications of a doctrine constructed from ideas of divine being (or beyond-being) and hypostases, can then be outlined positively as follows: God as Creator is the very subsistence, the ground underpinning the resulting creation, as the creation can then be said to subsist in God, a bi-focal subsistence or hypostasis. God in the hypostasis of creator can therefore be known, at the very least known to be, in and through the creation itself. And since this creation is continuously created and itself co-creative, it is characterized as much by continual nothinging as it is by continual evolving into being. And therefore the kind of knowledge of God the Creator which some creatures can have through such a creation, is characterized by a mixture of trust and hope, eros and faith, and not by anything approaching apodictic certainty. But that trust and hope, eros and faith, is strengthened by every experience of transformation that takes one through the deformations of accompanying nothinging, just as it is weakened by every death-dealing self-serving strategy that in effect reroutes it toward the human subject itself as its origin and goal.

Then this process of divine creation in which we humans participate as co-creators can be broken down into the twin processes of intelligent design and enlivening power; twin processes that we can see are ever operative in the created and creative universe, bringing the world to ever higher levels of complexity at the same time as they bring the world to life ever more abundant. So that it makes good sense to conceive of God the Creator as being the subsistence of these processes in particular, and of these particular processes subsisting in God. If only because it enables us to say that God is something like the intelligent beings and the life-giving beings we know. And although that may add little to our knowledge of

God, since God is no doubt infinitely superior to the intelligent, living and life-giving creatures we directly experience in the world, it still does mean that we can say more about God than that God is creator or ground of being. At the very least the addition of the hypostases, the subsistences of Intellectual Principle (in myth, a son) and of Soul or Life-Former (in myth, a spirit or breath of life) to that of Creator (in myth, a father), directs us to an access to experience of the divine that exists in the inner-most reaches of our own consciousness, in addition to the access we have in contemplation of the whole living and evolving universe.

The doctrine of the Trinity then in its essence and its varying forms is a conceptualizing, a theology, and a myth of God as Creator, built up from our experience-from-within of the continuous process of the divine cre-ation of our universe. The formula "one divine being in three hypostases" simply sums up a living monotheistic faith and trust in a divinity that subsists in the continuous creation itself, with its twin characteristic and constitutive features of intelligent design and life-giving force. But what then of the other dictionary meaning of *hypostasis* as an overnight camping site? Before dismissing this as a slightly bizarre example of that polysemeia of words which makes language the flexible and inventive means of inves-tigation and expression that it is, it is worth considering if this meaning also cannot contribute something valuable to the present question. The relationship of an overnight camping site to subsistence on a great and hazardous journey, together with the master image of the existence and life of creation itself as a journey from God and back to God again, has already been mentioned, and it is along these lines that that otherwise weird-looking meaning of the term *hypostasis* is relevant here.

The Three Overnight Camping Sites on the "Mystical" Way

The clearest light that can be cast upon the triune being of the Creator by means of this further meaning of the (loci of) divine subsistences as overnight camping sites, is seen in the writings of the so-called mystics, or in the so-called mystical passages of the writings of other theologians such as the Pseudo-Denys or Plotinus. But this light from such sources will shine on this subject only for the one who realizes that, contrary to the prevailing modern understanding, both common and scholarly, mystics are not mystics, nor do they describe what they describe, as a result of some especially vouchsafed experience that is generally unavailable to the majority of human kind. Quite to the contrary, just as the theologians just mentioned, and many others just like them, describe the three (loci of) divine subsistences that mark the journey of creation out from God — the One subsisting first as Creator-source; then as Mind or Reason-like fashioner; then as Soul or Spirit-like enlivening, energizing force — so the journey back by persons like our ordinary selves to union with the One, is pictured by them as our passing through the same sites or loci at which we are guided by Mind and strengthened by Spirit, and so propelled by the great Creative-process ever surging in and all around us, sending us on our way back into the formless fullness of Beyond Being, and the still center of the awesome storm of creation, from which we came.

In short, these theologians are describing how, as all come from God the Creator through the existential process of creation, all can always return to the culmination of a never-broken union with that same God through that same process of divine creation. That is to say little more than has been said already: that as we live through the transformations that constitute continuous creation, we come to know God in us and in our world, in (though ever beyond) God's soul-like subsistence in the enlivening that takes us through the serial dying of old forms (through the dark nights of our souls), and generally in God's Creator-like subsistence as the infinitely full formless darkness, that is only darkness to us (a further dimension of the darkness that afflicts our souls) because our eyes cannot quite take in the infinite intensity of the light, the reflection of which in all created things, as John said, enlightens everyone who comes into the world.

This "mystical" journey that every human person makes, whether they recognize it as such or not, is often presented in literature as if it were a strictly contemplative affair, an adventure of the mind in its most mannered contemplative mode. And such presentation and impression is no doubt largely due to that crude soul-body dualism that continues to infect the great Platonic tradition. So that the management of the body, consisting largely of suppressing its instincts, is a mere preliminary to setting out on the "mystical" journey for which the soul alone is fit. But this is a further distortion of the true nature and commonality of the mystical way. For consider once more the characteristically incarnate nature of the human spirit. Consider the fact that the empirical universe reveals itself and all that is in it first in imagery, an imagery that is admittedly shot through with intellectual analysis, however elementary. And in general consider again the comprehensive fact that it is by acting in or on the world, and being acted on by the world; in short, it is through the process of co-creation that we humans at one and the same time come to know everything that is co-operative within it, from the meanest thing that moves to God within, as we make of this world, and co-create of ourselves, all that in such a God-indwelt universe we and it can ever come to be.

The more contemplative form of the journey to union with the divine, the form that too often predominates in self-consciously "mystical" writings, is merely the more conceptual-analytic account of what and how one learns from the very practical process of living and dying that is now, like emotion, recollected in tranquillity, and analyzed rather than represented artistically. That is why Gregory of Nyssa's *Life of Moses* is as central to an understanding of his mystical theology as are the much quoted "mystical" reaches of his theological output. And it is no accident that Gregory of Nyssa is at once the most erudite student of Plotinus and Neo-Platonism, and also recognized as the most "mystical" of the Cappadocians. For it is by living creatively, by experiencing my finite life-force constantly dying in one form to find an increase in another, that I come to recognize and to know behind all the finite life-forces that live and die and so evolve at each other's expense and to each other's benefit, the subsistence, the indwelling of something like a life-force, a spirit underpinning the whole dynamic process, yet always transcending all of it. This is then something I can acknowledge and trust (the *via affirmativa*, faith). Yet it is something I cannot fully comprehend, for it is so far beyond my finite scale (the *via negativa*, for the affirmation of its no-thing-ness). But still something I can attempt to perceive and portray in its utter transcendence, if only by analogy and metaphor (the *via eminentiae,* for the deep, dark intimations of something that is this, but eminently more). Or I can act as if my finite life-force has power enough to guarantee me life together with the world I would want to support it, and then the death I thereby deal to others and to myself will teach me the hard way the lesson I should have learned the easy way: the Self on which the life of the world and its fullest prospects depend is not after all my self-centered self. It is, rather, the Self that subsists in my finite life-force, and in which I, like all other creatures, subsist, live and move and have our being. I travel through and beyond the hypostasis of life-force or spirit, the hypostasis of continuous creation, on the journey of the incarnate spirit toward the One whose dwelling is in all of creation.

Similarly, as I contemplate my life, I see that I live by forming, deforming, transforming myself and others as they do me, in an orchestrated universe of intelligible forms that prove themselves all good and well in their sustenance and increase of life overall, and all beautiful in the composition and harmony, the fittingness of all forms together to make a universe. And I travel through the ugly deformations inevitably encountered on the way, borne along by the dynamism of the intelligible forms that are true and good and beautiful. Until I go through and beyond the hypostasis of the intelligible totality-in-harmony of these dynamic forms (overcoming all ugly disharmony on the way), beyond this mind-like hypostasis, to the eternal formless source of all, and to the concomitant possibility of infinite formation which even my little self-transcending mind can contemplate as a possibility. But then suppose that I take my current knowledge of cosmic forms to be definitive and final, even if I take this to be the work of a creator god, now very like a mind indeed, my mind in fact. And suppose that as a result of all of this I lay down immutable laws for conduct in the world, especially when I do this in this god's name. Then I commit a form of idolatry which is really an attribution of all wisdom to myself. And once again I play the adversary of life, the satan, which is to say that I deal death. And the only way to turn the inevitable dying of forms into transformation of life once more, the only way to hope that this universal transformation of life is eternal is, once again, to go through and beyond this hypostasis of mind-like Form and Fashioner, as every dynamic fashioning invites me to do, and place my trust in the Formless One, the beginning and end of life's journey for the whole of creation.

Then much the same treatment of the third hypostasis is indicated, the divine hypostasis, the subsistence, the (real) mode of existence, as Creator. I experience myself and my life as a thrown-project, in Heidegger's unforgettable phrase, *geworfene Entwurf*: something birthed, thrown into the midst of creation, yet arriving there as myself a creative project within an ever-creative-evolving world. And I can either see myself or my kind as the sole or supreme creators of our world, or I can realize that I should go through and beyond what is a hypostasis of creation, a mutual indwelling of creation and something like a creator, and arrive once more at the limitless life-force, the formless fashioner, the still center of the storm of pullulating life that is the evolving creation. And place my trust in that as I carry on creating as best I can, at any particular stage of evolution, on good days and bad.

All of this is what is meant by saying, as Denys Turner in particular has argued, that mysticism has nothing to do with some esoteric experience that differentiates a small but privileged group, the mystics, from the rest of humankind. The mystical experience, the mystical journey, is nothing more and nothing less than the whole of the possible experience of the creative creature in creation, which is predominantly an experience of the One in and through that One's mode of being as Creator. And it follows from all of this that, far from there being a problem about "reducing" the three hypostases of divinity to the One God, the three hypostases of this Trinity, properly understood, can telescope into two, or one. For a hypostasis is a constituent feature of the creation, an actual, active structure in the fabric of reality that at once hides and intimates the existence of something. In our experience of creaturely creation within the cosmos, the act of creation is characterized by the application of intelligent design, by the application of energy or force upon already existent material; so that these two structures of the whole fabric of reality can be telescoped into one, namely, the process of continuous creation, as each can be telescoped into the other to yield one application.

So that it really does not matter if, in the corresponding mythic terms, Jesus is said to be the incarnation of the Word (Intellectual Principle), or to have the Spirit (the life force) come on and remain in him, making him son of God (a Creator, like his Father). For the structures in question can then be said to reveal something like Intelligent Fashioner and/or Life-giving Force, and in either or both cases, Creator. In short, what is revealed is One who can be said to be like and unlike the one conceived of in one, two or three of these concentric but real structures. The advantage of using the three is that by multiplying the real structures of reality as structures in which the Creator subsists, and which correspondingly subsist in the Creator, we multiply the descriptions of the real modes of being of the Creator and thereby acquire more expansive detail in the kind of being that the One Beyond Being is like, yet infinitely unlike.

It might help here to look briefly at an example of mysticism from the great traditions of Eastern religions, Hinduism in particular. The example is taken from the Yoga Sutra, for what can be glimpsed from the briefest of accounts of that sutra's contents is a process and experience of the utterly Formless that is quite comparable to that of Western "mysticism." The Yoga Sutra, like the religious sensitivity of which it is so fine an example, shies away from the Western idea of a God defined without more ado as the Creator. For if that is all that Westerners think of God, then the Absolute is indeed likely to be conceived as Sartre's *Dieu Fabricateur*, a manufacturer of things that then are supposed to assume a reality that seems at first blush to enjoy some equivalence with their creator. They seem just as real as the creator, who is then a being like them, albeit an infinitely greater being than any of them. So the Yoga Sutra simply distinguishes what it calls the Principle of Sentience from the Principle of Insentience. These are mutually exclusive in terms of connotation and attributes. The first, the Principle of Sentience, just *is*. It does not change, and it is the innermost reality in all that appear. And in particular it constitutes the innermost reality of persons. The second, the Principle of Insentience, has activity, the activity of energy-matter. It is concerned with movement, change, development, and it can be called prime matter. It evolves as psyche (a subtle form of matter), reason (intellect), mind, the I-maker (individual ego), the inner-sense-organs (the eye-behind-the-physical-eye, the eye that consciously sees, etc.). So that what I am seen to do outwardly is all and only what the psyche does inwardly.

The Principle of Sentience then appears to be something like consciousness per se; not consciousness *of* anything, yet a principle that enables the psychic function to actually function: the inner senses to sense, the mind to know, the intellect to reason and understand. Now this seems similar to the impression gained when creation was studied at the outset of this investigation, an impression to the effect that the material world comes from a mind-like (Beyond) Being, through the mediation of intelligible and sensual forms, rather than, as all modern discussion of the mind-body problem rather senselessly insist, minds coming from matter. Then the journey back to the Principle of Sentience is described primarily in terms of praxis, rather than any kind of more theoretical contemplation. The praxis suggested in the Yoga Sutra is called the "arresting" of the activity and movement that is characteristic of the Principle of Insentience, and of the various evolutions of this Principle into such forms as those of the psyche, reason, will ("ego making"). And the first arresting praxis with respect to this Principle of Insentience and its evolving forms consists in the abjuring all evil-doing. Presumably on the grounds that the self-centeredness involved in all evil doing keeps one obsessed with the Principle of Insentience and its evolving forms, and thereby denies forever access to the Principle of Sentience that enables all forms of (perception of) reality to be. This fundamental praxis is then accompanied by breathing and other exercises of bodily posture, which are designed to ensure that the body is not disturbed by any adventitious sensations. There then results a withdrawal of the senses from objects with which they are too constantly concerned. Then an exercise in concentration in an intensification of the withdrawal, an exercise in meditation as an intensification came into the world because of original sin; although it is then still impossible to tell whether he means by death in that context simply the final dissolution of our current bodily existence, the last in a series of bodily transformations that make up our earthly lives, or the "death" of eternal damnation, or some metaphorical mixture of both. What he does say on such matters, and all he needs to say, is this: "Observe the inconstancy of things, life before death and after death, life; the just and godly enjoys both, and the ungodly sinner keeps one to his woe, losing the other that is blest." And at this stage of the series of sermons, in the attempt to bring home to his listeners the seriousness of the choice that lies before them at every moment of their earthly lives, he is by no means sparing of the imagery of strict judgment, possibly leading to hell-fire and damnation.

Then Columbanus goes on to give his listeners a concrete example that will illustrate the enjoyment of this life which yet avoids us occupying it (as a colonizer occupies a land, controls all the resources of life if offers for his own aggrandizement, and treats it as his personal home). The example he offers is the eucharistic-style example of how we are to treat the staff of physical life, food and drink. Eating-and-drinking is both feature and support of the current earthly life God gives all to enjoy. Therefore we should bless God for this earthly life and its supports for all. And we will follow this example, if we mean to, when we then decide to "eat with the poor, drink with the poor, share with the poor, that even so we may deserve to share with the poor in that place where they shall be satisfied who here for Christ's sake hunger and thirst after righteousness." Little wonder then that he should end the series of sermons with the instance and imagery of the eucharist, and at the same time sum up in Trinitarian terms all that we know of God precisely by living in this manner. Breaking the bread to others, pouring out to them the wine of our lives, means that Jesus is present within us as the one in whom the life that is the light from the Creator lights up our path in life. Thereby lighting the darkness that recedes with advancing life, and robbing of its impenetrability the darkness brought about us by the death-dealing original sin of our kind. It means that we are inviting Jesus, then and thereafter, to "inspire our hearts with the breath of your Spirit, and wound our souls by your love . . . for thus in loving (our souls) ever seek, while (they) are healed in being wounded." Eucharist then, as it names the kind of life we can enjoy to the full in these present conditions, and at the same time names a sacrament which, like all true sacraments, effects what it symbolizes, is an earnest of eternal life. For it brings us into the conscious presence of

of the concentration. Culminating, paradoxically as it might seem, in an intensification of that meditation which results in an identification with an object used in the meditation, a sound or a picture, so that the point is reached at which common consciousness is so totally absorbed by that object — or non-object in non-object-based meditation — that common consciousness, as it were, disappears into it, and the stillness and emptiness begins to emerge, in which the hem of the garment of the Principle of Sentience may be touched.

So briefly and crudely described, it is really unwise to say anything much about this piece of practical theology from the Yoga Sutra. The effort to practice it though, however imperfectly in one's own case, does leave one with the impression that it is a journey back through the structures of the derivative and, comparatively speaking, unreal world, to some encounter with the Principle of Sentience, achieved through the forms of, comparatively speaking, Insentience. And not perhaps a million miles away from the Greek and Christian encounter with the Absolute One, when properly understood and explained. Or indeed with comparable forms of Jewish Kabbalah or Muslim Sufi "mysticism." And a further strengthening of the view that all revelation of God is in and through the creation, and the way back to God for all is through the structures of that creation that all share, as a sharing in the house of God.

In Summary: Columbanus on How to Preach and Receive a Trinitarian Faith

It would seem to follow from all of this that only those Christians who can be reminded of the sophistication of myth should be allowed, and perhaps encouraged, to continue to talk in terms of the personae of the one God, and then only for so long as they are kept well away from the theology of the Trinity in the form of its Western tradition. For the abstruse metaphysical terms of that theology are nowadays incomprehensible to all but students of the history of Western philosophy. And the persistence of that theology in using the term *person* where the Greeks used *hypostasis* results in a mixture of myth and metaphysics that has ever since sent the combined theologies of incarnation and Trinity from one misapprehension to another, down to this day. Or if there is need to talk or hear about the Trinity in Christian circles at all, perhaps the best strategy is to have everybody stick to the early creedal formula: "We believe in one God, the creator of heaven and earth; and in Jesus Christ, his Son and our Lord, who was conceived of the Holy Spirit and born of the virgin Mary; who suffered under Pontius Pilate, died and was buried; who was raised to sit at God's right hand." Or one could follow the example in this matter of the great Columbanus, a mighty Irish abbot who ended his life in Bobbio in the early seventh century. In his extant writings Columbanus shows that he possessed the most sophisticated understanding of the best theology of the Trinity in his time, while warning his flock of the egregious error of thinking that it was through this or any theology that they could come to know God and come themselves to God at last.

In a single set of thirteen extant sermons Columbanus, with power and poetry, outlines the essence of the Christian faith. Since this is quintessentially a faith, a trust in God, he begins with what we can know of God, and how we can know it. And so he immediately takes up the imagery of God as Trinity. He says that we are authorized by scripture to imagine God as Trinity. Just two texts are enough to tell us so: the *Sh'ma Israel* in what Christians call the Old Testament: "the Lord your God is one God": and the command of Christ about baptizing in the name of the Father, the Son and the Holy Spirit. He then reminds his listeners very briefly that what we know of God as Trinity is summed up in the formula *unum substantia, trinum subsistentia*, one in substance, three in subsistence. That alone would tell us that Columbanus knew of the most sophisticated results of Trinitarian theology in his time. If only because he chooses "subsistence" instead of the usual Latin *persona* for the place of the Greek term *hypostasis*. But then, in case we should conclude that it is by theology that we know what we can know about God, and what it means to say that God is Triune, he embarks on quite a rant against theology. "But human argument or skill or any vainglorious philosophy, which is unsound even on the nature of the world, cannot be our teacher about God" "for whence could vain men have known the invisible God even up to the standard required for debate, not to say as far as a finished definition of God." And in this vein he goes on and on for quite a bit.

What then? "Therefore seek supreme wisdom, not by verbal debate, but by the perfection of a good life." It is by living in and with this world, as the best practicalist epistemologists always insist, that we come to know ourselves and our world and all that is operative in our world. So Columbanus, thinking now in particular about knowledge of God, goes straightaway for the imagery of indwelling, in fact for an image of soul-body indwelling that evokes the imagery of incarnation. God, who is omnipresent in the world, "resides in us like soul in body . . . if we are not

dead in sins . . . if we are worthy that He should be in us, then in truth we are made alive by Him as His living members." We know God by living the life God gives us from within, in a manner — the self-transcending manner, as it will appear instantly — in which God gives it to us. "If we are not dead in sins." So he has to say immediately what sin is, and how this God-given life could be opposed by death. And he begins by anticipating and ousting the idea that sin has some affinity with the body and the flesh, and not with soul or spirit: "idle is mere mortification of the flesh . . . unless it be accompanied by a fruitful moderation of mind . . . let us cleanse ourselves first from pride."

But then in what, precisely, does this death-dealing pride of the human spirit consist? In the terms of Columbanus's probing and poetic imagination, it consists of treating what he calls the "transitory goods" of our current forms of life as if they constituted the self-acquired and self-fulfilling substance of life, the be-all and end-all here. Treating this good world as our home, as he also puts it, rather than a stage through which our true, God-given life passes on the eternal way. And so the image of the journey comes to the center of these sermons, the oldest and most durable image of the divine creation, the journey out from God and, more apposite at the point at which we find ourselves in the current forms of our existence, the journey back. So without ever denying the goodness of all forms of life conferred by the Creator, and alluding only to how beautiful and alluring they are, Columbanus waxes lyrical about the transience of the present forms of existence. "What are you then, human life? . . . you are a way to life . . . you are to be questioned, not believed or warranted; traversed, not occupied. . . . (You are) a mirage fleeting and void or a cloud, uncertain and feeble and a shadow, like a dream . . . what is the difference, I ask, between what I saw yesterday and dreamt of last night? . . . for we must flee what flies, and so live in it that we must daily die."

Columbanus does refer to the original sin of the race, the sin of Adam, in the course of this rhetorical address to life in its present earthly form. Still poetically addressing this life, he tells it that it would be "true . . . if you had not been cut short by the sin of man's first transgression, (for) then you became prone to falling and mortal, in that you have allotted all your travelers to death." Since he has abjured all that vainglorious philosophy in which theology consists, Columbanus does not himself explain where on the spectrum of extant theologies of original sin his own views belong. But he seems, from what he does say, to take the view that death

the One who is the eternal fountain of life, the One who is correspondingly always in us as soul (that it, as source of life), as the incarnate Word,
Christ, who lightens the way for us, and as the Spirit whose love carries
us to our journey's end.

In this short set of sermons two things are made clear about a Triune
God and us, as things are seldom if ever clear in the course of that tortuous, esoteric, argumentative, and often arbitrary defining and reasoning
that constitutes the Christian theology of Trinity. The first is this: that it
is in and through the experience of living our lives in this creation that
we come into real, empirical and to a limited degree comprehensive and
explicable contact with the One who is supreme eternal source of all existence and life. But depending on how we see ourselves and decide to
live our lives together, that barely comprehensible and expressible contact
can be made either by the easy way or by the hard way. If we bother to
notice that existence and life is forever poured out in superabundance to
all, and if we use the creative powers with which we are undoubtedly also
graced, in order to share and mutually increase that life for all others, we
shall encounter a Source of life without limit and be blessed with a corresponding hope that can carry us through all intrinsic deaths of forms
of life constantly transformed. If, on the other hand, our native pride in
these creative powers of ours, or our premature fears of the dying that
has to take place in all of life's advance, tempt us to consider our status
and role as that of sole creators or guarantors of life in our world, the
only moral beings in existence, then we shall encounter the One in the
form of dealer of the surfeit of death and destruction we thereby bring
upon ourselves. And unless we learn the hard lesson taught by living life
in this proud and utterly self-centered way, we may never be blessed by
the hope of eternal life, but damned instead in this life to the darkness of
random fears and a to despair that always lurks just beneath the next plan
and just beyond the next apparently manageable project.

The contemplative life therefore, to which is so often attributed the
knowledge of God as Trinity, is not a life lived in one's study or monastery
and consisting mainly of mental prayer and mental exercises, the subjects
of which are often thought to be special inner experiences granted only
to some, and truths revealed especially to some and not to others. Quite
to the contrary. So that the phrase should be spoken and heard as "the
contemplative *life*," and not as "the *contemplative* life." For it refers in
reality to human life lived as it ought to be, and to some extent cannot but
be, a life of thinking creatures, a life lived thoughtfully, contemplated in

periods of tranquillity and planned as far as possible in these same periods of quiet and focused meditation. So in the monasteries men and women have always tended their common lands and vineyards and flocks, enjoyed their food and drink in moderation, kept their guest houses open to receive the stranger and to feed the hungry. They have sung their psalms that told of the beauty and goodness of the world and of the beauty and goodness and truth of the One who continually created and enlivened it, thereby salving it always from inevitable or self-inflicted destructions. They have preached that kind of life and the God who lived and moved within it. And in the Irish system of the first Christian millennium, where the monastic institution served in the place of an Episcopal-diocesan institution in much of the territory it covered, since the lay people they served could not be expected to live the rule that these spiritual athletes followed, they worked out rules by which the same laity could enjoy all the good things of this life while still not occupying it as their permanent home. And so they preached this self-same God to these fortunate people as they hoped could be seen clearly to be working through their own lives.

The second thing that comes clear, correspondingly, from this short set of sermons is the meaning of the Christian doctrine of the Trinity as a way of conveying something true about the God encountered and known by living in God's good creation. The key to the meaning of Trinity is then found in the image of the journey through the transient forms of our present earthly existence to the bosom of the One eternal source of all life. These forms in their very transience proclaim the One within them, in the mode of being as Creator. And, if we break down these finite forms further into their constitutive elements of intelligible forms and forms of the power to live and change in such interdependence and interaction as to fashion one living and evolving world, these forms then proclaim the Creative One within them to exhibit also the twin derivative modes of being (derivative, that is, from the mode of being as Creator) as Word-Wisdom and Soul-Spirit. So that we arrive at last at that union with the One, that double-immanence in which eternal *shalom* is ours.

For that arrival we might as easily borrow the equally poetic imagery and language of Plotinus. "Here we put aside all learning; disciplined to this pitch, established in beauty, the quester holds knowledge still of the ground he rests on, but, suddenly, swept beyond it all by the very crest of the wave of Intellect surging beneath, he is lifted and sees, never knowing how. The vision floods the eyes with light, but it is not a light showing some other object, the light is itself the vision. No longer is there thing seen and light to show it, no longer Intellect and object of Intellection; this is the very radiance that brought both Intellect and Intellectual object into being for the later use and allowed them to occupy the quester's mind. With This he himself becomes identical, with that radiance whose Act is to engender Intellectual Principle, not losing in that engendering but forever unchanged, the engendered coming to be simply because that Supreme exists."

There are authors, both Oriental and Occidental, who insist that this direct union with the One, now beyond all mediation through subsistences of It or in It, is possible during earthly life, although they come so close to those who insist, alternatively, that such unmediated union can occur only after death, as to think it an uncommon and occasional occurrence while we are still in this gross body. And it is seldom clear from those who insist that such union awaits only beyond death, what role if any death plays in our progress toward it. Is it that the death sinners must die can constitute in itself the final purging of that self-centeredness in which their sinning and consequent alienation from the Creative One originally derived? Or is it perhaps also that the utterly deformative processes that amount to the ending of our current bodily form of life are to be seen as transformative in the mode of cleansing the windows of perception of their more material increment, now become excrement?

Such speculation is no doubt inevitable, and will long continue. But it serves no further purpose in this context. For the principal intention here is to set our experience of God as trinity (or binity or quaternity) squarely within our experience of God the Creator in creation. So whether the One is encountered, here or hereafter, in a direct mode or still through forms of being and consciousness, it does appear that the One is truly encountered and in such encounters known, in the modes of existence that Trinity tries to name and define. And that means that God, God's ways with the world, and our ways to God are revealed by God the Creator, fully and without remainder, in and through the creation. All may therefore know God and God's way, the steadfast love that contents itself with creating life continuously and ever more abundantly, and may know this simply through living according to that way, by responsibly exercising co-creative ability and so making real in act that same steadfast love in return. Nor is it necessary to learn the advanced techniques of meditation, even if they also have their place, nor to study the highly esoteric treatises of theology, for these of themselves, even when they get things right, do not add one iota, one dot to what can be known and experienced by living a good life, as Columbanus insisted. While always allowing that such enterprises can be very useful when used well as skilful means to a way, a life and a truth that is always otherwise available.

The portrait of the God revealed in creation, according to Columbanus and these other myth-makers and theologians (if we omit the cruel vision of a divine judge meting out everlasting punishment — a matter that is to receive a more critical analysis later), is painted in a more accessible manner by the Irish poet, Cathal Ó Searcaigh; for the true poet is always the seer.

Sanctuary

Here in the hollow of the mountains
it is more peaceful than a country chapel.
I walk, cap in pocket, silently
down the mossy carpet of the aisle,
down between the grass-clump pews,
and at the altar-height, stand a moment,
while a faint breeze — the altar boy —
dispenses heather incense everywhere.

Yet in this mountain chapel there's no talk
of rule or regulation and I'm not plagued
by the brutal piety of the pulpit
threatening those who err with torment.
This is no God of Tears or God of Thorns,
God of Tyranny or God of Mercy,
this God I am now looking at
but a God indifferent to my hindrance or my help.

Here it is with his life rather than his words
that whatever God there is makes himself known;
ignoring signs of reverence, veneration.
The source of all energy. Creator of the Elements.
Enough for him to stir, blossom
and push towards the light in every new-grown shoot.
His joy is the lustre of every color,
he gives life to the air around me with his life.

With every breath I take
I breathe him from the pure air
as fresh as new-baked bread, as cool as wine.

Part Two

CHRISTIANITY:
THE RELIGION THAT
DEVELOPED FROM THE
FAITH OF JESUS THE JEW

Chapter Five

CREDO

"We are complete realists, and without belief or superstition": thus you thump your chests.

But how should you be *able* to believe, you motley-spotted men! You who are paintings of all that has ever been believed!

You are walking refutations of belief itself and the fracture of all thought. *Unworthy of belief:* that is what I call you, you realists!

All ages babble in confusion in your spirits; and the dreaming and babbling of all ages was more real than is your waking!

You are unfruitful: *therefore* you lack belief. But he who had to create always had his prophetic dreams... and he believed in belief!

— Nietzsche, *Thus Spoke Zarathustra*

The Definition of Religion

A religion may be defined as a structured social phenomenon that as a rule consists of four distinguishable elements, and these can be named as credo or creed, code, cult and constitution. It seems necessary to talk of four distinguishable structural elements existing "as a rule," because in some religions some one or more of these structures may be missing, or may be visible only in such jejune forms that they are scarcely distinguishable from other elements or from the structures of everyday communal living. In fact, it has been remarked that some cultures, and especially some that practice what some modern scholars call primal religions, have no word at all in their languages for "religion." What we would call religion is so absorbed into their practical ways of living in the natural world that they share with the rest of us, that it requires no special oral or written literature, no special codes of behavior, no special ceremonies, no special profession or vocation or office, and not ever a special term for itself; none of these over and above what the basic society itself requires for

survival and a cohesive grouping of human beings. The Australian aborigines among whom David Turner lived on Groote Eylandt furnish a
very good example of such total immersion of what our heavily dualist
Western minds would call the sacred in the secular.

There are more practical examples of this nearer home, if a little more
distant in time now than the example of the Groote Eylandters. In old
Irish society, for example, the king and the poet were both sacred persons, *nemed*, as indeed were the *aos dana,* the practitioners of the arts;
from the artist in iron, the smith, to the hereditary poet, the repository of
divine wisdom, which conferred on the poet the power to inaugurate or
dethrone kings, depending on the righteousness or the unrighteousness of
their reign. For the creative arts were the means of creation, then as now,
a good enough reason for asserting the comprehensive attribute of some
pre-Christian divinities — such as the king-god Lug — as *samildanach*,
practitioners of all the arts. The traditional *file* or poet then, precisely
because of his permanent access to the throne of divinity, had it in his
power to proclaim on his own terms that the current candidate for kingship was indeed a suitable spouse for the Sovereignty goddess. The king,
correspondingly, played a cosmic role in union with the Sovereignty, but
he functioned in that cosmic role precisely by fulfilling all of his kingly
duties in truth, the *fir flathemon,* the justice and right the origin of which
is ultimately divine, and that must characterize all true princely rule. The
Christian church in Ireland tried early and late to acquire the right and
practice of this inauguration of kings, together of course with some consequent control of kings. So, on the Continental model of Popes claiming
to inaugurate and, if necessary, to depose emperors, it sought to substitute
a priestly myth and ritual of its own for the traditional myth and ritual of
the pre-Christian Irish. But in Ireland this kind of displacement proved
impossible and the ancient myth and ritual lasted until the end of the old
Irish order with the final defeat of the Irish chieftains in the seventeenth
century.

Up to that point the old immersion of sacred in the secular was entrenched in Irish kingdoms. So entrenched was it in fact, that when
Anglo-Norman lords invaded Ireland from the twelfth century, and managed to carve out for themselves their own small kingdoms from existing
Irish kingdoms, they would often engage members of the traditional caste
of court poets in order to have these poets perform for them also their
most definitive task. Namely, the establishment of the legitimacy of these
Norman lords in their new kingdoms in the traditional fashion, the poetic

proclamation of the marriage of the new lord to the Sovereignty. And if one needed any further and convincing illustration of the functioning of this sacred-secular aristocracy without any further need of priesthoods or temples, one need only visit *Emain Macha*, Navan Fort, the traditional mound for the inauguration of the kings of the Ulster people. There, shortly before the Christian era dawned, the archaeological evidence informs us, this mound was in part created by taking sods of earth from every part of that kingdom. And a great wooden structure was built upon it, a great house with areas for different social classes, and of such dimensions that architects today sometimes wonder how it was roofed. Then the evidence shows that the house was burnt down very shortly after it was completed. That second act of a somewhat sacrificial nature is not likely to puzzle people who know something about natural religious imagery. In this case, the imagery in question is already seen in the Bible: the imagery of the cosmos as a house in which God dwells with God's people. In order to secure that imagery, and perhaps to prevent people from gradually getting the idea that the physical house contained, if not in fact confined divinity, it was burnt down and its ashes mingled with the earth. So that the sacrificed building mingled with the earth then symbolized the cosmos and the cosmic role of each king who was then taken there to be inaugurated.

That is a partial example of a people and a culture for which institutions of the sacred and those of the secular coincided, an example of natural religion, one might say. But this is a partial example because, although there were other institutions in addition to those which supplied government and the tradition of wisdom by which the little kingdoms lived — there was, for instance, the brehon law, the tradition of legislation, or code, and the legislature that continually developed the rules of behavior — there was also what one might call a professional class called the druids. The druids, among other things, seemed to have been responsible for religious ritual, a kind of priesthood perhaps. It is difficult now to reconstruct the figure and office of the druid, even in Ireland where records of pre-Christian religion are so abundant. This is largely because, unlike the case of the profession of judge, the *breitheamh* who gave the brehon law its name, and unlike the cases of the poet and the chief, the Christian church set its face so resolutely against any assimilation whatever of the druid order, that by the end of the first millennium it had virtually eradicated them. And so it had certainly wiped them as cleanly as possible from the memory of succeeding generations. The druids that hold their occasional meetings in Celtic countries nowadays are largely the product of the literary imagination of the eighteenth century, although what they do and what they contribute to the sum of human wisdom, need be none the less significant for that.

Furthermore, even when a religion exists as an institution separable from the other structured social phenomena of a particular society, and where the former is thought to represent the sacred while the latter are thought to represent the secular, great variations can be found from religion to religion in the matter of the number of elements of the four mentioned already that are manifest in any particular society. Or at the very least variations emerge in the degree to which one or more of these elements manifest themselves in relation to the others. In fact, a fair amount of such variation can be found among different branches of some of these religions themselves. In a small Buddhist temple in downtown San Francisco, a visit to a weekly ceremony with its prayers, hymns or chants, sermons and even the collection, might very well remind one of a very similar ceremony in a nearby Presbyterian church. Whereas in a Zen Buddhist monastery fifteen minutes away the purist practice and training centered upon meditation would seem to a Roman Catholic still on his religious quest to be so lacking in doctrine about divinity, in sacrament, in code for daily living, and in governmental structures for its membership in general, as to make him wonder if it could be called a religion at all. Not that the absence of such familiar features need prevent him from following a purer way and truth and life, if he found it in that version of Buddhism, more than in the version of the Christian religion to which he belonged.

A similar variation in the presence and degree of the four elements that make up institutional religion can be found in the Hindu religion and, no doubt, in others also. Indeed it can be found in Christianity, and it could be lavishly illustrated by anyone who would take the trouble to draw the lines that connect the instances and importance of all four elements — a detailed and required credo, a detailed code for daily living, a cult made up of sacrament and sacrifice, and a government that governs the lives of its members in all these matters — through the various Christian churches and fellowships, from the Roman Catholic, for example, apparently at one end of the spectrum, to the Society of Friends, for example, apparently at the other.

In view of all of this at first sight bewildering array of what passes for religion in the terminology and usage of the modern world, perhaps the best way to begin to interrogate Christianity the religion is to focus first upon the constituent elements that can comprise a religion, each of the four in turn. It seems best to look first to the presence of these elements in the make-up of Roman Catholicism, where each and all seem equally prominent and essential. Then in the light of all that has been discovered already about the faith of the Bible and of Jesus of Nazareth in particular, it should be possible to try to place each element in the four-fold institution called religion, somewhere on a scale that stretches from the essential and obligatory to the non-existent or perhaps even the prohibited. For only in this manner can one come to some confident degree of decision as the whether the faith that emerged in Part One, a creation faith, a faith fully and properly designated as a living faith, hope and charity, based and directed upon God the Creator and all of creation, needs a religion either absolutely or at all, or simply on some conditions of usefulness that can change according to the results achieved.

The Credo as Scripture

The credo of a religious community refers to its verbalized *weltan-schauungen* or worldviews, to its express views about the fabric of cosmic reality, the natures and powers that move within it. Then to the religious community's views of the origin and goal of the cosmos (if it seems to them to have either or both). And above all to the community's place within the cosmos, as the community has come to know and believe all of this, or whatever of it the community in question does come to know and believe, from all of their experience of and in their world throughout nature and history. And all of this now verbalized after the community concerned has meditated upon it in whatever tranquillity the struggles of life have afforded them. Now in order to come to an adequate understanding of the worldview of any religious community, it would really be necessary to live with that community, probably for some considerable amount of time. For their truth, it always turns out, is also a way and a life. However, and luckily enough for academics who want to write books like this from the comfort of their studies, the perusal of verbalized embodiments, particularly in writing, can offer a passable understanding of such worldviews. Although it does help considerably if the academic researcher has had some experience as part of a religious grouping. On the other hand, it does not help at all if she comes to the subject blinded already by one of these dogmatic presuppositions, usually of a materialist complexion, that are so often made to masquerade as science these days.

The first source for the credo of any religion is its sacred scriptures, but once again only for those who are not blinded by that other prejudice of the scientific age, the prejudice against myth, and who are therefore capable of reading such scriptures. And this prioritizing of sacred scriptures is not intended to suggest that religions that do not have sacred scriptures are any the less worthy of study for that reason. Sometimes the fact that the so-called world religions all do have their sacred scriptures is taken as a tacit judgment upon the alleged inferiority of religions then called primal, or even primitive, whose worldviews remained oral in expression and transmission. But this overlooks the fact that some of the so-called world religions were transmitted in oral form for some considerable time before their sacred scriptures began to emerge. More seriously, it overlooks the fact that some of these that are still counted as primal religions could claim world-religion status on the grounds that the worldviews they offer are at least as comprehensively cosmic and universally relevant as others to which the accolade is offered without question. David Turner compares the religion of the Groote Eylandters with world religions, and particularly with Christianity, and far from unfavorably.

The Bible as a compilation of sacred scriptures is often referred to as a canon of scripture, or canonical scripture. That description conveys two impressions simultaneously: since a canon means a rule, it conveys the claim that the scriptures offered to inquirers by members of a religion are to be regarded as the authoritative sources for the faith in question: a rule of faith. And it usually also conveys the fact that the community of faith came at some point to a decision to select from a larger body of written presentations of their religion the ones that truly or most adequately caught the essence of that faith and its distinctive character: a canon of canonical scripture. Religious faith communities then present their claims concerning a particular body of written literature in one or both of two forms. The claim that the content of these scriptures was revealed as such by God to some seers, and is therefore to be received as divine revelation (what Hindus call *sruti*, revealed), or the claim that these writings are the result of God inspiring the authors concerned to write down adequately and accurately the contents of revelation already received by some other means (what Hindus call *smriti*, remembered)

Of course when any group of religious leaders over a period of time try to reach final agreement on which writings from a number of writings that circulate and influence members of a faith are to be accepted into a definitive canon of authoritative scriptures, and which writings are not to be so received, the result is bound to involve some inconsistencies, some disagreements and perhaps even some social splintering of greater of lesser seriousness within the religious groups concerned. So, to take the Hindu example, although the Veda (comprising Brahmanas, Upanishads, Aranyakas and Vedas!) is considered to contain the divine revelation (*sruti*) as such, some later sacred texts, such as the *Bhagavad Gita,* wield a much wider influence on Hindu believers, even though these are thought to contain only memoirs (*smriti*) of that revelation. In the case of Buddhism the Theravada Buddhist scriptures comprise the *Pali Canon,* whereas Mahayana Buddhists regard the *Pali Canon* as something of a preliminary scripture and depend more upon the *Mahayana Sutras,* and in effect, particular Mahayana movements take the characteristic form and content of their religious knowledge and practice by focusing each on one or another of these sutras as their own. Christianity, as it developed into a new religion, say from the second half of its second century, followed the practice of Judaism in drawing up its own canon of sacred scriptures. In doing so it incorporated the Jewish canon, although it tended to incorporate the Greek Septuagint version of what it then came to call the Old Testament, rather than the Hebrew canon. And that process of arriving at a definitive canon of Christian scriptures cannot be seen to be completed much before the end of the fourth century. Indeed in one sense the process might be said to be still incomplete, reminding us still of the conditions and difficulties of the earlier process. The Wisdom of Solomon, for instance, so much referred to on previous pages, together with a number of other books of the Septuagint version of the Jewish scriptures, is regarded by Roman Catholics as canonical scripture, whereas Protestant churches regard these books as apocryphal scriptures. And that even though Paul, for instance, in composing his piece in his Epistle to the Romans, on our knowledge of God the Creator from creation, and our lack of excuse for turning to idols instead, seems to be virtually paraphrasing the argument, almost identical in set terms, in the Wisdom of Solomon. (Compare Romans 1:18–25 to Wisdom of Solomon 13.)

Now none of that all too common history of inconsistency, difference and division need disturb, much less dismay the Christian, or indeed the adherent of any other religion that offers a canon of scriptures to the world. (It will be interesting to see if the most recently founded faith, that of the Baha'is, will issue a canon of selected scriptures from the many writings of Baha'u'llah, the Bab, and Abdul Baba.) For it is clear that the very process of canon-formation in itself acknowledges the fact that these scriptures are all of them human constructs. So that, whatever one may say about divine revelation given to, or divine inspiration aiding, the human authors of these texts, the proclivity of all human beings to error, even religious error, together with the human ability to detect such errors, is itself assumed in the very process of forming a canon of scripture out of the habitually larger body of candidate literature that presents itself. The ones who make the selection or, as they might want to put it, the ones who simply recognize the texts that tell the truth, the whole truth and nothing but the truth, may well claim that God specifically enlightened them for the error-free completion of this very task. Yet the neutral observer still finds errors in the documents then selected, even errors in matters religious (like the image of Jahweh the ethnic cleanser), as Karl Barth freely allowed. So that the same observer is entitled to ask: what precise form does the enlightenment of the selectors take? A question that brings us back either to the idea of divine revelation, or to the more elusive idea of divine inspiration again. And brings us indeed to a further question: does such divine enlightenment or inspiration granted to the authors of scriptures and to selectors of canonical texts, and to copyists, and to translators . . . automatically overcome human wilfulness in writing out or reading into any text whatever things that clearly suit our own selfish purposes in the world? Any more than any other grace of God simply and automatically overcomes such adversarial human wilfulness in any other of our occupations, besides those of author or selector or translator, or even just the readers of divinely revealed or inspired scriptures?

The fact remains that leadership groups in a number of religions select from among the literature available to them the writings that seem to them to portray most accurately God's ways with the world and humanity's required response. The fact remains also that with different groups or at different times within the formative history of a religion, different selections are made, and indeed different assessments as to whether the select scriptures present all that is revealed about God and the world's destiny, or whether the writings chosen have to be supplemented from other sources. Some Jews, for instance, think that the oral Torah continued to gain revelatory increment long after the written Torah was definitively canonized. The fact remains, further still, that as some writings gradually lost out, presumably because errors in the presentation of the faith were thought to be detected in them, the prospect of some similar errors in the writings retained in the canon had to be dealt with. This problem was dealt with sometimes through allegorical interpretation of otherwise offensive passages, a methodology also borrowed from the Greeks who first used that very methodology in order to sanitize less savory episodes in their religious mythology. Or, alternatively, it could be proposed that the writings that were canonized, although they contained some falsehoods and false directions along the way, identified these within their own compass. So for instance the prophets in what Christians call the Old Testament criticized the falsifications of divine revelation that the religion of Israel had itself engendered in the course of its checkered history, and which are faithfully recorded in the biblical record of the history of that religion, as did the prophet, Jesus, in his turn. In fact the relationship between the members of the family of monotheistic religions, as they call themselves — Jews, Christians, Muslims and now, Baha'is — is often framed by a repetitive process in which each successive member, according to itself at least, recognizes the fullness and truth of the divine revelation granted to the one that went before. But then claims that the religion that went before distorted or betrayed the revelation in a number of ways. Jesus criticized in this manner the religion into which he was born. The Holy Qur'an, interestingly, in making this case against the Jewish and Christian religions, frequently points to the Bible itself and to persistent in-house prophetic condemnations of straying from the truth. And the Baha'is suffered their most serious persecution from Muslims for making a similar case for the necessity of a renewed revelation, which they now preach. Although they seem to have the humility to say (or is it the pessimism to predict?) that, given the proclivity of religious communities to corrupt divine revelation, this latest divine revelation in their favor would most probably have a shelf-life of some thousands of years at the most.

Since these are the straightforward facts concerning sacred scriptures in those faiths that rightly consider them the most comprehensive and authoritative sources for the content and character of each faith in turn; and irrespective of the claims made in these faiths concerning the direct divine revelation of the content of their scriptures, or the divine inspiration of the authors of the scriptures, and the help of God especially given to some or all of those who read and teach these scriptures, the manner in which they must be approached and used becomes abundantly clear. The rule for reading and use, as it is frequently formulated, is this: read and use so as to let the set of sacred scriptures in question interpret themselves. An example of such a reading and use, whether it be judged good, bad or indifferent, is provided in Part One of this book. The reading reveals a clear and basic pattern of connected themes: divine creation, human co-creation and congenital fall, divine-human creative salving involving the principal efficacy once again of a Creator God who dwells in many ways in and among us and is triune, that is to say, encountered in three modes of real subsistences, and all of that revealed and known by living in the power and presence of God the Creator in the whole of creation.

This unified and interactive collusion of themes is repeated throughout the grand symphony that is the Bible, with modulations and variations, in different literary genres: in prayer and poetry, in ritual symbolism, in preaching both catechetical and moral, and most persistently of all in the story-telling form known as myth. The disharmony that is the theme of the Fall and its consequences, is repeated and modulated throughout the symphony, and it is normally reconciled on each occasion to the theme of salvation. But there are occasions on which it is not so reconciled in the immediate context, where it appears rather as an interlude that might be meant and heard as a true part of the full and complex pattern of the symphony. Such is the movement, for example, that invokes the slaughter of people and animals alike, and the hewing to pieces of the enemy king at Gilgal. Nothing in the immediate context indicates that this is a classic example of the Fall, and that Samuel, the prophet who did the hewing to pieces, is there a false prophet in the service of a satanic spirit. However, a later and true prophetic passage, when it invokes the reign of the God who would have swords melted down and molded into ploughshares, shows this to be indeed an episode that exemplifies the Fall. As it simultaneously shows up the intervention of the previous prophet to have been false, portraying a false god and a fallen people as the true and the good. That is one example of what is meant by the rule of letting the Bible interpret the Bible. It is a rule that acknowledges the fact that God's revelation is sometimes itself distorted into falsehood by the residual fallenness of the recipients, just as divine inspiration is also in part resisted by human wilfulness. Yet the true revelation and inspiration continues to reassert itself, with a continuity that mirrors the continuous creation, and to show itself more clearly by the contrast with the errors in truth and way that are also so much an integral part of the story.

Should that rule be extended inter-scripturally from its intra-scriptural application? Should the scriptures of one religion be offered any credence when they explicitly or implicitly correct some parts or some proposals of the scriptures of another religion? Or should the scriptures of one religion be allowed to correct at least readings of these parts, or understandings of these proposals that have become current in another religion? Only someone who believes that God has left without witness all except the members of the religion to which she belongs can reject out of hand the real possibility of such inter-scriptural correction. The classic example here is the repeated insistence of the Holy Qur'an on the point that God does not have a son or offspring in a sense univocal with that in which human persons have sons and daughters. A point that can be put in another way by saying that in effect all talk of God begetting, of Israel or Jesus being sons of God, is metaphorical. That what we are dealing with there is the language of myth, used to convey the sense of the awesome power and presence of God in the man Jesus. In the teacher and prophet that the same Holy Qur'an acknowledges Jesus to have been and, for "the people of the Book," still and always to be.

Further, if the clear and basic pattern of connected themes that knits together into one unified whole the whole of the Bible, is as already described, then the possibility of people who belong to any religion, or even to none at all, managing to experience in their lives and to see clearly some rays of that revelation, is likely to be as widespread as the equal possibility of at least partial blindness to or wilful distortion of essential facets of that same revelation as a result of the pride of the human spirit and the consequent fall. For the experience of fall and of its disastrous consequences often of itself arouses the anxious desire to find another way, a truer path to life's abundance. As the increasing disaster finally shocks open the eyes of the death-dealing and dying to the force of life that pulses through continual self-offering to ever higher forms and fruits and enjoyment, beyond transitory suffering.

That seldom happens, it is true. For a self-defined intelligent species, we seldom learn anything from past experience. The terror of all war is more likely to spur us blindly to make war on terror, a kind of crass stupidity that passes itself off as foreign policy for too many nations at the opening of the third millennium. Yet it remains always possible to see the light that shines in and as the creation, the light that is the Creating Word and that enlightens everyone in the whole world, and by that light to distinguish the path of life from the path to death, and to walk the path of truth. And so the Christian canon of scriptures comes into existence and exercises its comprehensive authoritative function by the following complex process: The followers of the prophet, Jesus of Nazareth, look through a series of writings that has emerged both before and after his lifetime, in the religious milieu into which he was born and died, and the milieu that continued his own achievement. They have as their guide in reading these hallowed texts the faith handed down to them from Jesus the Jew, in the forms, not just of verbalized memory and its tradition (*smriti*), but of the characteristic behavior, the ritual forms, and if not specific governmental structures then the distinctive spirit in which these operate. But beyond all of this they have, quite literally, a worldview of Creator and creatures which can be verified daily in their own living and dying, which the traditions of word and ritual present and act out in their own symbolic ways. A veritable embarrassment of criteria with which to judge and select from among the best candidates for the position, the writings that could provide the best canon of scripture, in both senses of the term *canon*.

Such is the status of sacred scriptures then, the primary form where they exist of the credo of a religion. Such is the availability of multiple criteria for their truth and authority for selectors, readers and teachers alike. And the application of these criteria must be ever balanced by the realization that the scriptures themselves, together with every other element of religion that stands as criterion for their truth and authority is, like religion itself, a product of humankind ever subject to the original temptation to distort everything to its own self-centered ends. In the case of Jesus, the one to whom the Christian religion looks as to its own very founder, his subjection to that temptation is recorded in the Christian scriptures themselves. Matthew, Mark, and Luke place the story of the diabolical temptation of Jesus at the very beginning of his mission, enabling the author of the Epistle to the Hebrews to describe Jesus as "one who in every respect has been tempted as we are, yet without sinning" (4:15). And since the story of that temptation is in the form of myth, it must not be taken literally as something that happened only just after Jesus's baptism and before his public mission began. It must be taken as a temptation that is always waiting to surface in the forefront of his consciousness, as it regularly does to all of us, and as the text in Hebrews confirms. Indeed one can see specific evidences of that original temptation later in the story of Jesus's mission. For instance, he was tempted as a member of the Jewish people to see God as *their* God, when he was tempted to reject, and at first did reject the approach of a foreigner, and was saved by her faith from letting the temptation grow into a sin (Matt. 15:21–28). And in the garden of Gethsemane he was tempted to refuse the bitter chalice of cruel execution that fidelity to the reign of the Creator God at that point required him to drink to the very dregs (Matt. 26:36–46). His closest disciples, and those who would be the leaders of the community of his followers, were not simply tempted but actually fell on important occasions. Peter who at one moment was praised for his recognition of Jesus as the true messiah and son of God, was certified satanic by Jesus at the very next moment for refusing to contemplate the necessity of the cross for the new life and witness of Jesus and his followers (Matt. 16:13–23). Just as James and John had in mind for themselves places of honor and privilege in the government of a kingdom of God soon to be established in triumph (Matt. 20:20–28). And Peter denied him and all deserted him at his trial when it became obvious that the destiny that awaited them might be far different from the comfortable lordship that James and John, like the others also no doubt, anticipated as the reward for fidelity to the reign of God.

When James, the brother of the Lord, and some others took over leadership of the newly formed community of Jesus-followers in Jerusalem after the death of Jesus, they simply seem to have assumed that those who wished to join the fellowship would have to become Jews. So permanently difficult is it for all of us to give up the idea that God must be *our* God. Such a distortion by the followers of Jesus turns up and it is honestly recorded as it happened. But then in the same canonical scriptures of the Christian church, it is seen to be at least compromised when Paul is allowed to admit the gentiles directly, and without having them undergo the initiation rite of circumcision (Acts 15; Gal. 2) But there are also distortions that are not even compromised by the inclusion in the biblical text of the truer position. Rather are both positions allowed to stand as they are and without further comment, on the fact, for instance, that they are in obvious contradiction to the each other. The most obvious case of this must be that passage in Matthew, in which Jesus is quoted to say that there must be no limit to our forgiveness of our brother's sin against us; having just before that been quoted by the same Matthew to prescribe a very legalistic procedure by which you accuse your brother in person, then before one or two witnesses, and then before the church, at which point, if he does not confess and reconcile, he is to be treated as a gentile and a publican. How false that last position is, and how true the first, becomes blindingly obvious when one remembers that the immediate access of gentiles as such to the grace of God had been recognized by Jesus, and that publicans and sinners were the very ones Jesus had come to invite unconditionally into the kingdom of God (Matt. 18:15–23).

To err is human. All religions, including Christianity, in all of their constituent elements, are human constructs. And so the drama of creation, original sin and salvation plays out at all times in the history of the Christian faith. No section or level of the Christian community is exempt from the full drama; no form of the presentation and tradition of the Christian faith free of the distortions that derive from persistent human fallenness. But neither is any form ever lacking altogether in the true picture of that faith and the true story of its way of life, a picture that is also always available from living in and with the creation, and from other religions. So that the distortions can always be detected and transformed. It is in this broad context that the comprehensiveness and authority of sacred scripture as a primary source of the appreciation of the Christian faith can be seen and accepted.

The Credo as Creed

After the scriptures the next source of access to the religious worldview that constitutes and characterizes a faith is said to be its creed or creeds. A slight surprise there, perhaps, since "creed" is an English derivative of the Latin verb *credo*, meaning I believe that, or I believe in something. So that it is under the heading of creed that one might expect to look for the first source of the worldview sought after. But, apart from the fact that Christianity may be alone in producing and, after scriptures, relying on creeds, the creeds in question turn out to be little more than concise, and indeed very, very concise summaries of what is found in the biblical myth. In actual fact some Christian creeds do contain a little more than that, but that little more causes its own problems, which must soon be faced.

Briefly then, there are three Christian creeds that gained wide acceptance in the course of Christian history: the so-called Apostles' Creed, the so-called Nicene Creed, and the so-called Athanasian Creed. (So-called in each case because, contrary to appearances, no precise indication of exact historical origin is conveyed in any of these names.) First, the Apostles' Creed, versions of which can be traced back to Italy in the fourth century. It was a creed apparently used at baptism, and probably therefore used also during the preparation for baptism in the instruction of catechumens. So that it most likely served the twin purposes of providing a table of contents of the faith taught, and a summary of the faith to which the baptizand committed herself in requesting and accepting the Sacrament of Baptism. It is worth looking briefly at the most modern version of it, a version of it closest to the one standardized of old by the Emperor Charlemagne:

> I believe in God, the Father almighty, creator of heaven and earth
> And in Jesus Christ, His only son, our Lord
> Who was conceived of the Holy Ghost and born of the Virgin Mary
> Who suffered under Pontius Pilate, was crucified, died and was buried
> On the third day he rose again from the dead
> He ascended into heaven where he is seated at the right hand of the Father
> From there he will come to judge the living and the dead
> I believe in the Holy Ghost, the holy catholic church, the communion of saints,
> The forgiveness of sins, the resurrection of the dead, and life everlasting.

No need to go into much detail to show that this creed is indeed a concise summary of the myth elaborated through the whole course of the Christian Bible from beginning to end, and a summary, moreover, that is construed in precisely the same mythic imagery that dominates the Bible. But it might be worth noting one thing about it before looking at the other two creeds, and that is the manner in which it presents the matters later worked into doctrines of incarnation and Trinity.

The first sentence of the Apostles' Creed is to be read as follows: we (as it was originally) believe in one God, viz. the Father almighty, creator of heaven and earth. Thereafter the creed goes on to complete the story in two further parts, in both of which the Holy Spirit is in pole position. First, the Holy Spirit comes at the conception in such a way as to make Jesus son of the Father-Creator and Savior, now seated at the Father's right hand. Finally, in the last part of the creed, the Holy Spirit again heads up a series of things such as the coming to be of church as what Paul called the body of Christ, a communion that stretches beyond death, to those who have gone before and to those who are yet to be raised beyond death, to the overcoming of death-dealing sin, and eternal life, a new creation. This story structure of the creed clearly yields a mythic or metaphorical form of trinity in which the divine attributes of Creator, Savior, and Sanctifier/Consummator are personified separately in order to convey consistently that God who is subject of all three attributes is indeed a personal being, though infinitely beyond our human perceptions of personality. The more obtuse theological form of trinity can also find support from this creed, but with two provisos. First, provided that one does not attempt to read the first sentence of the creed as if it were written, "we believe in One God, that is to say, one divine being or substance that is now deployed consecutively in the hypostases of Father-Creator, Son-Savior, and Holy Spirit-Sanctifier." The One God in that first phrase of the Apostles' Creed cannot be taken in this way, but only as naming and being God the Creator-Father. And second, provided that it is realized that the creed can support a unity and a binity of divine modes of subsistence as easily as it can support a trinity of these. For the one conceived of the Holy Spirit is the "only son" of the Father, so Father and Holy Spirit can be seen as one and the same, as generator of this son. And then the one conceived of the Holy Spirit and who saves is the one who makes eternally whole, as the Holy Spirit does in the final part of the story — as Paul put it, the risen Lord is the life-giving spirit (1 Cor. 15:45). Which offers a choice of theological formulae comprised of one, two or three divine hypostases, all equally orthodox.

The principal difference between this and the Nicene Creed which is recited as part of the eucharistic liturgy, and the Athanasian Creed that also found a liturgical role in Catholic and Lutheran churches in the West, is that the latter two creeds incorporate phrases drawn from conciliar definitions that were designed to settle the theological conflicts that plagued Christology and Trinitarian theology in the early centuries. The Athanasian creed in fact elaborates on such material in a formulaic contrast of right and wrong propositions — one wag suggesting that it succeeds only by denying in every second phrase what it asserts in every first phrase — to the point at which the whole creed seems to be dominated by the objective of achieving doctrinal orthodoxy at last. The Nicene Creed, in its own pursuit of pure orthodoxy, adds to our belief "in one Lord, Jesus Christ, the only Son of God," that he was "begotten, not made," and "of one being with the Father." Then it adds also to our belief in "the Holy Spirit, the Lord and giver of life," that this Holy Spirit "proceeds from the Father and the Son."

The phrase "of one being with" translates into English the abstruse concept of *homoousios*, one in substance or being, and it was designed by some orthodox theologians to weed out Arians. But it was itself subject to much confusion as to its precise meaning, and its appositeness in the arguments adopted nevertheless at the council was also questioned, as the correspondence of some of those who voted for it at the Council of Nicea illustrates. The phrase was nevertheless adopted by the council in order to ostracize the Arian "heretics," who were among those that felt most strongly that the confusing range of meanings of which the term *homoousios* was capable gave them good reason for rejecting it in any case. The other added phrase, "begotten, not made," also raised questions concerning the practical wisdom of inserting into creeds, and particularly into creeds that are destined to have high levels of liturgical presence, crystalizations of complex theological conceptual structures that are of their very nature abstract, contrived and hence variable as between different cultures and even different times within any cultures that engage in philosophical analysis and argument. For the phrase "begotten, not made," when conceptually analyzed, would appear to apply to every human being, indeed every mammal, and if only for that reason it cannot be used univocally across the range that divides creaturely processes from processes that are believed to take place within the inner being of divinity. For such extended application the phrase must be used analogically in conceptualized form, or metaphorically if left in its original mythic form, and equally so with respect to both of the terms that are here contrasted, *begotten* and *made*. That means that since both terms are terms for the origin of one thing from its source as that process is experienced in the creaturely realm, neither term is univocally applicable both to divinity and to humanity. Therefore, neither is a priori likely to be more successful than the other in order to uncover and express what it known of such divine processes as they occur within divinity itself.

Instead it is the case that one can choose from a variety of terms — beget, breathe out, form, fashion, and so on — in order to metaphorically identify the status of the Father as *arche anarchos*, underived, source-itself-unsourced. And correspondingly then to identify the other(s), Son and/or Spirit, as "persons" or hypostases who are eternally derivative from that Source. So this move, this choice of "begotten" and not "made," will not deter the Arians from talking as if that which derives from the Source is of a lesser status than that which is its Source. For such subordination of status follows logically, no matter which term is used for the sourcing. But that does not matter when the language is that of metaphor and myth, when the three are not persons as we are persons, but rather personifications of the ultimate creative wisdom and life-giving power by which the One, who is personal in some analogous sense beyond our finite comprehension, is present and active in all of creation, and in Jesus of Nazareth in particular. The phrase "begotten not made," like the phrase "one in being," signals a rather forced theological argument that was not successful even in convincing the Arians. These phrases should never have been inserted into creeds for all Christians. And this not simply because the "begotten, not made" phrase cannot in fact achieve what the contrast of its terms was meant to achieve in the cause of orthodoxy, but because in neither case can the deployment of the phrases be properly understood and evaluated outside of the complex, and now long obsolete metaphysical systems in which they were deployed.

Later in the history of the Nicene Creed the Western church insisted on inserting the infamous *filioque* clause, which had little effect on the faith of the followers of Jesus, other than serving to aggravate the divisions that had long affected the relationship between Eastern and Western churches. This is not, or not solely, a case of improperly inserting into creeds the terms of abstruse and obsolescent metaphysics. It is something far worse. For in speculating so far into the innermost processes of the divine being itself as this *filioque* debate both illustrated and urged — for that term raised the question as to whether the Holy Spirit derived from the Father only, or from the Father and the Son acting as one source — the only thing that theologians were now proving was that in their growing and largely ungrounded pride, they had finally lost the run of themselves completely. Such was their confidence in the abstruse concepts and logic of ever-obsolescing metaphysics. And these remarks are even more apposite in the case of the so-called Athanasian Creed, which if anything imports even more of the abstruse metaphysical logic used in early Christologies and Trinitarian theologies, in cryptic forms, into instruments to be used by any and every Christian as aide-memoirs to the substance of the faith.

There is a third reason why such abstract philosophico-theological definitions of elements of the faith should not be made part of creeds, designed as these originally were to act as summaries of the story of creation, salvation and infinite hope. And the reason is this: such definitions import into a creed, and then tend to infect all creeds with, the aura of the authoritative imposition of doctrine and the fear of the anathema for any who cannot subscribe to the definitions proposed. For the phrases imported into the creeds do quite frequently derive from the solemn definitions of matters of faith by some church councils, issued at a point at which a fight to the death had been taking place between warring theological factions. So that the scenario of the origin of such phrases is that of the ecclesiastical authority having to step in, in order to impose some formula, and either break a dead-lock or anathematize some of the factions involved. It is interesting to note in this respect that it was sometimes Christian emperors rather than popes who in the interests of unity insisted that a defined formula be imposed, and they were at least as anxious for the political unity of their empires as they were for the unity of faith of the faithful.

It was the emperor Constantine who insisted on the imposition of the formula that, not without his influence, emerged from the Council of Nicea, and the emperor Theodosius took a similar stance in the case of similar formulae that emerged from the later Council of Constantinople. Indeed some centuries later still, it was the emperor Charlemagne who oversaw the standardized version of the oldest creed, the Apostles' Creed, of which there were by his time and in his view far too many variations. Then, as the Roman Papacy developed and increasingly imitated, not merely the governmental structures of ancient imperial Rome, but also the ethos of absolute power on earth claimed by its old pagan secular counterparts, the practice of imposition without appeal which first applied to conciliar definitions of the kind just seen in Nicea and Constantinople, spread further a-field. It spread, not merely to all future councils of the Roman church, but eventually to the popes' doctrinal decisions when they decided to pontificate on a matter of faith and morals, and in doing so invoked their plenary power over the whole church. By the nineteenth century these practices and claims were backed up by a further papal definition, the definition of papal infallibility. Quite possibly the most falsifiable doctrine ever defined and imposed upon the Christian faithful. And so the infection of the creeds with the virus of power and imposition continued to take ever greater hold.

The end result was that the original relationship between the scriptures and the authorized creeds was almost entirely reversed. Originally the creed served as a table of contents and an aide memoire to the detail of the canonical biblical montage of the story of God and the world, of creation, salvation, and eternal life in prospect. So that the Bible was then the primary verbalized source and "rule" of faith. By the nineteenth century however the Roman pope, with or without the rest of the hierarchy, was the supreme authoritative interpreter of scripture, or at the very least the supreme arbiter of theological conceptualizations of scriptural material, and their doctrinal distillations. The primary canon of faith was no longer the canon of scripture, but the canon or rule of papal-conciliar doctrinal definition and the canon or rule of creeds hi-jacked by insertion of similar dogmatic formulae into their ancient structure, or the more thorough composition of creeds from such formulae. The critical assessment of these latter-day developments of the ancient ethos of imperial Roman power must await the treatment of that element of a religion called its constitution. For the moment it is necessary only to add that some Christian churches insist that the received creeds offer only very secondary criteria of the true Christian faith, while some Christian communities, like the Society of Friends, or Quakers, remove creeds altogether from their profession and practice.

Yet it also seems necessary to say that some of the creeds, or confessions as they are also called, produced by Protestant churches — the Westminster Confession of Faith, for example — might need to have their actual use examined more critically. For, despite the hearty profession of the unchallenged supremacy of the rule of scripture which some of these confessions contain, there is more than a little evidence to suggest that their doctrinal deliverances, and perhaps particularly those that contain judgments on the doctrines and practices of other Christian churches, often seem to be read into scripture rather than read out of it, and so prove to be alleged contents of the true faith that are very suspect indeed.

The Credo as Theology

A theology, as the "-ology" suffix suggests through its roots in *logos*, means an intelligible construct or just plain reason, applied to God. And so, as the origins of Christian theology in the wholesale borrowing from the Greeks more than amply illustrates, theology is essentially a philosophical discipline. The massive presence of theology in the history of Christianity from the age of the Apologists, that is to say, from the third century onward, is one of the most obvious, and indeed distinctive features of the Christian religion. Yet, although not as massively present perhaps, theologies are also quite widely instanced in the religions of the world, and this is true both of quite local, even tribal religions, and of the so-called world religions such as Hinduism, Buddhism and Islam. Although quite frequently the theological element may be found interwoven as one thread in the unified fabric of a particular faith, rather than find itself issued as a stand-alone systematic exposition of that faith, intended to take its due place, as a Christian theology might be expected to do, alongside other formulations of the credo in question.

The best illustration of the claim for the widespread appearance of theologies in the religions of the world is probably to be found in Ninian Smart's immensely erudite volume on *World Religions*. In this encyclopedic work — and rather surprisingly and even bravely, given the attitude to theology found among so many contemporary philosophers, scientists, and even practitioners of Smart's own discipline, religious studies — he quite rightly offers brief but detailed and accurate accounts of the theological, that is to say, philosophical elements from each of the main areas of the religious map of the world and from different ages of their history. Yet Smart's book should really not surprise anyone on this account, or not anyone who realizes that a religious faith, whatever else it might be, is in essence what it has already been called on many occasions above, a *weltanschauung*, a comprehensive view of a world that we all know and share. The views of the world that are found in the faiths of the world are admittedly concerned mainly with reaches of reality that far exceed the more utilitarian aims of science in its instrumentalist mode. The religious worldview reaches toward issues of ultimate origin and destiny, concentrating at the outset at least on the characteristic chauvinism of *homo sapiens's* focus in its own species and on the cosmic powers and possibilities that that species encounters and tries to understand. And yet, however much such views on the world might extend beyond science, as that is currently and conventionally practiced, they are still views on the world, gained by reflection on living in the world and issuing in directions on ways to live in the world, for the best outcome for all concerned. Such comprehensive world views are quite clearly concerned with living and ways of living in that same world. As much as they are concerned with theorizing about it all, they seek a truth about a life and a way. And they are therefore in all of these respects verifiable and falsifiable in their way, just as the predominantly instrumentalist-utilitarian sciences of our time are verifiable and falsifiable in their way.

In theory then all religions can be expected to give an account of the faith that is in them, as Paul might put it, and indeed as Paul himself did when he presented his faith in terms of a true and false wisdom, the wisdom of the cross of Jesus contrasted with the proud wisdom of the world, and with the wisdom of the Greeks in particular, which Paul rather too harshly judges to be no better than foolishness. So that the account given of any faith should be rational and persuasive, as Paul's account was, for it ranges from the evidences of a creator in creation that he rehearsed in his Epistle to the Romans, to his insistence before the Athenians that their statue to the unknown God was in fact to that creator God that their own poets (read: mythographers) acknowledged behind the divine "personae" that in polytheistic myth personify the different creative hypostases of divinity. And the account given in any *weltanschauungen* normally ranges further, to the observance of the waste and destruction of life in everyone's experience of life, a process adversarial to life that follows and increases upon the dedication of human life to powers, such as that of Mammon, that although themselves creatures of *homo sapiens*, are yet entrusted by the same *homo sapiens* with the task of keeping death and its harbingers at bay. Consequently, such comprehensive accounts of cosmic reality may well conclude with the contrasting experience of a life blessed by hope and joy and tranquillity even in the face of suffering and death. A life that is lived by those who place their trust in the Creator who pours out life in abundance to all, and thus graces them with the power to pour out the wine and to break the bread of life unstintingly to each other.

It is indeed difficult to imagine anything that is more easily and regularly verifiable or falsifiable than these comprehensive world views. And it is important at this point to understand that the verifiability and falsifiability of such *weltanschauungen*, such as the Christian example of a religious worldview already offered above, are equally available to all of the following: to those who insist that the world view came to them by special divine revelation, erupting into the natural world from outside of it (whatever that might mean); to those who insist that it came to them entirely from within and through this world and its history; and to those, like Calvin for instance, who proposed that the full and blessed-making revelation of God the Creator in creation came originally in and through God's very creation of the world (the covenant of creation), but that this was then lost to view in the blindness induced by original sin, and restored only by its especial re-revelation by Jesus the Christ, a revelation now contained in its fullness and purity only in the Bible. The same verifiability *and* falsifiability is available in all of these cases. But more on that later when issues of general and special revelation and faith come up for analysis. The matter of original sin is already dealt with, and the *sola scriptura*, only-in-the-Bible position, can be assessed properly only in the course of coming to appreciate other options and other faiths.

At this point of the argument of this book it dawns upon the writer that a reader may suddenly awake to the impression of an intrusive and growing anomaly. We are well into a chapter entitled "Credo," translated as "I believe." Yet we now find ourselves discussing philosophies as forms of credos, despite the fact that philosophies have always been considered the most rational of enterprises and, certainly since the dawning of the Enlightenment, the self-styled Age of Reason, belief or faith has been thought to be something rather different, beyond reason, if not beneath it. The dissolution of this anomaly may be achieved by recalling some remarks already made, to the effect that reasonable philosophical or scientific positions may be regarded as reasonable beliefs, that is to say, positions for which there is, not an apodictic proof which is seldom if ever available, but sufficient evidence to make it reasonable to accept and hold the positions in question. Yet one senses that at this point of the argument of the book the coincidence of belief or, better, faith and reason is assumed to be so complete that a somewhat stronger solvent of the appearance of anomaly is called for. So the following recipe for such a solvent might be suggested. Elements of it have already occurred and will occur again in different contexts, but it is worth reprising them briefly just here.

Just as the acquisition of knowledge and even more so the acquisition of wisdom is, first and foremost, a matter of practical engagement with the world around us; so faith also is, first and foremost, a matter of walking the walk before talking the talk. More elegantly put, it is a way that is walked, a life that is lived, before it is talked up as an expression of truth asking others for assent. This is all the more true since we humans are conscious and responsible agents interacting with all other creatures in a continuously created and hence evolving universe. So that knowing reality can never be a matter of a factual description of its state and status at any particular, frozen moment in time. It is, rather, a matter of envisaging how it is now evolving, and how to contribute creatively to its evolution, for the best outcome for all involved, since the destiny of each creature is ineluctably entangled with the destiny of all. And that involves trusting in our knowledge of it, trusting it to behave as we think we know it, having faith that on the basis of this knowledge and trust, all will turn out for the best for all; in short, keeping faith. The man or woman who can see things as they are with a view that sees simultaneously how things will then work out for the best is the prophet, the seer. Who has seen this better than Nietzsche, as quoted at the head of this chapter? Admittedly he might have put the matter more kindly. Yet something in our breasts — perhaps a less worthy emotion — responds to his savage invective against the sons and daughters of the Enlightenment, of the Great Awaking, of the Age of Reason (they had it coming to them!). Presenting themselves as Realists, indeed; in short, capable only of describing reality as it momentarily is, thus achieving instantly allegedly universal truths that required neither the visionary nor the prophet. While in actual fact the whole mental furniture of these people consisted of mere "paintings of all that has ever been believed," a mixum-gatherum of the best and the worst philosophical ideas bequeathed to them since the beginnings of Western civilization. "You are unfruitful: *therefore* you lack belief. But he who had to create always had his prophetic dreams ... and he believed in belief."

A brief indication then is all that is possible or necessary now, a short survey of the role played in some religions by some philosophies. By some of those loving (*philo-*) quests for wisdom (*sophia*) that seemed to uncover a source of life and of the wisdom of life-giving ways so deep and comprehensive that it deserved the attribute, divine (*theios*), and the resulting communicable systems of thought (*logos*) about a world so sourced and enlightened could therefore be called theologies. First, the case of Philo of Alexandria has already emerged, with his Jewish theology made up, as later in the Christian case, of borrowed Middle Platonism. Thereafter theology never played in Judaism anything like the part it quickly came to play in Christianity. But there are significant instances of exception. In medieval times and in places ranging from Baghdad to Cordoba, where the Jewish populations had been overtaken by Islamic rule, Jewish philosophers like Sa'adyah ben Yosef in Baghdad and Moses Maimonides in Cordoba undertook tasks similar to that accomplished by Philo. Except on these occasions they were working with a version of Greek philosophical thought which had been developed by their Muslim overlords, and in which Aristotle, for instance, proved a more important influence than was the case with the predominantly Platonic philosophy borrowed by Philo and the Christian theologians in order to give an account of their faith. And this brought about a Jewish theology remarkably similar to that which the Muslims of the time were developing, and to that which, say, Thomas Aquinas developed for Christianity at the same time. A remarkable time and effort indeed in which these three members of one family of faiths shared a similar theological task, with very similar origins in the same Greek philosophical theology, and with very similar results in all three instances.

This medieval Jewish theology was followed by the emergence of Jewish Kabbalah, often regarded as a "mystical," if not an occult movement. But in fact it was inspired by Neo-Platonist-type views of the One, of the "emanation" of the world from the One through divine hypostases like Thought, Wisdom, Life-Power and so on. And it led in the end to a practical spirituality for us creatures that would bring us, saved, to unity with God once again. So that all of the criticism recorded above about describing this "mysticism" as some kind of esoteric experience, rather than the experience in this world of an itinerary all must follow, applies here to Kabbalah also. Simon Shokek's recent book on *Kabbalah and the Art of Being* offers a contemporary analysis, based interestingly on the Kabbalistic theme of creation, of the manner in which Kabbalah is a practical wisdom "for living, creativity and well-being that has long been integrated into the lives of Jewish people, shaping their faith and identity."

It was Arabic thought that provided the inspiration and format for such Jewish and Christian theologizing from early to high medieval times. And it in turn took its origin from the discovery by Muslims in their newly conquered territories of selections of Greek philosophical works that included a much stronger Aristotelian element than had the predominantly and almost exclusively Neo-Platonic philosophy transmitted to the fractured remnants of the Western Roman Empire by John Scotus Eriugena. These selections also carried the sense of continuity of philosophical thought across currently separated ranges of science, metaphysics and theology. And the revival of that sense of the unbroken continuity of philosophy from physics to theology can be attributed also to the stronger Aristotelian coloring of the philosophical treasures then acquired by the new Arabian conquerors of these ancient cultures.

The simplest way to characterize the resulting theology with which these Muslims then influenced Jews and Christians alike, is to comment briefly on two key terms. The Arabic *kalam*, used to translate the Greek *logos*, could refer either to the word of God in the Qur'an, or to the rational account of this Qur'anic word that is then known as theology. Then the second Arabic term, *falsafah*, is really the Greek *philosophia* pronounced by a speaker of Arabic. And it referred primarily to the Aristotelian-colored philosophy, both content and method, that these Arabs had discovered to their considerable enrichment. Now if one were to listen to experts in religious studies these days one would interpret these two terms to refer to two quite different, if not opposed types of exercise. The one, dependent on a fideistic approach to an alleged divine revelation, devoted entirely to the bare unfolding of the content of this, and called theology. The other an exercise in investigative reason that tries to comprehend the universe and all the agents and agencies operative within it.

Ergo — the modern scholar in such matters rudely interrupts — theology should not be allowed in universities, but religious studies should be allowed in, because religious studies, or the science of religion as it has come to be called more recently, simply studies religions as social phenomena. It studies religions phenomenologically, that is to say. It notes their credos, their rituals, their ways of life and social structures, and the effects of these on private, civic and political life, yet without any further interest in asking about the truth or falsehood of the worldview that any of these religions presents. But that interruption, rude or otherwise, represents a complete travesty of what was going on in Spain and the Middle East throughout the Middle Ages, in contemporary Islamic, Jewish and Christian circles, and what should be going on today, and what is in fact going on where academia shows any real sense of its full responsibilities. For *logos* connotes an intelligible formulation, like something produced by reason, and of which a reasonable account can be given. An account of what is there and how it comes to be there, and what is behind its being there, and where it might be going from here. An account which is then reasonable in both senses of the word: understandable and acceptable in view of the evidence available to verify or to falsify it.

For these three religions then, each carrying a central and authoritative set of sacred scriptures, from the moment that Islam began to take on ancient Greek philosophy, as Jews had done once before and Christians had done wholeheartedly some six centuries before, it was a question as to how the *logos* presented in their respective scriptures related to the *sophia* they happened upon in the cultures they occupied. Certainly in each case that relationship has been described both by some of those who experienced the encounter and by those who write up the history of these encounters, as a clash between fideists and rationalists. And there is no doubt that there have been scriptural fideists, called such by outsiders and sometimes accepted by themselves, in these and subsequent ages. Just as there have been rationalists, once again called such by outsiders and sometimes accepted by themselves. And no doubt also, in both cases those who attribute or accept such adjectives have a false, or at least an inflated view of faith and reason. For most, if not all of what passes for true human knowledge is in fact reasonable belief. That is to say, it is based upon what we know of all that we encounter in the world as a result of working in and with the world (a practicalist theory of knowledge once again). And that working-with is in its most important respect a trusting of ourselves to the world — a trust in both ourselves as worker-knowers and in the world — on the basis of experiences beneficent or otherwise that we had and have before we investigate any matter more reflectively.

It is instructive to note how a contemporary trio, Richard Martin, Mark Woodward and Dwis Atmaja, writing on *Defenders of Reason in Islam*, from the era now in question down to modern times, describe the encounter between rationalists — they are using the adjective simply to indicate the centrality of reason, *logos* — and scripturalists, that is to say, those who take their scriptures to be the primary, if not the sole authority on truth. They see this from their Islamic sources in the Middle Ages, not as an encounter between rationalists and irrationalists (most likely meaning fideists), but rather as an encounter between rationalism and "scriptural rationalism." And that does accord best with an encounter named in these early centuries of Islam as one between *kalam* (*logos*) and *falsafah*. In addition, there is the fact that the major authors of this medieval period, whether they be regarded as practitioners of *kalam* or *falsafah*, find themselves discussing, when all are taken together, virtually all the same matters. These matters range from creation through God's consequently revealed (or hidden) nature; through God's consequent relationship with the world and more specifically with the human race; through human freedom in the face of God's omnipotence; through human morality (is something right because God says so, or does God's law enjoin something upon us because it is right?); through human falling, and God's continuing efforts to bring humanity back to life; and finally to the "mystical" way to God, our destiny beyond death, and the final destiny of the universe.

Furthermore, in discussing these common matters, and particularly where they are displeased with Aristotle for taking a view of some matter that actually contradicts the Holy Qur'an, or that at least represents a clearly alternative view — matters such as the eternity of the material universe, the prospects of personal immortality, and so on — seldom if ever does the Islamic scholar, whether he takes himself at the time to be doing *falsafah* or *kalam*, simply state the relevant Qur'anic text as if that was the end of the matter. Instead reasons are regularly offered as to why Aristotle got it wrong in some respects at least. Something similar to what Aquinas does in his turn when he shows that Aristotle's idea of the soul as the form of the body does not in fact entail the end of the individual soul on the dissolution of the individual body. Or when Al-Ghazali, anxious for the full and accurate truth of the Holy Qur'an, criticizes the whole business of hypostasizing God's Word or Wisdom or Spirit, not just by quoting the Qur'an against such a practice, but by arguing from the absolute oneness of the One against all manner of incursive polytheism. A polytheism that he thought to be inevitable in such hypostasizing, as it well might be if the hypostases are glossed in terms of persons in the univocal sense, and not the metaphorical or mythic sense of personification of divine attributes.

It is both fascinating and instructive for anyone who wants to understand the role of theology as a form of the credo of a religion to work through these Jewish and Muslim philosopher-theologians, and then through the two great theological encyclopedias of Thomas Aquinas. He was the greatest Christian philosopher-theologian of the Middle Ages, and he also worked with the more Aristotelianized philosophy that came to him also via Muslims like ibn Sina and ibn Rushd, and that had taken hold in the University of Paris during his sojourn there. The two works of his that are most worth consulting here are: the one, the *Summa Theologiae*, looking inward at the Christian faith, as it were; and the other, the *Summa Contra Gentes*, looking outward toward his Muslim counterparts in particular. What is most instructive perhaps are the degrees to which these philosopher-theologians think the contents of their respective sacred scriptures can be represented in this common Aristotelianized but still predominantly Platonic philosophy. These degrees range from those in all three religions who act as if virtually all of their respective scriptural credos can be represented in this philosophy, to those who believe that virtually none of it can. More instructive still is the view that is taken by those philosopher-theologians when they do agree that some issue is certainly falsely presented in this incoming philosophy. Many believe, for instance, that Aristotle was wrong in thinking that matter was eternal. But do they then think that their sacred scriptures offer a truth about this matter that was simply beyond the powers of human reason? Or do some think, rather, that it is merely a matter of Aristotle making a mistake, and that the role of their scriptures is to offer a corrective? And is that a corrective that a more effective or advanced use of reason might have arrived at in any case?

Some of our philosophers, Al-Ghazali for example, take that last view of Aristotle's account of creation. Aquinas, however, simply states that human reason, depending upon the data of much later experience, could not decide, even from the doctrine of creation out of nothing, whether matter was eternal or not. For God's creation out of nothing is equally compatible with the eternity of matter and with its non-eternity. So that all we can say is that, as a matter of fact, the scriptures inform us of the temporal limits of this material universe at both origin and end. But then Aquinas also thought that the doctrine of the divine Trinity could not be achieved by human reason working on the data of our experience of the creation. Despite the fact, of which he was most probably ignorant, that the finest statement of that very doctrine of the Trinity in the whole of the Christian tradition had been borrowed from the Greek philosophers. On the whole then, and taken in the round, it would be difficult indeed to conclude that there is anything in the scriptures or the creeds of the Christian religion, or indeed in the scriptures or creeds of other members of that family of religions, that could not be investigated, and verified or falsified, by that reflection on our experience in and of our world, that constitutes theology as a philosophical discipline. And is there not a further lesson for this triune family of religions here, in the very medieval scenario of all three managing to deal with their religious faith by use of the same philosophical theology? For they even agree with each other on the points at which they found difficulty with that same Aristotelianized Platonism. And they very largely agreed with each other also in the strategies each adopted to deal with such difficulties. To the point at which one is forced to ask, with some bemusement: what on earth was it then that kept them still denouncing each other as false or falsified faiths?

Now, of course, all of that does not mean that theology as a form of credo is any less error-prone than are scriptures or creeds. In fact theologies are almost certainly more prone to error than are scriptures or creeds, at least those creeds which stick to summarizing the scriptural stories, and avoid including in their mythic texts distilled theological formulae. Since such inclusion would then result in giving the theologies from which the formulae are derived, together with their shortcomings and perhaps even errors, both a shelf-life that is too long for this species of human construct and a level of authorization that philosophies should not have. This is because theologies, being philosophies in essence, have certain inherent drawbacks to them that other constructions of credos, such as sacred scriptures and creeds, do not have. These drawbacks are connected with the abstract and relatively artificial units of which philosophies are made up, and which are worth noting briefly, if only in order to place theology in its proper place in the pecking order of credos that correct each other.

Theology in the strict sense of the term is fashioned first and foremost from concepts and their logical alignment, just as myths are made of images and their merging into metaphor and story. Concept is formed by the abstractive process of selecting a certain feature that runs through things, and the more things and species of things it runs through the more universal a feature it is seen to be, and the more extensive the heuristic results that its use promises. Think of the four dimensions, of the molecular structure of DNA, of the atomic structure of the whole material universe, or of yet more abstract nouns like substance and accident, or of Aristotle's prime matter and form. Yet these abstractions are to some extent arbitrary, at the very least in the sense that the most effective and operative ones can change from culture to culture, and from age to age. Think of Darwin's evolution theory before the birth of genetics; or of Einstein's demotion of matter as a fundamental concept in physics; or of modern philosophers replacing the substance-accident concepts in their reality-appearance mode with the concept of the phenomenon. So that no particular set of concepts, however logically deployed, can tell the whole truth about reality, not even that fullness of truth that imagery in its efforts to reflect the imprint of whole objects and constellations of objects can hope to attain. Or, better say, it can take many supplementary sets of abstractions to convey what one set of images can uncover.

The gradual accretion of abstractions and sets of abstractions is therefore even more necessary in order to tell as much of the truth as the human mind is capable of perceiving, than is the multiplication of images. For in any case, what the conceptual mind is abstracting from is the imagery that forms our primordial apprehension of reality. It is therefore doubly tragic for our ability to perceive and to tell the truth when we insist on treating any one conceptual system as the definitive truth for all times and places, the whole truth and nothing but the truth. So, ideally, what one should expect in any religion that bothers to produce theologies is a number of different theologies. Ideally also these should be contemporaneous, for that would help greatly the prospects for their mutual correction or improvement. And they should certainly be sequential, if only to keep up with the ever new conceptual systems that scientific and general philosophical developments bring into common usage in different cultures and at different times.

For an example of different theologies that have lived side by side, one might consult the great Hindu tradition, and the three Vedanta schools. Each one takes roughly the same selection of Hindu scriptures, namely, the *Upanishads, Vedanta Sutras,* and the *Bhagavad Gita,* and all three try to give a philosophical presentation of the main teachings of these sacred scriptures on the relationship between the Godhead (*Brahman*), the human self (*atman*), and the world. To note the differences between the three schools, it is only necessary here to observe the fact that, first, Shankara and his school taught an Advaita or non-dualist philosophy of Godhead and empirical world. At the level of everyday human experience and perception there does seem to be differences, if not a complete set of distinctions between God, self and world. But, a strictly Advaita philosophy maintains, such impressions of distinct realms of reality really represent nothing more than *maya*, ignorance or illusion. It is only when we break through to a deeper level of knowledge and truth that we come to realize true reality: Godhead, selves and world are basically one, always have been and always will be. Then came Ramanuja and his school, arguing what can only be called a modified dualism: the world is in fact God's body (where else have we heard that recently in the West?), and the blessed union with God in which our true being forever consists, does not imply total absorption. Finally, Madhva and his school came much closer to what is a general Christian view, namely, that clear distinctions and differences exist between the Godhead, human selves and the rest of the natural world, and these persist eternally.

It is difficult to look across these there schools of Hindu theology and then to look across at similarly different moves or reaches in the history of Christian, Muslim and Jewish theologies without beginning to get the impression that they differ mostly in the manner in which they emphasize one abstracted feature of the complex reality they all contemplate, if not to the exclusion, then to the demotion of other features. Might it not be then that it is in the inevitable partiality of the view, a partiality that is endemic to all systems of arbitrary concept, that the potential for falsification consists? And that this potential for falsification is realized only to the extent that any theological system is promoted to the position of claiming to tell the truth, the whole truth and nothing but the truth? In Shankara's case, the highest form of unity may seem to consist in complete absorption in the One, and complete absorption can seem to amount to annihilation, and annihilating is no way to unify something with something else. And there is then no point in saying that what is said to be annihilated was only an illusory reality in the first place, for an illusory reality is a real illusion, and that reality at least (for it is something; it is not nothing) has to be annihilated. Hence Ramanuja might be seen to be actually righting a potential for a final and quite serious imbalance in Shankara by insisting nevertheless on the (admittedly derivative and so infinitely lesser) reality of what the latter called illusion. And Madhva might be seen to be trying to simultaneously right the possible unbalances in both of the foregoing systems. Similarly, where a culture sees a change in the general set of philosophical concepts brought into use, different sequential theologies must be allowed to emerge. The partial view that each one offers could then be justified by seeing it as supplying something which previous ones could no longer supply. So that any insistence on treating some past philosophy/theology as the whole and immutable truth in the case of any religious faith, as in any other matter, must inevitably result either in popular misunderstanding and mystification, or in downright falsification of the truth to be told. The Roman Catholic hierarchy, by adopting ancient theological formulae and imposing them for all time as definitions of the truth, contributes much to consequent mystification, and at times to downright falsification of the Christian truth. An example of this will be seen in the case of transubstantiation as a definition of the real presence of Christ in the eucharist.

In the end, all that can be said about theologies, as about other forms of the credo of any religion, is that they can be corrected either by other theologies, or by renewed perusal of scriptures or creeds, or by looking humbly to other religions. And ultimately all that is contained in the credo of any religion can be verified or falsified by the ultimate test of living and dying. For the truth expressed in each form of credo, it cannot be repeated too often, is a truth about a way and a life that holds out the highest hope for life. So that if walking in the way that any form of a credo describes, even begins to be experienced as living for death, rather than dying for life, then that part is false, and no amount of Bible quotation, or loud confessing, or clever reasoning, can make it otherwise. By their fruits, as Jesus would say when the pretensions of any prophet or teacher came in question, by their fruits you will know what it is that you are taking from these forms of credo into your own heart and mind, its truth or its falsehood.

Chapter Six

CODE

When your spirit wants to speak in images, pay heed, for that is when your virtue has its origin and beginning.

Then your body is elevated and risen up; it enraptures the spirit with its joy, that it may become creator and evaluator and lover and benefactor of all things.

When your heart surges broad and full like a river, a blessing and a danger to those who live nearby, that is when your virtue has its origin and beginning.

When you are exalted above praise and blame, and your will wants to command all things as the will of a lover, that is when your virtue has its origin and beginning.

When you despise the soft bed and what is pleasant . . . that is when your virtue has its origin and beginning.

Truly it is a new good and a new evil: Truly, a new roaring in the depths and the voice of a new fountain!

No more to will and no more to evaluate and no more to create: Ah, that this great lassitude may ever stay far from me.

I offer myself to love, *and my neighbor as myself* — that is the language of all creators. All creators, however, are hard.

— Nietzsche, *Thus Spoke Zarathustra*

Is There a Christian Morality?

If religion in certain cultures simply refers to life, and is so much a part of everyday living in this extraordinary universe as to render the word *religion* itself practically otiose, something of the same might as well be said of the word *morality*. Morality simply refers to the kind of living that characterizes human beings in the world. It must remain a moot point for the moment as to whether the word applies also to the lives of other species. And just as religion carries a special reference to these same lives in

227

so far as they are lived in the presence of some perceived ultimate source and goal of all existence, so morality carries a special reference to human life precisely in so far as it is characterized by the qualities of freedom and responsibility. Or in other words, precisely in so far as human life is characterized by self-conscious creativity, by the capacity for being knowingly at least co-responsible for renewing or making something new. Further, just as religion on reflection finds expression in words, in scriptures, in creeds, and in theologies, so does morality find its verbalized expressions also, and in a variety of modes.

Morality can be expressed in the mode of morality tales, like *Aesop's Fables,* a mode similar though not identical to the mode of myth. But morality can also be investigated and find oblique expression when myth and indeed good literature in general identifies, without ever moralizing, the challenges, opportunities and dilemmas that human life constantly throws up. And especially when this literature then reveals the consequences for better or worse that follow upon choices made or paths taken that might otherwise seem preordained. In this mode the human imagination shows once again its heuristic primacy. And its prowess in investigating human life in all of its moral density and recurring confusion is all the more impressive in that it does not explicitly moralize — "whenever your spirit wants to speak in images, pay heed, for that is where your virtue has its origin and beginning." Instead of explicitly moralizing, myth and literature in general give insight into the processes by which we all of us act daily as moral agents. Furthermore, such literature, whether oral or written, does one other thing that is of more crucial importance to morality than anything else. It educates the emotions, the most elemental, embodied powers of the human spirit, that the crude dualist considers hostile to moral virtue, but that are in themselves both the primary heuristic means of seeking out good and evil, and in addition the primary motivating powers that take any moral orientation from insight to action — "then your body is elevated and risen up; it enraptures the spirit with its joy, that it may become creator and evaluator and lover and benefactor of all things." Much if not all of this could be claimed of course for other creative arts besides literature.

Morality can also be expressed in the language of conceptual abstraction and analytic and synthetic logic, and it is with this mode of expression that the literature of moral philosophy and ethics makes us most familiar. Both modes deal in the three main categories of the formulation of morality: the category of ideals, the category of virtues and the category of rules and regulations. The great moral ideals that are held up to us — goodness itself, justice, love, freedom, and so on — are sometimes defined at great length. Think of justice in Plato's *Republic*, or of love in the *Symposium*. But it does not take too much cynicism to observe that the use of appeals to ideals, especially in political rhetoric (and that includes ecclesiastical political rhetoric), is designed to be effective precisely by a lack of definition for which a surfeit of emotional effulgence is then substituted. As George Orwell put, better to have the ring of freedom in your ears than in your nose. Like the freedom that the American president with eye-watering sincerity, and the British prime minister with that telltale tremble of the lip, are currently bringing to the unfortunate Iraqis — or at least to as many of them as may manage to avoid being counted as collateral damage in the process — by the bombs and bullets of their liberators.

Virtues too need careful definition, if they are not to be too easily abused by those who should know better. As ideals name the active states in which the well-being of humans and others consist, virtues name the habitual powers and patterns of behavior that can be both innate and acquired with practice. So that some virtues and ideals share the same names, as is the case for example with love, or justice. Some are called cardinal virtues: in addition to justice there are prudence, fortitude and temperance. For they are commonly involved in the practice of all other virtues and in moral behavior in general. Christians sometimes call three of the virtues supernatural: in addition to love, there is faith and hope. Even though there is nothing obviously supernatural about any of these three. Moral living consists essentially in continuous co-creativity in a continuously created universe, and that requires faith and hope in all the creative powers involved, and most particularly in the ultimate creative power in the universe. And the virtue of love for all who are together involved in this cosmic creativity is also required, if only to prevent treating these as mere means to one's own self-centered ends — "I offer myself to love, and my neighbor as myself." And, finally, the virtues can be abused on the basis of lack of clear and cogent definition, just as ideals can be similarly abused. How much evil is daily inflicted in the name of love?

That brings up the third and most universal and frequent category of the formulations of morality that has been encountered in human society since history began: the category of codes of laws, rules, regulations. This category certainly makes up with a vengeance for that lack of clear definition that can otherwise leave other categories of the expression of morality at the mercy of abuse by the earnest eye and the trembling lip. By far the most frequently maligned of all the forms and modes of moralizing, legislation does attempt to carry the process of the analysis of human behavior, its conditions, circumstances and effects, to some final and comprehensive clarity. However, given both the enormous complexity and, even more significantly, the constant change and evolution of human life in an evolving world, the task of analyzing human behavior, if only to divide its actions and effects into the categories of good and evil, is a never ending and not even a truly cumulative task. It is for this reason that the most evolved human societies have the so-called separation of powers, in which the legislature, without mutual interference from or with the executive power and the judicial power, is a permanent feature of the leadership of these societies. It is permanent because it must be constantly engaged in passing new legislation, revising the old, and on occasion deleting the obsolete.

Such are the general features of human morality in what may well be called its natural state, features that are characteristic of human life itself in its ever-evolving, constantly created world, a world in which all agencies operative within it are essentially inter-dependent. The different verbal accounts of human morality across different cultures and different times are then the result both of the creative imagination that constantly charts what can and ought to be done to bring things forward, and of all of the past and present that it has thereby pictured and also carefully analyzed, in the course of making each successive step forward — or backward, as the case may often be. Given this elementary account of morality and its expressions, what can be said concerning the claim of a distinctively Christian morality? It would not seem wise to approach this question by concentrating first on moral ideals or moral virtues — prudence, justice, fortitude, temperance, faith, hope and love — for despite the claims of some Christians that the last three are supernaturally infused virtues, it would be difficult indeed to substantiate a claim to the effect that Christians historically exhibited either a monopoly of these, or even a greater adherence to these, or to any others on this or any other list. It might be best therefore to concentrate, initially at least, on those codes of rules, regulations, laws, on the third category of the formulations of morality mentioned already. For in actual fact it is predominantly in terms of the moral category of codified law that Jews to this day promote the claim that the Torah represents the earliest form of ethical monotheism, together with the twin claim to be God's chosen people, appointed to cast the light to guide the feet of the nations in the true way. And it is in the context of covenant, or testament, that this claim and this special relationship between morality and a religion was sought to be established, first, in the Bible, in the religion of Israel, and then in the Christian religion-to-be.

Human Codes and Divine Covenants

Covenants (Hebrew: *berit*) in the ancient world were solemn agreements entered into by, say, kings and kingdoms, in the course of which the actions or relationships to be undertaken by the parties, or their abstinence from some of these, were defined. The gods of the parties involved were invoked as guarantors, perhaps by sacrifices offered on the occasion. The agreement of the parties was often symbolized by a meal, the breaking of bread, and so on (Gen. 31:44–54). In the special case of the covenant between Jahweh and the Israelites, however, since there was now no question of an agreement between equals, or even between members of the same class or race, the format inevitably changed. For here the initiative was and remained with God who had already done, and would now bind himself to continue to do, quite literally everything for his people. While God required that, for their part of the deal on offer, the people should behave in certain ways now once more defined for them. These covenants were then more of the nature of grace than of mutually contracted obligation. More like wills or testaments than mutually binding covenants in the classical sense. Which is probably why the Greek Bible renders the covenant idea not as *syntheke*, agreement, but as *diatheke*, a will or testament, with grace on one side and, on the other, the responsibilities that naturally follows upon the acceptance of the favor in question. Like someone inheriting a great old house together with its extensive estate, and inheriting with that all the inherent obligations that go with such a precious inheritance.

The covenant theme in this rather revised form recurs constantly over both Testaments of the Christian Bible. As commonly listed, there is the covenant with Noah (Gen. 9); the covenant with Abraham (Gen. 15, 17); the Sinai covenant mediated by Moses (Exod. 20, 24ff.); the covenant with the royal house of David (2 Sam. 7); the recommitment to the covenant under Hezekiah (2 Chron. 29) and Josiah (2 Kings 23); the promise of a new covenant in the days that are to come, as recorded, for example, by Jeremiah (Jer. 31:31–34; 32:36–41 — "I will make with them an everlasting covenant, that I will not turn away from doing good to them"). Then Jesus, on breaking bread with his disciples at their last supper, took the cup of wine and called it "the blood of the covenant," echoing the words of Moses at Sinai: "this is the blood of the covenant." Paul however contrasts this "new" covenant mediated through Jesus with the Mosaic covenant which imposed the Torah, seeing the former as modeled rather upon the covenant with Abraham and the blessing it promised to all nations (1 Cor. 11:25; Gal. 4:21–31; Rom. 4); whereas the writer of the Epistle to the Hebrews prefers to see the new covenant mediated through Jesus the Christ, as the very fulfillment of the promise of a new covenant issued through the prophet, Jeremiah, even if, like Paul, he also sees this new covenant as the displacement, rather than the fulfillment of an "obsolete" Mosaic covenant (Heb. 8:6–13).

Now that represents a fairly standard textbook list of covenant texts and of the covenants that are recorded in the Bible. And there are just two things to be said about it. First, the Mosaic covenant stands out from the rest both in what Christians call the Old Testament (i.e., covenant) and what they call the New Testament. Although it stands out in a different way in the latter than it does in the former. In the former it is the covenant to which most space is given, and that mainly because the terms and conditions of the covenant, the responsibilities that fall upon the human partners to the covenant — or should one say, the beneficiaries of the testament — are gone into in great detail over many chapters of the book entitled Exodus. These obligations range over all three categories: ethical, ritual/cultic, and constitutional. The ethical obligations are outlined in the so-called Decalogue, the Ten Commandments, and subsequently in a long and rather rambling code of conduct covering most ordinary areas of human commerce and encounter. The cultic-ritual obligations and taboos, including a liturgical calendar of three major annual festivals and the Sabbath observance, are then laid down in even greater detail. And, finally, the leadership and governmental issues, the constitutional features, are interspersed with all of this.

In this covenant text in Exodus then, and in this alone, one reads a full account of the code of ethics, the cult and constitution through which the Israelites were to live out their responsibilities to God in God's good world. With the result that it is in this extended covenant text, it is in connection with this covenant mediated by Moses, that the fullest account of the credo, the faith of Israel is provided. And that remains, together with some later additions of the institutions of kingship and temple, for example, the acknowledged covenantal context of the full faith of Israel up to the time of the addition to the Bible of the Christian documents. A view further copper-fastened by the conservative Jewish insistence that the sacred scriptures of Israel consisted in the first five books of the Bible, the Pentateuch, and the attribution of their authorship to Moses. And it is by this very reason of its unrivalled position as the most comprehensive source of the faith of Israel, that in all the major texts on covenant in the added Christian documents it is the Mosaic covenant that is mostly before the minds of the authors. Whether the texts in question have Jesus at his last supper echo the words of Moses, or Paul and the writer of the Epistle to the Hebrews argue for replacement of the current (Mosaic) version of the testament, or Matthew suggest, rather, that the version of testament current at Jesus's coming is now really and finally being fulfilled. Matthew's suggestion to this effect is carried both by his allegory of the setting from which Jesus delivers the law, from the mountain, and in the words he places on Jesus's own lips, that one iota of the Mosaic law will not pass away, but all will be brought to fulfillment.

The second thing that has to be said concerning the list of covenants and covenant texts set out above is that it can be accused of a serious omission. The accusation refers to a particular one of these incidents of covenant making, one that is almost always omitted from the list. One which is much more than an incident of covenant making among other incidents, one in fact which is the foundational incident of all incidents, including the incident on Sinai and the incident of a certain last farewell supper in Jerusalem long ago. The reference here is to the incident of covenant making that accompanies all other incidents as their ultimate source and sustenance: the incident otherwise known as the creation of the world. Yet not all lists of covenants omit the creation of the world or fail to recognize the fact that the divine creation of the world constitutes in and of itself a primordial covenantal relationship between God and humanity in particular. The Westminster Confession of Faith, for example, recognizes a covenant made with Adam in the very course of creation, and refers to it as a covenant of works. By that this Confession must be taken to mean that the blessed destiny which the Creator intended in creating humanity could be achieved, in part at least, by the co-operative work of human kind. But then, under the influence on the Confession of that errant Augustinian-type idea of original sin transmitted to all members of the race at or by the very fact of their joining that race, the Confession goes on immediately to conclude that the very first transgression of Adam had the effect of canceling that covenant of creation. And canceling it in such wise as to make it necessary for God to secure the original intention for eternal human happiness by substituting a covenant of grace in Jesus Christ. The original sin element in this account of the matter is a classic example of biblical eisegesis, as is the consequent theology of salvation by faith alone, and not by works — a distinction that makes little sense, in any case, in view of all that has already been said about faith as a keeping faith with the Creator God first and foremost in the living of our lives. But the main point of this passage from this Confession remains. There *is* a covenant in or at the very creation of the world, and it is indeed as much a covenant of works, as the Westminster Confession acknowledges, as a covenant based on believing some statement about God and humanity.

To all of which it is at this point necessary only to add the cautionary remark: works and grace must not be opposed so as to yield the false impression that a covenant of works cannot also be a covenant of grace. For in reality all covenants between God and humanity are brought about primarily by the original and originating grace and favor of the will or testament of God, from which the moral and other active responsibilities of the recipients then naturally flow. Furthermore, it is a mistake to read Paul and other Christian biblical documents as if they were contrasting grace or faith with works, simply with works in general. What Paul is contrasting, rather, is faith or grace with *the works of the law*, the current Torah. And in doing this Paul is not just condemning Jewish legalism, but rather rejecting the forms that the Jewish religion, the Torah, had taken. Just as Jesus had done with particular paradigmatic reference to Sabbath observance and the Temple. That Augustinian-type doctrine of original sin has a lot to answer for, in the line of spreading confusion, and sometimes downright pernicious nonsense, throughout Western theology.

Needless to say, when there is talk of a covenant being constituted in or at the very creation of the world, that is not to be taken to refer to some specific act or incident of entering an agreement or publishing a will, some act or incident additional to the act of creation itself. Like everything else that can be known about God the creator, the relationships in which humans stand to God, and above all the covenantal relationship, are revealed and known at all times and in all places, through our experience of the creation itself. The form of creation myth that imagines God creating the cosmos through the agencies of God's personified Word or Wisdom, in which human beings can then participate in a most particular fashion (in the image of the divine creator), is then the form of creation myth that most clearly yields the revelation of the covenant of creation.

That is what the Westminster Confession of Faith really implies when it sets first in the list of covenants the covenant of creation. By the very action of creation the eternal God endows us with the prospects of limitless existence and life, together with all of its supports and enhancements. In and through that same action we are endowed with the wisdom that enables us to be co-creators of creation, after our measure of course. And simultaneously with our inheritance of this limitless endowment of life and wisdom, we incur our own special responsibility for its maintenance and development. These are the basic terms of the primordial and everlasting covenant of creation. And all that remains to be done now is to look as briefly as possible at the other main covenants envisaged in the Bible; with an eye to their relationship with the covenant that is daily renewed in the continuous process of creation itself.

The very next covenant recorded in the Bible, after the foundational creation covenant, is the covenant mediated by Noah. This covenant is presented in the text as a special covenant drawn up on a special occasion and in particular conditions, the pullulating sinfulness of the race. Yet it is no less a covenant of creation for that fact. For in this text the dominant images are those of the flood, that is to say, the watery chaos, the formless no-thing that is the antithesis and the mortal enemy of formed things, and particularly of those dynamically formed things that have and propagate life, the *tohu w' bohu* then that is the nemesis of all existence and life. The story form of the myth then imagines the Creator, faced now with the destructive force of human sin, simply sustaining this destructive force. Indeed God co-operates with the destructive force of human sinfulness, even to the point at which the whole world is submerged once more in primeval chaos. Yet God holds back from this final death of the world, by saving not just Noah and his immediate family, but a pair of every species of beast and bird and creeping thing. In short, the Creator is seen once more separating land from the watery chaos, and furnishing it again with all living things; creating anew, or rather continuing to create the world. As the order to Noah intimates: "be fruitful and multiply, bring forth abundantly on the earth and multiply within it." And all is then summed up in the explicit terms of a covenant: "I establish my covenant with you, that never again shall all flesh be cut off by the waters of a flood, and never again shall there be a flood to destroy the earth" (Gen. 9:7–11).

Clearly this is a covenant of creation forever renewed or, better, a testament of creation eternally continued, never to be destroyed. God will continue forever to create, to sustain the forming and advancement of existence and life over incursive chaos. And especially since no condition is attached to this covenant to the effect that this commitment holds only as long as humans refrain from sinning so much again, the implication clearly is that God will continue the creative process even at the point at which this continuous creation is the response to the recurring chaos-incurring destructiveness of human evil-doing; at all points, in short, at which creation has to become salvation from sin. This is then the mythic portrayal of God's commitment to a love that remains steadfast through all rebuff and abuse of it; the love, as Dante put it at the end of the *Paradiso*, that moves the sun and the other stars. This continuous creation-salvation is God's steadfast love, so often invoked in the rest of the Bible. And it is especially invoked when a corresponding steadfast love is invited from the human partners in the covenant of creation, and when it is pointedly preferred to cultic sacrifice. And as the Creator suffers the rebuff to creative love, in the wilful destruction of creation by the creatures put principally in charge of creation, that scorned love never ceases to show itself in act, even while it is visiting upon that favored species the penal consequences wrought upon itself and its world by its own self-centered evil-doing.

These two covenants then, the first implicit in the creation of Adam and his commissioning to rule the world as king by the wisdom of God available to him in creation, and the second explicitly mediated through the legendary figure of Noah, are both covenants in and of creation. Therefore they are covenants with the whole of humanity. For Adam in the Genesis text, as its mythic nature requires, can refer both to an individual and to all of human kind. Furthermore, Noah is father of all humanity, subsequent to all other living humans having been destroyed, and his three sons who were with him in the ark are regarded in the Bible as the ancestors of all the nations. Indeed, in the case of the Noah myth, the covenant goes beyond the human race and is explicitly referred to as a covenant "with every living creature," suggesting surely that all living creatures have a right to the life that is given them by God's continuing creation. But for the moment it is best to concentrate on this covenant with the whole of humankind, since some of the covenant texts now to come on stream seem to narrow that extent of reference. In the case of the next covenant encountered in the course of the biblical narrative, for example, a certain narrowing of the covenantal commissioning, even if not of its beneficial outcomes, begins to appear. This is the covenant said to have been mediated through Abraham.

There are two versions of the covenant with Abraham, in chapters 15 and 17 respectively of Genesis. In the first Abraham trusts in God's promise that he will procreate innumerable offspring even though he and his wife are old, and God promises that Abraham's great nation of descendents will be given the land of Canaan, "from the river of Egypt to ... the river Euphrates." In the second, the same covenant is offered to Abraham and his descendents, but this time a further condition is added: "every male among you shall be circumcised ... any uncircumcised male ... shall be cut off from his people." In neither of these immediate contexts is there mention of benefit for nations other than that comprised of Abraham's own innumerable descendents (through Isaac), who will live in the land of milk and honey, at that time occupied by Canaanites and others. But in two other passages, one before and one after the ones just quoted, it is specifically stated by God that "by you all the families of the earth shall bless themselves (or, shall be blessed)" (Gen. 12:3; 18:18). Paul, much later, desperately wants to see in this Abrahamic covenant a precedent and prophecy of the faith in God the creator that Jesus lived and preached, and of a resulting and equal access of the Gentile nations to the everlasting divine promises of life attaching to such faith without the need to join the Jewish faith by circumcision. Therefore he wants to see this covenant as a covenant with all of humankind. For he can then argue as follows: Abraham was found righteous by God as a result of his first confession of his trust in God, the creator of life forever. And it was as a result of that faith that Abraham and his descendents were promised everlasting life and blessing. So, all who shared the faith by which Jesus lived and died, and thereby shared the Spirit that enlivened Jesus, were descendents of Abraham, whether they were circumcised or uncircumcised. For circumcision was a condition that was added to the covenantal promise only in a later version, the one which then referred more exclusively to Abraham's descendents according to the flesh (Rom. 4; Gal. 3).

It is an interesting and attractive argument, and it could be said to uncover the true spirit of the Abrahamic covenant, especially if the relevant texts are read in the context of the foundational covenants of creation that had gone before. And there is also, at least on a first and straightforward reading of these chapters in Genesis at issue here, an impression of a certain inconsistency, and inconsistencies in original texts may often make room for more adventurous interpretations when such are badly needed. The inconsistency in question here in the Genesis text is an inconsistency incurred when, on the one hand, Abraham is pictured as the father of "a multitude of nations," an almost Noah-like figure, with Abraham's wife, Sarah, consequently pictured as "a mother of nations." But then, on the other hand, Abraham is pictured as the one from whom God will make "a great nation," Abraham who "shall become a great and mighty nation," presumably the nation of the circumcised who will occupy Canaan. The inconsistency is all the more pronounced in that it is precisely in the second version of the covenant mediated through Abraham that the references to "nations" and the "multitude of nations" occur, the very version in which it is decreed that any uncircumcised male will be deemed to have broken this covenant.

Leave aside for a moment any help that this apparent inconsistency might offer to Paul's adventurous argument. Leave aside the fact that the end result of that argument undoubtedly embodies the substantial truth expressed in the imagery of divine covenants, of the essential and eternal relationships between God and humanity as a whole. And the fact then remains that as it now stands, and as it was finally redacted by the priestly caste within the people and religion of Israel, this text of the Abrahamic covenant does begin to send out a clear and certain signal. It is a signal that points to the emergent tendency and wish to see God's will and testament benefit first and foremost the nation of Israel, at whatever expense to others. Thereafter to be to the benefit of all of human kind, of course, but perhaps then also at the price to be paid of some associative membership of the nation of Israel. Certainly it was a signal of sufficient strength to allow this people to do that which it is our primordial temptation to do: to set their feet on the path that eventually leads to Gilgal. To send them down the widening road that ends in ethnic cleansing and the hewing to pieces of Agag by Samuel, the prophet of the Lord, "before the Lord." Except, of course, that Gilgal was by no means the end of that particular road. As one would quickly realize if one listened to a contemporary Israeli justifying the brutal assault of his army, at the moment mainly on the Palestinians in Gaza, by saying simply, "God gave us this land; and you can't argue with God."

There are no intrinsic contradictions between God making a covenant that is clearly intended as a covenant with the whole of humanity, and God making a covenant that is clearly a covenant with a particular person or people, but which is equally clearly a covenant for the equal benefit of all people. The covenant with Abraham and with the nation that comes from his loins, it could be made clear, simply tasked them with the responsibility of proclaiming the primordial covenant of creation to all people, together with the responsibility of all involved, to share equally in the benefits of creation that God's pours out always to all. And there are signs in the text (for Paul's benefit) that this is how the text could be read. But there are also the countervailing and more effective signs to the effect that the text suggests a more sinister reading of the kind just indicated above. As the very next covenant text would serve to confirm.

Certainly by the time the Bible reader comes to the next covenant in the biblical series, the covenant mediated through Moses, the more sinister signs have become more unmistakable. The covenant is mediated through Moses to Israel, to a people wandering in desert country, separated from civilization, on a mountain there. By this covenant, if they keep to its terms of course, God will make of this people "a kingdom of priests and a holy nation" (Exod. 19:6). Priests mediate between God and (other) people(s), and holy means set apart, as the sacred is set apart from the profane. That this is a covenant based on salvation does not of itself contrast it with previous covenants based on creation, for as it has been argued before, salvation is simply creation continued in the face of destruction both natural and malicious. Yet the salvation that is God's earnest given for this covenant is rather exclusively the salvation from suffering and death in Egypt of this particular people. Then the terms of the covenant that are to codify the responsibilities of this particular people consist in a combination of ethical and cultic or ritual prescriptions that follow each other in such an unbroken sequence, both in the Decalogue and in the much more detailed and extensive codification of the chapters that follow, as to convey the clearest impression of one seamless code of conduct. And this no doubt represents the characteristic code of living of this people at the time this text was redacted. And finally, as the promise that is part of the covenant, there is the land flowing with milk and honey that God will give to this people.

It could still be said, of course, albeit with decreasing certainty, that there need be nothing even in all of this specific detail of the covenant mediated through Moses that inherently and of itself impedes the prospect of reading a covenant with this particular people as being at the same time a covenant for the equal benefit of all peoples. All the Israelites had to do was to recognize that this covenant mediated through Moses was still in line with, and in effect of the same character as the more obvious creation covenants that had gone before. Then their attitude to other peoples would be to the effect that as God the Creator gives them life and existence, and land flowing with milk and honey to support and enhance that life; so the same God gives life to all, together with all of the supports and enhancements of a land flowing with milk and honey. And as God in creating this particular people had entered a relationship of co-creativity with them, and had thereby incurred for them both responsibilities on their behalf which they would then seek to formulate in their own codes, and acknowledgment of such beneficial and promising relationships as they would then seek to express in their own versions of ritual and cult; just so, and in just these ways, this people should realize, did God the Creator and Father of all deal equally with all the peoples brought forth in the course of continuous creation, and with the same implications for their moral and ritual response.

Then, if the Israelites felt that God in some way had revealed especially to them the true nature and implications of the creation covenant, in part at least, so that they could then shine a light on those areas of ethos and cult of other peoples that had been darkened by sin and idolatry, they could have tried to persuade these peoples that the gods they worshiped really represented the true Creator God, as Paul did with the Athenians. They could have tried to persuade them of this by the manner in which they treated these people's cults. Many had harvest festivals much like the Israelites; many even practiced circumcision. Then, if they understood the covenant with them through Moses as a means of advancing God's covenant in creation with the whole of humanity, they should have found some other way of finding for themselves their fair share of land flowing with milk and honey. What other way? Almost any way other than the way of ethnic cleansing and wholesale slaughter, after the manner in which the Israelites themselves interpreted God's covenant with them through Moses. For that is how they interpreted their covenant, as may be plainly seen from their telling of the fuller story of Moses, his covenant, and the subsequent saving of his people as it culminated in their occupation of their allegedly promised land. Further, in the earlier part of the Bible, they seldom ceased to mock the religions of their neighbors in the Ancient Near East. Accusing these of crude and unethical idolatry, while priding themselves of making no images of the deity. Yet as they marched on the road to Gilgal and beyond, they projected an image of their God that was as self-serving, abhorrent and savage as Moloch.

Nor were the Israelites alone in this, nor the Jews to the present day. The two religions, Christianity and Islam, that took origin respectively from theirs in the family of monotheistic faiths, and who professed equal respect for the Bible, showed also an equal propensity for forcefully oc-cupying other people's lands and siphoning off most of their milk and honey. If not on God's command, then coincidentally and conveniently in the course of winning these peoples over to the worship of the one, true God. Islam in its turn overran these ancient territories through which the Israelites had passed, and by military conquest made them part of "the land of Islam." Islam also overran and occupied in the same manner much territory that Christianity had occupied by the more peaceful means of converting the Roman Empire. But then the Christian Crusaders of Me-dieval Europe arrived subsequently to "liberate," that is to say, to occupy some of these same lands and thereby save them from "the infidel." And in doing so they engaged, in the name of God and of Jesus, in a degree of ethnic cleansing especially of the cities of the Muslims, and with a de-gree of savagery, frequently including cannibalism, that would rival and indeed exceed anything that the Israelites of old had perpetrated in the name of the same God. For Christians now insisted that they replaced the ones they called the "perfidious Jews" as God's chosen people. The Fourth Crusade offers another illustration of the mixed motives — to put the matter mildly — of those brave men who went to kill or die (in that order), with the cross of Jesus emblazoned on their breasts. Enrico Dan-dolo, the Doge of Venice, led that crusade. He had been blinded in one eye earlier in life in the course of some political or business altercation in Constantinople. And so it happened that he and his fellow crusaders somehow had to go round by Constantinople on their way to the Holy Land, and winter there. They sacked the city, thereby accelerating the final break between the Western and Eastern parts of the old Roman Empire, now the Holy (Christian) Roman Empire.

Some centuries later, as the great powers of Spain and some other countries set about their imperial conquests of new worlds, they could present it all as the extension of the Kingdom of God. The *conquistadors* were simultaneously saviors of lands submerged in idolatry and darkness, lands that would then of course be theirs to rule by divine right. In the eighteenth century the Puritans fled their English Egypt and, recommitted to their covenant with their Christian, no longer Jewish God, went to North America, to their promised land and their manifest destiny. To the manifest dislocation, ethnic cleansing and, when necessary, massacre of the native Americans to the west, and Mexicans to the south. In the 1940s the Zionists were back, to retake by force and terror the land that they still maintained God had given them, with a generous estimate of the borders of that land that God had decreed was theirs. And at the present moment, as these words form on this page, a born-again Christian president and chief of the armed forces of the USA, asking for God's guidance, and claiming on occasion to have received it, is busy once more with the latest exercise of manifest destiny, "liberating" Iraq. For as he put the matter in his own words, after the bombing of the twin towers in New York on September 11, 2001, Bush felt that he was "being chosen by the grace of God to lead at that moment," if only because "our nation is chosen by God and commissioned by history to be a model to the world of justice." One has to hand it to all three of this family of faiths for their awesome consistency, if nothing else, in their common betrayal of the primordial covenant of God the Creator in the creation itself, the covenant that sits at the beginning of the Book, the Bible, that all three religions profess to revere in one version or another.

The next covenant encountered in the Bible, the covenant with the House of David, is merely a codicil to the Mosaic covenant with the people of Israel, to the effect that the House of David would rule that people forever. A promise manifestly never destined to be redeemed. Unless, of course, Jesus was, as Paul assumes, "descended from David according to the flesh," a member of a royal family fallen on hard times. And unless the promise was then fulfilled in a manner rather different from the way in which the original Mosaic covenant had been understood and, as far as possible and for as long as possible, had been implemented by the occupation of that holy land. Finally, as far as other covenant texts of the OT are concerned, in particular those prophetic texts that promise a new covenant sometime in the future, as in the Jeremiah text for example, only one remark is necessary. It is difficult to say whether or not Jeremiah's promised new covenant is meant to be seen as a replacement for the Mosaic covenant or merely a correction of a misunderstanding and a consequently mistaken set of responses to the Mosaic covenant on the part of the Israelites. On the one hand, the covenant terms promise that God's law will be written in human hearts so that it will not be necessary for anyone to teach anyone else, and this could be taken to be a direct rejection of Moses, who is presented in Exodus as the teacher of his people while alive and with them, and then, precisely as the mediator of the Torah, the teacher par excellence of the people of Israel forever. On the other hand, the text of Jeremiah is still talking about a covenant especially with Israel, but intriguingly now, a covenant that God himself commends

to them on the sureties of the Creator's works as the fathomless source
of creation:

> who gives the sun for light by day
> and the fixed order of the moon,
> and the stars for light by night...
> If this fixed order departs
> from before me, says the Lord,
> then shall the descendents of Israel cease
> from being a nation before me forever.

Intriguingly also, God's promise that "I will not turn away from doing
good to them," is pictured as being redeemed, not in the old killing and
ethnic cleansing ways, but by buying the land: "Fields shall be bought in
this land ... for money, and deeds shall be signed and sealed and witnessed,
in the land of Benjamin, in the places around Jerusalem, and in the cities of
Judah, in the cities of the hill country, in the cities of the Sheph'lah, and in
the cities of the Negeb; for I will restore their fortunes, says the Lord." All
of which does tie the covenant with Israel into the context of the covenant
implicit in creation, as it ties all of this also to a kind of ethical means of
exercising the responsibility of sharing God's good creation that contrasts
rather starkly with killing and taking by force. In this future covenant, it
would appear, Israelites would be expected to pay an agreed price for the
land they claimed the Lord had promised them. And that at least would
imply that *their* God also looked after other peoples of the race that God
had made co-creators of this good world, as well as rulers under God of
God's kingdom, the world.

The New Covenant Ratified in the Blood of the Christ: The (re)New(ed) Code Given Down from the Mountain

However all of that analysis of previous covenants may fare, persuasively
or not, one thing at least is beyond doubt in the Bible. The prophet Jesus
of Nazareth considered that by his time the covenant of God with his
people had been radically distorted, particularly by the religious leaders of
Israel. It had become distorted particularly with respect to the cult, with
respect to the code, and most tellingly of all perhaps, with respect to that
intermingling of cult with code that so often in religious *weltanschauungen*
make these two seem to constitute a seamless garment. Rather than a set

of separates, one of which could be worn, and might indeed be better worn, without the other.

So there was by Jesus's time this inter-weaving of Temple and Torah. As the story goes, the Temple when first built by Solomon was designated to house the ark of the covenant, the ark that contained the written terms of the covenant, the terms which in turn guaranteed the presence of God with his people, forever giving them life and making them whole. An ark and a covenant and a Presence that they had before that carried with them wherever they went, but that was now stabilized in the Temple in the capital city of the land that God had promised them, forever. An ark and a covenant that therefore made the Temple the principal, if not the only house of the one, true God in the world. A covenant that defined in the details of both ritual and moral law the terms and conditions that were Israel's as the partner people in the covenant. It was this whole complex, constituting the religion of his people as it was formulated, taught and practiced in his time that Jesus criticized in virtually every encounter he had with the leaders of that religion. According to John in particular, he accused that version of his religion of being little less than idolatry. Satan, he said, was the father of these leaders, not the Father whose kingdom he, Jesus, had been sent to restore. Of course, they answered him in kind: accusing him of being a false messiah, a blasphemer whose ruling spirit was Satan, an idolator.

Now as then people can only judge between these Jewish opponents on the issue of the true God and the true version of the Jewish religion, by considering the case that Jesus made and died for. The case ranges over all connected issues of temple, ritual observance and moral response, and much of it has appeared already on previous pages. It needs but a brief recall here, together with some additional attention to the more specifically ethical principles involved in any overview that focuses primarily on the centrality of the covenant myth to that whole complex of co-involved issues that runs from temples to moralities.

So we have already seen that Jesus was understood, and rightly so, to have rejected the idea that the Presence could be confined to, or even considered predominantly available for worship in, the Jerusalem temple. Or anyone else's temple, for that matter. (A Roman Catholic may think at this point about the pretence that the Real Presence can be encountered in their churches where the eucharistic bread is reserved, but not in other Christian churches.) In reality of course the house in which the Presence can be felt and followed was, and ever is, the house of creation. And although temples could help focus that cosmic encounter — like the sacred building built and then burned down at Emain Macha — if they provided for worship of the one, true God of all creation, no one of them could ever be said to be essential to that blessed, demanding and most promising of all experiences in that same creation. It is also already obvious how that intersection of ritual and moral obligation known as the Sabbath observance became a focal point of the deadly disputes between Jesus and contemporary leaders of his faith. For the Sabbath ritual of abstinence from all work was so interpreted as to suspend a moral obligation which, as it turns out, is the most fundamental moral obligation of the most fundamental covenant. It is the obligation imposed in the very act of God's creating creators and rulers plenipotentiary, to co-create in the course of God's own continuous creation and, as a crucial part of that very obligation, to make whole that which had suffered diminution of life. And, in this respect, as we have also seen, Jesus gave an even more general and radical instruction on the nature of the relationship between cultic/ritual precepts and moral precepts as these occur in the context of presenting religions as covenants.

The true nature of the relationship between ritual and moral precept was formulated by Jesus in his insistence that the Sabbath was made for man, not man for the Sabbath, and that principle is both general and radical in the following manner: Not only does it prevent the setting aside of a moral precept in any individual case, such as this one of Sabbath observance. It sets up a general, moral principle to the effect that ritual precepts must always give way to the needs and applications of moral principles. In more concrete and practical terms, ritual precepts must be constantly interpreted and critically assessed in the light of humanity's developing moral precepts. This would mean, for example, that the Hindu rite of suttee, according to which the dead man's wife joined him, as in life, now on his funeral pyre, would have to be revoked a soon as the evolving moral sensibility of humankind arrived at the stage of extending the moral precept, thou shalt not kill, to this scenario also. Indeed the extension of this precept, thou shalt not kill, to more and more scenarios in human life is probably the best barometer of the rising or falling of human moral sensibility in general.

There is a further and more general and radical example of the effect of allowing humanity's obviously evolving moral sensibility and subsequent legislation to act as critic and judge of ritual precept, according

to the principle laid down by Jesus. As one can see from covenant texts
in particular, ritual and moral precepts are set out as if they constituted
one seamless whole, covering the whole response of humanity to God's
gracious will and testament. And as such, if ritual precepts are not placed
above moral precepts since they seem to have to do directly with what
we owe to God rather than how we are obligated toward our neighbor,
these two codes are placed on all fours together. Both are in consequence
treated as expressions of the irrevocable will of the covenanting God, and
the moral precepts then appear also as straightforward divine impositions.
Rather than what these moral precepts are in reality, namely, inevitably developing codifications of the rules of relationships to God through other
creatures that equally inevitably change, as human beings engage in their
most fundamental covenant response of co-creating God's world — "that
(the human spirit) may become creator and evaluator and lover and benefactor of all things." This form of failure to observe the critical primacy
of humanity's evolving moral sensibility and its correspondingly changing
legal codification, by placing ritual and moral precept on all fours together,
is unfortunately reflected in many, if not most of the so-called world religions. And mostly, to take one salient example, in the discrimination
against women, if not their actual and daily oppression. All of which
leads us to examine the purely moral precepts in the covenants now under
discussion at this stage of the biblical story. For what we do find there,
in Jesus's sermon from the mountain, is the most radical revision of the
moral precepts recorded in the covenant according to Moses, and never
more radical than in the interpretation of the precept, thou shalt not kill.

In the revised code of the covenant according to Moses, in the revision
by Jesus that is designed to perfect, or to fulfil that code that has by now
become in part at least obsolete and counterproductive in interpretation
and praxis, the moral precepts are entirely predominant (Matt. 5–7). There
is no repetition by Jesus of his explicit views on what has by now gone
wrong with the understanding of the cult and the distorting domination
of ritual. Except obliquely perhaps, when Jesus decrees that people should
prefer prayer in private to public performances of ever more elaborate
liturgical prayer in synagogues, and offers instead the brief "Our Father"
prayer as an example of all they need to say. Or when he insists that being
reconciled with a fellow human being that one has injured in some way
takes priority over any and all sacrifices formally offered in temples (or
churches that have altars). The moral precepts, it can do no harm to repeat,
the moral precepts that define the human response to God's covenant

are entirely dominant in the Torah now handed down by Jesus from the mountain. It does no harm to repeat this, if only because few accounts of what Jesus did and taught give to this sermon on the mount the pivotal place it should enjoy in Christianity, the religion and the moral system. Furthermore, whenever this sermon is commented upon in the relevant literature, certain of its most demanding precepts are treated rather as counsels of perfection, as they are then called. Anything but the straight moral precepts that they are, and requiring, as moral precepts do, the compliance of any who would keep the covenant that Jesus restored and sealed in his own blood.

"You have heard that it was said to the men of old, 'you shall not kill,'... but I say to you": the contrast with the Sinai covenant could not be more stark than it is in this new interpretation of the Fifth Commandment. (Matthew does not include a statement of the Ten Commandments here in this sermon, though he does state it in summary elsewhere, and clearly presupposes it here.) And the contrast is all the starker because of the number of circumstances in which the older formulation of covenant law allowed one to kill legally. "Whoever strikes, or curses his father or mother... whoever steals a man (into slavery?) shall be put to death." And then the *lex talionis* is invoked: "you shall give life for life, eye for eye, tooth for tooth, hand for hand, foot for foot, burn for burn, wound for wound, stripe for stripe" (Exod. 21:15–24). And then Jesus: "But I say to you," that we are not even to be angry with each other. We are not to deliberately diminish each other in any way. If we do, we are to make up to each other as a priority to our cultic obligations. In sum, we are obliged to do nothing less than to love all enemies who intend and do evil to us, and to pray for those who persecute us. So that we may be sons and daughters of God, true offspring of our Father who is in heaven, who makes the sun to offer its life-giving light and heat to the evil and the good alike, and who sends the rain to furnish the necessities of life equally to the just and the unjust. And it is particularly important that we do not return evil for evil in those cases where we are maligned, made subject to false accusation and positively persecuted precisely for living out this law of the covenant in God's kingdom, the world. Because in these cases we reach the stature of God's prophets, and in sharing their fate we give the most complete testimony to that trust in the Creator in which the limitless hope of all humankind consists.

And that is the first and foundational precept of the reformulated response to the divine covenant according to Jesus: trust in the Creator, eternal giver of life and existence to all. Trust in God forever for life and all the supports and enhancements of life. This trust is not a passive trust. Rather does it involve our assuming our full role as best-equipped creators among all creatures. Becoming people who can themselves be trusted, and who are prepared to trust others to share life and all the affordances of life with each other. For what is at issue here is a trusting response to the eternal life-giving source that results in our ruling the creation in the wisdom and the justice toward all that is transmitted to us in the very rationale (*logos*) of the creation itself. "Seek first his kingdom and his righteousness, and all these things (needed for life) shall be yours as well."

The corresponding, negative precept reads, in two versions: "do not lay up *for yourselves* treasures on earth," and "you cannot serve God and Mammon." Here in those twin precepts the horrendous prospect comes into view of people acting as if they were sole creative providers and guarantors of life for themselves, the prospect of idolatry in one or other of its many mythic forms, worshipful trust in oneself, in a creature-god, in a satanic power. And the prospect of all the destruction and death-dealing that then inevitably flows from this upon human life and upon the good earth that now supports it. For us plenipotentiaries of the Creator God on this earth these precepts mean then that we take our true trustful part in God's own project and rule, in pouring out life and existence unstintingly to all things. And in particular to give of ourselves and of God's good things even to those who would try to take them from us by force, to those who would steal them, as well as "to him who begs from you, and do not refuse him who would borrow from you." For all God's creatures are so inter-related and inter-dependent in this one universe, that each comes into being, flourishes and even dies at the expense of others. But only if that expense — at once bodily-material and emotional-spiritual — is freely paid by each, can all continue to flourish and life continue to evolve and to abound. With no limit other than those an eternal God might wish to impose, but shows no signs whatever of wishing to do so. In what is possibly the oldest surviving fragment of Western philosophy, Anaximander who said that the source of all things was *to apeiron*, The Infinite, was quoted also as saying: "into that from which things take their rise they pass away once more, and they make reparation and satisfaction to one another for the 'injustices' [i.e., what they have to take away from each other], according to Time's decree." Or old Heraclitus, who put it even more succinctly in his aphoristic manner when he imagined in the case of both mortals and immortals, "the one living by the other's death, and dying by the other's life."

There is one other precept of the Decalogue that Jesus specifically subjects to a revised interpretation in the course of handing down the new law from the holy mountain. The new terms of the new covenant that looks more and more like the oldest, original covenant of all. It is the so-called Sixth Commandment: thou shalt not commit adultery. Jesus's revision of this precept consists in decreeing that divorce, which Moses allowed as a concession to people's hard and unrepentant hearts, is not to be sought. It is forbidden under the terms of the new (old) covenant from the mountain, and so, if any one marries a divorcee, the result for both is the sin of adultery. In other passages from Matthew and Mark Jesus claims as his authority for therefore forbidding divorce the ordinance of God's creation: "He who made them from the beginning [or, as Mark puts it: "from the beginning of creation"] . . . said . . . 'the two shall become one'" (Matt. 19:3–9; Mark 10:2–9). This reference to an ordinance of creation in support of a straight ban on divorce finds its rationale in the following analysis: God in creating the world does so out of an eternal, steadfast love for all, the self-same steadfast love we are asked to exhibit in always returning good for evil, so that God expects nothing less from us. All the more then does God expect such steadfast love from the two who join together in the most special activity of procreating the very species that represents (to the best of our present knowledge) the highest form of co-creation in the universe. Under the renewed reign of God, in the terms of the renewed covenant of creation, married couples will exhibit such steadfast love for each other, for their children, and for all of God's creatures, for as long as they live.

In the text of Jesus's sermon from the mount as we now have it, an exception to Jesus's total ban on divorce is included in the form of the phrase "except on grounds of unchastity," whatever that may be taken to mean. Scholars of the text suspect that the legal loophole was inserted in the very early church for its own reason and benefit. And this could very well be true. Because Paul says clearly that Jesus simply banned divorce, without qualification ("not I, but the Lord"). Yet a few sentences later Paul himself is permitting divorce for converts to the faith of Jesus, under certain circumstances. But in doing so he specifically adds that he has no record of a saying of Jesus to support such an innovation ("I say, not the Lord": 1 Cor. 7:10–15). So it is best to deal later with these and other changes to Jesus's remembered formulations of the ethical terms of the covenant that he mediated, when the handling by the followers of Jesus of these terms of the renewed testament comes up for investigation.

Finally, some further precepts from Jesus to guide our relationships to God and to the world that God created. First, we are not to swear, not to call on God as guarantor of the truth of what we speak or do. We are simply to speak and do the truth. By the fruits of our speech and action people will know whether it is true or right or not, and no ceremony of calling on God will change that fact. Anymore than our calling God our Lord, our Lord, will do anything whatever to make us in the least bit whole and hopeful of eternal life, if we do not keep to the moral responsibilities laid on us in and by the covenant of creation itself. For if we are not living truly and rightly, and not expressing that truth and right, then calling on God in order to profess our allegiance or to promote some advocacy for our cause, is to try to make God complicit in our own evil. "Let what you say be simply Yes and No; anything more than this comes from evil." One's word must be one's bond. The fundamental precept of the old Irish religion under the aegis of God in the persona of Fionn comes to mind here: *ceart 'nar gcroidhe, neart 'nar ngeag, agus beart do reir ar mbriathair:* truth, right in our hearts; strength in our arms; and our deeds in accordance with our words. Words that are the expression of the truth and right that is in our hearts and that governs all our deeds, bringing the precept full circle. And that is all that is necessary; anything added to it may more likely take from it. Particularly, perhaps, distorted motivation. For the good that I do, whether in pursuit of moral or of ritual participation in the covenant, may be done purely for purposes of my own self-aggrandizement once again. I may pray ostentatiously from the front pews in church, or make a public display of my charity to the poor, or even parade my fasting with gaunt looks before an admiring populace (though this might not work these days, when the ideal woman is meant to look like a stick insect), and the oldest temptation is in control once more, the fertile source of the oldest sin. God may not be used, nor right and justice bent in the direction of satanic service. Truth must be upheld and right secured, for their own sakes, in the mutual steadfast love that binds the Creator and the creation. And anything below or beyond that is of evil.

In the actual sermon, in the actual formulation of the terms of the divine covenant, the whole text of it is prefaced by Matthew with a picture of the perfect human respondent drawn along the lines, not now of moral precept, but of moral ideal and virtue. This preface has become known as "the beatitudes," simply because those who comply with the terms of the covenant, now couched in these alternative moral categories, are assured in every verse of this hymn-like composition, of companionship with all whose happiness in the presence of the eternal God is thereby guaranteed, now and in the future. For they are already citizens and agents of the kingdom of the eternal God: blessed are you.

"Blessed are the poor in spirit, for theirs is the kingdom of heaven." The poor in spirit, because the poor in fact only are just as likely as are the de facto rich to be self-centered, greedy and willing at first chance to take by deceit or violence what others have, including at times their lives.

"Blessed are those who mourn, for they shall be comforted." God will keep on creating life for those deprived of it in any measure.

"Blessed are the meek, for they shall inherit the earth." The virtue of temperance best translates into the categories of ideal or of virtue what is at stake here, namely, the opposite of going to excess and lording it over others in the quest for control of the sources of life and consequent power.

"Blessed are those who hunger and thirst after righteousness, for they shall be satisfied." The virtue and ideal of right, truth, justice will prevail.

"Blessed are the merciful, for they shall obtain mercy." The forgiveness, the first and most difficult exercise that is undertaken for the sake of the ideal and virtue of love will, like love, prevail also, blessing "both him that gives and him that takes."

"Blessed are the pure of heart, for they shall see God." Clear sightedness, and single-mindedness are meant here, closest perhaps to the cardinal virtue of prudence in that this concerns knowing what to do, and nothing in particular to do with Christian churches' obsession with sex, as if sex were the most important thing in the world to get right. The heart, the emotions are the foundational heuristic devices where moral insight is concerned. Their cleansing of all excessive or distorted accretion is something that can be encouraged by education and acquired like any other virtue.

"Blessed are the peacemakers, for they shall be called the sons of God." *Not* war-makers of any ilk or hue, or for any reason whatever.

Like Jesus, people who make peace — *shalom* — are sons of God, because as the phrase connotes they share in the Creator's prime characteristic of giving life, even through the very gates of death.

"Blessed are those who are persecuted for righteousness' sake, for theirs is the kingdom of heaven; blessed are you when men revile you and persecute you and utter all kinds of evil against you falsely on my account. Rejoice and be glad, for your reward is great in heaven, for so men persecuted the prophets who were before you." The ideal and virtue of fortitude is now unquestionably in view, though not of course on its own. For virtues and ideals, like precepts, must travel in convoy if they are to have any hope of picturing at once in detail and in the whole that most precious and promising thing that can then be called a good moral life. So, if in the face of persecution one can muster the fortitude to go through it, loving and forgiving the persecutors, with faith in the eternal Source of life and the consequent hope in one's heart, one can find no better way of living out the terms of this covenant established by God in the activity and results of creation itself. And if the persecution is to result in nothing less than death, and one can go through the gates of death with that same fortitude, that same faith, love and hope, then like Jesus in this also, one can seal the covenant in the shedding of one's blood. For there is no more definitive form of testimony than to die for that in which one believes, to die keeping faith more fully than one ever did during life. That then is the definitive seal on the human side; on God's side the definitive seal consists in bringing out of human death life eternal, as Christians believed happened in the case of the man, Jesus, because it happens for all — as Paul put it: "if the dead are not raised, then Christ has not been raised." (1 Cor. 15:16)

The Covenant Mediated by Jesus and Its Moral Principles

There can be no doubt about the fact that Jesus quite deliberately reformed (fulfilled) the covenant according to Moses as it had been interpreted by his time. There can be no doubt either about the fact that he did so in all instances by using as his criterion the covenant in creation. This is clear from his references to sun and rain, to the birds of the air, the grass and the lilies of the field, and the single sparrow that falls to the ground. It is especially clear from his references to the beginning of creation —

beginning in the sense of source — from which we can learn all the most important lessons about God's ways with the world, and ours with the world and with its God. It is also clear from the work that Jesus was sent to do and did, namely, the continuation of God's work in creating, most commonly in the form of making whole what had been subjected to self-inflicted or suffered destruction.

Further, there can be no doubt about the fact that the moral prescriptions, virtues and ideals, set out by Matthew as part of the mythic picture of the making of this re-new-ed covenant, do represent the strict terms of the moral obligations incurred by all who would be party to the only covenant God ever offered, does or will offer. And who would hope for the ultimate blessedness that this testament of God promises: eternal life from life's eternal Source.

There should be no room for vacillation here. What has been summarized and commented upon here, what would be far better read and meditated upon in Matthew's original report and, most likely, Jesus's own powerful and memorable imagery, this does present us with the strict terms of the covenant. None of these terms can be sidelined as counsels of perfection meant only for those who as a consequence can be described as more perfect Christians than are those who live their lives "in the world." Instead, what can and must be done with them continually is to specify and modulate them, if only because ideals and virtues, and even sets of precepts are often very general and difficult to relate to the very concrete situations that in sequence make up most of our ever-changing lives. Jesus in the course of that collection that Matthew presents as a single sermon, does just that for some of the general precepts, concerning killing and adultery for example. But that does not complete the task for all time, even in the case of these two precepts. For, apart altogether from the fact that people must forever be prepared to correct sets of rules that they are always liable to corrupt for their own self-centered purposes, life evolves, creativity continues, and therefore codes must constantly change in order both to facilitate and to reflect the advances of life in length and quality.

The most general and fundamental moral principle in the covenant of creation is this: act only so as to preserve and advance life for all, and accept or cause only such diminution of life as is necessary to pursue the constant transformation of life for all. That most general and fundamental principle, implicit in the Creator's will and testament to continuously create and advance life for all, cannot be deemed to be addressed solely to human kind. All other species play their due part in the general creativity of the universe, and as a consequence, as individuals, die gradually that others might live and, as species, are transformed and sometimes die out in the process, that other (versions of) species might emerge. The covenant then is with all, and certainly with all living things, as the creation covenant with Noah makes explicitly clear. The human race, endowed with reflective consciousness, is explicitly aware of these terms of the covenant of creation, and so these terms take on with humans the form of moral precepts to which they can willingly conform, or not. And that places the further obligation of the charge upon them to rule themselves and the rest as vice-regents of the One who rules with the love that moves the sun and the other stars. To rule the other species in justice, to enable them to live as all subordinate co-creators must live and die.

The covenant implicit in creation is then not simply between individual species and God their Giver of life, but also between the species themselves, and primarily in this respect between the human species and those less endowed with reason and a corresponding moral sensitivity. From this point of view, it might have been preferable if some of our biblical authors who quoted Jeremiah as the prophet of the covenant that came (again) through Jesus, had chosen Hosea instead. Hosea, picturing the day when Jahweh woos Israel back from her idolatry, back to the relationship that obtained "when she came out of the land of Egypt," has Jahweh declare: "I will make for you a covenant on that day with the beasts of the field, the birds of the air, and creeping things on the ground; and I will abolish the bow, the sword, and war from the land; and I will make you lie down in safety . . . I will betroth you to me in righteousness and justice, in steadfast love and mercy. I will betroth you to me in faithfulness; and you shall know the Lord" (Hos. 2:14–20).

It is here, incidentally, here where it is a matter of extending to others, to all other co-creative creatures, to all other dynamic forms of reality, the steadfast love that is the defining characteristic of all creators of life both original and derivative; it is here that the third intrinsic character of the whole of reality comes into its own: the character of beauty. Truth and goodness have already gone together, in every reference to truth and right or righteousness, justice: *omne ens est bonum; omne ens est verum.* The truth and goodness of all reality coincide in that the truth of a thing consists in its being and remaining itself through its formation, deformation, reformation, transformation, on its journey to its perfection and in the course of its mutual adaptation to other forms of reality during the evolutionary process. Truth and falsehood in accounts of things consist in success or failure to account accurately for such existential truth and falsehood. Good and bad consist in the same process by which things are formed, deformed, reformed and at all events transformed, again in the general process of mutual adaptation. Good and evil then are the names for that reality-as-process and all parts of it, and its outcome in transformation seen from the point of view of any of the agent-things involved in it. And because all the truth we may ever know of all these things with which we share the world comes from our interaction as thrown-projects with them, that truth is also formulated in an account of the matter in which, in fact, such fulfillment is or is not achieved, and can or cannot be achieved by each and all. And moral discourse — for that is the form of the account of the world-project that is now at issue — is then true or false as such, and adequate or inadequate, to the extent that it accurately or misleadingly accounts for the processes by which transformation does and can, or does not and cannot, come about.

Yet, in spite of how fine that sounds, the fact of the matter remains that the character of goodness in the whole of process-reality is always inclined to be seen predominantly in terms of the transformation of the human viewer. Just as the ancient, indeed original temptation with respect to that steadfast love that drives all transformation through the inevitable deformations on the way, and that is therefore the first, foundational moral ideal and virtue, is the temptation to cage that love within the confines of the self. To confine the most steadfast love to self-love, if not of the individual self, then of one's national or ethnic neighbors, or at the very most of one's fellow human beings, and excluding enemies of course in all cases. And that is where beauty, together with its contrary ugliness, comes in as the third universal category, the third metaphysical character of all reality, that as such then coincides with the other two: *omne ens est pulchrum*. And that is also where art comes in, creative art and the artists who produce it, the seers who see the beauty and ugliness of creation-in-process and are then the indispensable agents of the revelation to those who, caged in their very self-centeredness, stain the otherwise translucent world with their selfish yearning. As Brendan Kennelly, thinking of his own art, put it:

> Words are innocent,
> And are never free from man's power to corrupt them.
> Out of his cage he sends his cries,
> Impressing his slavery on free things.

Fields, cities, seas
Are stained with his yearning,
His blood stains the summer sky
And he wonders why
He tries to glorify
Himself
By turning the rattle of his chains
Into the music of a word called freedom.
Yet when I consider the stain
I know that only the same grimed heart
Stumbling on its happy words
Will wipe it clean.

For beauty it is that elicits love, even in the grimed heart, love which cannot be commanded, and is the source of all commands that have the least claim to be obeyed. For beauty truly is a matter of form, and not simply of the integrity of the dynamic form of the individual agent or species that drives it to pro-create and evolve according to its kind, but of the harmony, the fittingness of forms of agencies that interact and are so interdependent, that must mutually adapt for the transformation of what constitutes after all one world, a universe. To picture such beauty, together with its oft-attendant ugliness, in words or in any of the media of the visual arts, or in the elegant formulae of deep mathematics, or to compose its harmonies and disharmonies and their reconciliation in music, is to enable the greediest of grime-clogged hearts to expand toward love of "all poor foolish things that live a day" (in Yeats's phrase), and to cherish them in their own right and their rightful place in the transformation of the world.

This in itself is the participation by the appointed vice-regents and co-creators of the world, whether they recognize themselves as such or not, in the steadfast love that characterizes the ultimate Creator of all. For even the deformations that comprise the transient badness and ugliness that all transformation requires can be beautiful and are rightly portrayed as such. The deformation of the woman's body in pregnancy, even the slight heaviness or grossness of the facial features, have the beauty of the advent symbolism of promise of a new creation, a new world. The true artist, the true seer, can detect and present the beauty of such deformations in contra-distinction to the ugliness of deformations and stains inflicted upon the beauty of the world by evil-doing. All part and parcel of art's general ability to enable us to love the one and to be repelled by the other, even as we are moved to compassion for those who are afflicted by it. The truest education of our emotions and our moral sensibilities occurs here, without the least intrusion of overt moralizing, and indeed all the better for being without that, merely by enabling us to see the light of goodness and truth that shines in all true creation, and the darkness that occludes it upon the entrance evil.

That is not to say that without a goodly exposure to good art, we cannot come upon that vision of the beauty that shines through all things, and its vulnerability in particular to the incursions of ugly, evil forces. For one thing, art that is technically quite good can glorify evil by beautifying both its processes and its results: think only of the age-old artistic glorification of soldiering and killing in war. For another, any experience of true love in response to natural beauty, and most especially to the beauty we love in a partner or child, can literally change the world for us, instantly and utterly, opening our eyes at once and simultaneously to the fragile beauty of all the earth, to the joy of its goodness, and also to the sorrow of its constant and universal exposure to forces that could then look either indifferent or downright malicious, and might well be either or both.

Very few poems in the whole history of poetry express the beauty-born love of another human being and reveal the manner in which it infuses all of the natural world with the joy of its grace and sorrow for its threatening transience than Yeats' paired poems, *The Pity of Love* and *The Sorrow of Love*.

The Codification of Jesus's Renewed Covenant of Creation and What the Churches Made of It

The fundamental principle of morality is not now sufficiently captured in the old formulation: do good and avoid evil. That principle stands of course underneath all, but it needs immediate supplement for purposes of any and every practical application, and practical application after all is what all moral principle and precept is about. The suggestion has already been made that the immediate supplement should read something like this: create always, as a derivative and dependent creator engaged in the task; and create in such a manner and degree that the benefits are there for all fellow creatures, and that any diminution of life and existence incurred is only such as can be seen to be an inevitable part of that progressive transformation of life and existence, that evolution of life and existence that is so obviously the result and goal of the continuous Creator of all. There is not much difficulty in formulating that fundamental principle, and it could be formulated more elegantly and more clearly than that by someone more gifted in such matters.

It is in the further formulation of that fundamental principle, it is at the point at which it can be made to guide our actions in any and every one of the concrete projects we face, it is there that the difficulties crowd in. We can begin by reminding ourselves that everyone who engages with the world in which we exist as thrown projects will benefit from faith in this evolving world and in all the powers co-active in it. Everyone can benefit from the hope to which such active faith gives rise, and above all perhaps, from a steadfast love of all involved, born of the beauty of transformation ever already evident in the world. And we can remember that it takes prudence to judge what must be done in these conditions of existence. It takes courage to do all of this in face of countervailing sufferings either natural to the process or maliciously increased by those whose god is self. It takes temperance to ensure that one's aim in action is moderate, that one's own god is not self. It takes justice to see to it that one's creative in-put is to the benefit of all involved and in due proportion in each case. And that is all very true, and very practical and concrete. But it all still raises rather than settles the question for each particular project in which we engage: what in particular ought one to do here and now? My justice makes it obligatory on me to answer that question in particular detail. My love makes me want to answer without any talk of obligation. Yet, although love can make it a joy to do what I ought to do, and can guide me to some extent as to what I ought to do, if only by holding my imagination to that beauty and harmony between all things that first and always arouses love, the precision of particular precept remains a permanent task. That is why human societies should have, not just legal systems, but permanent legislatures, and judicial systems that are independent of the legislatures.

This is not the time or place to talk any more about moral codes made up of precepts, of their well advertised and inherent limitations, despite their prevailing necessity, and certainly not the time nor the place to offer even in broad outline such a code for this age. It is the place only to look once more to Jesus's reformulation of the code that was then attached to the Mosaic covenant, and to see what the followers of Jesus then did with his code of precepts. It is clear from the rNT — yes, the re-NEW-ed Testament, because of all that has been said about the covenant mediated through Jesus as the renewal of the ... no, not the Old Testament, but the Original Testament, still OT, the terms of which had become corrupted by the time of Jesus — it is clear from the rNT itself that Jesus's followers already revised in important respects and often, it would appear, in a backward direction, his code, his formulation of the terms of the covenant of creation. Paul revised Jesus's anti-divorce precept, as did Matthew. And Matthew also modified quite radically Jesus's precept to the effect that we should never return evil for evil, but that, in preparation for doing nothing but good to those who do us harm, we should always forgive all who do us wrong.

Matthew's revision reads as follows: if your brother offends against you, try first for reconciliation between the two of you. If he does not cooperate, try again before witnesses. If he still will not cooperate, bring him before the church, and if the church does not succeed with him, let him be treated as "the heathen and the publican." Now this revision occurs within a few lines of Matthew's text that contains Matthew's clear account of Jesus's precept that there should be no limit to the amount of times we should forgive our enemies, seventy times seventy, as a symbol for infinity. And in a context in which Matthew had apparently already decided either to forget or to ignore Jesus's precept and practice of accepting as one of ourselves, by breaking bread with them, publicans and other sinners. In short, Matthew replaces an ethos of limitless forgiveness with a strictly judicial system in which failed appeals to offenders to come to heel would be followed by judicial trial and specific sanction (Matt. 18:15–21). These cases of backward revision are due no doubt to the unwillingness, or at best the inability of the first followers of Jesus to accept fully his version of the reign of God, and the consequent inability to accept Jesus's moral portrait of a true son of the true God. More of this unwillingness and inability may be seen when the theme of judgment and second (third ... ?) comings come up for perusal. But it is in the case of the precept against killing, as Jesus radically revised it, that we have already seen the most radical retro-revision by the community that claimed to follow Jesus in the early centuries after his death. Particularly as that killing is instanced in wars, and especially in the wars of conquest in which Christian nations, like other religious peoples, engaged. For war is the most obscene example of killing, involving as it does managerial killing on a massive scale.

Take the case of a British army arriving in the land of the Zulu in order to bring that land under the aegis of good Queen Victoria. The commander of that army announces that just invading Zululand and "killing a few thousand Zulus" should be sufficient to accomplish the annexation. What further formulation of our most general moral principle, thou shalt not kill, should govern the behavior of the Zulu in this case? According to Jesus, that further formulation should read: we must not resist the evil of this newly arrived killing machine; we must not kill them that would kill us; we must instead give them what they would take from us, and more. Give them some land, or give them a livelihood, or enough to live on. And if they insist on ruling over us, let them have their share in government, but insist peacefully that such rule must be a rule of justice for all. Something like that? Gandhi's pacifist policy of rebellion against injustice? One has to be very resourceful and, yes, imaginatively creative, in order to prescribe for the kind of conduct that can adapt the precept, thou shalt not kill, to such extreme circumstances.

It does seem to be the case that over the first two centuries of its existence the Christian church did understand Jesus to have forbidden warfare. Christians therefore would not take up the profession of arms. But then, it also appears, at a time that suspiciously coincided with the movement to make Christianity the established religion of the Roman Empire, Christian theologians began to adopt from Platonized Stoicism the morality of the just war. The fact itself of borrowing moral method and moral precept from Platonized Stoicism should not surprise us. For Christians had already borrowed the Stoic-Platonic theology of God. On the grounds that, in both systems, one discovered the ethical rules that should govern the world, from one's daily and cooperative experience of the way in which God's Word/Wisdom continued to create and re-create that same world. Except that Jesus interpreted such creative activity of the Word that his followers said was incarnate in him, in a way which showed that God never returns evil for evil, but only does good equally to all, and so all sons and daughters of God should do likewise. Whereas Christian theologians now began to adopt instead the contemporary Stoic-Platonic reading of God's Word revealed in nature, and thereby claimed a share in the prevailing just war theory. Conveniently so, for secular rulers seldom fail to require some quid-pro-quo for their patronage of religion. Political theology prevails over natural theology, as the Greeks would have put it. Or else some other Jesus or Socrates must die.

So Christians borrowed such arguments as would make the wholesale, managerial killing called war "just," in just such general circumstances as the British in Zululand and, later, the Germans of the Third Reich created. This was and remains throughout history and to this day, the most massive betrayal of Jesus's vision and mission to restore the true covenant of the reign of God. There seemed to be some fleeting hope of ending the maleficent reign of just war theory when nuclear arms were invented and used. For people began to argue that such weapons were so massively widespread and indiscriminate in their destructiveness, they simply could not be reconciled with the "just war" embargo on targeting innocent civilians. It soon became clear, however, that people like the so-called Allies in the Second World War were prepared, as Hitler and countless other war-mongers before him, to commit such crimes against humanity as the deliberate targeting and bombing both by conventional and nuclear weapons, of hundreds of thousands of civilians in Dresden, Hiroshima, Nagasaki.... The same Allies who have since been prepared to terrorize hundreds of thousands of innocent Iraqi civilians, killing thousands of them in a "war against terror," while displaying the nauseating hypocrisy of presenting the killing of some three thousand in New York on 9/11 as "the day the world changed." In truth 9/11 was just another normal day in a persistently war-mongering world, and just another instance of what Americans themselves describe, often in tones of moral righteousness, as "what goes around, comes around." In other words, the words of Jesus: those who live by the sword, will die by the sword. And there is no end in sight of that disastrous delusion of "just war" with which churches and states replaced the morality preached by Jesus.

But there are more common and everyday circumstances in which the same Fifth Commandment needs more concrete formulations and applications. These circumstances refer once again to the general moral principle of the divine covenant in creation, and in particular to that part of it which enjoins on all to keep to the minimum the expense to others of their living well and living ever better. Look now to the most basic, physical necessity of life, food and drink. Is it permissible to kill other living things for food? Does the Fifth Commandment apply only to humans, and only quite conditionally to these other living things? Or does it apply to all sentient animals, birds, fish, but not to other living things like plants, if they are not sentient? And as humanity comes into more extensive control of the whole earth, what further responsibilities must then devolve upon the shoulders of this species, with respect even to other animal species that currently live, as does humanity also, "red in tooth and claw"? The covenant envisaged by Hosea will not come about by direct divine action. God the Creator creates through creatures, and specifically through human creatures, in the course of that creative response. And that means that we have to be as continuously creative in formulating precepts for what we have to do, as we are in doing what we are responsible for do-ing as derivative creators. There are no sets of absolute, immutable moral principles. And if a precept such as, thou shalt not kill, looks like one, that is only because in such brief and simple formulation it is still lacking in the necessary interpretation and in the concrete details necessary for its application in a constantly evolving and highly complex universe. The same is true, even more so, of that general principle already announced as the fundamental moral principle of the covenant of creation.

A current illustration of the first and more positive part of that funda-mental moral principle — thou shalt create life ever more abundant for all, acting as a derivative and dependent creator — is found in the present and increasing knowledge and mastery of the genetic infrastructure of the evo-lution of life. And more especially in the awesome and, more often than not, largely unknown prospects of incipient genetic engineering. There are many who would say, and do say, that we human creatures should not engage in such activity at all. That to do so is in itself a form of idolatry, a prime form in fact of the original sin of humanity: playing God. To such people human beings have no properly creative role at all in God's cre-ation. They are at best maintenance workers reading off from the natures that come from a static divinity's assembly line the unchanging rules for dealing with each and all. And any attempt on the part of human beings to initiate a creative contribution or to alter in any way the pro-creative process in which certain creatures, including themselves, engage would be tantamount to posing as rivals to God who is sole and exclusive Creator of the world.

This kind of false Christian moralizing is traceable to the fact that when Christians first borrowed the Stoic-Platonic theology of God the Creator, they took in wholesale also the damage that an inferior dualist Platonism had already done to the original Stoic theology. As the chap-ter on creation above explained, the wholly immanent and ever-dynamic, spirit-like, fire-like *Logos* was gradually removed beyond the world, hav-ing created it originally through the immutable Ideas or Forms in the divine mind. So now Logos/Word squatted outside the world, distinct both from the world (and the World Soul) and from the ultimate One — the application in Christian theology of the term *person* helped here. Leav-ing human beings, now no longer real co-creators, to read off immutable moral principles from the largely static natures of things that make up creation.

The classic example of that false theology of creation, and its consequently straightforward "reading off" from a certain current feature of human nature, namely, the human reproductive cycle, a misleading, in fact a false moral ruling, occurs in the case of the papal prohibition of the use of any form of "artificial" contraception, rather than the "natural safe period." The hidden reasoning behind this latest example of misleading the faithful in matters of morality must be something like this: one must leave it to the divine Creator alone, to create new human beings as and only when the Creator alone wishes. The best way to do this is to keep on copulating regardless; the next best way is to abstain from sexual intercourse, perhaps by confining sexual intercourse to the notoriously unreliable "safe period," which nature, and therefore God has ordained for this purpose.

But it is the attempt to ban in the name of Christian morality all potentially salvific-creative genetic manipulation, it is this that represents the more serious outcome of a false theology of creation, and a consequently false fundamental principle of human morality. If only because the vast majority of the people to whom it was addressed have long ceased to pay any attention to the papal decree on contraception in any case. For one thing, such comprehensive condemnation of creative-salvific genetic manipulation distracts from a most urgent moral task of the moment. This is the task of detecting and weeding out the real immoralities that are only too prevalent at this time in the practice of genetic modulation. These are, first, the cynicism of pretending that the solution to the problem of world hunger lies with genetically engineered crops, rather than the reform of persistent economic pillaging and oppression by the developed countries for the sake of their own enrichment and self-aggrandizement. Second, the consequent use of the so-called developing countries as guinea pigs for growing GM crops well before sufficient research has been carried out in order to calculate the risk of the whole enterprise. And, third, for the same greedy, self-centered Mammon-motives, the patenting by business enterprises of the kind of knowledge and know-how from which, of its very nature, all human kind, and indeed other living species, should benefit equally and simultaneously. And so it is that the most advanced instance of humanity's exponentially growing powers of co-creation becomes at one and the same time a show-case for the persistent destructiveness of the oldest form of fundamental sinfulness, and the fullest and most persuasive example of the nature of human moralizing as a continuous creative elucidation of the fundamental moral principle of divine covenant in ever changing sets of concrete precepts. "No more to will and no more to evaluate and no more to create! Ah, that this lassitude may ever stay far from me." Yes indeed, and Ah also, that this newest prospect of human creativity at the genetic level be rescued from the sinners, and pursued properly by the just.

Is what has been outlined just now as the ever-evolving ethic that goes with the covenant that Jesus renewed, a Christian ethic then? Well, yes and no. Yes, in the sense that in so far as it is a morality that maintains and develops as necessary the moral principles that Jesus himself bequeathed to his followers. But no, in so far as one can see that the priests and teachers of the new religion, called Christianity, which Jesus neither intended nor even foresaw, have reversed in many instances the moral directions explicitly laid down by Jesus, and have furthermore over the centuries so changed for the worse the true biblical and theological context for right ethical thinking, that their moral teaching can result in wrong rather than right valuation and conduct to this day.

And no, also, in a more general sense. In the sense that the moral positions that Jesus adopted and outlined, and by which he lived and died, are quite recognizably derivable from the covenant in creation, as part and parcel of our human response and responsibility. Being, as we are, beneficiaries and subordinate partners in that covenant. In other words, the Word that was enfleshed in Jesus is the self-same Word that creates the world and thereby enlightens everyone who is born into this world — as John put it in the prologue to his Gospel. Therefore, the moral vision and formulation that occurs in and with the imaginative, reflective creativity to which all humans are called in this covenant, is both a possibility and a vocation for all of humankind at all times and places. As the epistemologist says, we know the world and all that is in it — including God — when we imagine and know simultaneously what it is and what it can and indeed ought yet to be, in so far as our limited human spirits can at any time know all of this. Human beings as such are natural moralists, equipped for this vocation by their very nature and position in creation. And they are designated moralists in and through the very course of being whatever else they are: scientists, politicians, farmers, entrepreneurs, tinkers. . . . And whether they are members of some religion or of none. And they are none the less fully qualified moralists for being none of the above, being numbered perhaps among the unemployed, those described by the poet as the ones, "who only stand and wait." Those who follow Jesus take him to be a special revelation of the true morality of creation, especially to those of them still partially (never totally) blinded by the original evil that forever seems to afflict our race.

Judgment

Whenever morality, responsibility, accountability and so on, come to be discussed in terms of formulated principles and codes of precepts, a discussion of the issue of judgment cannot be far off. A legislature is commonly accompanied by a judiciary that is charged with deciding what breaks the law, and that in itself can be a service to the law, if only because it can often entail interpretation of the law and the possible pointing up of flaws or insufficiencies in the current formulations of the law. Indeed the legal reference to decisions handed down by previous judges becomes in effect a body of "case law," an expansion in effect of a legislative code. And when a judiciary is attached to a legislature, some penal or at least restitutionary system frequently follows in its wake. That can offer a further service to the law and to its successful application to human behavior in society. For provided that it is conceived in a just, humane and constructive fashion, a penal system can act so as to save law-abiding citizens from further damage to their lives and livelihoods. And it can deter both law-breakers and law-abiding citizens alike from the wrong-doing to which all are tempted at one time or another. As it can also prepare the law-breaker for a return to a law-abiding life, if it contains some restorative elements. It is not surprising then that all three elements — legislative, judicial and penal — are found together in the biblical accounts of creation, and in accounts of the relationships, responsibilities, rules and consequences of behavior that are entailed in the very creation of the world.

The Bible, in its predominantly mythic mode, imagines the creation occurring a long, long time ago, "in the beginning." Just so, in the same mythic mode, it imagines the great judgment happening a long but ever-shortening time in the future, "at the eschaton." And every now and then in the course of human history the alarm is raised, and the cry goes out that the time is very short indeed, as was the case apparently with Paul. But in both forms of cosmic myth, dealing respectively with origin and eschaton, it is always necessary to remember that the time of the activity in question is a time-out-of-time, a time therefore that coincides with all parts of inner-cosmic time. For the cosmic myth seeks to identify all the cosmic agents, relationships and activities that make the cosmos to exist and to develop as it does. In the case of judgment myths, as in the case of creation myths in general then, we are trying to imagine what happens now, and from here we try to look backward, but mainly forward, as best we can.

What imaginative form does the myth of judgment take? There are many forms of cosmic judgment myth in the history of religions in particular, but the two forms that are also found in the Bible are of most interest here. The first form takes its master image from the tribunal in which a magistrate examines the conduct of individuals or groups, and hands down a verdict. The second form takes as its master image an apocalyptic scene in which some cosmic catastrophe, often involving a great conflagration, puts an end to all that is corrupt and contrary, and allows only the unalloyed good to come through triumphant. In the Bible, the great tribunal sets out the criterion of judgment clearly, fully and very simply indeed: did you, or did you not salve-create as Jesus did? And then it cobbles on the imagery of fire, for those who fail the criterion are condemned to the "eternal fire." In biblical apocalyptic scenes however, it is often water rather than fire that is evoked as the agent of destruction, likened by Matthew to Noah's flood, where the water it is that now washes away all that is evil (Matt. 24 and parallels; 25).

There is even at the end of the opening Genesis myth of the fall, a hint of the same eschatological use of new-creation-by-fire, when both "the cherubim, and a flaming sword that turned every way," are set to keep the way to the tree of life. Access to this eternal source of life, presumably past the flaming sword, is then prophesied in the last chapter of the Bible, although at this point the water imagery is prevalent once more: "blessed are those who wash their robes, that they may have the right to the tree of life." Fire and water are equivalent ciphers for creation, and the Creator can be envisaged as source of either or both of them. The water in the watery chaos is both source of life and, particularly in flood stories, instrument of the destruction of all that has become evil and contrary, and of the return of all of that to nothingness. Fire simultaneously consumes and so purges what is evil and contrary, and transforms the creation into the pure gold of life that springs ever-new through the gates of death from the eternal source, the Creator. Given the equivalent symbolism of fire and water in the present context, we may stay with the fire imagery of continuous creation, if only for brevity's sake, and because fire is the dominant attribute of the Creator Spirit.

So, fire we know as the prime symbol of creation, and in particular of continuous or evolutionary creation, in which forms of life and existence are consumed in the very process of forging the new. Fire is therefore the most apt image for the divine Creator as destroyer also, destroyer in the very act of continual transformation of the cosmos and all that goes into its very constitution. The Creator God is lord of life and death: "making *shalom* and creating evil, I am the Lord that does all these things"(Isa. 45:7, 18). But further, much further to this, the Creator Spirit is directly implicated in those other levels of destruction and death-dealing, far and away beyond that transient consumption of forms that is part of all transformation. When a human being turns satanic and for her own self-aggrandizement deals out deprivation and death to others, who is it that sustains and empowers that one in these very satanic actions? And when these others are thereby incited to come and destroy the grandeur of the self-deified, and to pay back death-dealing with even more death-dealing, who is it that sustains that incitement and empowers the destructive and vengeful onslaught? "I will bring strangers upon you, the most terrible of nations; and they shall draw their swords against the beauty of your wisdom and defile your splendor." (Ezek. 28:1–13). God will send the suicide bomber against those who despoil the suicide bomber's people. It is the same Creator Spirit who never does anything more, or less, than to keep on creating through the creatures, even when that continuous divine creation, because of their evil choices, empowers them to spread destruction and death indiscriminately to innocent and guilty alike. And it is God as Creator who then again keeps on creating, pouring out life increasingly to all alike, innocent and evil, despoilers and despoiled.

All are always invited, empowered, incited even by the overflowing grace of life and existence that they constantly receive, to share with the others in the others' need, to give as they have received, of their goods, of their lives. And when instead they take life and its necessities from each other in self-enhancement or vengeance, they are always already forgiven: "your sins are forgiven," Jesus sometimes says, even before he is asked anything about either sin or forgiveness. Then the recipients of his beneficence are urged to break the vicious circle by not resisting evil with evil, but by doing good to their enemies; yet they are still forgiven if they keep the vicious circle turning, still given life and all the supports of life from the eternal Source of life. And what of punishment then? Simply this: they are punished by that Source with nothing other than the destruction and death that, as free agents, they have themselves dealt out and brought upon themselves. So then, in terms of the dominant imagery of fire, the Creator Spirit could be said to be fighting fire with fire, fighting the fire that results in destruction, whether natural of malicious, with the fire that continues across all of these set-backs to transform and so to renew life and existence for all.

These myths of judgment are as much part of creation myths then as are myths of the fall. They tell more of what happens in and as creation, and therefore more of what can be known of and from the creation itself, than do creation myths and fall myths in particular and alone. They therefore tell us what happens in the world, what always happens in the world, not what happens in some other world, nor even what happened or will happen at the temporal beginning or the temporal end of the world, if such beginnings or ends exist. So neither do these biblical myths of judgment, unless tampered with, tell of a hell or purgatory outside of this world, whatever that might mean, or of a heaven outside of this world either. At most they hold out the hope of a new age when all the dross of evil is finally burnt out, and only the gold of the good life remains. In fact, hell and purgatory can be distinguished from each other only in this way: the horrors of evil that we and God inflict on ourselves constitute purgatory in so far as they succeed in purging us of our evil ways and acts, and they constitute hell in so far as they do not purge us, but merely incite us to prolong our self-destruction indefinitely. Given our legendary, long attested and seemingly interminable stupidity as so-called rational animals, never learning the lessons taught us from time immemorial, we seem set to fight "just wars": thereby to multiply into the future hells for most, and purgatory only for the less affected and lucky ones.

Then, in spite of all of this hell and purgatory on earth, there is of course also at all times and in all places heaven on earth. Whenever and wherever people live in mutual love-in-action, creating life and happiness for each other out of the bounty of God-given life and of the good earth, there is heaven. John the evangelist, who in respect of this matter also proves himself to be the most perceptive of all rNT writers where the common tradition of Jesus's life and teaching is concerned, has Jesus say that, although he came to save and not to judge, yet at his coming the world is always already judged (John 5:24; 9:39; 13:31; 16:11). By the standard and Spirit of Jesus, enfleshed in his life and consummately in his death, and set out as a rule of life in his interpretation of the covenant of creation, we are all of us already judged, and our sentences already being served.

Do our individual deaths make any difference to this scenario? Has death got any role to play in securing the justice of God who, in punishing us only with the punishments we inflict on each other, seems thereby to share responsibility in the rampant indiscriminacy with which that punishment falls on the (relatively) innocent and the guilty alike? The Creator does after all endow with the same wisdom and the same power the evildoers and the good, all of whom equally live and have their being in God. And the ensuing indiscriminacy is the most obvious feature of all human history. The psalmist who says he never saw such a thing, is either deceiving to flatter, or blind. In point of fact, it is largely this perception of widespread injustice by God in dealing out punishment to us in this world that persuades people to posit a general judgment and hells and heavens in another world, where and when justice will finally be readjusted for eternity for all.

It can of course be pointed out that this implicit complaint against God's justice is based upon too individualistic a view of human nature. Humans are social animals, whatever about being rational ones. So quintessentially are they social that the more isolated from birth a human life may be, the less human it seems to become. The most advanced study of human self-consciousness adds to this social impression: from the moment of birth, and indeed before that, human consciousness appears to be inter-subjective. That is to say, the human being is conscious of self only in the process of being conscious of other persons. In any case, it is only in and as communities that human beings by nature live and either prosper or decline, fare well or ill, and do and experience good or evil. Those who commit original sin seldom arrive on our borders one at a time. And in any case, some element, not only of the original temptation, but of its translation into action, appears at times in most if not all individual lives, and thereby builds up to the falling and active sinning of tribes and nations, of corporate bodies, national and international. The punishment then falls likewise on communities rather than individuals as such, and more often than not, rightly so. For all or most are complicit to one degree or another in all the good and all the evil that one nation or people does to another.

That is all very true. And yet it does remain the case, although it may not be calculable in individualist terms, that the punishment for evil-doing falls unevenly. And in light of this further refinement is it still possible to say that the unevenness of punishment for sin, and indeed of the general sequence of deformation that culminates in the most definitive deformation that ends our life in its current bodily form, our death, might be said to be evened out by that very death? It is pertinent to observe that the most persistent and unrepentant sinners who continue through life to enhance and sustain that life at such destructive cost to others, must experience death, even in long anticipation, in a way that is vastly different from the way in which the ones who follow the rule of the eternal Source of life experience death. For the former, death is the focus of the darkest despair. Not even to be thought about, for it advertises unmistakably and in advance the impotence in the project of securing life of all the finite things grasped at and accumulated for that purpose. Yet lurking in the depths of the consciousness of every mortal person, making its chill presence felt in unguarded moments of wakefulness at night, extending its frozen grip at every incidence of death's harbingers, illness or injury, and eventually turning the taste of all of the good things acquired and expected to be enjoyed, to the taste of ashes, the prospective death of the evil-doer creates a hell in the heart, cold hell from which the heart cannot be warmed. (In old Irish mythology, and carried forward into Christian times, beneath the hell of fire there was the *ifreann fuar*, the cold hell that corresponded to the greatest despair, a kind of living death, a life continuing over which death has retained its frozen grip. A bleak vision of hell captured in literary form by that third and largely unacknowledged member with Joyce and Beckett of Ireland's trio of great writers of the twentieth century, Brian O'Nolan, in *The Third Policeman*.)

That is one extreme. At the other extreme is the one who lives out the precepts of the covenant of creation in the footsteps of Jesus, following and continuing to develop his stated and interpreted precepts in the same spirit of acknowledgment of the eternal Source of life given liberally to all, and of the consequent enablement to give of one's life and livelihood to others. Such a one lives by keeping faith with the eternal Creator of life, and lives up to the responsibility of creating life to the extent of a creature's creative powers and also for the benefit of all, at least all others within range of one's limited power and presence. And to such a one the blessed hope sits at the heart's center, the hope that death will not see the end of life under the rule of the good Creator and the promise of a closer relationship to that Creator and to all others in what Paul envisaged as a spiritual body. So that where the unrepentant sinner is damned by despair at the unavoidable approach of death, the one without sin is blessed by eternal hope in the promise contained in the very character of creation and Creator. Death is then the great leveler of the otherwise uneven punishment for sin. All the more so since most, if not all of us, live out our lives in between these extremes of goodness and badness.

The picture that is painted of judgment in either and both of the parts of the diptych devoted respectively to an end-time tribunal or to an end-time apocalypse is this: heaven and hell are already here on earth, since end-time myths, like beginning-time myths tell a truth equally about all times in between an actual moment of beginning of the cosmos, if there was one, and an actual moment of its ending, if such there is to be. Hell consists in the evildoing and suffering that we inflict upon each other as an inevitable result of our falling for the original temptation of our kind. That suffering that we inflict upon ourselves is the only punishment there is for our original sin, which manifests itself in and as all that can be counted as individual sinful deeds in our lives. God is actively implicated in this punishment, but only as creative sustainer and enabler of all the activity that constitutes our existence. For as such God is facilitator of that quintessential freedom on which depends the dignity of our co-creative cosmic role. And if creatures of such dignity are to exist God can neither prevent the evil they freely commit, nor turn that to triviality by intervening in each case to prevent the suffering it causes to evil and innocent alike. God assumes the distinctively divine responsibility for that malevolent evil and suffering, as for the suffering that accompanies all transformation to higher modes of being, as the relevant texts from Isaiah and Ezekiel above illustrate.

Further, and for all that has just been said about death, the great leveler, it must remain impossible to say for sure if death can ever altogether level out the sometimes gross and always recurring inequalities between individual human suffering in this world and individual contributions to the original sin of this world. This inequality may remain a feature of existence for at least as long as our current grosser bodily form of existence obtains. All that God can do about it all, if we follow Jesus's understanding and living-out of God's reign, is to carry on creating and re-creating life for all, the good and the bad. And so to inspire all of us to do likewise, as the only way of sending our original sin into remission, and of restoring paradise as a permanent state even during our sojourn in these material bodies. For only in such manner can heaven entirely supplant hell in this age, or in any age to come.

There is a prayer in the Book of Wisdom that paints in cameo this picture of the God, the lover of life, who loves all that exists with a steadfast love, and infuses all with the divine creative and imperishable spirit. Just before the cameo passage here quoted the author has reminded God of sufferings that we humans have endured for sins committed, but only "so that they might learn that one is punished by the very things by which he sins." And that they might learn from this to change their hearts, so that they could thereafter keep faith with their true Lord, and emulate God's steadfast love in all their dealings with each other:

> "In your sight, Lord, the whole world is like a grain of dust that tips the scales, like a drop of morning dew falling on the ground. Yet you are merciful to all, because you can do all things and overlook men's sins so that they can repent. Yes, you love all that exists, you hold nothing of what you have made in abhorrence, for had you hated anything, you would not have formed it. And how, had you not willed it, could a thing persist, how be conserved if not called forth by you? You spare all things because all things are yours, Lord, lover of life, you whose imperishable spirit is in all. Little by little, therefore you correct those who offend, you admonish and remind them of how they have sinned, so that they may abstain from evil and trust in you, Lord."

And the witness of the great poets to all of this? This is best found in T. S. Eliot, though with a solid contribution from Yeats. Eliot, especially in *Little Gidding,* deploys the traditional symbols for the Creator, the Dove descending in tongues of "flame of incandescent terror" and, as fire does, burning away old forms in order to fashion in the same fire the newer and truer. Anxious to stress that it is as the Divine Love that the Creator weaves about us what we so frequently regard as this "intolerable shirt of flame," Eliot is anxious also to extend the creative-purgative effects of the burning Flame of Love from its daily chore of burning off the old in the process of transformation, to the redemptive burning off of all that belongs to "sin and error," as we daily suffer the destructive effects of the satanic fire that burns so steadily in all of our own hearts. Fighting fire with fire, as forest fires are often fought. So that, whether in daily living or daily dying, too often by our own hands, we are in Eliot's own words, "consumed by either fire or fire."

Yeats, in *Sailing to Byzantium,* seems to apply that ancient and awesome imagery more particularly to the natural death of his body, "a dying animal," when he prays to the great saints in heaven who were the very incarnations of Sophia, sages now "standing in God's holy fire," to come from that Fire and, presumably through that fire, to gather him "into the artifice of eternity." Although such special death-scene revelations of such imagery, however special they undoubtedly are and deserve to be, must be balanced with the conviction that the Fire that creates eternal life through all daily dying, whether natural or malicious in origin, thereby offers and makes accessible that same life eternal in every passing moment and part of what we experience as space-time. Eliot knew and said that "history is a pattern of timeless moments," and he also knew that the Bible ends with eschatological stories of final purgation and perfection of *shalom* that mirror exactly the stories of origin with which the same Bible begins: the story of paradise always lost and always regained. So, again in *Little Gidding,* Eliot imagines the goal of life's daily exploration of what this Fire of Love draws and drives us to, as an arriving "at where we started," and yet "knowing the place for the first time." As he joins the ancient image of the fiery tongues of flame to the equally ancient image of the rose, so beloved of Yeats, as an image of "the tongues of flame in-folded, "like a "crowned knot of fire" in the still center of which, as in the heart of God, we are always held in eternal *shalom.*

The Variety of Judgment Myths in the Bible

Yet it is not possible to end this matter here, not in any case for a theology of the faith of Jesus that claims to be based entirely upon the Bible, the whole Bible and nothing but the Bible. For there are too many texts in the rNT that are really too specific in describing a distinctive divine punishment applied by God at the inauguration of the new age to the specific sins of those who die unrepentant or unshriven, for anyone to be able to ignore such texts. What then is to be said about these texts?

The earliest judgment text of the rNT clearly states that when the Lord Jesus is revealed from heaven (the "second coming") with his mighty angels in flaming fire, he will condemn to "eternal destruction and exclusion from the presence of the Lord," "those who do not know God and who do not obey the gospel of the Lord Jesus." This text is clearly set in the context of vengeance, "since indeed God deems it just to repay with affliction those who afflict you" (2 Thess. 1:5–12). Just as in Paul's first letter to the same Thessalonians he had declared of those "who killed both the Lord Jesus and the prophets, and drove us out," that "God's wrath has come upon them forever." And in that first letter he apparently failed to see the sheer incongruity of reminding his readers of Jesus's own command: "see that none of you repays evil for evil" in their preparation for "that day" when Paul envisages Jesus as judge doing precisely what Jesus had commanded his followers *not* to do — to return, in this case, an infinitely excessive evil, for whatever evil their present opponents were guilty of in their finite ignorance and limited malice. And one can only hope that no one will try to evade this incongruity with the explanation that the reason God wants *us* to refrain from returning evil for evil, is so that *God* could do all of that and more at some final judgment. For then the God of Gilgal is certainly back in business, and quite literally with a vengeance, and God is even more monstrously portrayed in the coming age than in any ages past. For now God waits in order to sentence the evil-doers to eternal torment, instead of having them hewed to pieces on the spot. Indeed in this scene God does not even show enough mercy to give sinners the option of being hewed in pieces, or even to be annihilated, rather than suffer eternal torture by fire.

In one of the latest documents of the rNT, the Second Letter of Peter, a somewhat similar scenario is envisaged, as the writer counteracts the scoffing of those who say there is no sign of this much prophesied day when the Lord will return for final judgment, and no reason to expect it. The writer counters by reminding his readers that God did once before punish the sinners of this world by destroying the whole world with water. They can therefore be assured that the Lord will certainly come again, this time to destroy the world with fire, in a "day of judgment and destruction of ungodly men," when a new heavens and a new earth will be created, in which those found to be righteous will live" (2 Peter 3) — the ungodly having been annihilated in the fire? But of course this argument from scripture succeeds only by a blatant misreading of the myth of Noah and the flood. A misreading mainly achieved by omitting the part of the myth that contains God's solemn promise never (again) to destroy the good creation. A promise further reiterated and further specified in Jeremiah's prophecy of a new covenant. One can only wonder at the manner in which rNT authors deliberately distort the point of previous sacred scriptures, in order to arrive at a meaning that can serve their own correspondingly questionable interests. Recall Paul's twisting of the point of Moses veiling his face on his descent from the holy mountain and the presence of the glory of the Lord (1 Cor. 3:7). And one might well suspect that the interests in question are of the kind to which people are tempted by the original temptation of the race: to have even God as *their* God, made in their image, to see themselves and their fellow religionists as God's own people, recipients of all God's eternal benefits, as others and certainly those who oppose them must then be recipients of God's wrath.

However, in between these texts both early and late that portray a final judgment that condemns the enemies of Jesus's followers and the traitors among them to eternal torment, are texts that embody the true vision of judgment, the one that accords best with the covenant of creation, especially in its Noah version, and with Jesus's understanding of the reign of God the Creator, who reigns through continuous creation. There is Paul's truer vision seen when he is not seething with anger against his (mainly) Jewish persecutors: "each man's work will become manifest; for the Day will disclose it, because it will be revealed with fire, and the fire will test what sort of work each one has done. If the work which any man has built on the foundation survives (and Christ is the foundation which Paul is convinced he has laid down), he will receive a reward. If any man's work is burned up, he will suffer loss, but he will himself be saved, but only as through fire" (1 Cor. 3:13–15). Such a text keeps alive the true vision of God the Creative Fire. So that even the dark and dreaded death of the gross material body of the one who tries to sustain life by grasping at its material supports, at whatever expense to others, can be seen as the final purgative event for that one, preparing her for eternal life in a spiritual body.

There is also another example of eschatological myth also used by Paul other than the myths of eschatological floods or fires. These are myths of restoration. However, they carry the same import as the myths of eschatological floods or fires, but without the explicit use of that imagery. The finest example occurs in Paul's famous chapter on resurrection (1 Cor. 15). Clearly in this chapter belief in general resurrection from the dead is taken as a first and essential premise of the whole argument: "if there is no resurrection from the dead then Christ has not been raised." So all are raised. Clearly also God's raising of all from the dead takes the form of creatively sustaining the transformation of our physical bodies into spiritual bodies, to use Paul's own terms. And this in turn means that our currently "mortal nature must put on immortality," that is to say, must enjoy eternal life. The gist of this myth then is that eternal life is the natural destiny of all, or at the very least of all of human kind. And this picture is filled out in this Pauline passage by a description — reminiscent of the phrase from the prayer from the Book of Wisdom: "you whose imperishable spirit is in all" — a description of God through Jesus, in whom the divine spirit is incarnate, destroying (burning out again?) the last vestiges of all satanic reigns in the lives of all, and overcoming the last enemy death (or at least taking away its sting for the sinner), so that thereby God becomes all in all, as that phrase that forms the triumphal end of the chapter puts it.

Such myths of restoration in which the eternal pouring out of life is itself and simultaneously both salvation and eternal *shalom*, possess an internal logic that runs counter to any scenario in which the eternal God, instead of meeting satanic sinfulness with restoration and even enhancement of life, continues to create life beyond the death of our current material forms, but now with the purpose of punishing sinners with eternal torment. Just as that latter scenario runs counter to everything to which the mortal Jesus bore witness in his healing ministry and his occasional remarks in that context concerning sin and suffering and forgiveness. And above all it runs counter to that law of the covenant of creation which Jesus came to reactivate for all who were engaged in breaking it: imitate your heavenly Father, return only good and more good for any evil ever done to you or yours.

It is important to note at this point that judgment myths cast in the imagery of tribunals do not as such run contrary to judgment myths in the form of eschatological fires or floods; or to eschatological myths of bringing all to final *shalom* that do not use the fire or flood imagery. It is only tribunal myths that invoke scenes in which specific penalties are applied by God to the specific sins of specific persons or groups that run contrary, simultaneously, to all the other eschatological myths of judgment, and to Jesus's clear embargo on thinking of God as judge meting out specific penalties for specific sins. This is the embargo expressed so clearly in John's words placed on the lips of Jesus, when the disciples asked him to identify the sin that brought about the suffering of a particular man's blindness from birth: "It was not that this man sinned, or his parents, but that the works of God might be made manifest in him." And with these words Jesus proceeded to make the man whole. So most myths of judgment as tribunal are quite compatible both with this teaching of Jesus on divine punishment, and with the view that punishment for sin is the punishment we serve on ourselves, the view that hell is here and now.

When John's Gospel, as already noted, tells us that at Jesus's (first) coming the world is already judged, and the first Letter of John adds, "we know that the Son of God has come and has given us understanding to know what is true; and we are in him who is true, in his Son Jesus Christ. This is the true God and eternal life" (1 John 1:20). It is clear that we are reading a myth of judgment that is fully compatible with the fire or water myths of judgment as purgation. It would be possible to argue such compatibility in the kind of judgment myth that Matthew's Gospel offers in his scene of the great judgment at the end of the age (Matt. 25:31–46). It would be possible to read it in the sense of our being always already judged by the rule of God by which Jesus lived and died, healing the sick and so on. Were it not for the fact that, first, Matthew had already replaced Jesus's rule of unlimited forgiveness with a church judicial and penal system in which specific penalty is applied to the un-made-up-for offenses of its members. And, second, the myth ends with very specific reference to the eternity of the punishment.

In fact, this very feature of these tribunal myths, the feature that sees specific punishments applied to specific sins, and added as it were to any damage intrinsic to the sinning itself, destroys the very mythic nature of such stories. For it turns them into mere stories, stories of specific future events that then mirror specific past events also recorded in story. Whereas myth proper reveals features of all the events that constitute reality at all times. So, in Paul's Thessalonian correspondence, as in 2 Peter, God's punishment of those who mock, oppose and even persecute God's newest chosen people, mirrors exactly God's past punishment of the opponents of God's original chosen people that culminated in Gilgal. The "second coming," as it came to be called, in these particular myths of retribution, is now meant to even things out, in a way that God's tolerance for such sinners seems to be failing to do in this age. And thereby a central feature of Jesus's portrayal of the reign of God is radically undermined. In fact, it is virtually set at nought.

The Second (or More) Coming(s)

How are we to explain the fact that these false myths and true myths sit side-by-side in the same rNT? Indeed, at one point they seem to sit side-by-side in one piece of text, as does Matthew's record of Jesus's rule of unlimited forgiveness and Matthew's own reversal of it. The end book of the Bible, Revelation, has a judgment scene in which Death and Hades give up the dead in them at the end-time, and Death and Hades and any whose names are not found in the book of life are then thrown into a lake of fire where, with the devils, they are tormented for ever and ever (Rev. 20:10–15). Whereas the very last chapter of that last book of the rNT depicts the restoration of paradise. So how to understand then how these tales of severe, not to say excessive criminal justice with their characteristic second comings, tales posing as future history rather than cosmic myths, came to sit beside true and truly cosmic myths that properly portrayed a Creator Spirit whose ways with the world and whose wishes for the world's ways are characterized exclusively by steadfast creative love?

It would seem that some understanding can come to this dark area of Christian thought that has persisted from the earliest rNT writings to the present day, only if one faces up to a persistent failure of followers of Jesus to see or to be willing to see (none so blind as those who will not see), what in all of his life and death Jesus showed them to be his Father's way with the world and the corresponding way to the Father. This failure to see or to be willing to see, this propensity to hear while remaining unwilling to heed, this it is that enables even those followers Jesus called to be closest to him to record and remember both the words and the deeds in which Jesus showed the way to life eternal, while at the same time modifying and down-sizing this portrayal of the way and the life and the truth to the level of what they could manage in their own interests.

John, with his usual superiority of insight reveals this aspect of the reception of the mission of Jesus by his closest and most constant followers, when he has Thomas ask Jesus to show them the way to the Father. Thomas is clearly not satisfied at all with what he is seeing so far; something more acceptable must be produced. And when Thomas is told that in seeing and hearing Jesus he is looking at the way to the Father, this reply proves merely to be an opportunity for Philip to pipe up and suggest, "Lord, show us the Father and we shall be satisfied." Another dissatisfied customer who can only be told — and a little exasperation could be pardonable here — that the Father is seen in the Son, for to be son means, in the idiom used in the rNT, to be the spitting image of the father in one's form and ways (John 14:1–11).

And so it goes on, right up to the very death of Jesus, and beyond, indeed right up to the present day. Peter's grand confession of the messiahship of Jesus earns him the status of foundation of the new community forming around Jesus (although in Ephesians 2:20 the foundation is the apostles and prophets, and in Revelation 1:14 it is the twelve apostles). Only for Peter to be reduced immediately to the status of a satanic adversary when it appears that he has in mind something quite other than a reign of God that could require one's death in order to keep faith with the God of everlasting creative love. Peter would clearly prefer something more like the glorious reign of those victorious ones, like king David, that son of God of old, over all their enemies. The kind of reign perhaps that

James and John also have in mind when they ask, through their mother, for seats at the throne, and have to be reminded that the only question they have to ask themselves is whether or not they can give their lives. Peter at the end finds the courage to follow Jesus to the place of his final trial, but then recedes into denial of the way and the truth, the Spirit and the life that finds in this darkest hour its most glorious revelation.

In the earliest post-death stories about Jesus, at the original end of Mark's Gospel, an angel appears at an empty tomb telling women to tell his disciples that they will see Jesus in Galilee. Yet in Mark's original gospel, which on the authority of major manuscript traditions and other patristic evidence ended at chapter and verse 16:8, there is no return of Jesus, no second (or third . . .) coming back by Jesus to the scenes of his earthly mission. The references in Mark 14:28 and 16:7 to the risen Jesus going before them and being seen in Galilee, in the absence of any reference by Mark to an actual second coming to Galilee, can be more plausibly read as Mark's version of the point made by Jesus to Philip and Thomas. This point was to the effect that they were seeing all there was or would be to be seen of the revelation of the Father in his uniquely beloved Son, in Jesus's one and only earthly ministry, largely conducted in Galilee, though consummated by his death in Jerusalem. And this in turn harmonizes quite well with a general tendency in Mark's Gospel to contest the followers' persistent and importunate wishes for a far more glorious and triumphant son of God and savior than they seemed to be seeing in the life, ministry and death of Jesus of Nazareth.

After Mark the ends of the other Gospels and the odd testimony of other documents of the rNT then refer to many appearances of Jesus himself. That is to say, they refer to returns of Jesus to the stage of this earthly life, second, third . . . comings. These appearances/comings are as such neither part of resurrection itself, nor proofs of either Jesus's resurrection or of ours. For the raising of Jesus consists essentially in his elevation to the status of son of God in power, as Paul put it, and only secondarily in the consequent prospect and reality of eternal life in and with the Creator Spirit. And that raising was accomplished by the imperishable Spirit possessing Jesus and being bodied forth by him, a process that achieved its culmination on the cross. As John's account of Jesus's "hour" makes plain, and as Matthew implies by having resurrection occur at the hour of Jesus's death. And that elevation by imperishable Spirit means for Jesus as for others into whose lives Jesus breathes that same imperishable Spirit, eternal life as sons of the Father, as he was son. So that the only proof of that resurrection, that raising, lies in the experience of sonship as the earnest of eternal life. The real point or points, then, of the narratives of appearances, of returns, of further comings of Jesus can be gleaned only from the obvious concerns of each such "appearance" story in turn.

Matthew repeats Mark's account of an angel delivering a message to some women to be transmitted to Jesus's disciples, about his going before them to Galilee. He then adds another story of a coming of Jesus to meet the women in person, and to repeat to them the same message about Galilee. Why? Is it to point more than once to an actual coming to Galilee, because of the importance to Matthew of what will transpire during that encounter? For Matthew, unlike Mark, does add an account of an actual post-death coming of Jesus to meet the said disciples on a mountain in Galilee "to which Jesus had directed them" (Matt. 28:10). And the concern of that meeting then turns out to be this: to have the eleven remaining apostles conferred by Jesus with his own supreme authority ("all authority is given me in heaven and on earth"), for their commissioning to make disciples of all nations (Matt. 29:16–20; see Dan. 7:14). That must remind a reader of Matthew's binding and loosing text, and of the authority that would surely be needed if they were to modify Jesus's own rule of unlimited creative forgiveness of those who do us wrong, as Matthew himself had already modified it. The impression is unavoidable, that his followers still do not quite know, as Thomas put it, the way that Jesus lived out before them, or they are still not quite satisfied with certain aspects of it, as Philip clearly implied. They either cannot or will not see it as Jesus portrayed it, and need authority to formulate it as they see it. Thereby yielding a model for the treatment of sinners — deciding which sins are to be forgiven and on what conditions, and assigning suitable penalties — on which Paul also could construe the "second" or, rather, final coming of Jesus as judge of all the world at an eschatological tribunal.

Luke (chap. 24) repeats in essence Mark's story about the women and the angel(s), but the message to be transmitted by the women now concerns something Jesus had told them "while he was still in Galilee." He told them that the son of man had to die by crucifixion in order to be raised, the one thing that some of the closest of his disciples, disappointed at the kind of son of God they seemed to be getting, could not accept. These words of the women therefore seemed to them to be "an idle tale, and they did not believe them," in Luke's laconic comment. The same disappointment then, after Jesus's death, in fact increased by his death, as Luke's very next story of the two disciples on their way to Emmaus makes clear. Jesus comes to meet these two disillusioned disciples on the road and does his best to persuade them from the scriptures that it was "necessary that the Christ should suffer" in order to enter into his glory. (This argument from scripture is present implicitly in the passion narratives of the Gospels, in which the story of Jesus's passion and death is dressed in a collage of implicit and explicit quotations from the OT.) But his exegesis does not appear to have succeeded. Only in the eucharist to which he invited them at journey's end — "he took bread and blessed, and broke it, and gave it to them" — did he become recognized, known to them as their risen Lord. It is too trite, though it has sometimes been suggested, that it was some table-fellowship convention, or even some idiosyncrasy of his that allowed these disciples to recognize a recently executed leader transformed by his experience of death/resurrection. Rather, what they now recognize, what they now know through this or any other eucharistic celebration, is something of which the most accurate and eloquent exegesis had failed to convince them. Namely, that the risen Jesus as the very incarnation of the life-giving Spirit, as Paul called him, was precisely the one who gave his life for others. For that is the incarnate Creator Spirit that breathes through every eucharist in which Jesus's followers break the bread and pour out the wine of life, of their own lives if need be, to all. There in the effective symbolism of this sacrament of creation (as must be explained more fully in the next chapter, on Cult), celebrated in *anamnesis,* the would-be followers of Jesus conjure up, know, recognize, truly encounter that incarnation of the Creator Spirit named Jesus of Nazareth. Provided only that they engage in the drama of this sacrament for what it truly is: a means of testing the world and registering its deepest realities as these are revealed in the whole of our lives and in the whole of the creation, of which these lives are such an integral part.

As Luke's story continues that insight is confirmed. Jesus comes to the place in which the Emmaus travelers rejoin the eleven and some other disciples and displays his wounds. In confirmation of the lesson that he had tried in vain to teach them during his life: that it is the vulnerable self-sacrificing human being who is the incarnation of the Creator Spirit or, as John would paint the picture implicitly and so powerfully in his Gospel, that it is precisely the crucified one who is the glorified, glorious and triumphant son of God. And Luke ends, fittingly then, with a commission from Jesus to his disciples that is far truer in its terms to the faith that Jesus inspired in his followers than was the commission according to Matthew. As the reader would see if she considered Matthew's stress on teaching "all that I have commanded you," when read in the light of Matthew's earlier insistence that Jesus gave his church discretion over conditions in which it should offer God's forgiveness of sins, as well as on the matter of specific penalties to be attached. Jesus's commission, according to Luke, is that the ones to which he has just returned should have as their mission to spread to others that *metanoia*, that change of heart, accompanied always by already accorded forgiveness, by which all people would keep faith with the Creator Spirit. Creatively co-working for a better life for all, at whatever cost to themselves, and never placing the same faith in themselves as providers of life, at whatever cost to others. So Luke formulates Jesus's commission to the disciples as follows: "that repentance (*metanoia*) and forgiveness of sins should be preached in his name to all nations" (Luke 24:47).

Having said so much in Luke's favor, however, it must also be said that there is some disturbing evidence elsewhere in Luke's Gospel to the effect that even Luke did not understand the terms of Jesus's faith and of his consequent commission to his followers, precisely as Jesus himself would have understood them. For Luke at one point in his Gospel does seem to slip somewhat toward Matthew's default position on the church's forgiving or refusing to forgive particular sins, when he has Jesus tell his disciples to forgive a brother who sins only as often as the brother repents (Luke 17:3–4). Which probably illustrates no more than the known fact that when a misapprehension, even of some central issue, enters a system, it is then likely to be found even in contexts in which one would not otherwise expect to find it.

John (chap. 20) having given his own version of women and others at the tomb, adds his own story of a return of Jesus to a room, presumably in Jerusalem, to confer *shalom* on the disciples assembled there, to breathe the Spirit on them, and say: "Receive the Holy Spirit. If you forgive the sins of any they are forgiven; if you retain the sins of any they are retained." These words must surely be understood in the context of Jesus during his ministry informing his disciples that "all sins will be forgiven the sons of men...but he who blasphemes against the Holy Spirit will not be forgiven" (Mark 3:28–30; Matt. 12:31–32; Luke 12:10). In short, once again, like God their Father, Jesus's disciples are to forgive all sins, even to the positive point of doing good to those who sin against them, to the point of loving their enemies. But the one sin they cannot wipe out is the sin of those who persist in blasphemy, that is to say, those who persist in thinking that the God in whose name Jesus and his disciples act is a satanic god like their own, like Mammon for instance, who manipulate others for their own self-aggrandizement. (On second thoughts perhaps it is in this sense that Luke's passage about forgiving only those who repent might be read.)

John, like Luke, also includes in that scene of the return of Jesus a showing of wounded hands and feet, and a repetition of this a week later for the benefit of Thomas who, it will be remembered, originally failed to see in the Jesus they experienced up to his death the way to eternal *shalom* with the Father of all. This, as in Luke's case, is usually interpreted as a "proof" scene, and so it is. But it is crucial that we be not misled on the point of what it proves, and how. It would be disastrous for our present enterprise if we were to trivialize this showing and poking of wounded hands and feet as a proof that it was the same Jesus who was crucified on Friday who was now alive and well some days or weeks later. (Just as some features or idiosyncrasies of Jesus's table-fellowship in Luke's Emmaus narrative are often trivialized as evidence that it is the same Jesus who died who is later seen alive.) For we might then be inclined to think that in stories of poking wounded hands and feet we are being offered proofs of Jesus's resurrection. A perspective on the matter that would reduce resurrection itself to the revivification of a corpse, and then reduce the resurrection of Jesus itself, as has too often been done, to a proof that all that Jesus and his disciples said and claimed about him was true. The very kind of sign and wonder that only adulterous generations seek and would not, according to Jesus himself, be given, ever. But the resurrection of Jesus consists in his raising to the status of Word or Spirit incarnate, son of God in power, life-giving Spirit, Lord. A process that was begun at his very coming into the world and consummated by his death on the cross. And the only proof of this raising of his to the status of son of God in power that we now have or could ever need, consists in our experience of that Creator Spirit breathing in us through Jesus, and facilitating our keeping faith with that same Creator Spirit through death and into eternity.

No, what these stories of wounded hands and feet open for inspection on Jesus returning to his old haunts are meant to prove is something we can all verify in all our eucharistic lives. It is something that Thomas and Philip and Peter and so many others refused to accept at the time. Something that so very many of us have refused and still refuse to accept to this present day. Something indeed, if we were to be open and honest about it, that all of us decline to accept in practice during most or our lives. Namely, that it is the one who would give his life for others, and did so; it is this one who is son of God in power and Lord, and the one who shows the way to eternal *shalom* in this age and in any age that is to come.

Then, John's Gospel ends with what many scripture scholars call an epilogue (chap. 21), in which a further coming of the risen Jesus to one of his old haunts, the Sea of Tiberias, is recorded. This epilogue contains a miracle story of multiplying a catch of fish and what seems to be a eucharistic story of sharing fish and bread, followed by a discourse that appears to be concerned with Jesus settling some issues that had apparently arisen about the roles of certain leaders in the early community of his followers. About Peter in particular, and the beloved disciple, commonly thought to be John himself. Paul too, in his famous chapter on the resurrection (1 Cor. 15) lists six return visits of the risen Jesus, the last of which was to Paul himself. These are normally thought to be concerned with the commissioning of leaders in the early community. (Although the "appearance" to a group of five hundred does not easily fit this scheme.) For it is the coming of the risen Jesus to Paul in a phenomenon of light and voice on the road to Damascus that is normally thought to refer, not just to Paul's conversion, but to his commissioning as an apostle (Acts 9:3–6). And finally, it is presumably all of these return appearances, ensemble, that the Acts of the Apostles has in mind when they are imagined to have taken place during a forty-day period "after his passion." This passage clearly identifies the purpose of all of these returns or post-death comings of Jesus, not as the purpose of offering evidence for the resurrection of Jesus, but rather for the stated purpose of "speaking of the kingdom of God." But this is the very purpose that consumed all of his earthly life, in word and deed, and that achieved its consummate communication in that same passion and death (Acts 1:3).

What then, in sum are we to make of all of this? Leave aside the sometimes anxious desire to know if there are any common features that characterize the experiential basis of all of the post-death "returns" of the risen Jesus recorded in the rNT, ranging as they do from a recognizable or an unrecognized body, to a disembodied light and voice. Simply acknowledge the fact that all of these, and more, are part and parcel of the greatly varied imagery in which the Spirit (of) God, and therefore the Risen Lord as life-giving spirit are pictured making special appearances in a world from which they are never really absent. Light is naturally the medium of such comings of the divine, when God's hypostasis as the Glory occurs in the context, as with the shepherds at Bethlehem. The voice from above is the medium for the epiphanies of the divine at Jesus's baptism. Angels, that is to say, messengers, often in human form, are often the media, personae or personifications of God speaking on a particular occasion for a specific purpose.

The fact of the matter is that this imagery that ranges from light shining to speaking voices is, understandably enough, the conventional imagery for the expression of the conviction that God through the continuously creative Word or words (*logoi*) in creation "enlightens everyone in the world" (John's prologue). Or that the Creator Spirit that continually creates the world and enlivens humans in their innermost conscious beings, thereby communicates the practical wisdom of the true way of the world; and so forms in us that mind that was also in Christ Jesus, as Paul would have it. For, as Jesus said, we could comprehend the way of the reign of God if we simply noted how the sun treats equally the good and the bad, and the rain serves the just and the unjust. Or that the same Spirit that was incarnate in Jesus forms that same mind in us, and thereby makes us members of the extended body of Christ in the world. So that Jesus can be said to in-spire us and others who encounter us, for example, as we share in, and learn in practice from participation in the symbolic praxis of eucharist, like the disoriented disciples at Emmaus. The followers of Jesus and others, both before and after his earthly sojourn, are spoken to, communicated with, enlightened by God and Jesus in all of these interlocking ways.

Leave aside, consequently, the issue of the objectivity of such sightings and hearings. For the fact that they all belong to the genre of what is known as vision literature, does not in the least take from the possibility of the objectivity of the "appearances" and other epiphanies, and therefore of whatever truth they are thought to communicate. God, and God acting through Jesus, is just as objective a presence in the lives of Jesus's followers after Jesus's death, as before that consummate event. And if biblical exegetes are, quite rightly, not at all worried about the objectivity of the angel's message to Joseph when he discovered that Mary was pregnant, even though it is said that the angel appeared to Joseph in a dream, then neither should anyone be worried about objectivity with respect to the rest.

Concentrate instead then, as the account of these return appearances above has done, on the purposes, the concerns served by each and every story of Jesus coming once again. And simply recognize the fact that if the presence and permanent appearance of Jesus to his disciples before his death could allow them to distort his words and deeds by passing them through their own preferred vision of the reign and sonship of God, there is literally no earthly reason why they should not continue this distortion after Jesus's departure from this earthly life. Or why they should not continue with such distortion even after those special encounters with God's permanent presence through Jesus, such as Paul experienced on the road to Damascus, and others no doubt experienced and described in other ways. Encounters that are then remembered in the community as quite singular experiences of that presence during the earliest years after the death of Jesus. Add to this the fact of that common experience of all of us: that when what is being said is what we definitely do not want to hear, then what we actually do hear is not quite what actually was being said. And the persistence of Christians, and even Christian leaders in distorting the vision of the reign of God is understandable, if not even to be expected.

Remember Paul claiming, in the very context in which he directly dismantles Jesus's rule about divorce, when he admitted that he had no saying from Jesus that would permit him to do this, that he thought nevertheless in doing it that he had the Spirit of God in him? Is this not strictly parallel to the claim made by certain magisterial leaders of Christian churches down the ages, a claim to specific comings of the Holy Spirit on them? This is a claim to the effect that the same Spirit that came upon and formed the life-giving spirit of Jesus of Nazareth, guides them also and unerringly on those special occasions on which they set themselves to teach to all who would be followers of Jesus the message of Jesus in all matters pertaining to faith and morals, as revealed in the life, death and destiny of the same Jesus. Perhaps these leaders should more often remember the advice they give to members of the faithful when these claim certain supernatural visions, namely, that the content or import of the vision should be compared to the true faith and morals of Jesus, as by far the best means of securing its authenticity, and preventing the incursion of the satanic. Just so must one compare, from the biblical texts down to the present time, programs of faith and morals that are preached or practiced, to see if they comply with the account of the living faith of Jesus that is also so clearly portrayed in the same Bible.

Just as his followers managed to convince themselves, as Jesus during his earthly lifetime with them revealed to them in word and act the true reign of God, that he was not after all making such radical changes to the traditional faith they shared with him — though he did seem at times to betray a penchant for exaggerating for the sake of effect! — so they were prone to believe that his more spiritual presences with them after his death also perfected their traditional faith, but without rejecting out of hand so many of its features that happened to suit their more selfish interests. Interests such as the punishment of those who resisted the spread of their faith or, in Paul's teaching on divorce, the retention of increasing membership of their new community of followers, and so on.

Finally then, and in particular, it is in the light of these persistent states of still not knowing, or not being satisfied with the reign of the Creator Father as revealed in the Son's way of steadfast love, in which evil is never to be returned for evil, in heaven or on earth, but to be met with the creative forgiveness of doing good: it is in this light that one must read all of these expectations of an end-time tribunal that will condemn some to eternal torment. So some of the earliest followers of Jesus were unable or unwilling to see, hearing but not more than half heeding, what they nevertheless faithfully recorded. And the Bible continues to the end to prove itself a record of a larger truth than those advocates of a narrower infallibility can allow themselves to see. As it illustrates the persistent betrayal of the divinely revealed truth to which, from beginning to end, it always also witnesses.

The misrepresentations and betrayals continued, of course, into the history of the religion that took the name of Jesus the Christ, whom it claimed as its founder. Already in the early 50s of the first century of their existence, well before the community of Jesus's followers had emerged as a new religion separate from Judaism, as it did about one hundred years later, we have the strong beginnings of the old original temptation of all religions. This is the temptation to believe God's gifts to be franchised solely or principally to them, and God's wrath correspondingly reserved mainly for outsiders, and in particular for those who set out to oppose them. That attitude reached its apogee in the medieval Christian church: outside the church, its officers now proclaimed quite peremptorily, there is no salvation. And after the Protestant Reformation of the sixteenth-century Christian churches condemned members of other Christian churches to hell. All of them, as their sinful theory and practice of church proves, distorting the revelation of Jesus and of the covenant he mediated once more: the covenant of creation. For that is the true revelation, preserved in the Bible by the very people who then in the Bible betrayed it, and yet preserved it in all the Christian churches, if only by their preservation of the Bible.

In any case, this true revelation of the way, of the eternal God's steadfast creative love for creation and humanity within it, no matter where, or how often, or how so ever it is betrayed, continues to come through the creation itself. And since the poet is the seer, a poet of sufficient depth of vision will see the revelation in creation and speak that true revelation. The Irish poet whose vision, after Yeats, was deepest and truest is Patrick Kavanagh, who penned the lines: "Heaven/ is the generous impulse, is contented/ with feeding praise to the good." In another poem that with characteristic quirkiness he entitled "Miss Universe" he caught and held the vision of an ultimately non-judgmental Creator, and caught a clear glimpse of the steadfast love that, albeit often through unavoidable violence, brings all to eternal *shalom:*

> I learned, I learned — when one might be inclined
> To think, too late, you cannot recover your losses —
> I learned something of the nature of God's mind,
> Not the abstract Creator but He who caresses
> The daily and nightly earth; He who refuses
> To take failure for an answer till again and again is worn.
> Love is waiting for you, waiting for the violence that she chooses
> From the tepidity of the common round beyond exhaustion or scorn.
> What was once is still and there is no need for remorse;
> There are no recriminations in Heaven. O the sensual throb
> Of the explosive body, the tumultuous thighs!
> Adown a summer lane comes Miss Universe
> She whom no lecher's art can rob
> Though she is not the virgin who was wise.

Chapter Seven

CULT

This, however, was the beginning of that long meal which is called "The Last Supper" in the history books. And during that meal nothing was spoken of but the *Higher Man.*

— Nietzsche, *Thus Spoke Zarathustra*

Cult may be taken here as a term to include all behavior designed to deal directly with divinity: prayer, of course, and also liturgy, the public engagement in ritual; whether the public concerned is confined to the family, and the prayer and ritual is conducted perhaps by the head of the household and in the home. Or whether a more extensive community is involved, and the prayer and ritual is conducted also by persons officially ordained for the purpose, and in public buildings designed for divine service. All of these forms were in evidence in the cult of the religion into which Jesus of Nazareth was born, and in which he died. Therefore, the first question to be answered in the course of this chapter on Christian cult concerns Jesus's own stance with regard to the cult that constituted the practice of his own religion in his time. And that is a question that is not too easily answered, as any interested reader of the rNT may quite easily observe. First and partly, because Jesus himself appeared to have been on something of a learning curve when it came to assessing access to the faith he preached and promoted as the essence of the advent of the reign of God. Remember his encounters with the faith of some petitioners for salvation from him who did not belong to his own religion. Second and more substantially, because it is very obvious from the most cursory comparison of documents that make up the rNT that Jesus's own immediate followers in the prophetic movement he started interpreted in widely different ways, in both word and action, what they believed to be his stance with respect to their common Jewish cult.

Matthew in the scene in which Jesus, the new Moses, hands down the new Torah from the mountain, has Jesus insist that this does not involve abolishing either the (old) Torah or the previous prophets. What is involved, rather, is their fulfillment. Fulfillment? Their perfection, perhaps, their accomplishment? However that term *fulfillment* is understood, if one goes lightly on the phrase "not an iota, not a dot, will pass," the idea of perfecting or fulfilling can be made to cover quite an amount of reformation, of correction even. And yet, however much correction one may want to smuggle in under the cover of fulfillment, one will still remain a very long way from abolition. At the other end of this argument then, the end that comes closest to abolition, is the Letter to the Hebrews. The aim of this epistle, described in its introduction in the Revised Standard Version as "the longest sustained argument of any book in the Bible," is that of proving "the preeminence of Christianity over Judaism." That phrase is a little bit anachronistic, since at this point of history there is as little evidence of the existence of a new religion called Christianity as there is of Jesus ever having wanted to found it. However that may be, the further aim of this letter is to prevent recent converts to the cause of Jesus from "returning to the Jewish beliefs and practices of their ancestors." The letter argues specifically for the end of the Temple and its priesthood as points of reference for Jews converted to the following of Jesus. Indeed, that particular piece of argument goes so far as to insist that, since Jesus can now be imagined as the High Priest who has gained for all a direct access to the Throne of Grace, there is no longer any need or room for any cultic priesthood whatever to act as intermediary between the faithful and their God. This piece of biblical argument should surely concern those Christian churches that, despite this letter, insist on such priesthoods and altars and sacrifices as part of the Christian religion.

In between these extremes different positions seem to be taken by different leaders and groups among those who constituted the early following of Jesus. And these to a certain extent reflect the traditions and interpretations of the words and actions of Jesus that were handed down in the tradition of this new community. It is obvious from the Acts of the Apostles and from letters of Paul that the leaders of the Jerusalem community of Jesus-followers continued to attend the Temple and to follow "the Jewish beliefs and practices of their ancestors." Whereas Paul himself, while also going to the Temple and to the synagogues, held passionately to the controversial position that the rule of circumcision as well as other ritual rules concerning food and so on, were not binding upon his converts. Similarly with the tradition of Jesus's own words and actions. Some of these could be interpreted within a general intent to reform the priesthood and the Temple — his "cleansing" of the Temple, for example. Whereas some reported words of his could as easily be read in such a way as to suggest that temples and their retinues, and not just the Jerusalem temple were redundant. For as Stephen too proclaimed in his speech from the dock, the whole of creation constituted the true house of God. In his response to the Samaritan woman who wanted his views on the respective claims of the temples on Mount Gerizim and Jerusalem, Jesus could certainly be taken to suggest that neither would be necessary when people came to worship God in spirit and in truth. And then there is his far more sweeping condemnation of the whole religious leadership of his people as belonging to the party of Satan.

What can be concluded from all of this when the question of a cult for the community of the followers of Jesus comes up? Mostly negative conclusions, must be the answer. He certainly did not ordain any priests to perform particular cultic duties for his followers, and no such cultic priesthood appears in that early community. Nor are any officials of that community described as properly cultic priests for some centuries after the community, now called Christian, separates from its Jewish matrix. Nor was there any question in these earliest centuries of setting up distinctive Christian temples, altars or other public places of worship. The houses of leading converts were the gathering places in which whatever praying and preaching and ritual they then engaged in were then practiced. Jesus did, it appears, set some kind of leadership over the inner circle of his chosen disciples, the leadership of the Twelve, but it is not very clear how this leadership structure fared in the light of subsequent events. That however is a matter for the next chapter, on the constitution of this early community. The point for now is that this leadership did not appear to have any particular cultic role, unless one counts under the rubric of cultic, the proclamation of the good news of the reign of God and the incitement to the kind of faith and trust from which its eternal benefits could be expected. But that would be to stretch the meaning of the cultic beyond the range of manageable meaning, and to complicate current matters by the introduction of functionaries such as Paul introduces in his list of charismatics — apostles, prophets, teachers, healers, and so on — that are better dealt with elsewhere (1 Cor. 12:27–31). Is it best then to conclude from the above that Jesus left it open as to whether one could or should try to reform the Jewish religion of his time in order to remove from it some blockages to the triumphant extension of the reign of God, or alternatively to create some other cult, or perhaps to do without any cult, and even without any religion in that narrow sense of the word *religion* at all? The best way to proceed is to look at the rituals in which his earliest followers engaged, and which survived the break with Judaism, and to compare these with what is known of the witness of Jesus's own preaching, life and death as already outlined above.

Prayer

Matthew gives us permission to be quite brief about prayer, if not quite as brief as Jesus's own injunctions about brevity in prayer might lead us to be. In fact, these injunctions are so brief and to the point as to be worth quoting in full:

"And when you pray, you must not be like the hypocrites; for they love to stand and pray in the synagogues and at the street corners, that they may be seen by men. Truly, I say to you, they have their reward. But when you pray, go into your room and shut the door and pray to your Father who is in secret; and your Father who sees in secret will reward you.

And in praying do not heap up empty phrases as the Gentiles do; for they think that they will be heard for their many words. Do not be like them, for your Father knows what you need before you ask him. Pray then like this:

Our Father who art in heaven, hallowed be thy name. Thy kingdom come. Thy will be done, on earth as it is in heaven. Give us this day our daily bread; and forgive us our debts, as we also have forgiven our debtors; and lead us not into temptation, but deliver us from evil."

It is perhaps worth adding some other relevant sentences from the same Sermon from the Mount: "Therefore I tell you, do not be anxious about your life, what you shall eat or what you shall drink...your heavenly Father knows that you need them all; But seek first his kingdom and his righteousness, and all these things shall be yours as well" (Matt. 6).

There it is then. Not only an injunction to brevity, but an actual example of just how brief you can be, and still pray for all you ever need to pray for. For the "Our Father" is clearly the prayer of the kingdom of God, and as such it is the prayer for the kingdom of God. For the reign of God is the rule of creative love and bounty, so that everything that you could ever wish for is always already given to you before you ever get round to praying, thy kingdom come. Life is given and all the supports of life, the bread of life itself and the wine of hope and happiness. And all the salving of life, up to and including the victory over death itself. You have only to take it, and to bless God for it: "hallowed be thy name." Not because God is insatiable for praise, and not simply for the sake of good manners, but because this simple acknowledgment of the limitless bounty of creation is the surest source of the inspiration that will enable you to translate this experience of infinite and unconditioned grace to you into a corresponding generosity and grace to others. Food to the hungry, healing to the sick, love to the enemy. For it is your very self that is otherwise the obstacle to the experience and hope of life ever more abundant, an obstacle simultaneously for yourself and for others, as you seek to commandeer the bread and the wine of life for your own security and self-aggrandizement. For this you must ask regularly for forgiveness, although God knows that you have need of that too, and has always given it before you ask — "your sins are forgiven," said Jesus, before he was even asked.

Just as in the case of the request for the daily bread of life, what you are really asking for is the realization that what you ask for is already given, and the ever-emerging belief that it will always be given, since the giver is the eternal creator of all who does not change character or falter, the one whose reign takes the form of steadfast love. So that this is still the prayer of the kingdom of God, for the kingdom of God. For that reign that alone promises eternal life cannot come to you, and to some extent it can be prevented from coming to others, if it is your will to replace it with another rule that is adversarial to it, the reign of the satanic spirit. And it is not that this forgiveness, that you rightly and regularly ask for, is conditional on your forgiving those who have sinned against you. That is not the true import of the phrase "as we also have forgiven our debtors." Rather is the connection the same as in the case of the request for daily bread: just as the appreciation of the bread of life and the wine of life's highest hope and happiness engenders in you the spirit that breaks that bread and pours out that wine to others, so the anticipatory divine forgiveness that actually always takes the form of the eternal creator pouring out life and hope to all, to the good, the bad and the indifferent, is itself the spur to you to forgive your enemies, to make them the objects of that same steadfast love of which you yourself are the eternally cherished beneficiary.

"Forgive us our debts" — there you go again, always in danger of forgetting that God already knows what you need and is already giving it. So that this petition also really asks for your *realization* that the superabundant outpouring of life is itself forgiveness. And that *making real* must have the natural consequence for you who are now ruled by God in this manner, of letting that life pour through you to others, in the course of which it will constitute the most positive form of forgiveness of those who have, do or will sin against you. The form of steadfast love that will not return evil for evil, but instead do good to those who hate you. Still a prayer of the kingdom of God, for the reign of God in each and every heart.

Finally, "lead us not into temptation, but deliver us from evil." That is sometimes translated or interpreted to read, "lead us not into the trial," and it would appear that, for the English language at least, both forms are necessary. For the term *temptation* reminds us more of that primal temptation of our race, to make of ourselves our own god, sometimes rather thinly disguised as another kind of being, called Mammon perhaps, or less thinly disguised as Nietzsche's Superman. And the only prevention of that temptation consists once again in the realization of the reign in our hearts of the one, true and eternal Creator of life. But then the term *trial* directs our attention to the form of the "Our Father" that Jesus used in the garden of Gethsemane: "Father, all things are possible to thee; remove this cup from me; yet not what I will, but what thou wilt" (or "thy will be done on earth, as it is in heaven," the self-same sentiment; Matt. 26:39). Here Jesus, and we, may legitimately pray that we be spared from such trial and death as Jesus in fact suffered, prudent as we must ever be about our known prospects of resisting the oldest temptation to survive at any cost. But if, in our cases also, it is not in God's providence that we be spared this ultimate test of our keeping faith, this dying rather than kill those who would kill us for what we preach and live, then we are back to praying for what we know God always gives: deliverance from this death and into eternal life. So that still, even at this extreme point, the prayer remains a prayer of the kingdom of God for the reign of God. For to die in these circumstances for that reign is to breath the Spirit of it most powerfully into an ever-dying and death-dealing world, and so to extend the reign of that Creator Spirit and with it the blessed hope of all humankind for life eternal.

Is that all that is to be said about prayer then, on behalf of Jesus and his followers? Well, yes, certainly it says all that it is essential to say on the subject. For this is a prayer to the Creator for the creation. Its purpose is, not to get God to do anything that God as Creator would not do anyway, but to make humans realize what God the Creator does in all eternity. And to realize this in the double sense of acknowledging it, and accepting and setting themselves to their essential part in it. So that the work they then do in the world is the real prayer, more real than the mere recitation of the words. For words might turn out to be just that, mere blather. Whereas creative work done in faith and trust in the ultimate Creator is prayer made real in act, and thereby blessed with the hope and happiness of unlimited life. That is the truest prayer, prayed through the way that one walks through the whole of one's life, prayed with few words, and often none at all.

There is therefore not any need, and perhaps not any real place for, petitionary prayers for the success of individual ventures, like passing an exam. Or for individual healings, in which God seems to be expected to act for this cancer patient while not acting for other cancer patients, either because they have not asked, or do not believe in God, or for some other unfathomable reason. Unless perhaps such prayers are really meant as mere exemplary formulations of the general prayer to the Creator to provide us always with the expertise and the means of salving life as much as possible. As much as possible? Yes, for as the great Sean Connery put the matter, memorably, in one of his films, "we all have to die of something." And we are back to the "Our Father" again, and to a prayer to God to provide all that is always provided: all the material to feed and clothe and shelter all living things, all the medicinal substances and the methodological ingenuity to heal the ills of the race, and so on, and so on. And we are back to the realization that it is not any failure on God's behalf to respond to individual cases of suffering and need that is the cause of the massive amounts of unnecessary suffering and deprivation in the world. But rather the maiming and massacre, the uprooting and starvation attributable to the warmongers of every age. Or the denial to millions of medicines (for AIDS for instance) because those needing them most cannot pay enough to meet the overriding profit motive of the pharmaceutical companies (old Mammon, again), and so on, and so on. So that the prayer of the kingdom of God for growing among us of the reign of God is in fact the only prayer that is necessary. Once it is said in sincerity in one's room or one's heart, it is on the way to being already efficacious. For it already floods the mind with the kind of faith and hope in the world that can both inspire and guide the kind of action that could rid the world of all unnecessary suffering and failure, disease and destruction.

Nor is there much need to say that prayer very often. Memories of a Catholic childhood reproduce the bizarre scene of a priest administering the sacrament of Penance and telling the penitent, "for your penance say the Our Father five times." What in God's name did this priest think of this prayer, that he could command it to be recited five times, in quick succession no doubt, and as a penance? To say it regularly, but not so regularly as to make it a routine, would seem to suffice, provided that one said it very thoughtfully and with a ready willingness to the commitment entailed in it. But are there other kinds of prayer? For surely one could follow Jesus's embargo on too much prayer talk in all the churches of his self-proclaimed followers, but without cutting the whole exercise back quite as much as that? The answer to that question depends much on what kinds of recital or exercise one wants to include under the category of prayer. For example, there is the prayer of praise, and that could be seen as an extension and a series of particular illustrations of the blessing of God for his creation that follows immediately on the opening address of the Lord's Prayer. But there is need for some care here also, for this kind of prayer, in conjunction with the highly questionable doctrine to the effect that God created all for his own glory, courts the very real danger of presenting God as some sort of self-obsessed megalomaniac. Whereas the glory of God resides in God's goodness, God's infinite and steadfast love, from the overflowing of which, as Plato too acknowledged, the whole creation and all its infinite promise resulted. So by all means bless God for the overflowing goodness that the whole of creation proclaims, as so many of the psalms do in so poetic a fashion. But that is still within the range of the Lord's Prayer, and comes equally under the embargo of too much talking, particularly when there is so much work to be done.

There is also what is sometimes called the prayer of contemplation, popular with those who lead what is called the contemplative life. That too most definitely deserves a place in any account of prayer, and has played a prominent part in the prayer forms of the Christian tradition. Even if, as in the case of traditional Christian theology, it precedes Christianity and finds its role at the particular cultural origins of Christian contemplative lives in the contemplative lives of the Greek philosopher-theologians. In a way, Jesus himself could be said to have recommended it to us, and in such a way that it lies behind the prayer that Jesus taught us, and implicitly at least accompanies that prayer whenever it is thoughtfully recited. For when the question arises as to how we are to come upon that trust and faith that are coincidentally and implicitly expressed in every petition of the Lord's Prayer, the answer is already given by Jesus in the very course of his instructions from the holy mountain as to how we are to pray and what we are to say. We are to contemplate the creation, to pay attention to it, to attend to it with that prayerful waiting that informs the profession of the poet and is rewarded with the deeper vision of all that is, from dark source to bright future, that makes the poet a poet, a seer. We are to attend to the sun and the rain, the grass and the lilies of the field, the birds of the air and the single sparrow that falls from the sky . . . we are to attend upon the creation for the vision that can support the trust and hope and love that must then inform the Lord's Prayer if we are to be enabled to pray it properly (and the contemplative part of it all requires even less talk, than do the other parts). And that prayer, the Our Father, with that grounding and sustenance, can then be described finally as the prayer of the creation, for the creation. In fact, in both cases, the prayer of praise and the prayer of attending to, of waiting upon, of contemplation, there emerges naturally an element of blessing God for it all, as the opening phrases of the Lord's Prayer and of the eucharistic formula alike illustrate. A surge of gratitude arises that inspires our eucharistic action of giving from what we have so abundantly received. And that in itself, if anything will, moves us quickly from word, thought and symbolic act, to a kind of living and a kind of dying under the reign of the steadfast love of God.

Sacraments

It is under this title that the dominant and distinctive forms of Christian ritual are most commonly listed. Yet there is little enough need to go too deeply into the etymology of the term *sacrament* in order to set up this section, or analyze the ancient usages of the term to denote certain procedures of the courts of law, for instance, or of recruitment to the army. It is quite sufficient for present purposes to think of sacrament as a species of sign or, better, of symbolism. In particular, that kind of sign, more properly called a symbol, that participates in and begins to effect that which it symbolizes. These signs can be made of words of course, but they can also be made of the elements and media used in all of the arts and crafts. In fact the most comprehensive kind of participatory and effective symbol is perhaps that which is comprised of a play, a drama, a performance that can include all or most of the arts: words spoken or sung, music, pictorial and architectural representation, movement or dance, and in general acting with the elements of the world and especially with persons. Sacrament as symbol in this convention does not involve words alone. A creed is a purely verbal symbol, giving expression to our faith in the *weltanschauung* it delineates, and reinforcing our commitment to it. It is like a piece of high prose, or a poem. But a sacrament is a play and the play, as the Irish playwright, Stewart Parker, too soon taken from us, put it, "is how we test the world and register its realities. Play is how we experiment, imagine, invent and move forward. Play is above all how we enjoy the earth and celebrate our life upon it."

By a Christian convention that was accepted by the medieval church of Christendom at the Council of Lyon in 1274 C.E., seven sacraments were identified as the central and essential sacraments of the Christian faith: baptism, confirmation, eucharist, penance, matrimony, holy orders and extreme unction. All other rituals were relegated to a lower order of sacramentality, some eventually called sacramentals. The criteria for this selection of seven is itself a matter of some uncertainty and controversy. Was it the coverage of the ages of human life and the essentials of communal living: birth, growth to maturity, communing, procreation, empowering intermediaries, redressing disorders, preparing to die? Or was it a claim to specific institution of these sacraments by Jesus himself? Or both? Or others? It would take too long to try to answer these questions here and, frankly, no result achieved would be likely to be worth the trouble. At the Protestant Reformation of the sixteenth century the seven sacraments were reduced to two: baptism and eucharist. And already in the thirteenth century Thomas Aquinas had concluded that all other sacraments were ordered to the eucharist as to their end. Which meant this much at least, that the eucharist could achieve in itself what all the others could achieve singly and together. It should suffice then for present purposes to deal with baptism and eucharist, accepted by all Christian communities as the central sacraments of Christianity — with the exception of Quakers, for instance, who do not believe that any such rituals are required for the following of Jesus — and to add some brief comments on some at least of the other five.

Baptism

Since Jesus during his earthly existence does not appear to have ever thought of founding a new religion, or to have had any inkling of the fact that a new religion would be devised by his followers who would then claim him, and not without some justice, as its founder, one must look hard to see if there is any evidence at all for the contention that he instituted sacraments. Take first the case of baptism. There is little doubt

about the fact that Jesus, at or before the outset of his own public prophetic mission to his own people, had some association with the mission
of another prophet, John the Baptizer. There is little doubt that he had
in fact been baptized by John, that is to say, he had undergone the ritual
by which all followers of John entered upon the way that John preached
as constituting the reign of God. There is then some evidence in both
the Gospels and the Acts of the Apostles (19:1–7) that there were some
questions in the minds of John and his followers as to what exactly Jesus
was doing. Especially since, according to the Gospels, Jesus announced
his mission in precisely the same terms as John had not long before that
announced his: "repent, for the kingdom of God is at hand" (Matt. 3:2;
4:17). And these questions must have been given point and some sharp-
ness by the knowledge that Jesus had been baptized by John. For if Jesus
was baptizing, then he really did have to say if he was doing so as (still)
a convert of John's, or whether he was doing something different from
John, and if so, what? This may be the reason why the other John, the
evangelist, interjects into his narrative of baptism by the disciples of Jesus:
"although Jesus himself did not baptize, but only his disciples" (John 4:2),
and other evangelists also make John the Baptizer say that Jesus is vastly
his superior and baptizes with the Holy Spirit and with fire.

It is all very confusing, and all that can with any confidence be concluded from it is this: the followers of Jesus did quite quickly introduce
baptism as an initiation ritual for their growing community as they began
to spread the gospel of Jesus far and wide, and as Matthew makes Jesus
specifically commission them to do: "Go therefore and make disciples of
all nations, baptizing them in the name of the Father and of the Son and
of the Holy Spirit" (Matt. 28:19). That conclusion urges upon us the
crucial question that needs to be asked of all of this, namely, what is the
reality of this life in this world that this symbolism of baptism participates in, begins to effect, tests and registers, for John the Baptizer and
his disciples, and for the disciples of Jesus? And the clue to the answer
lies, obviously, in the nature and function of the cosmic element, water,
its properties and usages.

After air, water is the element that living things can do least longest
without. It is therefore a fundamental necessity of life, so fundamental
that it is a natural symbol for the source of life; it is a continuous source
of emerging and continuing life. This symbol participates in the reality
it symbolizes. (Hence the anxious search for traces of water on some of

our nearby planets.) No surprise then at its universal presence and functioning in all known religions, in rituals of sprinkling it or pouring it over people, or immersing people in it. In pre-Christian Irish religion, for instance, the places sacred to the creator goddess, Brigid, are so often wells or springs, rivers and particularly their physical sources. Just as the waters of the primeval deep in full and formless flood are those from which the Creator makes the whole living world to emerge. So that pouring it over people or immersing them in it is a natural symbol of associating them most intimately with the ultimate source of life in the universe, so that that life may flow into them unimpeded and flow through them to others. To baptize people in the name of Jesus, the son of God, is to baptize them in the name of the Creator Spirit that sourced the life of Jesus poured out for others, and to baptize them in the name of the Father, from the image of whose son the form of the true creativity appears, the form of creativity that gives life eternally and without limit. To baptize in this manner is to enable the people who accept this sacrament to participate creatively as recipients and channels of that same life while acknowledging its ultimate source and being blessed with the hope of life unlimited. The drama of the water, together with the words spoken, and whatever other adjunct symbols and actions may be added — lights, garments, anointings, commitments from significant others — symbolizes and effects the acceptance of life with acknowledgment of its eternal source, together with the responsibility toward life that this brings, and the hope and happiness that the implicit pledge contained in this life-giving also offers.

Water, its properties and usages, reveals also another function that offers the prospects of further symbolism. It is universally used for cleaning, for washing away the dead or useless matter that can clutter up or bring disease or decay to the living organism. And that side of its symbolism is also evident in its religious usage, and quite rightly so. For life in its creative evolution continually makes forms of itself obsolescent, or allows parts and pieces, or even whole species-forms of itself to die out in the course of their replacement by the new, and of these also the living and evolving organism must be rid. Furthermore life must be rid of the destructive and death-dealing practices that are deliberately introduced by, and may have become very dear to, those consciously creative creatures that are free to choose for themselves the life they want for themselves at whatever expense to others. All of that too must be flushed out of the living system, no matter how painful the process may prove. And for all of that side of the progress of life, the symbolism of water the universal cleanser is apt, illuminating and inspiring. Paul unites both sides of the symbolism in the account he gives of Christian baptism. He links the imagery of going down into the water and emerging from it again, all in the name of Jesus, to the imagery of dying to our old sinful ways, the ways that killed Jesus, and to rising again to new and eternal life, just as God raised Jesus. "Do you not know that all of us who have been baptized into Christ Jesus were baptized into his death? We were buried therefore with him by baptism into death, so that as Christ was raised from the dead by the glory of the Father, we too might walk in newness of life. ... We know that our old self was crucified with him so that the sinful body might be destroyed. ... But if we have died with Christ, we believe that we shall also live with him" (Rom. 6:1–8).

Baptism by water therefore offers a double-adaptor sort of symbolism. As one is immersed in and registers both the reality of the creative source of life, and the reality of the cleansing away of the detritus that represents life's dying continuously to self-obsolescent form. And it should go without saying that the manner in which this dual-focus symbolism is deployed or experienced conveys the most serious consequences for the manner in which the world is tested and its deepest and highest reaches of reality registered, evaluated, and responded to in subsequent praxis.

For example, despite the fact that there really are two sides of the coin, the side of the symbolism of baptism that features the cleansing away of the detritus of deformations is often permanently to the fore and customarily predominant in the practice of the ritual. Then the result is bound to be a reinforcement of our all too prevalent tendency to focus upon the *niedergang*, as Nietzsche calls it, the downside, the nothinging of forms of life, and especially that which is caused by our original sinning. Then it is little wonder that, when the perceptions and practices of baptism in which the cleansing side of the symbolism of water is unquestionably dominant, particularly when the baptism of infants becomes a common practice, baptism should become associated with that false doctrine of original sin as a real sin automatically transmitted to each new member of the human race at and by the very process of conception itself. But the cleansing side is never, and it should not ever be made to be the dominant side of the natural symbolism of water, whenever or wherever a drama with water at its center is used to test the world and to register its realities. It is the life-giving properties of water that are naturally to the fore and must predominate in any dramatic symbolism that centers upon water. Just as it is the continuous creative act of giving existence and life eternally that sheds obsolete or corrupt forms as an integral part of the creative élan of life to ever higher forms.

It is difficult to determine whether it was the distorted doctrine of original sin, largely due to Augustine, that distorted Christianity's understanding and usage of the symbolism of baptism down through the centuries. Or whether it was some reversal of the natural order within the dual symbolism of water that, partly at least, caused the distortion of the doctrine of original sin. It is difficult to decide which is the chicken and which is the egg. But does that really matter? Not as long as Christianity can be rid in any case of a dual distortion of the theology of sin and of baptism, of the kind that only too often resulted in what can only be described as thoroughly sin-driven Christian theologies. These are the kind of Christian theologies that set sin as the prelude and the very raison d'être of the good news, as if the whole activity of God that Christians were commissioned to preach consisted in God's necessary — although of course free and unforced — actions to counteract what humans had done. Thereby handing the initiative in a certain manner to humans, making the first part of the gospel preached thoroughly bad news indeed, and resulting almost inevitably in those distortions of the biblical metaphors for our saving from sin — the metaphor of redemption, in particular — that have been encountered already above. And resulting also, as far as the practice of baptism is concerned, in the sometimes unseemly haste of those driven by such distorted views to baptize neonates in case they should die without baptism, and as a consequence be rejected from God's blessed presence for all eternity. A rather revolting image of God that seemed not to deter those who distorted the symbolism of baptism in this way. And an image of God that is significantly similar to the equally revolting image of a God who would require the cruel death of Jesus as payment for the sins of human kind.

On the other and more positive hand, when the priority within the dual symbolism of baptism is kept in proper order, then and only then can the practice of infant baptism find its full and acceptable theological justification. In order to see that justification, and indeed in order to appreciate the full symbolic power of the baptismal drama, it is necessary to draw into the picture the other personae dramatis involved: the parents, god-parents, and the official representative of the local Christian community who normally takes the leading role in the drama. It is they, any or all of them, who pour the water over the child or immerse the initiate in the water. So that the fuller symbolism of the drama then signifies that the initiate is being introduced into the family (house-family and/or extended church family) through whose members the life-giving, Creator Spirit breathes. The same Spirit that breathed so specially through the man, Jesus, and now breathes through the body of Christ extended in time and space. The water then in which *they* immerse the child, by participating as water does in that creative power that eternally sources all life and simultaneously washes away any dying and death-dealing forms of life, symbolizes the eternal commitment of the Source of all life to pour out life indefinitely to this neonate. It symbolizes and in part effects the circumstances in which the Creator Spirit will pour this life into this newly arrived human being through the loving and co-operative creativity of fellow humans, especially those gathered round the font, and most especially of all the pro-creators of the child. And it symbolizes and in part effects the circumstance in which that divine creative act and that co-creative human activity of advancing life will serve to prevent the child from succumbing to the cultural force of the original sin, a force of temptation to which, because of its corporate dimension, all of humanity is destined to be subjected. In the case of adult baptism, the ceremony symbolizes and in part effects the *metanoia* by which the recipient, with the help of the community, sends into remission, washes away original sin and all of its previous manifestations.

Baptism is a natural sacrament, in that it is a sacrament of creation, in the dual sense of using a created source of the creation of life in order at once to participate in and to symbolize the deepest source and goal of the creation as a whole. Baptism symbolizes the eternal creative sourcing of existence and life by the dramatic action of ritually introducing the human person to water that is itself a derivative and participative source of life. Baptism can therefore be performed by people of any religion or of none, by any number or grouping of people. And as it tests the world and registers the reality of its deep and continuously active creative source, baptism simultaneously inspires and commits the participants in the rite to deal creatively with each other and indeed with all the world, so as to contribute to the procurement of life and life more abundant for all. And in that very process baptism moves those who administer it and those who receive it to strive to overcome in each and in all the destructive death-dealing which arises either naturally in the very course of continuous creation or in more dire and disastrous form from the proclivity of humans to fallenness.

All of these considerations apply to overtly religious movements in which the sacramental ritual of baptism is practiced, and so they apply equally to the Christian Sacrament of Baptism. Yet there was a doctrine developed in the course of the centuries of the Christian theology of the sacraments, known as the doctrine of *ex opere operato*. This doctrine proposed, very briefly, that the grace or favor, enablement or inspiration conferred in the course of the celebration of a Christian sacrament, was guaranteed by God. For the sacraments were instituted by Jesus, the son of God, and therefore the grace of God that they symbolized was conferred automatically to those who were prepared to accept it, independently of the disposition or character of the ones who administered the sacraments. The beneficial effects, that is to say, were conferred by the very process of the ceremony properly conducted (*ex opere operato*), and were not restricted by the moral condition of the minister of the sacrament in question, whether clerical or lay. Now there is a certain truth in that, but it needs to be carefully stated, for otherwise the sacraments must decline to the status of crude magic. It is true in the case of baptism that the ever creative Creator Spirit, symbolized in the pouring of water, will continue to create life for all, and by doing so overcome death and destruction from whatever source, and will thereby attract or inspire people to give up their death-dealing ways, no matter how badly or how long these people, whether they are acting as ministers of sacraments or not, persist in their sinful ways. That continuous creation and the steadfast love that finds expression in it, is then both God's grace and God's limitless forgiveness.

In that sense, what the sacraments at once symbolize and participate in never fails to materialize. And yet it may well fail to have its true and full effect upon me, whether I am a designated minister of the sacrament, presiding and playing a leading role in the bringing about of the sacrament, or a more general participant in the sacrament, or the recipient. For if I or anyone else involved in sacramental ritual, in whatever role or part, am a person who grasps at life and the supports and enhancements of life to the spiritual or physical destruction of others, and most especially, if I treat the very sacraments themselves, the means of making real our common access to the grace and favor of God, as means that are exclusively available to me and my co-religionists, then to the extent that I am such a person and treat others in this manner, I have turned the sacraments themselves into sin, the same old original sin that they were designed to overcome through their inspiration to participate in life and life more abundant for all. And then the sacraments — for this will be true of the eucharist as much as of baptism — will be not only null and void, as the canon law would express the matter, they will prove to be positively adversarial, satanic with respect to the effects they should have on the experience and hope of life poured out limitlessly and equally for all that they are supposed to register as the gift of the eternal Creator Spirit.

So did Jesus institute, as the term goes, the Sacrament of Baptism as a sacrament of initiation into the community of those who opted to follow him? The answer to that question is more likely to be no, rather than yes. First, there is the statement already quoted from John the evangelist to the effect that Jesus himself did not baptize, but his disciples did so. The reference in the immediate context of that statement to Jesus's disciples as the ones who did baptize in his name, is most likely not a reference to the disciples who accompanied him during his earthly sojourn, but to disciples who succeeded these and who introduced baptism as the initiation rite for Jesus's followers sometime after the death of Jesus. These later disciples did this, no doubt, with the conviction that this is what the now heavenly Jesus wished them to do. So much is suggested by the story that ends Matthew's Gospel, the story of Jesus's appearance to "the eleven" on a mountain in Galilee, and of his commission to them on that occasion to baptize "all nations." Certainly in the gospel stories of Jesus during his life on earth, sending out numbers of his disciples to preach the reign of God and make disciples of others, there is no mention of baptizing among the detailed instructions as to just what they are to do and not to do.

And then there is the complex picture painted in the Gospels, and in one reference in the Acts of the Apostles, a partly confusing picture of the relationships of Jesus to John the Baptizer. Jesus was baptized by John in what is explicitly described as "a baptism of repentance (*metanoia*, change of heart) for the forgiveness of sin." And that immediately raised some questions about Jesus. Was he not always sinless, then? And was he not then a disciple of John, a symbolically signed up member of John's movement? Whatever about the answer to the first of these questions, the answer to the second question is very likely to be in the affirmative. But then there is the more confusing aspect of the gospel descriptions of the baptism of Jesus by John. How is it that the Gospels have John, on the occasion of his baptizing Jesus, being made aware and publicly proclaiming that Jesus, far from being one of his converts and followers, is in fact inestimably greater than himself? So that he, John, is no more than a mere precursor to the one who would definitively (re)install the reign of God. And yet, sometime later in the careers of these two emissaries of the reign of God, when John is already incarcerated by Herod, he has to send some of his disciples to Jesus to ask if Jesus is truly the one who was to come; in short, is he, John, merely a precursor after all? Did John not know the answer to this question already as he baptized Jesus? Had he forgotten in the meantime? Or merely suffered the unsettling incursion of doubt? Or was the questioning simply for the benefit of his remaining disciples?

It is quite impossible to be definitive here, but the most likely truth of the matter might read something like this: Jesus was baptized into the movement of John, and it was from this moment, as Mark makes clear, that the Spirit filled Jesus's soul and consciousness with such keen awareness of overpowering presence, as to make it possible to say that the Holy Spirit indwelt him. So that Jesus, from the very moment of taking part in the symbolic drama, was already plumbing more deeply the steadfast creative love of that Spirit, and simultaneously sensing, more than John could do, the extent of the joyful responsibilities for co-creation for others that it entailed, as well as the extent of the sacrifices of self that it would demand and enable him to make.

There is just one direct hint of the truth of this interpretation in the brief gospel stories of the mission of John when compared to the vastly more detailed gospel accounts of the mission of Jesus. Just a hint, a straw in the wind perhaps, but perhaps also a striking indication of the direction in which the Spirit is moving. John as herald of the reign of God, and in good covenant fashion, is seen in the Gospels to go into some detail as to the responsibilities and obligations entailed in the encounter with the God of life that the Sacrament of Baptism both symbolizes and effects. And as one reads these details: soldiers are to be satisfied with their pay and stop terrorizing and pillaging; tax collectors are not to demand more than is due in order to line their own pockets; and the man who has two coats should share with someone who has none...suddenly one remembers another covenant condition about coats and cloaks. Jesus after his baptism by John, now handing down the law from the mountain, formulates it as follows: if anyone would take your coat, let him have your coat as well; if he forces you to go one mile with him, go two, for you must not resist evil with evil, but rather love your enemies and do them good. And as suddenly a whole new vista opens up, and a gap widens between John and Jesus as both the real height of promise and the real depth of sacrifice that emerge from the participation and channeling of the creative steadfast love of God come into view.

The width of the gap, the distance and the difference, is then summed up in the Gospels in terms of the difference between a baptism with water and a baptism with the Spirit, with fire. And indeed it is the case that the symbolism of fire for creation and re-creation is far more powerful than is the symbolism of water. If only for conveying the degree of the eradication of dying and death-dealing tissue, the degree of burn that must be endured in happy hope in order that the new creation of all reach its joyful fulfillment. It is likely then that Jesus realized that his following of John and his baptism experience at the hands of John had led him further into the appreciation and service of the reign of God than John himself had been enabled to go. It is likely that Jesus in the course of his own mission did not then use baptism, or enjoin upon his apostles to do so. For he and they had to supplant John's mission in order to make real the higher power and promise, as well as the deeper demands that Jesus understood the reign of God to enjoin upon them. The experience of the Creative Spirit breathing the fire of creation into and through them, was to come to people through their encounter with Jesus whose life, all that he did and was, and most definitively his death, served to make him a channel of that Spirit to others. And then that indwelling of the Creator Spirit was to come to other people through the people into whom Jesus, the very enfleshment of the Life-giving Spirit, had breathed it, through the extended body of Jesus in the world. That encounter of itself was to constitute for those who were able to benefit from it their baptism with the Spirit, their baptism of fire.

It is likely that John did wonder what Jesus was up to, and where he stood in regards to himself, whether he was superseding John or not. And whatever answers John may have received to these wonderings, if any, it looks as if nothing much was done by John or his followers to negotiate, combine or compete with the incipient Jesus movement. It looks as if both movements continued on parallel courses, the one increasing as history tells, the other declining. And when the Jesus movement did adopt baptism as an initiation rite, most likely sometime soon after the death of Jesus, the difference between the baptisms was still expressed in terms of baptism in the Spirit, a baptism of fire, rather than baptism in water (only). When Paul comes upon some who have been baptized with the baptism of John and asks the latter if they have received the Holy Spirit, the response is, "No, we never even heard that there is a Holy Spirit," followed by the explanatory remark that they had been baptized "into John's baptism" (Acts 19:1–7). The truth of the matter is that baptism into the

Spirit that breathed most fully into the world through the man, Jesus, though symbolized by water, must supersede the baptism of John. It is this truth of the matter that the evangelists place on John's own lips on the occasion of his baptizing of Jesus, together with the confession that he is merely the precursor of Jesus who is the prophet expected to come in the end-time.

Eucharist

Eucharist is the sacrament that all Christian bodies that promote the sacramental side of religion believe to have been specifically instituted by Jesus. And the most common view among these bodies is that the Christian Sacrament of Eucharist was instituted by Jesus during the Last Supper, as it is called, the meal he shared with his disciples on the eve of his execution. And yet, before settling on the story of that last meal with his disciples, in order to distil from it the clearest possible idea of the sacrament that was instituted and of how precisely its institution was achieved, it might be wise to look more broadly into the rNT, and particularly into the gospel stories about Jesus's mission, for other material relevant to the issue. The first thing that should then strike anyone who engages in such a wider search is this: unlike the story that is commonly taken to be the story of the institution of the eucharist at the last supper, which is told by only three of the evangelists, another story is told by all four. And although this other story is normally classified simply as one miracle story among many, many others, it is in fact and quite unmistakably a story of eucharist. It is the story of the feeding of the five thousand, a story similar in kind to the story of the feeding of the four thousand that is told by the evangelists with the exception of John, and that is also a story of eucharist.

Yet the story of the feeding of the five thousand is the more significant of the two sets of stories, if only because John does not include in his story of the last supper the words and actions of Jesus that are thought to constitute the institution of the eucharist. John clearly did think that Jesus instituted the eucharist, for he has a whole theology of eucharist in the very chapter of his Gospel that opens with the story of the feeding of the five thousand and continues with statements of Jesus to the effect that: "I am the living bread which came down from heaven; if any one eats of this bread he will live forever; and the bread which I shall give for the life of the world is my flesh." These sentiments are fully the equivalent of Matthew's imagery in his story that Jesus at the last supper, "took bread . . . and said, 'Take, eat; this is my body'" (John 6:61; Matt. 26:26). John then certainly believed that eucharist was very much part of the mission of Jesus in his efforts to establish the reign of God as he understood it. But John does not appear to have thought that Jesus instituted the sacrament at the last supper with his disciples. On the contrary, he suggests — and then, surely, the other evangelists can also be taken to at least allow — that eucharist was already there in the course of the mission of Jesus that led inexorably to the last supper. For both the descriptions of the feeding of the five thousand, as indeed the descriptions of the feeding of the four thousand, are unmistakably descriptions of eucharist ritual.

John's words in the course of his description of the feeding of the five thousand read: "Jesus then took the loaves, and when he had given thanks, he distributed them to those who were seated." Matthew's words for the same occasion are "and taking the five loaves . . . he looked up to heaven, and blessed, and broke and gave the loaves to the disciples, and the disciples gave them to the crowds" (Matt. 14:19). One needs only to compare these two ritual formulae with Matthew's account of the eucharistic ritual at the last supper — "Jesus took bread, and blessed, and broke it, and gave it to the disciples and said, 'take, eat, this is my body'" — in order to see that in both instances, as indeed in all instances of the stories of the feedings and of the words and acts of Jesus at the last supper where eucharist is depicted, the ritual is exactly the same. The term *eucharist* used for these meals takes its origin from the second action of the ritual: having taken or received the bread, the staff of life, one then thanks the gracious giver, in Greek *eucharein*. Or one blesses God for the gift of this necessity of life, another form of thanking. Either way one symbolizes the reception of life itself as a gift from God the continuous creator of all existence and life. Of course, at the last supper, it was the wine that was joined with the bread in order to compose and constitute the eucharistic ritual, whereas in the meals that took place as a result of the feedings, it is fish that accompanies the bread. But that should simply tell us something more about eucharist as a sacrament of the reign of God the Creator for the followers of Jesus. At least this, that it is the meal that is essential, rather than the ingredients of which the meal is made up. Indeed John seems to distance himself deliberately from the apparent consensus of the other evangelists to the effect that the last supper took the form of the Passover meal. For John has Jesus eat his last supper with his disciples on the evening before the evening of Passover. A further indication from John of the fact that it is the meal that constitutes eucharist. Not necessarily a meal of particular foods and drinks, and not necessarily a ritual meal already constituted as such, together with its particular food and drink. Although such a ritual meal could be made a eucharistic meal just as well as any other meal, by the simple addition of the eucharistic words and attitudes and actions.

There is one further indication in the rNT that is worth considering in order to secure the conviction that it was something about Jesus's comportment at ordinary meals, something about the way he conducted himself in the course of the table fellowship that constitutes our common rituals of eating and drinking, that made his disciples realize that table-fellowship was a significant means of pursuing his mission to establish the true reign of God. So that they might well have continued that ritual sacramental practice after his death, even if he had never told them explicitly to continue to act accordingly after he was gone from their earthly company. In the earliest of the Gospels and at the very beginning of his Gospel Mark tells of Jesus's baptism by John the Baptizer, his taking over from John, his preaching and going about his ministry of salving, and in particular his healing of the paralytic to whom, without being asked, he proclaimed God's already proffered forgiveness, to the clear offense of the "scribes of the Pharisees." And then immediately he goes on to tell of Jesus, "at table in his house." Mark describes Jesus sharing his meal with his disciples and with "many tax collectors and sinners." And he tells of the scribes of the Pharisees being further offended by this kind of conduct. After Jesus's earlier enigmatic response to their earlier objection to his declaration of forgiveness to the paralytic — "which is easier, to say to the paralytic, 'your sins are forgiven,' or to say, 'rise, take up your pallet, and walk?'" — the response to their objection to his table-fellowship with sinners must have been at least more intelligible to them, even if it was no more acceptable. Jesus simply said, "those who are well have no need of a physician, but those who are sick." In short, that ordinary meal in the house of Jesus was healing and forgiveness together for those who most needed both.

The sharing of the meal with these people who needed healing of one kind or another then, was part and parcel of the salving of them. A salving that was in turn part of the continuous creation, reformation and transformation of life by the Creator Spirit. A salving creation that was then both symbolized and effected by the activity of those truly ruled by this steadfast love of God, in breaking to these wounded ones the bread, the staff of life. With the recognition of the fact that life and all the supports of life were the gift of the Creator Spirit to all, and the consequent responsibility of all recipients to grace as they have been graced, and to give of their lives and livelihoods to others in whatever manners and measures the palpable needs of the others require, and at whatever the cost that the grateful giver could bear.

It is implicit then in that first account in Mark's Gospel of Jesus's table-fellowship, that the meal shared with publicans and (other) sinners was seen by him to be itself part at least of the healing of the invited ones. In the breaking of his bread to them and the pouring out of his wine for them (if he did serve wine), he was continuing to assert the status of food and drink as gift, assuaging their hunger and thirst, enabling them to trust in the creator's gift of the necessities of life. So that the publican need not continue to rob people in his efforts to secure life by himself for himself and at whatever cost to others; and the prostitute, for instance, could also learn such trust, and not be reduced to behavior so damaging to herself and to others in order that she too might be her own sole provider for her own life. At the same time these guests were drawn into a communal circle round a table in which steadfast love took the practical form of the sharing of food and drink, and that in itself constituted forgiveness for the robber publican and the prostitute, for instance, who helped damage human relationships by turning what should be an act of love into a commodity. And it cured the lonely, outcast condition of both, simply by drawing them into that communal circle of a true, practical and steadfast love. Healing as creation, food and drink shared as contribution to the creation of life with limitless prospect, the meal beginning to achieve what it symbolizes, as all truly sacramental symbols do. And all of this in the stories of Jesus feeding people — a few guests at his table, or thousands tired, hungry and thirsty after listening to his sermons — just ordinary stories of feeding and being fed. Well, ordinary in the sense that these meals were just meals with the simple purpose of feeding and being fed, irrespective of any miraculous facet to the provision of the food, but not special meals that belonged to a particular cult, not cultic meals.

For the meal, any and every ordinary meal, can be a natural sacrament: a natural sacrament of creation. Sophia, the Creator of the world, already suggests so when she glosses her insistence on acknowledgment of her as source of life and death with the imagery of her issuing an invitation to a meal: "Come, eat of my bread and drink of the wine I have mixed" (Prov. 9:5). Every meal eucharistically enjoyed, in which food and drink are thankfully received from the cosmic Source, then broken and poured out to others and received from others again, qualifies for the name of Wisdom's Feast. For our very eating and drinking in such a spirit and in such conditions is tantamount to breathing in, to ingesting, the very spirit and *modus operandi,* the way and rule of the Creator Spirit herself. Sometimes, as already remarked in the chapter on Creation, and as one sees repeated in the words of Jesus, a metaphor is used that is stronger than the bread and wine metaphor of partaking in Wisdom's Feast. In the *Wisdom of Jesus the Son of Sirach,* as in the words of Jesus quoted from John, the imagery is now of eating and drinking, not just the bread and wine on offer at Wisdom's Feast, but Wisdom herself, or Jesus himself who is Wisdom incarnate. "Those who eat me will hunger for more (of me), and those who drink me will thirst for more," so says Wisdom in Sirach (24:21). "Unless you eat the flesh of the son of man and drink his blood, you have no life in you," says Jesus according to John (6:53–54); "he who eats my flesh and drinks my blood has eternal life."

Now this stronger form of the metaphor of eating is not a late exaggeration that somehow slipped into the biblical tradition. It is traceable as far back in the Bible as the earliest creation story where its terms are those of the Wisdom tree of which the man and woman partake. Nevertheless it seems very necessary to say — especially in light of some theologies of Jesus's physical body considered to be "present in" consecrated yet common or garden variety bread and wine that we eat and drink — the stronger form of the imagery of eating Wisdom's self is equally as metaphorical as the weaker form of eating Wisdom's proffered meal. And both forms carry precisely the same metaphorical import. For to sustain and promote life precisely by eating and drinking in this particular way — taking these necessities of life from each other's hands as gifts created for all, even to the point of being prepared to die rather than kill so that others might live so fully — that is to ingest and imbibe and then live by the Wisdom through which God continually creates and thus rules the world, the Wisdom that his followers believe became incarnate as divine Spirit in Jesus of Nazareth. For Jesus immediately cashes the stronger metaphor in the currency of the imagery of double-immanence so beloved of the Bible. "He who eats my flesh and drinks my blood abides in me, and I in him." In other words, to partake of Wisdom's Eucharistic Feast is to ingest the Wisdom ever operative in creation or, equivalently, to breathe in the Creator Spirit, and so to keep faith with the eternal giver of existence and life. For Jesus was raised by the Holy Spirit to the level of life-giving spirit, as Paul would put it, so that the metaphor of breathing in the Spirit that made of Jesus all that he was, like the metaphor or ingesting Wisdom incarnate, can license the larger, more extreme metaphor of ingesting Jesus, of taking him into the operative center of one's very being.

(But — anyone may well ask who recognizes the continuity of this imagery with that of the Fall imagery in Genesis, the imagery of eating the fruit of the tree of wisdom as a metaphor for consuming Wisdom — is not such "eating" precisely what one was forbidden to do, according to that earlier myth? Any satisfactory answer to this question must note the flexibility and versatility of the mythic use of any given set of images, so that the closest attention to details of text and context is ever necessary for true insight into the disclosure in each case effected. In Eden the would-be consumers were after all-wisdom for their own aggrandizement, as witnesses the fact that it was under the impetus of the age-old satanic temptation that they wanted to eat, and did eat. Like the rich people that Paul condemned for using the eucharistic meal to flaunt their conspicuous consumerism at the expense of the poor, potential colleagues all, of the Prince of Tyre.)

As further intimations of the potential of every meal to be a sacrament of creation, consider also the fact that the perfection of life in its origin and eschaton is commonly described either in terms of the garden of plenty, water and fruit, food and drink, or in terms of the feast of fat things prepared by God, and prefigured by the land flowing with milk and honey. Consider also the fact that the meal is a much more effective sacrament of creation than uses of water alone can offer. For in the meal the social dimension of the symbolizing and effecting of the constant creation of life is accomplished much more fully and comprehensively than it is in baptism. For one thing, the bread itself and kinds of drink other than water are already results of the cooperative creativity of God and human persons. As part of the eucharistic prayer of the Mass expresses the matter: "Blessed are you, Lord, God of all creation. Through your goodness we have this bread to offer, *which earth has given and human hands have made.* It will become for us the bread of life." "Blessed are you, Lord, God of all creation. Through your goodness we have this wine to offer, *fruit of the vine and work of human hands.* It will become our spiritual drink."

The communal co-creativity of humankind is thereby already constituted as part of the symbolism before further reaches of communal symbolism begin to take effect. These further reaches of the symbolism are then constituted by the breaking of the bread to others at the table and the pouring out of the drink to them. This is the central part of the ritual of the meal, for it symbolizes and effects the precise nature of the co-creation of life that can promise life without limit for all. It consists in the giving to others of the very necessities of life that are crucial for one's own life, if necessary to the point of giving life itself, and then receiving the necessities of life, receiving life from others. Holding the bread in open, chaliced hands, the natural form of the gesture of offering it to others, has the kind of symbolic and effective force that is the very opposite of closing one's hand in on the bread, thus making a fist, and symbolizing and effecting the attempt to secure life and the supports and enhancements of life by oneself, for oneself, with the constant threat to the lives of others thereby also both symbolized and effective in the fist. And the wine is also in the open chalice, ready to be poured out by each to the others. In this powerful and insistent manner the usages of the food and drink that human beings have helped make, and that then constitute the common meal, symbolize and simultaneously begin to participate in the effect symbolized, namely, the effecting of the sacrifice of each one's life that is necessary for others who live at each other's expense. As well as the effecting of creative forgiveness, of healing of the wounds of their sinfulness for the ones who have hitherto made fists with their selfish grasping, by gifting them good things as all are already gifted, instead of doing them in turn even more harm than they are already doing them-selves. And, finally, the effecting of the happy hope for the limitlessness of the life for all that is thereby received and shared, beyond the deformation and destruction, both natural and wilful, that must be transcended along the way. The meal that is conducted by taking as gift, and blessing God for, and breaking open to others, friend or foe, the nourishment of bread and the refreshment of beer (the old Irish creator goddess Brigid turned water into beer, not wine), is easily the most comprehensive and effec-tive symbol of that most practical and steadfast love that binds together creator and creature in the promise of eternal life.

These increasing references to the (self)sacrificial elements in the eucha-ristic meal must recall once more the final meal of Jesus with his disciples on the night before his execution. And we are reminded of the long tra-dition of seeing that meal as a cultic sacrifice, or at least an integral part of a cultic sacrifice. Yet that last supper does not constitute a cultic sac-rifice in the proper sense of that word, nor is it part of a cultic sacrifice. Furthermore, if the terms of cultic sacrifice are used of Calvary which the story of the imagery of this meal anticipates, as happens in the Letter to the Hebrews, then these terms are used metaphorically, in the manner already explained. That is to say, the terms of cultic sacrifice in the Jerusalem Temple are used because of a similarity that also involves the difference of something that goes beyond cultic sacrifice and replaces it, as the Letter to the Hebrews also argues explicitly in the case of the self-sacrifice of Jesus. Yet as eucharistic substance and spirit can inform any meal, as Jesus saw and celebrated meals from beginning to end of his mission, so that same substance and spirit could inform a cultic meal, any cultic meal with the most probable exception of a cultic meal that formed part of a sacrifice of expiation. True eucharistic substance and spirit could then inform the Passover meal, a cultic meal celebrated in the homes of the Jews, as some of the Gospels suggest happened with Jesus's last meal. In fact, the Passover meal could be an ideal cultic meal for purposes of being transformed into a cultic meal for the followers of Jesus. For the Passover meal symbolized as it celebrated God saving the Jews from deprivation and death, an ongoing exercise of God's steadfast love, together with the sacrifices the Jews had to undergo themselves as part of the process. But the Passover meal would have to be modified if it were to serve the mission of Jesus and his followers. It would have to be modified in the same degree and manner as the terms of the Mosaic covenant in which the original Passover from Egypt culminated, were modified by Jesus in his sermon from the mount, and in the conduct of his life and death. Modified, that is to say, in the direction of restoring the original covenant of creation, in which people undertook to channel the life, the land, and all other supports and enhancements of life, to all and not just to the Jews, and at whatever cost to themselves, even life itself if conditions so required.

Yet there were, and may still be, some residual problems about celebrating Christian eucharist in the form of the Jewish Passover meal, however modified. The main problem would prove to be connected with the temptation to import into the Christian eucharist a sacrificial symbolism that once again carried the old cultic sacrificial import into the understanding of this sacrament. For all breaking of bread and pouring of wine symbolizes one's general willingness to sacrifice something of one's own and one's self for others. So that Jesus doing this at the meal before he was executed was bound to refer specifically to his by now inevitable death for his cause, as he well knew. The bread broken and the wine poured out now symbolized for him, first and foremost: "my body given up for you"; "my blood shed for you." And from that it is easy to see how failure to see such talk of his sacrifice on the cross as sacrificial language in the same univocal sense as such language bears when it is used for all lesser sacrifices we make in living under the reign of God, becomes part and parcel of the failure to take the cultic language of priesthood-sacrifice on Calvary as metaphorical language. If only because there was in any case an old-style cultic sacrifice of lambs in the Temple involved in Passover at that time also. Perhaps that is why John unlike other evangelists seems to want to tell us that Jesus's last meal was not in fact the Passover meal. Because John, the most persistent and adamant of the evangelists in judging Jesus to have brought them beyond the Jewish religion of his time, may have feared that any endorsement of a modified Passover meal as the central sacrament of the faith of Jesus, might simply result in the kind of backsliding that would see the necessary modifications gradually swallowed back into the bowels of the religion whose leaders were involved in having Jesus killed in its name.

In any case there is early evidence that the meal celebrated in memory of Jesus was celebrated as a special cultic meal in the communities of his followers. When Paul complains bitterly to the Corinthians that, whatever they themselves might think, "it is not the Lord's supper that you eat. For in eating, each one goes ahead with his own meal, and one is hungry and another is drunk... (and you) humiliate those who have nothing" (1 Cor. 20–22), he is in fact saying that the conspicuous consumerism of some that adds humiliation to the hunger of others, is a sacrament of original sin rather than a sacrament of salvation. And he is more than hinting that the rich should be feeding the hungry instead of humiliating them. But when he then asks rather querulously, "Do you not have houses to eat and drink in?" he seems to be suggesting a separation of ordinary meals, which the rich should see to it are adequate for the poor also, from the eucharistic meal as such, in which perhaps a token piece of bread and sip of wine is used to symbolize and effect God's continuous creation of life coming to us and through us to all others, at whatever cost to ourselves. And that of course is the case with eucharist as it is celebrated in Christian communities ever since, it is celebrated as a special cultic meal, in church.

For all that, however, there is nothing in the practice and preaching of Jesus himself that requires eucharist to be confined to such a special cultic meal confined to special cultic buildings. That last supper that Jesus celebrated with his disciples, including the sinner, Judas, like the meal that Mark recorded at the outset of Jesus's mission, might well have been just an ordinary meal, with no particular attachment to the formal cult of their religion. And as such it could seal the renewed covenant of creation as successfully as older versions of that covenant with a vengeful God were sealed with cultic sacrificial meals. Any meal in any home that begins with the grace before meals, and continues with the ritual of people then taking the life-giving gifts of food and drink and offering them to others, serving others first, and then receiving from the others these necessities of life . . . any meal, wherever it takes place, that so symbolizes and effects the channeling of life to others, is eucharist in the full Christian understanding of the sacrament of creation that it re-presents. Provided only that the food and drink on one's table, like the table itself, is ever ready to be shared with those in need.

But then it must also be said that a properly eucharistic meal shared outside the Christian community can realize, in the fullest sense of that word, the same presence of the same life-giving Creator Spirit, but now without any concomitant realization of the enfleshment of that Spirit in Jesus of Nazareth. The invitations to eat and drink in those passages of the Bible that deal with Creator and human creatures — like the Wisdom text quoted above — convey the same promise of creative and saving presence of the life-giving Spirit, as Jesus conveyed in asking his followers to consume eucharistically the bread and wine. For in doing so they would be taking into them the same life-giving Spirit that was enfleshed in Jesus's own body and blood, and they would then become members of an even more extended body of his in the world, enlivened and enlivening others by the same Creator Spirit that made of them one body. That is the meaning, and the only meaning of "real presence," a phrase that is too often bandied about in popular preaching on the Christian eucharist. Real presence does not refer to some mystifying presence of the life-giving-Spirit-in-the-physical-body-of-the-historical-Jesus-in-the-bread-and-wine. For one thing, Jesus no longer has the body he had at the last supper. Paul says it is with an altogether different kind of body that we are raised, a spiritual body. And, for another, it is not in the *bread,* nor for that matter in the *wine* as such that the presence of life-giving Spirit, whether as embodied in Jesus or not, is realized. But in the whole eucharistic action of the meal, and only for those who truly understand and commit themselves to the intentionality of that dramatic symbol that participates in the reality it symbolizes. John, who has Jesus describe most graphically the eucharistic meal as the eating of his flesh, naturally follows this with an account of the puzzlement of Jesus's disciples as to how this could happen, and then has Jesus move against any crude image of ingesting the actual body of Jesus, by haranguing them rather, as follows: "Do you take offense at this (his talk of eating his flesh and drinking his blood)? Then what if you were to see the son of man ascending where he was before (body and blood gone up to heaven; no longer there for the eating)? It is the spirit that gives life, the flesh is of no avail; the words I have spoken to you are (about) spirit and life" (John 6:61–63).

This then is the Sacrament of Eucharist as the Bible bears witness to it. Two questions about it remain.

First, can we say that Jesus instituted the Sacrament of Eucharist? No, and yes. No, in the sense that meals in themselves contain the possibility of being natural sacraments of creation. This possibility was realized when Jesus in his turn took it up, put his distinctive mark on the symbolism of the meal, and by doing this released the fullest capacity of that symbolism to reveal and realize the immanence in the creation of the life-giving Spirit that is source and, in a sense, goal of the whole of that creation. But this possibility in the meal was revealed and realized before Jesus took it up, as is evident from the Bible itself, and from the fact that so many religions have meals at the heart of so much of their ritual. But yes also, in the sense that Jesus does appear to have given back to this symbolism its potential for revealing and realizing the truest nature of the Creator Spirit, and the nature of that Spirit's method of continuously creating this universe from within its co-creative creatures, and the nature of the whole conditions, hazards and promises of that creative élan. He allowed the natural symbolism of the meal to reveal and realize these conditions, hazards and promises in particular through the meal's natural concentration of that most creative of creatures, *homo sapiens*, thus envisaging what Nietzsche would call "the higher man."

And yes, also, in the sense that this alone of all possible sacraments seems to have been the one to which he himself was committed from beginning to end of his mission. As his disciples remembered, and therefore continued to make it their distinctive sacrament after his death. In his memory and to keep his presence alive in the world through their status as his extended body in the world. There is an interesting theory to the effect that the appearances-presences of the risen Jesus recorded in the rNT are really instances of eucharistic presence. The paradigm example is found in the story of the disciples on the road to Emmaus. The disconsolate disciples did not really know his presence in his bodily company on the road, but only in the meal, in the breaking of bread. And there are other cases of meals mentioned or hinted at in rNT stories of appearances, comings, real presences of the risen Jesus. And there was the Church Father (was it Cyril in his *Catecheses*?) who warned his catechumens that if they entered the eucharistic celebration with the wrong motives and expectations (like the ones in Corinth who flaunted their wealth and humbled the others by eating and drinking to excess?), they would die rather than live and, further, they would keep Jesus in his tomb.

Second, is the eucharist in the Christian churches today the eucharist that Jesus in these ways instituted? In order to attempt the least adequate answer to this question, it is first of all necessary to observe that it most probably would not have mattered to Jesus in what precise manner the communities of his followers then institutionalized the celebration of eucharist in memory of him. For instance and for all that John the evangelist might say, they might have institutionalized it as their modification of a Passover meal, as some of the Gospels suggest Jesus's last supper to have been, to be celebrated once a year at Passover by the community of the new and universalist Israel. Or they might have institutionalized it, as early "house churches" seem to have done, as one or more of the ordinary meals served up in the home, incorporating significant features such as the blessing, the sharing with outsiders, and so on, and with consequent degrees of frequency, on the model of Jesus's first recorded meal. Or they might have decided, as in fact after some time they did decide, to institutionalize it as an extraordinary meal, in which token sharing and consumption of food and drink symbolized and made present the life-giving Spirit as embodied for them in Jesus of Nazareth. Given such a range of valid possibilities for his followers, the question asked is more quickly answered by looking for aspects of later celebrations of eucharist in Christian communities that seriously diverge from the eucharist that Jesus instituted.

Unfortunately, examples of damaging divergence, and some so damaging as to make one wonder if the communities involved are celebrating eucharist at all, are found in most if not all Christian churches that include this sacrament in their practice. It must suffice to list here, and to discuss in some brief detail, the most enduring and the most serious of these. Now, paradoxically enough, it seems to be the case that the largest Christian denomination in the world, the one called the Roman Catholic Church, harbors the most damaging and enduring divergences, and perhaps the most divergences *tout simple*. So that in giving some account of these, one will have gone as far as it is necessary to go in a context such as this; members of other churches can then wear whichever of the caps fits, or whatever number of them fit.

The change seems to have set in as soon (toward the end of the third Christian century?) as some leaders of the Christian communities began to think of themselves as cultic priests who therefore offered cultic sacrifice. These then began to read into accounts of Jesus's last supper things that simply are not there: a priest ordaining as fellow priests the designated leaders of his followers, and offering the cultic sacrifice for which he himself was the victim to be duly slaughtered. In succeeding centuries these priests, if they were to be real priests "different in kind and not merely in degree" from a loosely metaphorical "priesthood" of the *laos*, the people of God (as Vatican II puts it) needed a sacrificial victim to offer. Yet they have, as the eucharistic prayer still puts it, only "this bread . . . this wine to offer," and that as the liturgy makes obvious, is offered to each other, the bread of (that is, symbolizing and effecting in the offering of it, the gift of) life, and the wine symbolizing and effecting a drinking in of the Spirit, "our spiritual drink." And that is not nearly enough for a cultic sacrifice. So it is necessary to have Jesus, the risen embodiment of the life-giving Spirit, present, and since all that one seems to have to offer is bread and wine, the most obvious move is to make Jesus present in the bread and wine. The priest then is thought to be empowered by the Sacrament of Orders, to do something prior to the offering of cultic sacrifice, which is what ordination to priesthood normally empowers one to do. He is thought to be empowered to make Jesus present in the bread and the wine, by repeating over bread and wine words Jesus is reported to have used at his last supper. Words the meaning and intentionality of which on that occasion bear not the slightest resemblance to the intentionality with which they are now imbued, as John the evangelist was at pains to explain. The result of all of this then is that this priest can offer Jesus, the crucified Jesus, as the slaughtered sacrificial victim to God again, and again, and again. . . . At the height of this praxis, hundreds of thousands of priests offered this "holy sacrifice of the Mass" daily, a great many of them with no more of a community present than a single altar-boy, if even that. A more successful way of side-lining the quintessentially communal nature of eucharistic symbolism could scarcely have been devised, even if one set out deliberately to do it.

Was all of this not sending the new religion in the opposite direction to that which is implicit in the mission of Jesus, particularly in its cul-mination outside the city and its temple, and explicit in the teaching of the Letter to the Hebrews? Did it not send the new religion backward toward priesthoods standing between God and humanity, and offering slaughtered animals (sometimes human ones) in order to acknowledge and perhaps appease the Lord of Life? Yes, it did all of that, and more. This theory and praxis of eucharist also perverted the reality and meaning of real divine presence, both as to what was present and as to how it was made present. For what was now said to be made present, and said ever more clearly as the centuries rolled by, was the earthly "body, blood, soul and divinity" of the man, Jesus of Nazareth, and in the particular state that resulted from his being crucified on Calvary. And the method of his body and blood being made present was then described as some mystifying, if not downright magical process, by which a priest especially ordained and empowered to do so, "changed the bread and wine into the body and blood of Jesus" — accompanied, of course, by his "soul and divinity."

The making present in this quasi-magical manner of the physical body of the man, Jesus of Nazareth, in the bread and wine, it is then explained, means that, despite appearances, the bread is no longer bread, and the wine no longer wine. Despite the fact that, to all possible investigations of science or the common senses, the bread and wine of the eucharist remain bread and wine before, during and after its sacramental usage The only things that the bread and wine are changed into in the symbolic eucharistic process of taking, eating and drinking, and then metabolizing are, first, the human bodies that are nourished for life and built up by these elements of bread and wine. So that, at this stage of metabolism, there is supplied a further and essential feature of the effective symbolism of the eucharistic sacrament. For at this point of the process of the meal the bread and wine participate in the reality they symbolize. This is the reality of the supports for life gifted by God equally to all, and co-fashioned by human beings who then co-operate with God in making them and the life they support and enhance available to all. So that now, as these elements actually, if in part, enter the living fabric of the human bodies concerned, they promote and enhance these human lives that advance in dependence upon each other and ultimately upon the source-giver of life and of all of its supports and enhancements, our daily bread. An effective symbol, surely, at this point of the metabolizing of the elements also, of the life-giving Spirit acting creatively through human co-creators within the very lives of human beings, thereby making whole co-operative communities of them, according to Paul's master image, into the one body of Christ, the incarnation par excellence of the Creator Spirit.

Second, the elements of bread and wine change, also in part, into "the remains." These "remains" do not refer to the "appearances of bread and wine" that somehow remain after their "substances" have somehow disappeared. They refer rather to feces and urine, for example, but this part of the process also adds its own essential dimension to the effective symbolism of the meal. As we speak of "the remains" of a person being laid in its grave, so here these remains of the metabolism of the meal remind us forcefully, once we face up to the full natural reality of the eucharistic meal, that the progress of one stage or form of life and life-giving involves the death of others, though that very dying can then contribute in its own way to other advances of life. Even at this extreme the presence of the eternal Creator Spirit who gives life through death is effectively symbolized in elements and processes that are truly sacramental in that they participate in the very reality they symbolize.

The medieval era produced a theory as to how, during the meal of bread and wine, when the priest uttered a particular verbal formula, Jesus of Nazareth who was raised to the status of life-giving Spirit could be made bodily present in bread and wine. This took the form of a highly sophisticated metaphysical theory, based upon highly abstract, esoteric concepts of substance and appearance. It was called the theory of transubstantiation, for one substance, that of bread, was transposed into or transplanted another substance, that of the human, bodily substance of Jesus. While the "appearances" of the substance of bread remained, but the corresponding "appearances" of the body of Jesus did not become apparent to the communicants. (It was called the theory of consubstantiation by Lutherans later, who wanted to say that the bodily Jesus was present in the eucharistic bread and wine, but the substance of bread and wine remained.) There really is not much to be said here about transubstantiation or consubstantiation. Except perhaps this: the concepts of substance and appearance as here defined and used are so abstruse that they might conceivably succeed in permitting someone to think that this version of what is really present at eucharist and how, might offer a tolerable enough explanation of some form of presence. But apart altogether from the fact that this kind of metaphysics of an invisible substance or essence hidden beneath the appearances or phenomena has been subjected to a corrosive critique by modern metaphysicians from Hegel to Sartre, a critique to which modern physics and biology make their own contribution, the very abstruse and esoteric nature of the medieval theory puts this explanation of real presence out of the reach of all but the most historically erudite of scholars. And there are very few of these in evidence at any level of church membership.

But the real problem with transubstantiation theories whether simple or sophisticated remains. The problem is that, however the philosophically sophisticated might understand this medieval metaphysics to offer a true account of the real presence of the Creator Spirit "found in human form" in Jesus, the development of that metaphysical account over the centuries has served only to distort the true view of what it is that is really present in the eucharist. And it has proved even more misleading with respect to the way in which what is really present is made present, and its presence known and realized. For what is present is not the flesh and blood of Jesus's earthly body — Jesus now lives on in what Paul called a spiritual body — but rather the life-giving Spirit that has long ago taken on the persona of Jesus, and that is now transmitted as such in the historical Christian community in formative, creative inspiration and praxis. And the means of making this life-giving Spirit especially present in this persona and in this community of Jesus-followers — it is, of course, also always present and active otherwise in the world at large — does not consist in some mystifying manipulation of the nature or substance of bread and wine, but rather in the whole of the sacramental action of partaking as gift, breaking and pouring to each other, sharing out the necessities of life and life itself. In this way the presence of the Creator Spirit who took on the persona of the Jesus we knew and know so well is actually realized among us, in the many senses of the word *realized*. We become conscious of the presence within us of the Creator Spirit in the persona of Jesus, in accepting as gift the dynamic life-giving forms of food and drink, as we become conscious of our own co-creative role in making them such. We are then inspired to exercise our own co-creative responsibilities further. First by ceasing to block the flow of God's creation of life through us, either by seeking to secure life for ourselves only, or by returning the violence of others who behave in such a self-centered manner. In this way we are made into positive channels of the eternal divine creation of life for all, media for the eternal Creator Spirit. This is the Spirit (of) God that constitutes the fundamental reality of our very existence, and at the same time confirms the promise of unimaginable fullness of life and happiness. That is what is really present in eucharist, and that is how it is really present.

The distortions of the eucharist as Jesus instituted it do not begin or end with the intrusion of cultic priesthoods and transubstantiation-type theories. Further distortion took place, perhaps by some sort of transposition to all participants in eucharist of the purity code for the cultic priests of old, but in any case in the following manner. Those who wished to take a full part in the eucharist by consuming the bread and wine — and since the eucharist is essentially a meal, that is the only way in which one could properly take part in it — were warned that they should make sure that they were "in the state of grace" with God before they did so. To partake of the meal at the table of the Lord while still sinners, people were assured, would be sacrilegious and would serve only to compound the sinfulness of those who dared to do so deliberately. Now this ruling about the eucharist involved a double distortion. Because Roman Catholics were still ordered to go to Mass on Sunday, but if in unshriven sin not to approach the communion rails, this ruling confirmed the distortion of thinking that the real presence was in the bread (and wine), and it made of the Mass little more than "a visit to the Blessed Sacrament," as Roman Catholics call it. Mass was now like a visit to Jesus in the tabernacle in the churches where the consecrated breads were kept, but with the added experience of witnessing the ritual means by which Jesus got there. And that showed something of how seriously distorted this view of real presence could be. For it clearly conveyed the impression that the really real presence of the Lord and Savior was confined to the temples of this religion, that the dwelling of the Lord was not the whole world. But the twin distortion is equally serious, for as the story of his first table-fellowship on his mission observes, in response to his critics — who saw what he was doing in this eucharistic meal far more clearly than these subsequent distorters of it — Jesus described that table fellowship as the healing of the sick. In other terms, it constituted the forgiveness of the sinners invited to his table. And that is what that table fellowship was and, undistorted, it still is. Divine forgiveness, according to Jesus of Nazareth, consists primarily in doing good to those who commit evil offense against each other, and the doing good in turn consists in God offering and our channeling to them life and the necessities and enhancements of life, which is precisely what the eucharistic meal symbolizes and effects.

The eucharist, as Mark has Jesus uncompromisingly declare, is instituted for the sinners rather than the righteous. So when one sees some Christian churches, whether at the Roman Catholic or the more evangelical extremes of the range of Christian churches currently on view, refusing to share the table of the Lord with members even of other Christian churches, on a variety of grounds but all of which involve accusations of failures or betrayals in Christian belief or practice, then one is seeing the further damaging, rather than the salving of whole churches. One is seeing a comparable distortion of the eucharist to the point of serious suspicion as to whether some of these churches can be said to be celebrating a "valid" Christian eucharist at all. It would be funny, were it not so tragic, to see the Roman Catholic authorities give as the main reason for denying the validity of eucharist in some other churches, the charge that these did not have a properly ordained priesthood, and that in turn because they did not understand eucharist as Jesus instituted it. Given that the introduction of a cultic priesthood in itself represents the central misunderstanding of Jesus's institution, and is then at the center of other distortions of eucharist, such as transubstantiation ideas, and so on.

The question that obviously obtrudes at this stage is, if so much distortion of the eucharist as Jesus instituted it, is evident in so many churches organized in his name, and if some of the distortions reach the point at which, as Paul would say, "it is not the Lord's supper that you eat," what are the members of such churches to do? Until their theologians can persuade these churches to reform their eucharistic praxis and corresponding theory in the spirit of Jesus (quite literally, in the Spirit of Jesus) as the vocation of theologian in any Christian church requires them to do, there are many other things that Christian people can do about eucharist in the meantime. They can, for instance, revert to earlier Christian practice, and hold proper eucharists in their homes, presided over by the mater- or pater-familias. Or, despite the fact that the president of the eucharist in their local church seems to think (erroneously as it happens) that he is a cultic priest with power to change bread and wine into the body and blood of Christ, and then offer it as a cultic sacrifice, and despite the fact that the priestly hierarchy declares that only the virtuous people already united and of one mind are then rewarded with Holy Communion, such people, sins and all, can just go and take full part in that celebration. Treating it as the sacrament it really is and thereby receiving its healing, and experiencing the real presence of the Creator Spirit through the persona of the risen Jesus, empowering them in turn to be channels of life more abundant for all, and blessing them with hope. And they might do this in churches of different Christian denominations consecutively. For then they and any others acting like them in any particular congregation will "bring about eucharist," however much any others in the respective congregations may act to impede or render that eucharist null and void.

Or they can forget about eucharists as formal cultic meals as such, considering these perhaps to be so distorted by Christian churches that they are for all practical purposes beyond reform. And then just take their food and drink together in the true spirit of gratitude that greets any gift, and break and pour out to each other, and sometimes at least open their table to the poor, and sometimes even to the rich who have done them wrong, and thereby experience in all of this the presence of the living Spirit flowing through them. For this will then be a meal celebrated in the spirit, if not with the letter, of this traditional Irish "grace": "Blessed be you, O Lord, in this food we are about to eat, as we ask you, O God, that it may be good for our body and soul; and if there is any poor creature hungry and thirsty walking the road, may God send her into us so that we can share the food with her, just as He shares his gifts with all of us alike." This will then be a meal like the first meal that Mark has Jesus serve to disciples, publicans and sinners alike. Just such an ordinary meal, and not recognized or recognizable as a special cultic meal either by its critics or its defender on that occasion.

Other Christian Sacraments

Baptism and eucharist are the two Christian sacraments recognized by all Christian communities that use sacraments. And it is not even necessary that a Christian church that wants to have a sacramental side to it, would need to use both of these sacraments. For the Sacrament of Eucharist can do everything that the Sacrament of Baptism can symbolize and effect. Clearly eucharist can receive initiates into the body and life-giving Spirit of the Christian community, make them members of the extended body of Jesus the Christ in the world and its history. And eucharist also supplies the creative-healing forgiveness, the creative overcoming of sin and its effects with which God, according to Jesus, anticipates every fledgling expression of trust, every change of heart of which human beings prove capable.

But it is also obvious that eucharist can accomplish all that is accomplished by some further sacraments that have been introduced in the course of history by some of the more sacramentalized Christian churches, and in respect of which the case for their institution by Jesus must conclude somewhere along the range from the highly unlikely to the almost certainly not. Take the case of the Sacrament of Confirmation for example.

This involves a rite of anointing with oil that seems to have been part of the baptismal ritual in the very early church, but that later separated to become a free-standing ritual that symbolized and in part effected the supple strengthening of the young person growing into adult maturity. The eucharistic ritual of the shared food and drink also symbolizes and in part effects the strengthening and refreshment of the person, young or old, for the journey of life toward its fullest and final form. The same could be said for the sacrament that used to be called Extreme Unction, because it strengthens one for the last part of life's journey, the part that takes us through the gates of death. The same could be said for this same sacrament now that it is called the Sacrament of the Sick, for it now symbolizes and in part effects the strengthening that can see us through serious illness or injury, whether or not these be the immediate harbingers of death. The eucharistic usage of food and drink for these hazardous journeys through such threats to life, symbolizes and in part facilitates the presence of the life-giving Spirit, and as such render the two other sacraments at least supernumerary.

Something similar could be said for the Sacrament of Penance, designed as it was after some fierce controversy in the early church concerning the manner in which the church should deal with post-baptismal sin. The rather uppish idea that communing membership of the church allegedly founded by Jesus was for the sinless only was already being promoted in certain quarters. According to this party there was therefore to be no "second penance" after the first comprehensive forgiveness of sin was symbolized and effected in baptism. Then, ignorant of or ignoring the fact that Jesus's table fellowship was itself the most creative form of forgiveness of sin, and as such available at all times to any who accepted an invitation to that meal, the eventual victors over the uppish devised a ritual in which sinners would have to undergo very stringent and at first public penal regimes, before being ceremoniously admitted back into the eucharistic community. A move by which the victors thereby agreed with the uppish that eucharist truly was for the sinless only.

Within a few centuries, and largely under the influence of those mighty Irish monks who spread their superior learning and their particularly Irish version of Christianity through the continent during the so-called dark ages, the ritual of penance became a private affair conducted, that is to say, between monk and penitent. The Irish practice of private penance had in mind a pastoral model in which the monk would act as *anam cara*, soul friend of the sinner, helping to open up to the light the disease of sin and to apply curative remedies: fasting to the gluttonous, long wakefulness to the bed-addicts, silence to the liars, the calumniators and the back-biters, more prayer to those too busy to think about their God. But in due course the legalistic imperative of making the punishment fit the crime overtook this more pastoral form of the ritual of the Sacrament of Penance also. Then the legal model spread to the whole of this new sacrament, and all the talk was about the tribunal of penance, in which one was decreed guilty by confession (often after some interrogation by the residing magistrate), a penal judgment was handed down, and on these conditions an edict of forgiveness was issued, at and from the issuing of which the divine forgiveness itself was in effect.

At the point as which private penance settles down in the finished form of a judicial tribunal, one notices even more readily something that one could have noticed in the earlier era of public penance. One notices both the need of Matthew's binding and loosing powers for church officials, and the change that Matthew made to Jesus's teaching on forgiveness, which was the context in which Matthew has Jesus confer the powers of binding and loosing on "the disciples" in the first place (Matt. 18:18). Matthew had Jesus confer these same powers especially on Peter, and he had Jesus come back after death to say to "the eleven disciples" that, like the Son of Man of Daniel 7:14, all authority in heaven and on earth is his, so that he can commission these disciples to pass on to all nations what he has commanded them, including of course their prerogative of binding on earth what would then be bound also in heaven (Matt. 16:19; 28:16–20). For of course, since Matthew had changed Jesus's teaching on forgiveness, precisely by insisting that those who sin against others and prove recalcitrant be brought before a tribunal of the church for judgment and penalty, he has to have Jesus confer the power of binding and loosing — rabbinical terminology for deciding upon the forbidding or permitting of certain action — and even to have Jesus return after his death to confer such power as would hold both in heaven and on earth. We are already well on the way to a church that decides who, when and what God's forgiveness will reach. And all of that then only needs to be formalized and ritualized along the lines of a judicial tribunal of penance, an ecclesiastical court capable according to itself of releasing or withholding God's forgiveness for the sinner. We have already come a long way from Mark's first story of Jesus's table-fellowship with sinners.

After so many centuries of distortion of the nature and (un)conditioning of divine forgiveness of human sin, when compared to what Jesus had to say on the matter, it is not only necessary to say now that eucharist is a true locus of the event of divine forgiveness, such as to make the Sacrament of Penance also supernumerary. It is necessary also to add that unless and until the Sacrament of Penance is reformed to such an extent that it can truly symbolize the ever-anticipatory forgiveness of God, it should be replaced by the Sacrament of Eucharist. The very recent history of Irish Catholicism in fact provides a startling and rather puzzling example of such positive replacement. Startling in this way, that some thirty years ago now and without any warning a very large majority of Irish Catholics simply stopped going to confession, as they called the Sacrament of Penance, on Saturday evening, in preparation for Mass on Sunday. So that soon only a truly tiny number took the Sacrament of Penance before going to "Mass and communion," as they would put it. Puzzling in this way, that there appeared to be no discussion among the people at large concerning the relationship of these two sacraments, before the masses voted with their feet to replace the traditionally twinned sacraments with the Sacrament of Eucharist alone.

They surely did not think themselves any the less habitually sinful than they had ever been before this radical change in their religious practice suddenly materialized. So they must have felt that divine forgiveness is available to them anyway in their communing with the Lord. In any case, they arrived at an orthodox conclusion in this matter, to the effect that a special Sacrament of Penance is supernumerary. And they arrived at this conclusion without the professional help of any of their theologians. That should be a matter of consolation to all theologians. For it means, if this was not already entirely obvious, that we theologians have done as much to bowdlerize the Christian faith as had any self-proclaimed priest or other leader in the Christian community. And that the Holy Spirit can move well and widely without moving through any of the above.

Of the remaining two sacraments of the seven celebrated by major Christian denominations today, the Sacrament of Matrimony and the Sacrament of Holy Orders, the former was certainly not instituted by Jesus. If it had been, the church that took the name of Jesus as its founder would surely have known that, and would have behaved from the beginning as if matrimony had to be one of its sacraments. As it happens, the church did not treat or talk of marriage as a sacrament until well toward the end of its first millennium. It is difficult to fix upon an exact date for the church's institution of matrimony as one of the seven sacraments decided upon as the central sacraments of Christianity in the Middle Ages.

But it certainly did not happen in the first five to seven centuries. During these early centuries the Christian church left the whole business of marriage to the inherited customs (that is to say, laws) of the people and thereafter to the civic authorities, where it rightly belongs. By the whole business of marriage is meant everything from decisions as to what constituted a valid and legal marriage: the rites involved, the commitments and the manner in which these were expressed, the dramatis personae and their various roles and actions, the responsibilities of the married to each other, to their children and to their wider families, the provisions for subsequent breakdown, and so on. It is interesting to note in this connection that when the church at last did decide to elevate matrimony to the status of one of its sacraments, it did not introduce its own formula for the conduct of a valid marriage, as if it had any such formula revealed to it by God. Instead it opted, not for the form of betrothal and marriage that Jesus would have known at the time he talked about marriage, but for the form for marriage that had been developed over the centuries by Roman law for the Roman empire.

At the very most in the early centuries of the existence of the Christian church, the church's efforts to have something to do with the regulation of marriage were restricted to such things as bishops advising or attempting to ensure that Christians married other Christians, or offering a blessing after the marriage had been duly constituted according to secular law. Then when the church did finally decide that Jesus had instituted as a sacrament of the Christian church an institution of marriage that had long preceded him, it then proceeded to use a rather peculiar logic. This was a logic that could find a home only in Christendom, that is to say, in a form of society (sometimes called a theocracy, although calling it that would seldom be fair to God) in which religious and political leadership were so united or intertwined that the former could claim precedence over the latter. By such a peculiar logic the church proceeded to argue that the regulation of marriage, or at least the marriage of Christians in society, was entirely the prerogative of the church, rather than the responsibility and duty of a state. Christian churches that have behaved like that, if only with respect to the marriage of Christians, and who try do so to the present day, on the basis that Jesus instituted the Sacrament of Marriage, have never acknowledged the fact, and it is a fact, that they are as unworthy as they are normally unqualified for this task. For the regulation of the institution of marriage is both integral and crucial to the whole social fabric of any state or people. And these same Christian churches, through their clerical officers, are in any case unworthy to do so in the name of the one they call their founder. Because the Christian church from the very beginning, as one can see from a variety of sources that range from Paul's letters down to the current Roman Catholic *Code of Canon Law,* introduced divorce. Divorce was confined to conditions specified by the church itself of course. Yet Jesus, it seems clear from an overall view of the scriptural testimony, held to the ideal of a steadfast love that bound married couples together until death did them part, whatever the cultural form of marriage that may have been in use. Those who lived under the reign of God's steadfast, creative love for all would surely show that same steadfast love to a partner who is in a very special sense now a co-creator, and would not reject such a partner, but would forgive any and all offenses committed.

Paul, as Matthew did with forgiveness, quite deliberately modified Jesus's teaching on divorce, having just stated it precisely (1 Cor. 7:10–15). Paul also thought of matrimony, not as a natural sacrament of creation, an effective symbol of God's steadfast love in ever creating life more abundant for all, a symbol now constituted by the partners letting that creative love flow through them, not just in all of their co-creating of the world, but especially in their speciality of pro-creating other members of this most co-creative species. Instead, Paul now thought of marriage as a symbol of Christ's relationship with his church. And these two changes in position are related: the introduction of divorce and the change of symbolism from creation to church. Because the reasons given by Paul for divorce have to do with his wish that a Christian partner married to a non-Christian might live unthreatened in the practice of his or her Christian faith and membership of that faith community. So then the terms and conditions by which the covenant of creation is operated and fulfilled for all, have to be modified in favor of a particular faith community. And authority for some further binding and loosing has to be found, for something which Jesus did not appear to have contemplated in his lifetime. "I think I have the Spirit of God," says Paul (1 Cor. 7:40 — but was that Spirit not incarnate consummately in the life and death of Jesus?) For these binding and loosings are now in favor of the community of Christians. What is symbolized is Christ's love *for his church.* ("See how these Christians love *one another,*" the early Christians' boast of what was said of them by outsiders, forgetting momentarily perhaps Jesus's command to them to love *their enemies?*) This is a step, hardly a very large step, but a significant one nevertheless, to the state in which Jesus found the law of

Sabbath observance, a law that was just and right because it was a law of and for this faith community, to the membership of which God's graces were franchised. This law, in the state in which Jesus found it observed, was not made for humanity at large. Humanity was made for it, for the faith community and the laws which distinguish it as source of God's grace for others.

The final wrong-headedness of such traditions of modifying Jesus's code of the kingdom while claiming to have the Spirit of God endorsing if not inspiring such moves is revealed in the hypocrisy (or is it plain ignorance of both law and fact) displayed when the Irish bishops sought to persuade the Irish Government not to introduce divorce legislation because, they argued, the introduction of divorce, for however restricted a set of reasons or causes, would ruin "God's plan for marriage." This from an ecclesiastical authority that had divorce legislation in its own *Code of Canon Law*. Yet not even all of that should be thought to prevent a Christian community from numbering matrimony among its sacraments. But if that community wished to follow Jesus rather than modify the terms of the covenant he mediated in order to suit itself, it would have to get rid of its divorce legislation in favor of its own members. It would instead have to hold faithfully to Jesus's ideal for matrimony, and thereby strive to have marriage function, as by its nature it should, as a true sacrament of the Creator's eternal love for the whole creation.

That does not mean, of course, either in this case of Jesus's edict on divorce, or in the case of Jesus's general precept in the Sermon on the Mount concerning our treatment of those who do us evil, that a separation of the evil doer from the marriage, or the restraint of the evil-doer may not be arranged, especially if serious measures of physical or mental cruelty are involved. Nor does it mean that a marriage may not be queried if other conditions of ignorance or deceit or questionable motivation are shown to have materialized. For none of that nullifies the duties of steadfast love to evil-doers and incapacitated alike, whatever the outcome for the survival of a particular marriage.

In sum, a Christian church must recognize that marriage, like eucharist, is a natural sacrament of creation. Matrimony is a ritual symbolism which participates in and signifies a love that is both spiritual and sexual, and that thereby binds the contracting man and woman in a union that is directed toward the procreation of the race. Any church is therefore authorized to see in matrimony a candidate for the status of a cultic sacrament both within its own community and in the wider society. Although, as history shows, the church did not originally decide what were to be the valid forms, conditions and entailments of marriage, even in the lands of what used to be called Christendom. And it should not therefore try to pretend that such decision is ever exclusively within its power. However, on the grounds that Jesus in his life, his teaching and his death revealed the truest terms of God's covenant in creation, a Christian church, having purged itself of any of its own ignorance and hypocrisy in the matter, can insist that the only true and full ideal of marriage is the ideal of the steadfast love until death of those who enter that blessed state. But then also, recognizing that marriage is a natural sacrament of creation, just as it was to God's act of creation that Jesus pointed in setting out his ideal for marriage, a Christian church would have to open the Lord's table to all those married by means of whatever legal and valid forms the surrounding society had authorized.

And if, as is most likely to keep on happening, some people through the hardness of their hearts end up with broken marriages and broken lives, that same community of Christians would have to offer to such people always the healing-forgiveness of the true eucharistic table of the Lord. For it is such people, sundered and suffering from their own fallenness, who need salving, more than the ones in whose marriages all goes well. The ones present at the first table fellowship that Jesus himself inaugurated were publicans and sinners, and he insisted, in the face of the pious offense taken by "the scribes of the Pharisees," that his table-fellowship was primarily for them. Nor can a Christian church exclude from the table of the Lord divorced people who have married again, for the proffered reason that they are now "living in sin." Given all that has been said concerning the original sin of the race, which of us is not living in sin to one degree of another. Jesus's advice to those who would punish a sinner, "let him who is without sin among you, cast the first stone," is too soon forgotten. Besides, whatever sinfulness any partner in a marriage has incurred in the course of the irretrievable break-down of that marriage, this is always already forgiven by God, and that forgiveness may not be gainsaid in any way by a church that pretends to have Jesus as its founder. Nor can the second marriage be automatically described as a state of sin. If only for the simple reason that, as is happily not infrequently the case, the partner(s) concerned may find that now, the second time around, they manage to rise to that steadfast love that usually they failed, in the manner of all human flesh, to make real in act in their first attempt, with all the usual punitive consequences for themselves and their children that follow with such characteristic indiscriminacy from the ubiquitous original sinfulness of the race.

Eucharist, the one sacrament that Jesus certainly instituted, if only by raising the meal to its highest potential in respect of its natural sacramentality, is a natural sacrament of creation. Accordingly there is no problem about the followers of Jesus developing the cult after the death of the one they called the founder of their religion, by instituting other sacraments that by their parallel symbolism accomplish what the Christian Sacrament of Eucharist symbolizes and effects, but in more precisely focused contexts. In other words, the separate sacraments now seen to be instituted in the church after the death of Jesus (sometimes centuries after the death of Jesus) — baptism, confirmation, matrimony, penance, anointing of the sick — can focus the spirit of eucharist, the Spirit by which Jesus lived, died and was raised, on specific, critical passages in the coming and going of human life: birth, growth to adulthood, founding the basic units that pro-create human society, entering crises caused by falling into the original temptation and the call for *metanoia*, encountering serious illness and death. So the fact that the Sacrament of Eucharist can symbolize and effect, can accomplish all that all the above sacraments together can accomplish, offers no sufficient reason for rejecting these sacraments from the Christian cult. Always provided that these focus sacraments that help us through life's natural crisis points, by acting as rites of passage, do truly re-present the spirit of eucharist, the Spirit that took on the persona of Jesus.

All the sacraments so far considered fit these criteria, with the exception of the Sacrament of Penance. For once that sacrament came to be dominated by the symbolism of the tribunal, and divine forgiveness had to wait on the priest's pronouncing the sentence "I absolve you from your sins," it had clearly run contrary to the life-giving Spirit made really present in the Sacrament of Eucharist. The Sacrament of Penance then needed, and still needs, reform. Perhaps by reverting to the old Irish system of the *anam cara*. Or, until reform is achieved, a replacement by the Sacrament of Eucharist, as the faithful have already divined.

What then of the last of the seven sacraments, the Sacrament of Holy Orders? This sacrament as we now have it in the Roman Catholic Church is said to confer on its recipients the status of cultic priesthood, and the requisite power to change bread and wine into the body and blood of Christ. So that the priests should have a victim to offer in what could then be known as a proper cultic sacrifice. Jesus did not institute this sacrament, for he did not ordain any priests among or for his followers. And what happened when this sacrament was instituted some centuries after his death or, rather, when some traditional rituals were understood to confer a Sacrament of Holy Orders in this sense, is that eucharist itself became quite distorted in its symbolism and effect. And, although the question of chicken and egg is not easily answered here either, the eucharist then stood in need of radical reform in itself, as it still does in churches that think they have cultic priesthoods. For the original operative symbolism of eucharist was then overtaken by the symbolism of cultic sacrifice, and a consequent distortion occurred in our understanding of what was made present in eucharist, and how. It is difficult to avoid the conclusion that, in order to rid eucharist of such serious distortions, the Sacrament of Holy Orders simply has to go.

Or is that perhaps too harsh a judgment on the Sacrament of Holy Orders? Could it not be modified so as to assist rather than occlude the eucharistic spirit? There are clues in the Bible as to how this could be done, as it has been done in some Christian churches that were formed since the Protestant Reformation of the sixteenth century. The main clue lies in the stories of the Jesus's last supper, first in the synoptic Gospels and then in John's Gospel. In the synoptics, the false myth of the ordination of cultic priests at that supper proclaims, it was those disciples who were to be leaders of the community of Jesus's followers who were ordained priests. So the falsely imagined ordination to priesthood was for leaders. But then in John's Gospel the ritual that Jesus introduces during the meal is the ritual of the washing by Jesus of the feet of his disciples. A ritual that symbolizes and effects the service, in fact the most menial service possible to those who looked to him as their leader, a service that only slaves would normally perform. Jesus had already instructed those who would be leaders among his followers that they were not to lord it over others as gentile leaders did, that the ones who would lead must be the least of all and servants of all. So Jesus according to John could just as easily be said to have instituted at the last supper a sacrament by which leaders were to be formed and appointed in his community. A sacrament the parallel imagery of which echoed a central element in the operative imagery of the meal — the operative imagery of serving others, rather than oneself.

That would certainly seem to chime in with Luke's understanding of the matter in his version of the story of the last supper. For although

Luke does not include in that story any separate ritual of foot-washing, he does follow the story of the ritual of the eucharist meal, immediately, with the command of Jesus to his followers to the effect that those who would be leaders among them must act as servants of the rest. And he points for illustration and example to the manner in which he on that fateful evening, as always, was not like one who sat a table to be served, but the one who serves (Luke 22:14–27). Is there not here sufficient biblical evidence to say that Jesus himself instituted a sacrament by which people could face that critical point in life at which they were to assume the role of leader in the society of their fellows, offering a further rite of passage, consisting in the menial ritual of washing the feet of those to be led? And is it not also possible to say of this extra sacrament, both that eucharist itself can accomplish what it accomplishes, but that as long as the extra sacrament concurs through its parallel symbolism with part at least of what eucharist accomplishes, its addition to the cult is justified by its focusing of the total symbolism and effect that characterizes eucharist upon another important rite of passage in human existence? Sacraments have been said to have been instituted by Jesus on far less evidence than that. But even if the institution of such a Sacrament of Orders in which the higher orders of society truly serve the lower, the very opposite of what happened, particularly with the orders of Roman society in Jesus's time, even if this cannot be attributed to the historical Jesus, it has as much right as any other of the sacraments to be included thereafter. Provided that this Sacrament of Orders was understood, on the model of orders in the society to which this terminology points, to install the recipients, not in the Roman order of aristocrats, but in the order of servants or slaves.

Should the Christian community ordain a special leadership for the eucharistic meal-ritual? Or should they use instead some of the other leaders that emerged (were ordained?) in the church, either some of the so-called charismatic leaders that Paul mentions, prophets, teachers (there is some evidence in the early church that these presided over eucharist), or some of the more administrative types, like deacons or bishops? This became an issue from the time the little communities outgrew the original house gatherings. It is an issue that has lasted up to modern times, even though, once again in the Roman Catholic Church for example, the issue has long been resolved by the priestly caste, as they think it to be, monopolizing virtually all of the various leadership roles in the church. It would not seem to matter, on this issue, what option is taken, other than one that involves cultic priesthood. Practical considerations would no doubt prefer some options over others. But all must realize at all times that it is the gathered community that brings about true eucharist, and that the president of the Sacrament of Eucharist, as that person is now sometimes called, or the minister (servant) as Reformed churches prefer to say, simply acts for the congregation in this central cultic ritual of the Christian religion. Correspondingly, whatever rituals are adopted for whatever leadership roles any Christian church at any time chooses to adopt, these rituals must not themselves become the monopoly of some self-propagating clerical caste. Finally, such rituals must always use such symbolism, like the one used by Jesus, as will faithfully re-present the spirit of eucharist, and especially in this case the spirit of service that is at the heart of eucharist.

Chapter 8

CONSTITUTION

"O Zarathustra," answered the pope, "forgive me, but in divine matters I am even more enlightened than you. That stands to reason."
— Nietzsche, *Thus Spoke Zarathustra*

The constitution of an organized community of persons refers to the designated plan by which they are organized, a plan for leadership structures,
for offices and officers by which the community is governed, that is to
say, held together, advanced, administered and regulated. In the case of
the community made up of the followers of Jesus of Nazareth as it expanded rapidly and extensively within decades of his death, the picture
of its leadership structures painted in the earliest relevant documents, the
rNT, is both complex and fluid. It is a picture of a community of communities, the original one having its center in Jerusalem, and the others
scattered far and wide as missionaries began to move about the Roman
empire with the gospel of Jesus as their pressing charge. The picture becomes both complex and fluid as a result of a process by which available
forms of leadership and leadership structure in civic and religious societies
are tried out, adopted and adapted by this new fellowship of faith. The
briefest survey of this process must suffice for present purposes.

Begin with Paul's leadership list: "God has appointed in the church
first apostles, second prophets, third teachers, then workers of miracles,
then healers, helpers, administrators, speakers in various kinds of tongues"
(and by implication, interpreters for the latter) (1 Cor. 12:28). Is that
list complete for the time it was written? Perhaps not. Can it be divided
into establishment and charismatic types of leadership, the former formally adopted by the community as part of its permanent establishment,
the latter depending on the Spirit breathing special community-building
charisms where It wills? Only with doubts and difficulties. For when Paul
wants to defend his title to apostleship, he appeals to the palpable suc-
cesses of the Spirit breathing through him into the hearts of his converts.

And there is this more general point in any case: the whole community is held together and achieves its growth by allowing the same Spirit that had taken on the historical persona of Jesus to breathe eternal life through it to others. Although it can be observed that the Spirit of Jesus enables different individuals to promote that life for all, by giving them different gifts from the list that Paul had offered as a sample, just before he wrote out the list of leaders.

First apostles. The title means someone sent, commissioned, delegated to carry out some special assignment on behalf of the sender. In the case of the followers of Jesus, it would first and foremost apply to those especially commissioned to go out and spread the gospel, the way, the true life under the reign of God, for which Jesus lived and died. In such a sense Paul claimed the title of apostle for himself, and equally for some missionary companions of his, Sylvanus and Timothy (1 Thess. 2:7). He also uses the title for yet others that he names as "those outstanding apostles, Andronicus and Junius" (Rom. 16:7). Church tradition has carried down the ages the view that there were only twelve apostles, appointed by Jesus himself. But that represents a conflation of two separate categories of leader; and the conflation can hardly be held innocent of the charge that it prejudicially supports a particular view of the government of the Christian church in the world. A view that was formed later, and that must shortly receive some critical attention.

There certainly is sufficient evidence to indicate that Jesus chose from among his general band of disciples an inner group to which he gave a special mission. A group smaller than the seventy-two he sent out to preach during the course of his own mission, a group referred to as the Twelve, or the twelve disciples. Matthew has Jesus at the last supper, "at table with the twelve disciples," and Mark says quite simply that "he arrived with the Twelve." Luke, on the other hand, has Jesus "at table, and the apostles with him," and this surely suggests, since the Twelve could be called either disciples or apostles, that they were in fact a special group from within those called either disciples or apostles, there being no etymological reason why the seventy-two could not be called apostles. In other words, the special twelve did not exhaust the category of apostle any more than they exhausted the category of disciple, and they had a quite distinctive leadership role all of their own.

The most satisfactory explanation for the historical Jesus appointing a special group of leaders called the Twelve, and the most intelligible account of their role and function, is therefore something like this. With no intention of founding a church or religion other than the one he grew up in, and no intention of going to the gentiles other than through the religion he felt it to be his divine prophetic commission to reform, Jesus set up among his disciples a leadership group called the Twelve. This group was to symbolize and effect the coming into being of the new Israel, and of its renewed status as the son of the true God, who creates and cares for and thus promises life and life of indefinite abundance to all. The Twelve would then be an operative symbolic grouping of leaders, as if constituted of twelve leaders of the twelve tribes of Israel. That seems to have been the understanding of the matter among the earliest leadership group in Jerusalem. It was perhaps also part of the reason for their apparent concern at Paul's apostleship to gentiles, an apostleship conducted, as he came to see it, without the need to go through the structures and rituals of the religion of Israel. But the moment did come when it was decided by the "apostles and leaders" of the church in Jerusalem, of which Peter was apparently "one of the pillars," that Paul should have his way and accept converts to Jesus the Christ without their having to be first circumcised as Jews. Paul claims that on this or another occasion in Jerusalem, "James and Cephas and John, who were reputed to be pillars, gave to me and Barnabas the right hand of fellowship, that we should go to the Gentiles and they to the circumcised." And with that the circumstances in which the Twelve could form the government of the growing community of Jesus-followers were already passing away (Acts 15; Gal. 2:9). Although the office of apostle continued, as Paul in his letters amply illustrates.

According to the opening chapters of the Acts of the Apostles, the Twelve were involved in a number of activities. Among these was the choice of Matthias (by the advanced Human Resources technique of casting lots), to fill the vacancy in their ranks left by Judas. Then the Twelve appointed by the ritual of the laying on of hands, seven of the disciples who had been selected by the body of the disciples of Jesus, to perform some administrative duties within the community, and in this way to free the existing leaders for dedication to their primary role: the preaching of the word of God, and prayer. The seven thus ordained are traditionally known as the first deacons. Although it is very clear from the very next story of Stephen, who was one of the seven, that he also preached and taught the gospel, so passionately and effectively in fact that he was martyred for doing so. Thereafter, there is mention of *presbuteroi*, presbyters or elders, and *episcopoi*, bishops or supervisors, with one passing hint that the deacons might have been assistants to the latter, the helpers or administrators in Paul's list, perhaps (Phil. 1:1). Elders, presbyters, would have formed the town council in the local government system of ancient Israel; overseers, bishops, having a similar role in the wider civic culture of the empire. But these leaders also, it is clear from the stories about them in Acts, as well as from references to them in various *Letters*, were also preachers and teachers of the word of God, and indeed that was always their prime calling and responsibility. Although none of these officers or leaders in the Christian community, as it later came to be called, were in these early years needed to preside over the eucharistic meal. All in all then a moving and complex picture of a community experimenting with ways of organizing and governing itself. Borrowing existing structures of secular civic and political society, making it up as they went along, and especially as the growing split with the native religion of Jesus saw the obsolescence of the only leadership institution that Jesus himself seems to have bequeathed to them, the institution of the Twelve.

When we pick up the story of this experiment in the structural engineering of this growing and increasingly far-flung community from documents outside the rNT we find early evidence indeed of the beginnings of a very successful streamlining of the complex and fluid state of affairs as the rNT tells of it. The author of the *Letter of Clement*, written from Rome during the last decade of the first century, has God commission and send Jesus, Jesus commission and send the apostles, now confined in number to the twelve, and the twelve apostles in turn commission and send "bishops (aka presbyters) and deacons," in order to make disciples of all nations and to guide and rule the new people of God. Other leaders too are active, it appears, prophets in particular. But the line of commissioning that gives the community its constitutional structure is already being straightened out and certified through the bishops. So that when a century later Irenaeus, in his battle with the ubiquitous Gnostics, wants to point to the institution that can guarantee the truth and the true way and life that comes down from Jesus, he points again to the "apostolic tradition" handed down in an unbroken line of command through the succession of bishops in each of the churches. And first and foremost among them he placed the bishop of the church of Rome, a city whose bishops descend in their line of commission from Peter, the leader of the Twelve, and from Paul also. For Peter and Paul according to legend both died in Rome in the course of founding the church in that primatial city of the empire.

And the rest is history. The Christian community in the world is clearly borrowing its leadership structures from the Roman empire, and not only the names and forms of office, but the administrative divisions of the empire also. The bishop of Rome, still the center of government of the empire, comes to be called *papa*, father, for that was one of the titles of the Roman emperor. Bishops of other great metropolitan centers also come to be called *papa*, but the bishop of Rome, like Rome itself, will never give up the claim to be first among these. Why should it? Add to this the fact that bishops come to be described as priests, eventually in the proper cultic sense of the term, and the constitutional terms that place the whole organization and regulation of the church in the hands of a priestly caste are already in position and need only to be written up and presented in a formal, legal constitution. Therein lies the beginning of a Christian foundation myth of the Christian church in the world, a foundation myth that was then faithfully developed down the centuries, and most consistently developed to this day by the Roman Catholic Church. So, for the sake of brevity, this whole history of the development of what may be called the constitutional law of a new religion, now illustrated from the example of the oldest and still functioning form of church government, may be summarized here from the most authoritative documents of that same Roman Catholic Church in recent times, the Documents of the Second Vatican Council of the 1960s, and from the most recent, twentieth-century revision of that church's *Code of Canon Law*.

"And the Word was made flesh and dwelt among us, full of grace and truth ... and from his fullness we have all received ... for ... grace and truth came through Jesus Christ." How is that grace and truth that came with Jesus of Nazareth carried to all down to the present day? That is the question that the old foundation myth still maintained in good order by the Roman Catholic Church answers, in fidelity, it would claim, to Irenaeus and all the orthodox Fathers and teachers in the church through all the centuries between. As elaborated in documents of Vatican II such as the Dogmatic Constitution on the Church, the Decree on Bishops, the Decree on Priests, this twentieth-century version of the oldest, still functioning foundation myth, focuses first on a priestly caste that is distinct in essence and not just in degree from what is more generally and metaphorically known as "the priesthood of the people," the "priesthood" of the laity, or "of the faithful." Priesthood properly so called is a cultic priesthood, indeed a hierarchical priesthood, in that the bishop rather than the ordinary parish priest enjoys "the fullness" of this priesthood. And this distinctive essence of priesthood results from the conferring upon chosen men — women need not apply — of a "sacred power," the nature and effects of which are illustrated in the assertion that it enables the men who receive it to do two things: to "bring about the eucharistic sacrifice," and to rule "the priestly people." A sacred power then that, once conferred on certain men in a special Sacrament of Orders, sets them apart as a distinct clerical caste, whose role it is to rule the rest of the followers of Jesus and to provide these with eucharist.

The key to the puzzle as to how the conferment of one "sacred power" can be said to enable the recipients both to "bring about eucharist" and to rule, is found in a combination, as in the combination that opens a combination lock. Except that here we have a combination of ideas rather than numbers. The combination of ideas is this: the idea of eucharist as a cultic sacrifice for sin (already criticized) and the source of all forgiveness, healing and whole-making; the idea of original sin as an actual sin of Adam transmitted (by divine decree) on the occasion of each human conception; the idea of divine grace as some sort of supernatural entity over and above nature as we can know it; and the corresponding ideas of revelation as knowledge or information beyond our natural powers of detection (the two latter ideas receive some final critique in the Epilogue). When these ideas are put together, they open the door to the following view: the answer to the question as to what precisely happens when those who are uniquely empowered to do so bring about eucharist, namely, that *grace* is infused and wipes away sin, and heals and sanctifies, that answer must be especially *revealed* to some special people (for none of this can be perceived naturally), and the ensuing knowledge about divine grace must be passed on to human kind, without failure or error. Revealed to and unfailingly passed on by, presumably, the ones originally empowered to bring about eucharist. These same ones, therefore, must possess the ultimate authority on earth to teach this truth about eucharist (and other sacraments), about grace, sin and salvation. And indeed, as well as the supreme authority to teach the way and the truth, in this case called magisterium, these same ones must possess also a power to rule, a power of jurisdiction. This is a power to make rulings concerning all of the above matters: about the forms and so on of sacraments to be administered and received, about the way people ought to live their lives, about the relationships of hierarchs to others, as legislators, judges, enforcers of laws and penalties.

It is worth noting here something about the full rigor of the logic of this combination of ideas. The rigorous application of that logic that would virtually monopolize all power of fullness of priesthood, of authoritative teaching, and of (other) law-making and enforcing, was not really in force in the Roman Catholic Church much before modern times. In the high Middle Ages the chair of the theologian was separate from, and in its own way equal to the chair of the bishop; the one, the *cathedra* or chair of the theologian-teacher, was to be found in the university, where such chairs still exist, especially in the more ancient universities. Whereas the *cathedra* or chair of the bishop was found in the cathedral. Furthermore, the churches that formed as a result of the Protestant Reformation of the sixteenth century maintained in honor the institution of the *Doctor Ecclesiae*, the teacher of or in the church, separate and distinct from the other leadership structures with which they replaced the papal-episcopal institution. Only indeed in more recent times has the Roman Catholic Church tried to legislate for the role of theologian by insisting that the theologian should really be confined to promoting, explaining and defending where necessary, the teaching of *the (authentic) magisterium,* a magisterium that coincides entirely with the ruling hierarchy itself. Thus in effect the role of principally authorized and authoritative teacher in the church is monopolized by the papal-episcopal hierarchy.

This particular play of monopoly, it is worth adding here, had and has a deleterious effect on the leadership role of teacher in the church. For the teacher, the theologian is responsible for studying the faith of the followers of Jesus, both in the Bible and as it is kept faithfully alive under the breathing of the Spirit of Jesus in the whole church. And she is also responsible for the equally faithful communication of the nature and content of that faith to the whole church in terms intelligible to each time and place. Therefore, for the faithful accomplishment of this task, to the very best of her ability, the theologian is responsible first and foremost, not to the hierarchy of the church, but to the whole church. For the teacher, the theologian, although she may well prove to have a gift for, and may well work hard to attain the knowledge of the faith, and perhaps even the wisdom in respect to that faith that Paul mentioned among the gifts of the Spirit graciously given to the leaders he lists for the church, yet she has herself no power of jurisdiction. Nor indeed has she any authority whatever other than the inherent authority, or acceptability and persuasiveness that the whole community finds in what she writes or otherwise teaches. That does not prevent the hierarchy from exercising its wider power of jurisdiction over the teaching that goes on in the church. Especially on these occasions when the community of the followers of Jesus is threatened with tearing apart by such different versions of the teaching of the faith that reconciliation between these teachings seems impossible. For serious error must then be suspected, and every effort made by "the officers of good order," the overseer or episcopal functionaries in the church, to have the truth restored. Yet everything will depend on how this kind of potentially disastrous emergency is handled by the officers of good order. In particular whether they call a council representative of all church members, or simply maintain for themselves some monopoly of the conservation of the fullness of truth, together with what must then seem like its imposition on all others, through the exercise of a power of jurisdiction that is itself wider than the power of magisterium.

In sum and in pursuit of adequate accuracy, it might be worthwhile to take the terms of the constitution of the Christian religion according to the Roman Catholic Church from that church's own *Code of Canon Law.*

The power of governance, or the power of jurisdiction, "which belongs to the church by divine institution," is exercised by those who are in holy orders, although it is allowed that lay members of the church, by delegation, can cooperate in the exercise of this power (canon 129). This power of governance is then "divided into legislative, executive and judicial power" (canons 135ff.), but this distinction does not lead to any provision for a theory or practice of the separation of powers in the Roman Catholic Church. The distinction serves only to assert the fullness of power in all forms of its exercise for those for whom its sovereign status is claimed. And only clerics can obtain offices the exercise of which requires the power to govern, and a person becomes a cleric for this purpose by the reception of the diaconate (canons 265, 273). When the issue of sovereignty, of the *summa potestas* or, in the English translation of the code, the "supreme authority" of the church is raised, the locus of this is first said to be found in the office of the Roman Pontiff. "Consequently, by virtue of his office, he has supreme, full, immediate and universal ordinary power in the church" (canon 331) That this power includes judicial and executive, as well as legislative power, is clear from the whole context, even if it is not already clear from canon 333: "There is neither appeal nor recourse against a judgment or a decree of the Roman Pontiff."

Yet it is then said that the College of Bishops is bearer of supreme and full power over the universal church (canon 336). For those initially puzzled by these apparently contradictory claims to the locus of sovereignty, an explanation is forthcoming to the effect that the Roman Catholic bishops as a college are bearers of this supreme power only when in union with the head of the college, who is the pope. Furthermore, it is the pope who chooses the ways in which the college can act, and no consensus of the college can achieve the status of an act of supreme power unless he agrees to its proclamation, or at the very least accepts it freely. The most solemn form in which this collegial power is exercised is that of a general council. But then a general council must be convened by the pope, he must preside over it, set its agenda, approve its decrees, and transfer, suspend or dissolve it (canons 337–41). It would take a clever and most erudite lawyer to estimate the real amount of supreme power left over for the college of bishops when that of the Roman Pontiff is subtracted in any one instance of its exercise, or in all.

There is another college with which the papacy is closely involved, the college of cardinals. It is the college of cardinals that elects each pope. But it is the incumbent pope, and the pope alone, who selects all of those who are promoted to the college of cardinals, and who creates each cardinal simply by papal decree (canons 349, 351). That surely adds to the pope's unrivalled power over the church during his years in office a further means of influence over the kind of pope he would like to succeed him. All bishops also must be appointed by the pope as his free choice, whatever rights might be held by certain parties in the church to submit lists of suitable or preferable candidates for the office in their part of the world. Or whatever traditional rights some (very few) parties might still have to conduct a kind of election for the post (canon 377). Add to this the fact that the pope himself also exercises "ordinary power" over the diocese of each individual bishop, and despite the fact that this arrangement is said to "reinforce and defend the proper, ordinary and immediate power which the bishops have in particular (diocesan) churches" (canon 333), it surely also emphasizes even further the awesome extent of the sovereignty that Roman Catholic constitutional law confers upon the pope, and makes one wonder once again about any residue of real power left over even for bishops.

Some might wish to soften somewhat the impressions of awesome sovereignty here claimed for the Roman Catholic hierarchy, by suggesting perhaps that this power is thought to be properly exercised only over Roman Catholics. Yet when the matters over which this sovereign power of magisterium and jurisdiction are more closely analyzed, some unease may register as to the possibility of such containment. The matter over which this sovereignty is exercised is described as a "deposit of faith." Now the phrase most frequently found in the section of the canon law that concerns the promulgation of this "deposit of faith," this "revealed truth" (canons 747–54), is the phrase "matters of faith and morals," or "doctrine concerning faith and morals." And the canon law is certainly not shy about this church's claims concerning the morals part of the deposit of truth it claims to possess: "The church has the right always and everywhere to proclaim moral principles, even in respect of the social order, and to make judgments about any human matter in so far as this is required by fundamental human rights or the salvation of souls" (canon 747). Laying down moral rules *everywhere,* as required by fundamental human rights *or* the salvation of souls? The prospect of containment seems to recede even further as the canon law goes on directly to claim the prerogative of infallibility for the pope, and for the college of bishops in union with the pope, in those instances of their definitive teaching on faith and morals that are directed to the whole church, so that any such teaching requires from their subjects a response of "divine and catholic faith."

The adjective "divine" here implies the divine origin of the teaching or ruling. It makes the idea of divine revelation directly relevant, as the condition under which such rulings are promulgated. Yet the precise nature of the process of divine revelation thought to be involved is not always clear. There is reference to "the word of God" in the deposit of faith, presumably a reference to an original (verbal) revelation contained in scripture and handed down in tradition (canon 750). But other church decisions refer to a divine law allegedly revealed in nature. And that is bound to make the student of this constitutional system to wonder once more whether, in the case of its moral teaching at least, it can really restrict its claim to sovereign jurisdiction to card-carrying members of the Roman Catholic Church. In any case, we are in the presence of rulings for conduct, the content of which come from divine revelation in history and nature, and the office for the imposition of which is itself divinely instituted and endowed with absolute sovereignty. And all of this is made finally clear in those canons which state that, even in cases where the "assent of faith" is not required, those addressed are to offer "submission of intellect and will" (canon 752). That does seem to remove any real role for the rational minds and wills of those addressed, particularly in moral rulings. Simple assent, instant consent seems to be the order of the day.

Now that may be the constitution of the oldest still functioning form of Christian church government, but it is not of course the only constitution for a Christian church that has been proposed in the course of Christian history. The multiplication of mutually separated Christian churches began in earnest with the split between the Eastern and Western parts of Christendom which probably became irreparable by the thirteenth century (and not least because of the exploits of our aforementioned Enrico Dandolo, Doge of Venice, and the crusade he led). It continued with the further split between mainstream Eastern Orthodox Christianity and some uniate churches of the East that, as that name implies, maintained a union with Rome. It increased greatly with the split that occurred on the occasion of the Protestant Reformation of the sixteenth century, and then within Protestant Christianity itself. All of that would paint a picture sufficient for most purposes, though still not quite a complete picture, of the continuing growth of the number of churches into which Christianity the religion has differentiated itself over the last two millennia. It would be as impossible as it would be unnecessary to list here all of the constitutions of these Christian churches. But before some general critical comment is offered under the heading of constitution, it would surely be helpful to give a brief description of the constitution of one other Christian church that flourishes today, this time from the Protestant family. And long personal familiarity and appreciation suggests the choice of the Presbyterian Church of Scotland.

According to the Westminster Confession of Faith, the subordinate standard of belief adopted by the Church of Scotland (subordinate, that is, to the supreme rule of faith, the Word of God as contained in canonical scripture), "There is no other head of the Church, but the Lord Jesus Christ" (xxv, 6). Yet the Lord Jesus "appointed a government, in the hand of church officers, distinct from the civil magistrate. To these officers, the keys of the kingdom are committed" (xxx, 1–2). The confession contains no further guidance on the protocol of church government, except to suggest that "for the better government, and further education of the church, there ought to be such assemblies as are commonly called synods or councils" (xxxi, 1). It is this factor that makes Cox in his *Practice and Procedure in the Church of Scotland* declare it a principle of Presbyterianism that it be "conciliar in polity." Cox's collection of the constitutional documents on which the particular structures of this church are based reveals the following deployment of "synods or councils," now called "courts."

First, at parochial level, the lowest court is made up of one teaching elder or presbyter, that is to say, one ordained to the ministry of word and sacrament, and a number of ruling elders or presbyters, who are ordained for life to that second form of the office, and the whole is then called a kirk session. The next court above that parochial one is the presbytery or, to give it its formal title, The Right Reverend The Presbytery. This court is responsible for an area covered by a number of parishes. Its members are made up as follows: the teaching elders or ministers of the parishes involved, together with some other ministers, and a representative ruling elder from each parish involved, together with such other ruling elders as will make up the number of the teaching elders. The next higher court is called the synod. This is made up of all the members of a number of adjacent presbyteries, together with "corresponding members" from adjacent synods. The supreme court of the Church of Scotland is called The General Assembly, and it is made up of equal numbers of teaching and ruling elders chosen and sent by all the presbyteries of the church.

Individual parish congregations issue a call to a prospective teaching elder or minister, but it is Presbytery that acknowledges the call and ordains to the ministry of Word and Sacrament. Presbytery also, as bishop, proposes the ruling elders that are to be ordained to the office of minister for individual parishes. The Church of Scotland then is not, or not fully, a representative democracy. But, apart altogether from the fact that the lay/clerical distinction would be quite controversial in Presbyterian circles and much resented by many Presbyterians, neither could the governing power be described in any circumstances as a clerical monopoly, as is the case with the Roman Catholic Church. In the lowest court the ruling elders must outnumber those ordained to the ministry of Word and Sacrament, and in the three progressively higher courts parity of numbers of teaching ministers and ruling elders is always maintained. The Presbyterian Church is therefore fully conciliar in polity, as the Westminster Confession says a church should be, rather than fully democratic in structure, and the extent of its conciliar nature is further emphasized in the so-called Barrier Act of 1697. This Act was designed to prevent hasty changes of a substantial nature, but it succeeds simultaneously in preventing power from coagulating at the top, for it proposes that any acts which the General Assembly ("The Venerable") might wish "to be binding rules and constitutions of the Church" should then be remitted to the presbyteries. The presbyteries would report on the matter to the General Assembly of the following year, so that there might then be revealed a "general opinion" in agreement, or not in agreement, as the case might be.

When it comes down to the question of sovereignty, the *suprema potestas*, it would appear that, as befits a church of Protestant Reformation origin, the Church of Scotland holds a position very different from that of the Roman Catholic Church. For it claims "to acknowledge the Word of God which is contained in the scriptures of the Old and New Testaments to be the supreme rule of faith and life." As remarked already, this church takes as its subordinate standard the Westminster Confession of Faith, but it claims the right to modify, interpret and further formulate this subordinate standard in accordance with the Word of God. It recognizes liberty of opinion on matters that do not concern the substance of the faith. But in this, as in the case of modifying its subordinate standard, this church also claims to be the sole judge of what is of the substance of the faith, and of what modifications may be made. In short, this church is sole judge of the agreement with the Word of God in scripture of any suggestions made, under either of these headings. So, the one to be ordained to the ministry of Word and Sacrament, as well as offering assent to the point about the Bible as the supreme rule of faith and life, promises also to be subject to "the superior courts of the Church," the supreme court being of course the General Assembly.

The differences between this constitution and that of the Roman Catholic Church must be only too obvious to the most desultory of readers. And yet there are some elements of similarity that are worth considering. First, there is that curious combination once again of the teaching role with the sacramental role of the one who is called the teaching elder or minister. This is surely reminiscent of the sacred power that combines in the Roman Catholic Church the role of those enjoying the fullness of the priesthood in bringing about the eucharistic sacrament, with the role of magisterium, even though the rest of the ruling role in the Church of Scotland is in the hands of the ruling elders or presbyters. And there are some who think that in Presbyterian practice the eucharistic role of the minister is closer to that of the Roman Catholic priest than the good reformed teaching on the subject of priesthood should allow. A university colleague who had spent many years in the mission fields of Malawi often remarked on the odd fact that on Sunday mornings he had to ride his motorbike to several well-scattered parish churches in order that they should have someone to preside over the Holy Eucharist. Exactly as his friend and neighbor, a Roman Catholic priest had to get on his bike and ride off in all directions, because there were not enough priests to serve all the parish churches in the area. Just as there were not enough Presbyterian teaching elders or ordained ministers in what was clearly a parallel case?

But the more substantial similarity certainly resides in the issue of a church's claimed authority in ruling on matters of truth, church practice and morals. For the Church of Scotland it is the Word of God in the scriptures that functions as "the supreme rule of faith and life," a phrase remarkably similar to its Roman Catholic counterpart, "faith and morals." As with the Roman Catholic Church we may be left in some doubt as to the nature and extent of the Word of God or divine revelation, particularly in the case of moral rules for living. Many Protestants, suffering perhaps from a certain phobia with regard to what is called natural theology, either because they wrongly believe that its defenders think it to be based on something other than divine revelation in the cosmos, or because they estimate at close to nil the ability of the fallen mind to perceive that revelation any longer, refuse to entertain the traditional Stoic and then Christian idea of natural law morality. Yet they do speak of "ordinances of creation." But however all of that may turn out to be, the fact of the matter remains that the Church of Scotland does describe itself as "sole judge," in particular through its supreme court, the General Assembly, of the agreement of any human formulation of doctrine on faith and life with the contents of the Word of God in the scriptures. And that stance alone must bring it close indeed to the kind of claims made by the Roman Catholic magisterium to have the power and authority to be the supreme authentic teacher in matters of faith and morals, an authority which includes the role of supreme judge in matters of the interpretation of the same Christian scriptures.

So impressed are some people by this similarity between these two Christian churches, so apparently at odds with each other in so many other ways, that they begin to wonder aloud about the reality, or at least the substantiality of some of the other much advertised ways of differing. For example, the Protestant church claims that the Word of God in the scriptures is their supreme rule of faith and life and that, on the contrary, the Pope in the other church arrogates to himself just that same supreme rule, despite the latter's protest that he serves that same Word of God in the scriptures. But since both claim that in this matter of teaching what, and only what is compatible with the scriptural Word of God, they are "dependent on the promised guidance of the Holy Spirit" (or words so similar as to make no difference), it must be doubtful whether any real difference emerges here either. Much the same could be said with respect to infallibility. One church, on behalf of the Roman Catholic magisterium, claims it; the other regards such a claim as a piece of infernal cheek.

Yet if in effect both churches claim to be supreme judges in matters of divinely revealed truth about faith and life, what difference does it make whether one claims to be infallible or not? Nothing separates the supreme judging of truth and falsehood in matters of faith and life, as between the churches, except the offices and manners by which such judgment is issued.

There is no intention to pretend that these two Christian churches are representative of all Christian churches, the one representing the "Catholic" camp, the other the "Protestant" camp. Nor should there be any suspicion of the pretence that these two represent the two extremes between which all other self-designated Christian churches can be made to fit. There are some small "uniate" churches still thriving, that are so far to the "right" of Rome (in terms of constitutional law) as to make Vatican officialdom look like doe-eyed liberals. There are churches so far to the "left" of Presbyterians as to make these seem suspect of secret hankerings after Vatican-style government. But it would be as impossible as it is unnecessary to offer even the briefest survey of all of them. All that is necessary here is some summary notice of some of the main features that the constitutions of all Christian churches, written or customary, explicit or implicit, must cover. For that is enough to sustain a reasonable critique of the constitution factor as illustrated in so many ways and so far in the course of the history of the Christian religion.

There is in fact not very much that needs to be said by way of critical comment on this constitutional element in religion. Of the four major elements that go into the make-up of a religion, the constitutional element is of the very least significance, but that is not to say that it is of no significance at all. The way in which a religious community governs itself, the way in which the ones in office treat the others or see themselves with respect to the others, can in its own way give the broadest of hints as to the kind of God to whom the members of that community entrust their lives, and as to the kind of treatment the members can expect from that divinity. And if that broad hint runs counter to all that is otherwise conveyed in creed, or cult, or code, or in the worst case, all three, it can damage, if not indeed in extreme cases negate, the very best of all that is otherwise conveyed in the preaching and practice of that religion. The image of the human government of Christian churches cannot but affect to some extent their image of the reign of God, both for the members of these churches and for others who look at, or even look to these churches, for some light along the way of life.

Every human community needs some structures of leadership in order to hold it together, to regulate its communal life, and to develop it into the future. So that a human community bound together by common religious categories, if the person it looks back to as its founder did not bequeath to it some defined structures of leadership, must simply create such structures for itself, or borrow some from surrounding societies. And there is this much to be said for the idea of borrowing the governmental structures of surrounding societies whenever a growing community of the followers of Jesus want to organize themselves; if there is an example to be given, not just to all people as to how to live their lives under the reign of God, but to those in the authority of public office, as to how to do this in their own very circumstances, then the example can be all the more effective if the religion operates exactly the same kinds of governmental structures as do the outsiders. Example is always more powerful than preaching alone.

Therefore, when in time the Christian church, now grown to the width and breadth of the Roman Empire began to adopt for its localized episcopal structures the further hierarchical structures of the Empire, with Rome itself at the head, and with metropolitan centers of provinces, and so on, that too was all to the good. Or at least it would have been if the bishops who governed through this hierarchy continued from the beginning to do so in the spirit of service that Jesus had enjoined upon all who would be leaders among his followers. But they did not do this for very long. Gradually what happened was that instead of the ethos of service infiltrating the Roman Imperial form of government from a church that soon after Constantine became in effect the established church of that empire, the opposite occurred. The ethos of imperial power, the practice of lording it over people and making one's authority felt, seeped into the government of the Christian church. The seepage had reached saturation point by the time of Pope Boniface VIII and his doctrine of the two swords. So alike were the two imperial powers, the secular and the sacred, in both ethos and practice of government, that rivalry for the higher place on the same scale became inevitable. Boniface stated the desired outcome of this rivalry when he put the prevailing ecclesiastical view of the matter in the metaphor of the two swords. These are the swords respectively of secular and spiritual power, snugly together in the same scabbard. God gives this scabbard with its two swords to the Pope, who then gives the sword of secular power to the Emperor. And if the latter does not wield it justly, the Pope can take it back again. That is to put the matter rather roughly;

but it is mentioned here only in order to show how similar the ethos of power had become in the minds of these two imperial administrations.

As it passed through the Middle Ages, this already imperial church took on the trappings of feudal lordship and serfdom. So powerful in fact was this further but linear metamorphosis that Luther, who rightly wanted to reform the Roman church, was yet quite appalled at the peasant revolt. Quite unable to see the conclusions that these peasants were drawing from his own restoration of the biblical ideal of human life and relationships, Luther sided against them in the bloody battle that ensued, and not just on the grounds that they should not have taken up arms to gain their goal. But it was the Roman church, against which Luther rightly railed, that carried the identification with feudal overlordship to its highest degree. And to this day the trappings of that lordship are evident, not just in raiment and in social etiquette — ordinary Christians expected to kneel before the lord bishop and kiss his hand — but in the constitutional law just noted above, with its constant stress on sovereignty, *suprema potestas*, vested in one imperial figure, and with the express proviso that none of his judgments require the consent of the church. It would be funny, were it not so tragic, to hear contemporary popes going on and on about secular values and the secular spirit infecting and destroying the church, while they themselves in their understanding and exercise of their office represent what is perhaps the most ancient, and certainly the most notorious form of the secularization of Christianity in the whole tainted history of its existence.

Other churches must decide for themselves what, if any, of this configuration and ethos of power, as Jesus said "the gentiles" exercised it, has come down in their cases. And it would be foolish to think that dictatorial power — for that is what is at issue here — can be found only where there are popes and bishops of the Roman Catholic ilk. A biblical fundamentalist church leader can be just as dictatorial and judgmental, and as willing to condemn to hell any one who does not agree to the letter with his interpretation of scripture, as can any pope. Service is service as slaves provide it, with no claims to power, and leaving others utterly free to accept their service, or not to accept it. This ideal of service can become the ethos of any particular form of government — imperial, monarchical, conciliar, democratic — with any particular types of office and officer, borrowed or newly created. Although it would be wise, for the sake of the power of example over mere preaching, if borrowed forms of government and office reflected faithfully the patterns of leadership in the secular world, and changed when these changed. So that imperial forms should have by now given way to democratic ones. For it is human beings that create the structures by which they are organized and regulated, and who change and develop these as time goes on. That, as history shows, is no different in the case of societies of religious people than it is in the case of secular societies. So that, as already stated above, if there is to be a "Sacrament of Orders" in any Christian church, then it can only take the form of a symbolic ritual that "ordains" leaders to the order of servants (or the nicer word, ministers). And if Christians want to believe that Jesus himself instituted a special Sacrament of Orders, then they really have no option other than to reinstate the ritual he himself performed, according to John's alternative account of his last supper: the ritual washing of the feet of the members of the eucharistic community by the one who would preside over it in that or any other leadership role.

It is very unlikely indeed that the Christian religion can now boast, or indeed has ever been able to boast of having among the plethora of churches its history has seen so far "one, true church," whether attended by all Christians or just by some. From the earliest times recorded in the rNT there is ample evidence, not just of differences between the little churches in different places, but of varying degrees of decline from the teachings of Jesus, if not indeed downright reversals or betrayals in respect of his teaching and embodiment of the true reign of the one, true God. Sometimes the differences took the form of factions created by overzealous promotion of particular leaders, but at the expense of the leadership of Jesus: I am of Paul, I am of Apollo, I belong to the party of Cephas. At other times there were more serious differences as one can see, for example, from the position condemned by the Epistle to the Hebrews, and by other references to "the party of circumcision." And there were other distortions in the teaching and praxis of the churches, such as the abuse of the eucharistic meal that made Paul round on his Corinthian converts. For what was at issue there was quite literally a matter of life or death, and Paul has no hesitations in saying so. Hardly has anything that could be called "the one, true church" as yet come into view before the end of the period covered by the rNT. And since the end of rNT times, the history of Christian churches reads as much like a constant repetition of their lapses as of their intermittent efforts at reform, with the further spectacle of both lapses and attempted reforms more likely as not resulting in further break-away churches.

So it remains for each church that claims to re-present Jesus the Christ and to be part of his extended body in time and memory, to examine itself against the biblical Jesus and such evidences of his Spirit as the contemplative and prayerful can detect either in their own or other Christian churches, or for that matter outside of Christian churches altogether, in other religions or in none. In that way each church can learn from others, and perhaps also as part of that same process offer to others some improvements or even corrections of which they might stand in need. And do all of this without the need to impose conformity to any existing church. For just as it is most unlikely that there is now extant any "one, true church" in terms of total fidelity to the revelation that Christians claim in the form of the life, death and destiny of Jesus of Nazareth, it is equally unlikely that there is any set and unalterable forms of credo, code, cult and constitution by reference to which any given church could ever be called completely true. If anything is obvious from the inquiry conducted already, it is the need for a continuing creativity in the endeavor of construing each and all of these four elements of religion in order to see the Spirit of Jesus best embodied through changing worlds.

It is worth noting one example of such creativity, and of the diversity it introduced for the best outcome for all involved. It is an example of creativity in the matter of church constitution, an example of the way in which a people converting to Christianity can modify their own cultural constitutional forms of government, rather than have imposed on their culture ancient Roman imperial constitutional forms. The example is taken from the earliest history of the Christian religion in Ireland. Ireland had a high culture in the fifth century, but not a civilization in the strict sense of that word; it did not have any *civis*, any city or town. Irish society was not organized around towns and cities. Therefore, although some missionaries like Patrick came to Ireland as bishops, and no doubt bishops were ordained in Ireland from early times, the papal-episcopal structure for church government that fitted so well the lands to which the Roman Empire extended, simply did not fit the governmental structures of early Ireland. What then do we find instead? Ireland was divided into small *tuatha*, or kingdoms, each ruled over by a chief or, in broader European terms, a king. Furthermore there were groupings, families one might say of such *tuatha* over which one king held some overarching power, the others being client kings. Then, from the beginning, Christian monasticism came to Ireland, and the creative innovation came about through the process of adapting papal-episcopal government to a system of monastic government. The example of Iona, founded by Colm Cille, can best illustrate what is happening in this example of a major Celtic form of the enculturation of Christianity, a religion already thoroughly enculturated in Greco-Roman categories of imagery, ritual, thought and institution.

Colm Cille, like other monastic founders, received large tracts of land from the chiefs or kings of the small kingdoms, and where there was no diocesan-parochial administrative structure in place, these monasteries in effect became the "parish churches" for surrounding districts. Then an abbot like Colm Cille would found other monasteries in other areas, and he would remain in a position of overlordship with respect of these other monasteries and their abbots — like the over-king and the client-kings in the secular realm. In this way Colm Cille and his successor-abbots of Iona eventually ruled over a *familia* of monasteries in large donated tracts of land that stretched over the northern part of Ireland, much of Scotland and the north of England. These lands were then the *paruchia*, the parish of Iona and its abbot. When one realizes, further, that Colm Cille was in line of succession for the kingship of the O'Neill dynasty, for he was within the narrow degrees of kinship for that purpose (the Irish were not foolish enough to confine succession to primogeniture), and when one notices that the next eight at least of the abbots of Iona succeeded him in that same close family lineage of princely descent, one can easily see how closely this ecclesiastical constitution of this particular Irish church mirrored the constitution of the secular government. In a manner similar to that in which a quite different ecclesiastical and a quite different secular constitution were parallel in the Roman Empire at large. And for as long as the old Irish order and the native Irish monastic system remained intact, one can trace the benefits of that parallelism for the introduction of Christian values from "church to state," as well as the failures that at times brought the worst of the ethos of the secular form of government into these monastic churches.

The main difference in terms of government between these local Irish churches and the church of the Empire at large, and the one that best illustrates the creative innovation that was necessary in this new outreach for Christianity, is focused in the office of bishop. The monasteries each had a bishop among its functionaries, but it was the abbot or abbess, who was not a bishop, that ruled his or her *paruchia*. The bishop was necessary mainly, if not only, in order to ordain priests. The monastic bishop no longer had the place, highest after the pope in the chain of command within the church as such, as he otherwise had in the papal-episcopal constitution of the church. The papacy, needless to say, did not like this arrangement at all. But the Irish did not think this sufficient reason for overlooking its advantages, not to say its necessity. And one of these mighty abbots undertook to explain to a pope why this piece of Christian pluriformity, far from weakening, the papal constitution of the church, in fact strengthened it. This was the one called Columbanus (in order to distinguish him from the other "dove" of the church, Colm Cille), whose *paruchia* of monasteries stretched from the Vosges to Bobbio in northern Italy, the monastery in which he died (now therefore in territories in which there was already episcopal administration — the Irish plainly thinking that their form of church constitution, comprised of abbots and their monastic regimes, was at least the equal of any other). In letters written to Pope Boniface toward the end of the sixth century, Columbanus stresses his allegiance to the primacy of Rome: "for all we Irish, inhabitants of the world's edge, are disciples of saints Peter and Paul and of all the disciples who wrote the sacred canon by the Holy Spirit, and we accept nothing outside the evangelical and apostolic teaching . . . but the catholic faith as it has been delivered by you first, who are the successor of the holy apostles, is maintained unbroken." Rome, he adds a little later in the same letter, is renowned in the whole world because the chair is there, hallowed by the relics of Peter and Paul, the twin fiery steeds of God's Spirit that enabled the charioteer, Christ, to reach "even unto us."

If he had left matters there, he might just have received a grudging acceptance of his position from Rome. But no, Columbanus's sense of the superiority of his own culture, or of what he calls "the freedom of my country's customs," leads him on to lecture the pope on the nature of the primatial authority that he has just acknowledged in such fulsome terms. Primatial power, he explains patiently, does not belong to any pope simply as a result of some conferment ritual, such as Jesus enacted by symbolically giving the keys of the kingdom to Peter, to be handed on down the line to all future popes. Nor does primatial power accrue to any pope simply by any other protocol of succession. "You ought to know," he warns Boniface, "that your power will be the less in the Lord's eyes, if you even think such a thing in your heart." What, then? "Power remains in your hands just so long as your principles remain sound; for he is the appointed key-bearer of the kingdom of heaven, who opens by true knowledge to the worthy and shuts to the unworthy; otherwise, if he does the opposite, he shall be able neither to open nor to shut." For, as he adds a little later, "it was his right confession that privileged even the holy bearer of the keys, the common teacher of us all" (Peter he means, the first pope). He is undoubtedly referring here to the powerful ideology of the *fir flathemon*, the truth, right and justice, ultimately of divine origin, by which alone kings can rule, so that, in a pre-Christian Irish ideology that in many ways parallels the wisdom theme in the OT while being in no way dependent upon it, the ruler who commits injustice is no longer king, and should no longer live. And that goes for popes as much, if not more than for any other constitutional ruler.

Nor does he stop there. His lecture on and to the papacy continues to cover in some detail those circumstances in which a pope fails in his duty to the truth. If a pope's witness to the fullness of truth he claims from Christ is found to confuse rather than enlighten and strengthen the faithful; and much more seriously, if it is found to be false, then those who have kept the true faith, whoever they may be, even though described as the pope's subordinates, will be "the head," and the pope's judge. For it is "the unity of faith in the whole world (that) has produced a unity of power and privilege, and in such wise that by all men everywhere freedom should be given to the truth, and the approach of error should be denied by all alike." Columbanus's vision of the church is more than conciliar; it is communitarian. And finally — there is no extant reply, but one can imagine Boniface reading this letter and wondering if this intractable Irishman is ever going to let up — he lectures the pope on admissible pluriformity, rather than a rigid uniformity, within the world-wide community of Christian believers. For there are more matters than just this one on the constitution of the church that must be allowed to form part of the rich variety of forms that the following of Jesus of Nazareth may take. And in the end, Columbanus simply reiterates the same criterion that Jesus urged people to use when trying to decide if a teaching or praxis of any kind, though different from the one other Christians adopt, is yet in accord or not in accord with the Spirit by which Jesus himself lived and died: by their fruits you shall know them. As Columbanus put it, the church should "contain us [who differ] side by side, whom the kingdom of heaven shall contain, *if our deserts are good*." Not a bad model at all, one might well argue, for an ecumenical movement that currently seems to be running into the sand, with the Rock of Peter still threatening some of the worst prospect of its eventual wreckage. True ecumenism must always involve the richness of that creativity that is necessary for construing all four main elements of religion in order to see the Spirit of Jesus best embodied through a changing world. True ecumenism must then begin by embracing the richness of that creativity that is already offered in the very variety of Christian churches. Further, it would seem that it is through the mechanism of a truly ecumenical, that it to say, world-wide council of churches that ecumenism can best and most effectively move toward its goal of the mutual inspiration and, where necessary, the mutual correction of these churches. Provided that that council is truly a forum for encounter in mutual love and respect, and not an instrument for the advancement of or toward one church in which the self-same credo, code, cult and constitution must be observed by all. There are better, more mutually beneficial, and certainly more mutually enriching ways for all followers of Jesus to be united in his Spirit and promise, than for all to belong to one, and only one, true church. Similarly, there should be no problem about Christians changing churches. In fact, it should be seen as a strict obligation, especially by Christians who have no intention of changing churches, to partake of the table of the Lord occasionally in churches other than their own, and otherwise to share in their prayer and praxis. That would be real ecumenism, rid at last of the unseemly jockeying for position for one's own leadership structures and constitution to which some current negotiations still seem to be increasingly narrowed.

Epilogue
CHRISTIANITY AND
OTHER RELIGIONS

The Essence of Christianity: The Covenant of Creation

The Bible makes one thing clear about the religion in which Jesus was born and died, and toward which he acted as the last in a long line of reforming prophets, the prophet of the end time, the final prophet, as his faithful followers saw it. The "new" covenant that he proclaimed, more, that he made real in act in all his living and in his very dying, its inner essence and its detailed terms, was in effect the oldest covenant of all. It was, and is, the covenant of creation. It was and is then a renewed covenant rather than a new covenant. It is new in the sense of something that had been badly damaged, and is now made new again, renewed from the human side of the covenant. From the divine side, as a testament, it had never changed, nor would it ever change. The eternal Creator Spirit in and through the very act of creation willed and wills existence and life to all creatures that are formed in the course of this continuous creativity. Further, in the very act of creating the things that are, by forming them rather than simply shouting them into existence, the Creator Spirit brings about forms of existence and life that are themselves creative forms. And never more so than in the case of the species of beings that rather fancies itself as far and away the most advanced species in the universe, *homo* as they call themselves *sapiens* or, as one sometimes finds the phrase, *homo sapiens sapiens*, in order to stress a point? (God help the universe if this is the wisest entity it has to boast about.)

In this way the Creator Spirit gifted this species, *homo sapiens*, not just with existence, and not just with life, but with the power of imagination and thought, and thus equipped them for a greater role in creatively advancing the creation, than that role which is both incumbent upon and enjoyed by any other species of which these doubly wise persons are currently cognizant. Not indeed that this pampered species is the only species, or even one in a select number of species that are endowed with creative powers and can therefore take their real if subordinate part in the continuous creation of the universe. All species, and all forms of things in the universe are endowed with forms that have within themselves a source of development (as Aristotle's definition of the term *nature,* or *physis,* so accurately observes). And in point of fact, it is through the patient creative labor of these other forms of existence and life in the world; it is through a process that science calls evolution or emergence, that these wise ones are brought into existence in space-time. A fact of the matter that seldom elicits much in the line of appreciation or gratitude (eucharist), but rather elicits much more in the line of a greedy and self-centered pillage that threatens to turn this almost immeasurably tiny part of the universe inhabited by these wise ones, this still patiently and creatively laboring earth, into a wasteland. The prospect has become real in our time, that a wasteland may soon not only cease to produce any more or more advanced species, but may fail to sustain all it has so far brought forth according to the franchise given it in the act of creation, in the words of Genesis, to bring forth living things.

Now the terms of the franchise given in the very act of their creation to all existing and living things, the mechanisms by which all of these can play their secondary but substantial, indeed essential part in the process of the continuous evolution/emergence of world(s), seem to involve something of the order of self-organizing structures, all of which obey the laws of physics and so on, but which nevertheless result in "that which is produced by a combination of causes, but cannot be regarded as the sum of their individual effects" (as the *Oxford Universal Dictionary* defines emergence). In the case of most of these creative forms (natures, *physeis*) it would seem that they are not themselves conscious of what they do or how they do it. Although some may be conscious of some of this in the form of the operations of instinct. In the case of humankind, however, and perhaps of some other "higher" species, there is not only an increasing awareness of one's own creative powers and of all the other co-operative powers in the world, there is also self-consciousness. So that one is not only aware of the responsibilities laid upon one in the very act of being created as a co-creator, and able to learn how to co-create for the mutual benefit of all creative creatures; one is also aware of being aware of this. And thereby one is free to act creatively or destructively, but not free with respect to taking the consequences of one's actions in either direction.

Human beings can therefore express the laws by which the co-creativity of the world proceeds in terms of (an also evolving) moral law. It is in this form that the terms of the covenant given in and with this most creative form of divine creation are expressed by human beings for human beings. Jesus gave expression to the terms of the covenant of creation in the paradigmatic Sermon on the Mount, and elsewhere of course in his teaching and debates about his conduct. He did so in clear opposition to terms that had been, or had become part of the Mosaic form of the covenant of creation, and for this eventually he was executed.

So the testament of creation becomes the covenant of creation as the bequest of existence and life unlimited empowers creatures, and thereby lays on them the responsibility to creatively advance existence and life. From the ongoing activity of creation therefore one can know what can be known in this life of the first source of existence, the Creator Spirit conventionally called God. One can know simultaneously as much as one's powers of thought and imagination can allow one to know of God's ways with the world. First, that apart from the first eternal creative initiative that sources all existence at its uttermost beginning, the Creator Spirit eternally pursues its creative act through the created creative forms of existence, and does so from the "moment" of their coming into being. And, second, that the creative activity that is pursued through their agency is itself an act of sharing out and advancing life and existence to and for others. From this, one can read off from the creation further terms of the covenant that now exists, just as Jesus did, and now in particular the terms of humanity's ways with the world and with God. The co-creative creature must be creative for the advancement of all, must share out life and the necessities and enhancements of life with all others as much as is possible and, especially in the case of fellow humans, quite irrespective of their deserts. Just as God sends life-giving light and heat and water, having the sun shine for the good and the bad, and the rain fall for the just and the unjust, so that good must be returned for evil, and never evil returned for evil suffered.

From the same testament-in-action, the eternal creation and advance of existence and life, one can read off also what might be called the negative terms of the resulting covenant of creation, the terms concerning destructive evil-doing or sin. For it is not difficult to see what the creation myth in Genesis did not fail to include in its account. Namely, that it is the very high degree of humanity's wisdom and power of co-creativity that forges for that so self-admired species its perennial temptation to act as the sole supreme guarantor and enhancer of life for itself, whatever the different, more concrete circumstances that might trigger the fall into that temptation on individual occasions. And the consequences of that fall, as constant as human culture itself, are even more easily read off from the sorry suffering history of the depredations wreaked by that race on itself and on its planet world. Breaking that term of the creation covenant that requires all to give life as they have received it and continue to receive it from others, and that requires of all in consequence that they be prepared to go through loss for the sake of the advancement of life for others and for themselves, this fall always consists in the aggrandizement, indeed the idolatry of the human self, individual or group. And it always results also in the inevitable deprivation of life for the others involved, a deprivation well beyond what can be joyfully accepted in the course of freely serving to each other life with all of its supports and enhancements.

The nature of salvation from this sin, the mother of all sin, can also be read off from the ongoing activity of divine creation. It cannot consist in serving up to the perpetrators a punishment that fits the crime in some crude like-and-equal fashion, as in the *lex talionis*. For that simply spreads destruction and death ever wider where creativity and life alone should be in force, and where only such death to previous forms of life as life's advance of itself demands should be required. God, according to the Bible, takes part of the blame for empowering people who have suffered death and deprivation to destroy the grandeur and the lives of those who aggrandize themselves at the expense of others, and seeks to neutralize part of the blame taken, by presenting the matter under the heading of teaching to all a good, corrective lesson. Yet, Jesus is adamant, salvation is nowhere to be found as yet in the course of such a response. A wider view of the divine activity of continuous creation must notice that the God who brings enemies to destroy the self-aggrandizer, always also at the very same time offers the largesse of creation, life and life ever more abundant, equally to all, evil doers and correctors alike. True salvation from this sin then, as Jesus illustrated in his doings as much as in his preaching, consists in assuaging the hunger and thirst and healing the wounds of body and spirit, for both perpetrators and victims of this original sinfulness. And then this salvation is in itself a kind of forgiveness that quickly outpaces the declaration, worthy in itself, of putting out of mind without more ado the offense suffered. It is a creative kind of forgiveness that puts life and the limitless promise of life at the forefront of the human agenda once more, as it appears to be the exclusive agenda of the divine. What God does in order to salve is no different from what God does in order to create: God gives and advances life for all, through the creative co-operation of all, and when testament becomes covenant, that is how human beings must behave also.

That then is the covenant between God and creature that can be read off from the ongoing activity of divine-through-creaturely creation. The covenant, like the testament on which it is based, can be characterized in its essence and in its terms as a covenant of steadfast love. That love, as the term *steadfast* implies, includes fidelity or faith, and hope or trust. From God's side, from the point of view of testament, the love exhibits faith or fidelity in face of all infidelities from the other side. And, yes, it implies hope and trust on the part of God that those equipped with the abilities and responsibilities of co-creating will always act to enhance rather than diminish or destroy the lives of others, the hope and trust that they will not turn satanic. From the human side and from the point of view of covenant, the corresponding love equally involves faith or fidelity in face of all the self-inflicted or other-engendered set-backs to life's advance, as well as a hope and trust in other creaturely co-creators of life. But most of all it involves a hope and trust in the continuous creativity of the Creator Spirit who works through all. Particularly in those cruelest of conditions in which deprivation and perhaps death is threatened by the evil-doer, it is necessary that whatever love has grown in the heart as a result of God's gifts of life through others, should enable the threatened one to keep faith with, to trust in the eternal giver of life to all, and to hope for life then, beyond all present threat and through all destructive experience.

Now that trust and hope can come to that high point of intensity before the threat of death itself, only if all the days and nights of ordinary living have proved to be a training ground for trusting and hoping in the eternal Creator Spirit, by the giving of lives and livelihoods to others out of that same love that is shared with the Creator Spirit who breathes it through all of our lives and deaths. For just as the Creator Spirit shows that love with its faith and hope in the continuous activity of the creation of life, a continuous creative activity that always creates through the creature, so the corresponding covenant love with its faith and hope from the human side, can be shown to God only through the expensive activity of human creativity directed to and through the fellow-creature. As God creates through other creatures, there is no loving of God except through the love of other creatures, expressed in the form of the highest creativity that can be mustered for the benefit of all. Those who urge people to love their neighbor for God's sake are so far mistaken as to have turned the matter entirely on its head. Besides which it is demeaning to anyone to be told that she can be loved only for someone else's sake, even God's.

As for the case of those Christians who permit themselves a gentle boast by quoting a remark made by outsiders, "see how these Christians love *one another;*" one can only ask, is there no limit to the extent to which they can get the message of Jesus wrong? As the author of the First Epistle of John puts the matter, rather bluntly, "If anyone says, 'I love God' and hates his brother, he is a liar; for he who does not love his brother whom he has seen, cannot love God whom he has not seen" (1 John 4:20). "Love must be made real in act," as the poet put it, but you cannot do any good directly to God. You can only fulfill your part of the covenant of creation by acting creatively for the good of other creatures. Jesus in the judgment scene he painted repeats the phrase "as long as you did it to one of these brothers, you did it to me." And who is brother, who is neighbor? Just one's fellow Christians? Hardly. Whoever is in need, even if it is the enemy who comes to pillage and kill, for that latter is the one most in need of the benefits of creativity that are then a form of creative forgiveness, the most costly and the highest form of love.

This covenant of creation, restored to its pristine purity by Jesus in his teaching, his life's work and his death, is faithfully caught in the earliest forms of credo, code, cult and constitution. The terms of the code that goes with this creation covenant are summarized in the Sermon on the Mount, and summarized much more crudely above. The earliest credo, known as the Apostles' Creed, begins with an expression of faith in one God, the Father Almighty, Creator of heaven and earth, and ends with faith in the Holy (Creator) Spirit and the hope of life everlasting. As far as the earliest "constitution" is concerned, it appears to consist in a community that at first "held all things in common," a kind of commune, served by those who could best minister to its needs and to its missionary obligations, as Paul lists these, and in its more purely administrative functions served by those who would genuinely serve it in both respects, and not attempt to "make their authority felt," as would happen later with those long lines of reverends, lordships, eminences, holinesses and other such titles for supreme potentates on earth, vicars, as they would have it, of the supreme potentate in heaven.

In the case of the cult, Jesus himself formulated the paradigmatic prayer, and he chose a eucharistic meal as the only sacramental ritual (other than the washing of feet, perhaps) for which we can be sure of his own personal endorsement. The Lord's prayer, the "Our Father," asks simply for the reign of God in our lives, and that is equivalent to a prayer that we be able to uphold our side of the covenant of creation. The eucharistic meal, finally, is a sacrament of creation. That is clear from the central appearance of the symbolism of the meal in the Wisdom tradition of creation imagery and theology. Food and drink, symbolizing the source and staff of life, explicitly accepted from the Creator Spirit who is ultimate source of all life and who is acknowledged, blessed for that. Food and drink to which human co-creativity has contributed, for it thereby symbolizes the manner and extent to which we procreate life for each other in co-operation with the Creator Spirit. Food and drink now divided and broken out to others in symbolic commitment to continue, each and every one, to give of our lives for each other, thereby living and dying under the rule of the Creator Spirit, and becoming again and again the channels of the steadfast love that rules the whole of creation.

Christianity and Religion

The twin biblical records of testament and covenant (the OT or Original Testament and the rNT, the renewed Testament) provide the most prominent headings under which to organize the story of the tradition of a faith that spans the religions of Judaism and Christianity. This is the case not because that imagery of testament-covenant is so very frequently in use in the Bible. For compared to the imagery of divine creation, for example, which is so frequently in evidence over the whole of the Bible from beginning to end, the imagery of testament-covenant is very infrequent indeed. Yet that latter imagery does occur at crucial stages of the story of this particular tradition of faith. It occurs when the story wishes to point to a founding prophet, Moses. It occurs when subsequent prophets complain about the breaking of the founding covenant of the religion of Israel, as a means of explaining the miseries that have befallen those on the human side of the covenant. Yet these same prophets unfailingly give God's word that God's steadfast love will renew the covenant for those who wish to return to that love and to the forms of faith, fidelity, hope and trust it both engenders and requires. It occurs at the moment when the prophet, Jesus of Nazareth, is about to seal his life's commitment to the terms of that covenant that God still offers, by shedding his blood in final fidelity to that living faith that co-creates life for others rather than ever attempt to kill them.

The testament-covenant imagery is also made prominent, of course, in the course of the convention adopted by Christians for the naming of the two parts of their Bible. The part that Christians took over from the Jews they called the Old Testament. And the part that these Christians added in order to form their full Bible from the gradually selected documents such as Gospels and letters for the purpose of witnessing to the faith of Jesus, they called the New Testament. Yet even all of this prominence might fail to convince some scholars of the truth of the claim that testament-covenant imagery provides the best heading under which to organize the story of the tradition of a faith that spans the religions of Judaism and Christianity. Unless of course they realize that the covenant in question, and in all biblical versions of it — whether initiated, promised, or corrected and renewed — is a covenant of creation. That is to say, it is a testament that is operative in the bequest of existence and life itself, and a covenant that is entailed in the creation of creatures that are themselves creative. The covenant is initiated by the One Who Causes To Be, with those who have the freedom and responsibility to advance or oppose that project, from which God in Exodus is named. Hence wherever the creation theme occurs in the Bible, as it does from beginning to end, the testament-covenant imagery is also implicitly present in the argument of the relevant piece. To take one large example from matters already mentioned: in the rNT that which results from the life and death of Jesus is called a new creation. That means that salvation in fact is an ever-new or renewed creation, that Jesus, He Who Saves, is the creative channel for the continuous creation of life and life more abundant by the Eternal One Who Causes To Be.

It is because of its inherent and constitutive imagery of divine creation then that testament-covenant imagery can best be used to organize the story of a faith that made its way from the religion of Israel to the religion that later emerged as another fully formed religion called Christianity. And that fact of itself raises some extremely serious questions for the Jewish and Christian religions. And for Islam also most probably, a religion that originated, in part at least, from perceptions of the failures, often self-advertised failures of the religions of Israel and Christianity. Failures to live up to the promises and responsibilities of the true reign of God as that had been truly revealed to them. When one is trained to see in the image or idea of divine creation an account of nothing more than the first instant of the coming-into-being of the universe, one may well fail to see that same image or idea of divine creation elsewhere and in a much more expansive role in the rest of the Bible. One sees what one expects to see, and one frequently fails to see what one does not expect to see, even when one is looking at it. So that, having been alerted somehow to the continuing centrality of the image of divine creation throughout the whole story of the Bible from origin to eschaton, one is then less surprised to see almost as frequent a role for this foundational image throughout the *Holy Qur'an*. And when one begins to see all of this one may then be open to the idea that this primacy of divine creation imagery in the faith that moves from Judaism to Christianity to Islam, may raise the same or similarly serious questions for other religions also. What questions are those, then?

Too peremptorily put perhaps, and collapsed into one most radical question, these questions boil down to this one: if the relationship between God and creation, and especially with humanity, together with the terms under which these relationships can result in the most permanently and fully blessed of destinies, can be known from the continuous creation itself, is there any need for institutional religion at all? Put like that, the question may indeed appear too blunt and too radical by half. Yet it surely gains some legitimacy for Christians at least, from the rather fulsome condemnations, seeming at times to amount to dismissals, to which Jesus treated major elements of his own religion in his time. The question gains some further legitimacy from the uncertainties, to put it at its best, that surround every effort to give details of Jesus allegedly founding a new religion. And the question gains some final legitimacy from the list of things contrary to the faith of Jesus that now characterize the Christian religion, as seen in the revisiting of Christianity so far accomplished in this book. That list could be quite easily lengthened.

It does seem difficult to exaggerate the degree to which Jesus approached dismissal in his critique of the chief institutions of his religion as these were conceived and operative in his time. The principal institution of his religion, covering the cult and the constitutional leadership, consisted in the Jerusalem temple and its priesthood. Jesus did apparently adopt a familiar prophetic attitude to the cult, to the effect that God preferred steadfast love to cultic sacrifice. But that is compatible with seeking to reform temple cult and priesthood, something that, as it is recorded, he also tried to do on at least one occasion. However, at times his attitude to the temple and its priesthood seemed to go beyond attempted reform of its self-conception and its *modus operandi*. He is remembered to have suggested that if, or when the temple came down, it could be replaced, and not by another temple. And that true worshipers could worship, not in any particular religion's temples, but in spirit and in truth, in the wide and capacious house of all creation. As Stephen, who also fell foul of the temple priesthood, apparently took Jesus to have taught. Together with the priests, Jesus criticized the scribes, the scholars and teachers of his religion. But there again he was not satisfied, apparently, to stop at arguing them into a reformation of what they were teaching about God and God's reign and rule.

Rather did he gather to himself an inner group of his first followers — at one stage they were numbered at seventy-two — and commissioned them to go and preach the good news of the true reign of God. And he appears to have chosen from among his followers a smaller group, entitled the Twelve, with Peter at their head, who would lead this mission into the future. Taken from among all those that Jesus himself, and they and the others he commissioned could make into disciples, the Twelve would continue into the future to symbolize Israel of the twelve traditional tribes. For Jesus in his life-time appears to have been convinced that "salvation is of the Jews." In other words, the good news was indeed good news intended for all by God the creator of all. But it was his own people's privilege to have been chosen for the particular responsibility of shining the light of that truth to the nations of the world. Jesus does appear to have hoped that his people would be converted again to this mission of theirs by his disciples, with just this one leadership structure of the Twelve, with or without temple or priests, or the institutionalized teachers, "the scribes of the Pharisees," or of any other faction. This people with just this leadership structure for the purpose of preaching by behavior and word this credo of God the creator, healer and Father of all, and this code of the mutual creative provision of life by all for all, would be all the institution that would then be necessary for the expansion of the true reign of God. Jesus also used the natural sacramentality of the meal as a ritual access to the experience of the reign of God and the inspiration to live by the Creator Spirit that reigns in all of creation. But his purpose at this point, as his practice shows, could be accomplished either by use of some existing cultic meal, or simply at any otherwise ordinary meal.

There is not a lot in all of that to show that Jesus depended upon a fully institutionalized religion, either the one into which he was born and could succeed in reforming for the task, or one he would himself institute for the purpose, to spread to all the reign of God that he made real in all of his life and death. And some Christian theologians, like Barth and Bonhoeffer, have before this suspected that Christianity in origin is not really a religion at all, but rather a faith. So then, should the faith of Jesus ever have been turned into such a fully fledged institutional religion as happened in the course of its history? It does seem that the process of forming a fully established religion, boasting its own credo, code, cult and constitution is all too often accompanied by the temptation to then believe that God has given over into the care and responsibility of a particular person and/or group of people the grace, and the truth about that grace, by which God is to be truly known and by which they and the rest of human kind are to be brought to the fulfillment of eternal life. That conviction is usually expressed in the course of what has been called above a franchise theology. And it seems so often to be characterized by an unacceptable degree of exclusivism. There is a tolerable of degree of exclusivism that can be connected to a verifiable claim that the grace and truth that God makes available equally to all, seems to be made especially available to certain individuals or groups. But only for the purpose of opening the eyes of others to that grace and truth that is there for all to see, and to which they have been blinded in one way or another. However, to go beyond that is to risk an intolerable exclusivism that pictures God as first and foremost the God of this privileged group, *their* God, and the God of the others effectively only through them. Jesus and his faithful followers lambasted the religious establishment of the Jerusalem temple in particular for their subscription to that particular conceit, that intolerable form of exclusivism, just as they themselves hoped to convert their people to the preaching of God the creative Father of all, who was always accessible to all in the house of the creation that God shared with all.

Yet the followers of Jesus themselves soon enough seem to have managed to convince themselves that the fullness of grace and truth that was especially revealed in the life, death and destiny of Jesus of Nazareth, was now entrusted by God exclusively to them, and even more exclusively still to their institutional leaders. And they thereby set about excluding from God's saving grace and truth all but those who would join their religion, which they by then had rather fully established in the Roman Empire and its subsequent patchwork of kingdoms. They even, indeed especially excluded the Jews, not quite seeing that in this they were simply rejecting in others precisely what they were now practicing on their own account. At the base and foundation of this kind of exclusivism lies a certain view of truth and grace, a view of these that is quickly caught by the term *supernatural*. The tolerable exclusivism of the one especially chosen is turned into the intolerable exclusivism of certain religions, precisely by the conceit — of which the select ones themselves are seldom guilty — that the truth in question must be especially revealed because it is beyond the bounds of nature and particularly of human nature to embody, acquire or transmit. And the grace or gift of God is equally beyond the bounds of nature to receive or transmit. Hence the enormous stress on the term *supernatural* by religions themselves, and then not surprisingly by outsiders who are sometimes tempted to inspect or even sample their wares. Hence also these dichotomies between supernatural divine revelation and what can be achieved by human reason and imagination, and between supernatural grace from God, and nature as we otherwise know it. So it is to the dichotomy between revelation (and faith), on the one hand, and reason (and imagination and so on), on the other, and to the dichotomy between nature and grace, that some critical attention must turn, if the issue of different faiths and religions is ever to be successfully resolved.

The Nature of Grace

However it all came about, and however long ago it began to come about, religion nowadays and normally is set down securely upon the territory of the sacred, the other-worldly, the supernatural. It is then separated from the profane, the secular, the natural by a well-defined border. A border anxiously policed and well defended on both sides, from any who would either seek to ignore it or, much more seriously, who would seek to annex some or all of the territory on the other side. Yet if the account of the faith of Jesus already given is at all true and fair, if the foundational status of the covenant of creation survived through the prophetic changes he made to his own Jewish religion, then there would appear to be no basis in history or in fact for any dichotomous distinction between nature and divine grace. Not even the level of distinction envisaged in some Catholic theologies that talk of grace perfecting nature or, like Rahner, of nature representing no more than a "remainder concept" of what would be left over if God's still supernatural grace were to be, quite impossibly, subtracted from the history of the natural world, and particularly from the history of human nature as we know it.

Take the word *grace* to mean initially at least a gift or favor freely given. Then existence, life itself, is God's foundational favor, the fundamental and formative free gift from the Eternal One. And that primordial, everlasting gift includes all the affordances and enablements that are necessary for the existing world to continue to emerge in the course of what is called evolution, according to the "laws" of evolution and in particular, among these, according to the "law" of new life ever emerging from the death of its older forms. From the point of view of one living species in particular, *homo sapiens*, thus enabled to evolve to the highest level yet known of reflective self-consciousness, this grace or gifting by God involves above all the gift of wisdom, which is the gift of creativity in its highest form and, in consequence, the gift of the highest known form of freedom as to the manner in which this species will continue the creative task of all creatively formed creatures, or indeed as to the choice of whether it will co-create or turn satanic and destroy.

The grace of wisdom (*sapientia*) comes to humans (*homo sapiens*) in particular and that enables us not only to know the ways of the world, but to do this through working with these ways, thus envisaging how these ways can be developed to the point of bettering ourselves and our fellow creatures. That enlightenment that comes to us from the Creator Spirit or Word, as John the evangelist put it, enlightens everyone in the world. That self-same gift of wisdom can be broken down into constitutive gifts according to categories of the kind that Paul, for example, lists for his converts at Corinth. The gift of wisdom itself comes first, then more particular constitutive parts of that comprehensive gift: the gift of knowledge (*scientia*), which in the old world would correspond to something like today's science (historical, human, social, as well as the more physical sciences), the general gift of knowing how the world works as a necessary part of knowing how to work with it. The gift of prophecy, of being capable of speaking the right word to one's time and circumstance. The right word being that which embodies the Creative Word for that particular time and circumstance. The gift of discernment of spirits, of distinguishing in effect whether the spirit that moves people to co-create is truly the Creator Spirit, or some other, adversarial or satanic spirit (remember Jesus and his opponents taking dramatically opposite views on this subject). The gift of healing, of salving.

Practical gifts, such as the gift of being ministers and administrators in the government of human communities, bring to mind the fact that wisdom, the mother gift, comes with her more practical as well as her more theoretical offspring, the cardinal virtues. Prudence is the name for the gift of making the right practical judgment in the most concrete of circumstances; justice the gift of knowing how to act so as to co-create for others, as well as for oneself; temperance the gift of knowing how to control one's desire to have life and its affordances to excess and at the inevitable expense of others; and fortitude is the gift of the courage that enables us to practice, through the suffering of the inevitable diminishment involved, the virtues of temperance and justice. So all of these virtues we learn and acquire from the wisdom that is gifted to us in God's gracious activity of continuous creation.

Finally, love comes to us, embodied and inspiring, made real in that same original and eternal gift of the creation of life and its perfection in eternal *shalom*. For God has no ulterior motive in creation, nothing more than the love of the goodness, truth and beauty of the resultant creatures. And that love comes with its natural born children also; its steadfastness, that is to say, its fidelity or keeping faith, and the hope it engenders in the hearts of giver and receiver alike. Love draws a corresponding response from those it makes and moves, to love all God loves in the course of creating, and through them, and only through them, to love God the creator, both in the most practical of ways (1 Cor. 12:8–11; 27–31; 13).

The so-called supernatural virtues then are as natural as any of the other things that make up the category of divine grace. So there is no special kind of supernatural stuff that is infused upon or into our human natures in order to raise these to a supernatural level, to empower these natures with supernatural "faculties," or to impel them to particular good choices and actions. All that counts as divine grace, from life itself to the latest good and gracious act that anyone has performed, as Pelagius tried to explain, is the love of God, or God's indwelling Spirit made real in God's eternal act of the creation of life, and life ever more abundant. Undoubtedly that divine grace, at least in some or other of its embodiments and manifestations, is not received always and in the same degree by all human beings. Indeed some of the rarest individuals in human history exhibit such degrees of wisdom and steadfast love that they are recognized and received as founders of faiths. But in general all of these graces of the Creator Spirit are delivered alike to all, to the just and the unjust; for they are delivered in and by the foundational activity of continuous divine creation that includes all of the affordances and enablements of existence and life.

This kind of creation theology of grace can be derived as easily from pre-Christian Irish religion, as it could no doubt be derived from other so-called primal religions, and as it has been seen to be derived from the Original Testament that records the earlier religion of Israel. In old

Irish religion the principal gods are all creators of the world, making the primeval flood depths recede from the land, clearing the wilderness and bringing forth springs to fertilize the land, and so on. And they are also saviors, restoring peace and harmony and prosperity, in particular after the ravages of war, like Lug does, after the theomachy known as the Battle of Mag Tuired. They appoint kings on earth, who are then united with the creator God, now in the persona of the Sovereignty goddess, and who thereby rule the world wisely for prosperity and peace for all. The ethic of responsibility that flows to human beings with this comprehensive grace, and that emerges through the final practical reaches of that grace as wisdom, is summarized in this catchy triplet, attributed to the divine persona of Fionn:

> *Ceart 'nar gcroidhe*
> *Neart 'nar ngeag*
> *Agus beart do reir ar mbriathair*

(truth, right in our hearts; strength in our limbs; and the accordance of our deeds with our words — words which speak to each circumstance the truth and right that is in our hearts, so that this first ethical principle forms a full circle, a wheel of life that we can drive forward to life's fullest and happiest realization). In fact, when Christianity came to Ireland with all of its talk of grace, the Irish did transliterate the Latin, *gratia,* as *gras* or *grasta.* But they did also use to translate the term *grace* a traditional Irish term, *rath.* This refers to a free gift, of cattle for example, to a young man seeking to establish himself independently in society, with the expectation that he will work with that gift in order to develop into a self-supporting family unit that will later become a net contributor to other members of that society. A very apt and suitable term for God's grace of life-and-wisdom, to be developed by each for life more abundant for all.

All of this, of course, might well be criticized on the grounds that it paints the kind of far-too-cozy picture that is sometimes painted in the new theologies of grace: all is grace in this world, and all manner of things are graces, and there is nothing that is or that God does that cannot be counted as grace. But that is clearly not the case, and neither is it a fair and proper assessment of the comprehensive Christian theology of creation here set out and adopted. For God, it has been explicitly allowed, is equally complicit in the diminution and destruction of life in which creatures constantly engage each other, and none more so than *homo sapiens.* As God is also complicit in humanity's positively creative and responsible endeavors.

God is the ultimately creative source of the evils that human beings bring upon themselves in the course of their continual efforts at selfish aggrandizement. "Because you consider yourself as wise as a god. . . . *I* will bring strangers upon you, the most terrible of nations, and they shall draw their swords against the beauty of your wisdom and defile your splendor." God is the ultimately creative source of the evils that they suffer in the normal course of living by each other's gifts of the necessities of life. God is the ultimately creative source of the even more normal course of humans living as material creatures in space-time, and therefore of the final mortality of their current forms. And although the latter two instances of God's complicity in the diminution and destruction of life may be acceptable on the grounds that each is part and parcel of life's ever upward élan, both instances nevertheless share with the first instance the absence of qualification for any simple inclusion in the category of grace. For even if examples of the first class of instance can sometimes act as a corrective and therefore be deemed a grace of sorts, in our experience the suffering and deprivation brought upon us by the evil-doing of our own kind very seldom does act as any kind of future deterrent against repeated evil-doing. Rather does that experience of suffering and deprivation join the other instances of more natural deprivation and suffering, in that these also often become part causes of our resorting to the original temptation to secure our lives at whatever cost to others, and the vicious circle of evil rolls on its miserable way once more.

No, all is not grace. Far from it; and our hope then rests ultimately on the eternal grace that is the infinite largesse of life flowing from the steadfast love of the immortal Creator Spirit. Aided perhaps also by the hope that the dark, despairing death we face, all the darker and more despairing the more we diminish the lives of others in a hopeless attempt to secure our own, will prove to be sufficient punishment for and correction of the evil we have done to others and to ourselves. Or perhaps we can hope that as we pass over to the life of a spiritual body, as Paul called it, and come nearer to God, we shall all be able both to give and receive from each other that creative forgiveness, that returning of good for evil, that so often escaped our abilities and even our intentions here in this current bodily form. There are faiths that envisage our spirits returning to current earthly forms until they have purified themselves of evil sufficiently to enable them to participate in eternal happiness. Christianity too, in some of its versions, envisages a kind of purgatorial in-between world in after-life. All such speculations are either of equal value or of no value at all. There is no way of knowing for certain; eye has not seen nor ear heard. But the hope is there in the experience of the steadfast love of the Immortal Creator that the grace of creation must triumph in the end for all.

So the whole of natural existence and life is not grace. Nevertheless the term grace always does refer to natural life and existence, seen as a gift from the Creator Spirit, and most especially when it reaches the status of eternal life. Is there any room at all then for the term supernatural, and for any distinction between natural and supernatural? Given all that has just been said, there is this answer to that question: there is an optional use of the term and the distinction, but there is no etymological or logical necessity to use either of these. Aristotle's definition of nature, *physis*, best explains the matter: a form (of existence) that has within itself the source of its own movement, change, development. In the sense that the Creator Spirit is not a formed entity; it is not a nature, or a natural thing, for form, shape, outline, entail limit, and the creation of all actual and possible entities, and more specifically the creation of creative entities, cannot be attributed to a being that is itself limited. Since the limits of an entity are also the limitations on its powers of production. So one could say that the Creator Spirit is supernatural, in order to indicate that it is not one formed entity, not one thing among others. It escapes the category of the formed, and to be formed is part of the definition of a nature, or nature. But in this usage of it the term *supernatural* would have to be reserved for the ultimate Creator of all, and it could not be extended to any of the gifts of the Creator Spirit, all of which are formed, themselves creative, but derivatively creative, and therefore always natural.

Yet that usage of the terminology of the supernatural, together with its distinction between natural and supernatural, must always be considered to be at best optional. The great Irish theologian, John Scotus Eriugena, entitled his own major work *Periphyseon*, in Latin, *De Divisione Naturae;* because according to his usage of the term *nature* (*physis, natura*) was capable of a range of reference that covered everything from the Creator to the limits of the material world. And that also is a defensible usage of the terminology, if only because, although the Creator lacks one element in Aristotle's definition of nature (form, limit), the other element of the definition is present and indeed characteristic par excellence of the Creator: the element of being the source of the movement, change, development of all thereby formed, created things. This is a usage of the term *nature* that stretches its analogical meaning all the way toward reference to a God beyond all limited human comprehension. For in this usage of the terminology in question, the distinction between Creator and creatures is not indicated in any differentiation introduced within the language of nature — all is nature and natural — but rather by a differentiation such as that between the infinite, unformed, and the formed and therefore limited, within the overarching category of nature, *natura, physis*. Spinoza's *Deus sive Natura* can provide us with another version of this usage of the terminology of nature. As can the Stoic theology that Christians borrowed wholesale instead of developing their own. For in both of these philosophical theologies also the Creator is entirely immanent in the creation, yet always transcendent also as the self-same Creator ever and ultimately sources all of the world's existence, activity and life in a manner that enables it to transcend its serial stages. And no, this has nothing to do with pantheism, even if it is sometimes called by the rather similar name of panentheism (within everything). There is no logical connection between saying that the Creative Source forms everything from within, and saying that the entities thus formed are nothing other than the Creator Spirit itself.

Revelation: Faith and Reason

What now of reason and revelation? These frequently twinned terms normally suffer the same fate as nature and grace. They become divided by a well-patrolled border that ensures as clear-cut a separation of territories as that between nature and grace. That border remains a deterrent to any common ground that reason and revelation might hope to occupy. For some who deal in reason declare that, at best, reason does nothing to support religious commitment, if not that reason positively destroys any pretensions concerning revelations of the divine that superstitious people might entertain. Then there are some who insist that reasoning can lead an inquiring mind across its own territory and up to the aforesaid border, and can then help the enquirer onto the wall at a point at which the inquirer can jump, if she wishes, onto the territory in which divine revelation can be closely encountered. Yet even they are then likely to caution the inquirer to the effect that, as the grace that saves and that promises eternal life is of the supernatural rather than the natural order, its very existence is concealed from natural imaginative reason and from all of its investigative and visionary powers. So that one must still leave reason on its own side of the border beyond which it hinted one might have a happy encounter with the divine. Having leaped over the wall — and that is a leap into the unknown as far as reason is concerned — these religious adventurers must realize that they have left behind the territory of nature and reason. They must hitherto keep to the territory of the supernatural, and of the correspondingly supernatural revelation of the ways of God with the world, and of the way of the world back to God.

The resulting dichotomous distinction between reason and revelation is then sought to be copper-fastened by linkage of revelation with faith, and not with reason. But not now with faith as we have recently seen it, not with faith as a keeping faith with, an entrusting to all that we can see in the world of the Creator's most promising grace of a good life to be made ever better. The faith that is contrasted with reason is faith as blind and obedient assent of mind and heart to whatever has been supernaturally said to us, in whatever miraculous manner it is thought to have been revealed. So that, even in that last version offered above of their territories and affairs, reason and revelation must emerge as a kind of doppelgänger dichotomy entirely corresponding to that of nature and grace, in the form of that latter that has just been subjected to critical examination. But then, as the dichotomy of nature and grace disappears with the critical realization that grace refers to the freely given ambience of all that is positive and promising about the very existence and life of the natural world, and of that world alone and in its entirety, so does the coincident border between reason and revelation, as that is so commonly construed, disintegrate before one's eyes. Like the fall of the Berlin wall, in more ways than one.

For one thing, and quite to the contrary of the usage of reason and revelation exhibited by the anxious guardians of a non-existent border between them, the self-revelation of reality is always and at all levels of perception and knowledge, a prior condition to anything that reason can do about it. First, reason as imagination. It is suggested that the term *intellect* (from *intus legere*, to read into, to see into) can as easily indicate imagination. We attend to, we contemplate the images that the world continuously unveils, that is to say, reveals for us. We note that they are images of evolving, creative reality, so that we simultaneously try to envisage through these moving images how things could receive our own creative input, and all advance together. Then, reason as reasoning or more abstract logic. We do the same kind of thing, except we now abstract certain features of the rich and concrete reality that is unveiling itself to us in images. And we endeavor to combine these abstractions creatively also, according to the logic of development they already reveal. And we do this, once again, in order to advance that development by our own contribution, or at least to reverse its failures and setbacks, as when we find ways to cure disease. And in all of this faith and hope is naturally evoked and heavily involved. Faith, trust in the world that is revealing itself as one works with it, in the multiple sense of faith in the world's life-giving, life-sustaining, life-evolving features, features that we share with the world and with all that operates upon us and with us within it. But faith also in the truth of the revelation of these co-operative entities, and in our true, if always improvable apprehensions of them. And, thirdly, fidelity to the joint project in which we are involved with the whole reality of and within our universe; and the love even, and the hope that all of this experience both inspires and elicits in return. Therefore, reason and revelation, far from relating to separate regions of reality divided by some permanent border, relate together to one and the same region of reality, indeed to the whole of reality, comprising also what some describe as the supernatural.

Mention of the supernatural once more copper-fastens the insight to the effect that the false dichotomy between reason and revelation usually has a doppelgänger, another false dichotomy, this time between natural and supernatural. And that these two find their mirror image, if not their formative cause in yet another false dichotomy: that between immanence and transcendence. This last dichotomy relies on the image of a border or, better, "an infinite qualitative distance" between, on the one hand, God as a supernatural being and God's supernatural gifts for eternal life, and the supernatural knowledge of these, and on the other hand, natural life in the natural world together with our natural knowledge of it. The addition of the adjective *qualitative* to the distance across the chasm that is imagined to separate Creator and creation, is designed to neutralize the otherwise crudifying effect of a spatial version of that distance. Yet in actual operation, and especially when glossed with references to being "outside of," or "beyond" the created universe, that imagery of distance-transcendence introduces surreptitiously once more the cruder spatial elements that proponents of the idea of infinite qualitative difference try so hard to avoid. The image or idea of being outside of or beyond space-time does not really make any literal sense. So that it is more than defensible to say that the divine Creator eternally transcends from within, the world that is thereby continuously created, and that this Creator can therefore be known to do so, as part and parcel of that natural knowledge that relies upon the natural revelation of all the realities that are operative within the same natural world. When saying that divinity is transcendent — for, as Feuerbach established at the beginning of *The Essence of Christianity*, the human spirit also enjoys a capacity for transcendence — one is using the terms of transcendence and immanence as co-ordinates rather than contraries, and the false dichotomy between immanence and transcendence disappears. We transcend the world from within it, by acting creatively for our own evolution and that of the whole world. Divinity can also be said to transcend from within us and our world, by continuous creation, but since God creates the world by forming creative forms, God eternally transcends from within both us and our whole world, all that is or ever will be in and of it.

Investigation, contemplation of our world, with its claims and counter-claims concerning encounter with God, is constantly be-deviled by the active presence, often implicit, of these false dichotomies between reason and revelation, natural and supernatural, immanence and transcendence. Take philosophy first, and much if not most of what passes for philosophy of religion: proofs and disproofs of God's existence, and the question of miracles. Both proofs and disproofs of God's existence do really disqualify themselves from serious rational consideration in so far as they regularly take themselves to be discussing a god who exists outside the universe, who acted on one occasion to put the universe there, and who is then said by religious people to return on other occasions in order to interfere with, or to set aside, its natural processes. Set up on such implicit assumptions then, both proofs and disproofs are inevitably guilty of the following logical oddity. One first defines the kind of entity a god must be, and then sets out to prove, or to disprove, the existence of this god. Seldom does anyone engaged in this very odd procedure pause for a moment to ask the most obvious question. If we had never in our time and world encountered this being that could be called god, how could we even begin to describe, much less define it? And if we had encountered it, what would be the point of this whole elaborate exercise of seeking to prove its existence? Philosophers of course might answer: we simply took over these alleged proofs from religious folk and dealt them a dose of our own fine critical acumen. To which the only relevant response must be: no excuse; your own fine critical acumen should have been first to tell you that you should not take over for such lengthy, persistent, and entirely odd logical treatment any description of an entity that you cannot naturally encounter.

Miracles then are treated in philosophy of religion as instances of by-passing, if not defying natural agencies and processes and the scientific laws which govern these. But to treat miracles like this is to treat them as instances of contributory proofs of a previously defined divinity. And apart altogether from the fact that the so-called miracle stories in the Bible are never used in this manner; the same logical objection applies as apply in the case of the so-called proofs.

For the consciousness, the knowledge of the existence of any entity, created or divine, must be a case of encounter with a power, a creative presence, and not a case of proof of something habitually absent, or else-where at least at the time of the inquiry. And if the God question really does come down to a case of encounter, then surely that question must be allowed to fall within the concerns of those whose profession and privilege it is to actively engage with, and to contemplate and query all of the creative-evolutionary agencies that operate within the world, their genera and species, and all of their modi operandi. The God question must fall, that is to say, within the remit of the scientists. Indeed, even since the coming of the age of science in the modern era, some scientists do profess to see in the natural world, as they actively investigate in increasing depth its universal processes, traces of the power and presence of a divine creator. Many others, however, contemplating these same deep and universal features of the universe, say they see no divine creative power and presence, merely a most remarkable and, yes, a most mysterious universe still, but a universe that shows every possible sign of being a self-made, self-making totality.

A common scientific view of the origin and existence of all that now comprises the universe is roughly as follows: At Planck time 10^{-43} seconds into the Big Bang our universe emerged, from a state of complete disorder. Emergence, already noted, refers to a process of truly creative evolution by which unpredictable, irreducible, in short, truly novel elements and features of the cosmos appear. These are then said to be brought about by structures that self-organize in accordance with the laws of physics and by taking opportunity from chance. Indeed it is found that a small number of relatively simple structures, principles, formulae-driven processes can by sheer dint of repetition give rise to ever more complex systems. Biological systems arise from interconnecting biochemical processes within even more highly complex structures; and this, the emergence of life, continues the self-same pattern with even more fascinatingly unpredictable results. For a living thing has DNA, a structure that one scientist has called a "semiotic representation" of its environment, a recorded memory of its past by which it organizes both its survival, its future, and its persistently unpredictable evolutionary forms.

In every case of emergence the novel exercises a downward influence on what went before, and some argue that life introduces such a degree of novelty and corresponding influence upon the world that gave rise to it — especially when life emerges in the form of *homo sapiens* — that the very process of emergence itself now means that the world has purpose and significance, spiritual significance even, which it did not have at previous levels of its existence. Others argue the opposite, like Richard Dawkins, a recent evolutionary throw-back from the ranks of the biologists to the days before the physicists abandoned reductionism. It is all still a case of self-organizing structures, forms, principles of the laws of nature creatively evolving the universe we observe so that, as Dawkins puts it, "the universe we observe has precisely the properties we should expect if there is, at bottom, no design, no purpose, no evil, no good, nothing but blind, pitiless indifference."

The difference between these two very different assessments of the self-same process of emergence or creative evolution, as far as the god-hypothesis is concerned, would seem to be this. The one sees the very emergence of purpose and acting for a purpose, especially where such purposive action becomes a spiritual consciousness, as being compatible with, if not indeed the very trace of the presence of the Creator God of an evolving universe. Whereas the other sees nothing of the kind; nothing but the blind operation of structures, stateable formulae, all composed according to the laws of physical nature, and mindlessly giving rise to the cosmos as it has arisen and continues to arise. Not only is there nothing in this scenario in which one could reasonably claim to encounter a Creator Spirit; there is no gap in the emergence of the cosmos into which a divine creator could be introduced. How then to judge between those opposing assessments of an agreed scientific-cosmological scenario? It is difficult indeed to judge between them on their own terms. The question concerning the provenance of the "completely disordered" universe before Planck time 10^{-43} seconds, can safely be left aside. Partly because a completely disordered universe can mean nothing. It sounds like a contradiction in terms, because that is most probably what it is. But partly also because, even if God is invoked to put the "disordered" universe there, God is thereafter superfluous to requirements. Since the self-organizing structures take over from the moment when our universe began to emerge.

And partly, finally, because scientists like Stephen Hawking hope to give an account in accord with physical law of that prior state of universe that only lasted for 10^{-43} seconds, so that an account of the "how" of the universe as a unified set of self-organizing structures, then covers back to the absolute beginning.

The difficulty of discriminating between the two opposing views is compounded further by the fact that people who favor compatibility of this science with religious faith of one kind or another, sometime seem to suggest that only when life emerges and with it truly purposive activity, is there a basis for belief that the whole universe may have a purpose. For that could then support belief in a divine promoter of the whole cosmic drama, whose overall purpose this is. Without the emergence of life's purposefulness, the picture that would come across would remain one of self-organizing structures that simply determine all that would come to be. And then, even if some creator god were postulated in order to instill such a design of self-organizing structures into the universe, such a god would thereafter be as superfluous to cosmological requirement as the god postulated merely to put into existence the prior "completely disordered" universe.

It all amounts to a quite peculiar, confusing and possibly confused run of seemingly logical reasoning. Entities such as self-organizing structures, or genes even, act for ends such as self-propagation and advancement, yet they are not described as purposeful? Are we to attribute purpose only at the point of evolution at which self-consciousness and rational thought emerge? And is purpose to be further reduced to conscious purpose? But why so? The set of organizational principles that produced life from non-living forms is no different in essence from the set of organizational principles that produced sentient life, then self-conscious, rational life, and thereafter all the advances of this new spiritual life that rational imagination can create. And at each and every stage of this serial evolution, that same set of organizational principles has every bit just as much right to be described as being just as purposeful. Simon Conway Morris talks about life advancing itself, not by using brand new structures, especially invented for each advance, but by seizing upon existing structures, co-opting and re-engineering these in order to give rise to the unpredictable. The end product, he suggests, is a paradox because the processes of emergence implies blatant jury-rigging and improvisation, yet at the same time, on looking back over any series of processes of emergence, they seem to reveal (at least to our eyes) a seamless and beautiful adaptation. Even the new and unpredictable set of principles or structures known as life itself, emerged in just as seamless a fashion from sets that preceded it, from interconnecting biochemical processes within very complex structures, these last having emerged presumably from a relatively small number of simple self-organizing structures by sheer dint of repetition.

It certainly seems as if the only way to clear up all or most of this conceptual confusion is this. First we must recognize that these self-organizing structures, principles, formulaic processes based on natural laws, and acting in combination throughout the whole of emergence-evolution to bring about the universe as we know it, are in fact the creative forms which in the best creation theology are seen as the agencies of creation by which the divine creator creates. For structures, principles, laws, formulae and such-like do not hang about on their own, like the smile on the face of the Cheshire cat that smiles on one even after the cat has gone. And they certainly are not such agents as can act on their own to make things. Structures, laws, mathematical formulae, and so on, are all either mental abstractions from concrete existing entities; or at first products of agents' minds or mind-like entities. Considered in their abstractness they do not and cannot bring anything into existence, or any new version of things into being. The architectural plan for Jones's new home will of itself never house Jones. But a builder whose mind is informed by this structural plan may house Jones. These also, the so-called self-organizing, self-complicating structures by which the universe comes about, are equally products of mind, and only as such, only while being maintained as such by such a mind or minds, can they act. Not as agents in themselves, but rather as creative forms of concrete entities, by which an imaginative and intelligent agent brings about ever new and surprising stages of existence and life. This is a fact of the matter so simple and elementary, so entirely obvious, that it is often omitted from sophisticated discourse about self-organizing structures giving rise to ever more complex species of living things.

What one encounters when one investigates and contemplates this wonderful world either as a professional scientist or simply as everyman who every day lives and dies in and with it, is mind, or some mind-like entity. Forming, deforming and reforming the world by an originating and perpetual process that thus gives existence and life to the whole resulting universe, pouring out life without stinting. Life always evolving in this way to no foreseeable limit. And to what purpose? one feels obliged to ask; but only because some people seem to think that this is a crucial question, particularly for people who profess some kind of religious faith. To no purpose other than that, must be the answer. Simply for the purpose that life be given and shared and ever advanced across all obstacles to it, both natural and malicious; *le chaim;* until it is perfectly characterized by peace and prosperity for all; *shalom.* What we are seeing here is goodness overflowing, as goodness by its nature tends to do, in Plato's view of the matter of creation, or it is "love which must be made real in act," as Eliot put it. No ulterior motive necessary, or even welcome. Religious people who claim that God made the world for the prospect of being glorified by creatures ought to seriously reconsider their position. For, to paraphrase Dawkins, the universe we observe has precisely the properties we should expect if there is, at bottom, a designer with the purpose simply to confer eternal existence and life, eventually on free creative creatures, with the consequent emergence of good and evil, loving care and cold indifference.

It is not easy to understand how it is that some scientists cannot see the mind-like entity that reveals itself in the creation. Is it because they accept from some religious people all of this talk about transcendence as the contrary of immanence, so that what might be seen as the revelatory episodes of encounter with a presence, are mistaken for alleged evidence for the existence of an outsider, mostly absent one, who indulges in the odd intrusion? The kind of creator that so many philosophers of religion seem also to have in mind as they busily prove and disprove? Is it because philosophers and scientists alike are put off by images of God painted for them by self-proclaimed believers in the one, true God? A creator with ulterior motive? Or a god who requires the death of one man, however special, to pay for the sins of others? Or a god who is so much the god of a particular group of people that their ill treatment of others is allowed, if not even at times commanded? Or perhaps, in the case of contemporary scientists in particular, a much more mundane explanation may suggest itself. Namely, that modern scientists are mostly under the total influence of a dogma consisting of two parts: first, a crude dualism of matter and mind, in which the former must have no element of the latter in its composition; the second and consequent part, an image of matter as a body or bodies of hard stuff from which it seems to be truly impossible to explain how mind could emerge.

It could be all or any of this that explains the conceptual confusion and the deep disagreement on what is encountered at the depths of the universe. But in any event, the deep mystery that still inevitably surrounds a mind-like entity that is original source of all that exists and lives, even when the best efforts of human finite minds have been expended on investigation and contemplation, should not of itself prove off-putting to the scientist who operates at any of the levels of science, from the physical to the biological, the humane and the social. Quite to the contrary in fact. Although it must also be allowed that scientists in the name of science and with regard to its best prospects of success, may well invoke the needs of specialization and say that as scientists they should really stick to the quest for useful, practical *knowledge* of the formulae by which the cosmos operates and evolves. And leave to the moralist, the philosopher, the theologian, the quest for the *wisdom* that is revealed in those self-same processes.

Even if it is also fair to point out, in response to this point about specialization and the always rather artificial demarcation it involves, that those scientific endeavors to deal with the phenomena of mind and consciousness, their nature and origin, and their relationships to brains and bodies, would be greatly facilitated if it came to be seen that the human mind emerged from bodily matter already formed and, quite literally, always already in-formed by the infinite mind-like entity that is the continuous (from the point of view of space-time) creator of all. By comparison, talk of minds emerging from brains, consciousness emerging from matter understood in crude dualist contrast to anything that could be called soul, spirit, mind, consciousness, must be, and is proving to be most unpromising indeed. Especially since that crude dualist concept of matter, as Einstein recognized, can no longer play any fundamental role in physics. For the idea of matter that came down all the way from Democritus in ancient Greece to Newton in the Europe of the new Age of Science, was of something composed of small, hard but detectable entities, that interacted deterministically. Whereas spirit was conceived as something somewhat indefinable, hazy, but active especially in the creation of life. Physics would always be, quintessentially, particle physics, and the ultimate quest would be for the "smallest" particle of which all others, and everything was made up. But now in current physics matter, conceived of in such crude atomic-dualist terms is no longer seen as a foundational concept or image. Images of something like "fields" or "waves" from which the harder particles metamorphose, something that is resistant to much further definition through investigation of particles, hoves into view at the depths of the material universe. And it is this level of the material universe that now seems, as spirit once did, to be hazy and indefinable, but yet active in the emergence of the small, hard, formed particles that once seemed to determine the whole definition of matter.

These "fields" are forming forces, obviously, and they are themselves formed entities, for their properties can be discovered and expressed mathematically. So the question arises once more: what forms these? For the things that make up the universe only become things, they only *become* by being formed, according to a formula, a design. Without this forming, deforming, transforming there is literally no-thing. So the continuous forming requires the existence of some level of reality operative always within the universe that forms, deforms and transforms the whole universe through all of its interlocked parts. This can only be imagined as a mind-like entity, in that the human mind is the closest analogue we know for such an entity, however distant a cosmic former might be from the human mind. It certainly now appears that it is easier to understand the emergence of hard matter from matter that is always already formed by such a mind-like entity that simultaneously forms hard matter and space-time, than it is to understand the emergence of anything like mind, consciousness or spirit from matter as it has for too long been conceived and imagined in crude dualistic form. Especially if the matter of the universe as it existed before Planck time 10^{-43} seconds is imagined to have been in complete disorder (whatever that might mean) and innocent at first of any mind-like features or effects, such as self-organizing structures exemplify. In short, the suspicion now emerges that the solution of the problem of emerging consciousness, mind and so on, may well depend upon a Copernican revolution that tries to see matter emerge from some mind-like entity, rather than continue to explain how consciousness-mind can emerge from mindless matter.

In sum, there is purpose in the universe. Dawkins admits as much in countless references to genes acting for existential survival and advancement. And there is intelligence in the universe at large. Dawkins has "the selfish gene" work out ways in which to transform itself and its environment so as to advance its purpose, ever adapting its world and to its world, for the purpose of advancing its life. So far, so good. An apparently intelligent agent operates in the universe for the purpose of advancing its existence and life. Yet, left at that, the picture is as woefully oversimplistic as any picture painted by the dogmatic materialist and crudely reductionist physicist of a recently bygone age. There is a hint of such stultifying oversimplification every time a researcher in search of the explanation for a disease discovers the gene involved, but then has to look for an "epigenetic" factor in order to understand more fully how the onset of the disease is actually "triggered" in one person but not another. A small but strong hint of the need to understand that purposeful activity in the universe and the ensuing emergence of intelligent design occurs at the organic level, at the level of genera and species, and in the form of mutual adaptation, rather than purely selfish exploitative and enforced alteration of what are after all interdependent others. And that full picture, by its own ineluctable logic, reveals a cosmic purposefulness, to advance existence and life for the whole creation, as it simultaneously reveals the cosmic intelligence that supplies and ever applies the dynamic formulae by which that purpose is pursued.

What is dimly but increasingly perceived, then, in any truly cosmic contemplation is a shared purpose and a shared intelligence, some mind-like entity acting in and through the whole universe that drives its achievement through the application of dynamic forms. As ready remarked, that perception is not such as to deify the universe in some pantheistic fashion. Rather is the creative interaction of mind and matter best imagined as the interaction of these two ultimate types of reality, with the existential priority throughout all creation going to the former, something that is in fact depicted rather well in terms of the double imagery of the Bible. The mind-like entity lives and moves through all creatures, we live and move in it, and thereby is maintained a *uni*verse, instead of what would otherwise be an impending chaos of competing things, essentially destined for mutual annihilation. A local example of this otherwise possible fate is seen in the still dominant behavior of our own species, described in the Bible under the rubric of what later theology called original sin.

The whole history of the natural cosmos then comprises the revelation to imaginative-intelligent animals of the Creator Spirit, of that Creator Spirit's way with the world, and of the corresponding creative ways of *homo sapiens* that will lead to the life unlimited that is eternally on offer. The revelation inspires goodness for the goodness of life received, love for the love shown, faith in what is revealed, and in the formulations of it of which the best of humankind is capable. It inspires trust in the creative powers and processes discerned, by which life advances, and in which one must also discern and continuously reformulate one's co-creative contribution. And it inspires hope in the ultimate happy outcome for all. And it is all natural revelation, the revelation that comes through the natural creation and that constitutes as it does so the once and always covenant of creation, designating its signatories, its terms and its promises. According to this scenario, the process of human rational and imaginative knowing is one in which reality revealing itself from its very depths and increasing heights is perceived by *homo sapiens* — at least on the odd occasions on which she is wise — in the course of the very praxis of her cooperating with it in that dynamic activity by which she works with it for life and life ever more abundant, in fidelity and hope. Then the three graces known as revelation, reason and faith cannot be kept apart in separate compartments, with reason in one and revelation and faith in the other. Quite to the contrary, revelation, reason and faith are members of a true trinity, a veritable tri-unity, whereby the life-wisdom project of humanity subsists simultaneously in all three, and they in it.

But that, someone from any one of the particular religious faiths of the world might object, is to confine attention to what can be called general revelation. It leaves entirely out of account what can only be called special revelations. And even a Christian should know better than that. For after all, Christians do describe their active faith as a following of Jesus of Nazareth. If that does not imply that Jesus was the recipient and the embodiment of a special revelation from the Creator Spirit, why bother wearing the Christian insignia? Further, if it is allowed that Jesus brought to the world a special revelation of God, what on earth is there to prevent anyone from calling it supernatural? At least in the sense of coming from a transcendent realm above and beyond nature; impervious to the highest and best investigations of human reason, and in consequence, to be embraced by that very kind of faith that is so often rather archly dismissed by the (ab)use of the adjective, blind?

All that can be done in response to such pressing questioning is to repeat all that has been said above about the foundational covenant of creation, about its centrality in the Bible, and most particularly in the teaching and life of Jesus as that is recorded for us by his early followers. For there is nothing in that teaching, that life, death and destiny, nothing about life as the primordial grace of God, nothing about the glad cost and the natural manner of its sustenance and advance equally for all, nothing about the origin of evil, nothing about the suffering that has to be borne in the course of the only way to overcome that evil, nothing about the limitless hope with which we are then blessed, nothing that we cannot verify from our own natural experience of life in this universe. Although we may have to wait for the verification of the final part, and for the final confirmation of all of it, until we reach the last rite of passage, the death of our current bodily form of existence, and the entrance into a life we hope to be characterized by eternity rather than time. And if there is nothing that we cannot verify about all of this, then there is nothing about it that we could not have known in the first place. Yet knowing here does not refer to mere knowledge, but to wisdom, to knowing how to live a true life and walk in a true way to the fullness of life. And once we stray from that way and start living a destructive and a self-destructive life and set out on a path of perdition, it can be extremely difficult to bring us back onto the true path again. It almost certainly cannot be done merely by imparting to us some knowledge about the whole thing in more or less theoretical form. It takes someone who lives the true human life, to breathe into us once again the spirit that empowers and enlightens.

But that, according to all that has so far been said, is the Creator Spirit or Word, that enlivens and enlightens every one who comes into the world. It is the Holy Spirit who is at work equally in the inner mind and heart of *homo sapiens,* and whose presence is sometimes, somehow sensed there, if only in our dim and always form-mediated experience of a level of consciousness that has no distinctive form of its own, but appears darkly as unformed, unlimited, infinite. And neither then does that say any more about Jesus than can be said about the rest of us? No, except perhaps this: that the power and light of that Creator Spirit brought to bear on Jesus, both through the created world in general and particularly within the human spirit of Jesus, made of Jesus's life and death and teaching both the perfect human embodiment of that Creator Spirit, and the perfect inspiration and enlightenment of the human race. Something that can be expressed both in the incarnational terms of the indwelling of the fullness of the Godhead bodily in Jesus, and in terms of the Jesus thereby risen to lordship being described as himself sinless and a life-giving spirit. Whether the Creator Spirit put in more work, as it were, in revealing Spirit at work through the wide world and simultaneously in Jesus's own spirit, than the same Creator Spirit puts in with respect to the rest of us, who habitually make the Holy Spirit in our world and in our hearts share power over us with other, satanic spirits, we do not know, possibly cannot know, and most probably do not need to know. For when all is said and done, the claim that the writers of the rNT made concerning Jesus, final prophet and son of God in power, and the claim that we repeat as his self-proclaimed followers, is a claim concerning a historical fact. And so it is still a claim that, for others as for ourselves, can be verified only by the experience of our lives in their entirety.

The special revelation, in this Christian case at least, is then a special case or incident of the general revelation in all of creation. Jesus is the incarnation of the Word that enlightens every one who comes into the world, as John the evangelist worded the matter in the most popular incarnation text of the Bible. And that really should be the end our affairs with these invidious if seductive dichotomies of nature and grace, reason and revelation, immanence and transcendence, affairs which for too long tempted us to posture as the graced, enlightened and transcendent partners of inferiors all around.

Religions

Somebody quite important, someone like the Irish bishop-philosopher George Berkeley (but one cannot be sure), once opined that God was concerned very little, if indeed at all, with religion. Whoever it was that thus opined, certainly cast a cool, clear light on a subject that so often elicits from partisans and despisers alike far more fire and furore than light. And then there is the reasonably well attested fact that Jesus of Nazareth, to whom we trace the faith we call Christian, acted and spoke as if institutional religion was certainly not unconditionally essential in his vision of the future of that faith. He was very critical indeed of the central institutions of the religion into which he was born, on the grounds that these continued to corrupt a faith as old and available as creation itself, and he appears to have made little more than a symbolic gesture toward any religious institutions that might be needed to follow or, if that proved necessary, to supplant them. Further, John the evangelist's understanding of Jesus's vision of worshipers practicing their faith, not in temples or any such buildings, but "in spirit and truth," together with Stephen Martyr's understanding that the whole world was the house in which God provides for all people, suggests once again a faith in God and in God's good world that can be engendered, held and practiced without more ado in all of the natural world and so, presumably, in any and every human society.

The relationship between a religious faith and an institutional religion is both complex and shifting. And just as complex and shifting is the relationship between a non-religious faith — that is to say, a culture to which a people is committed, and which contains a comprehensive *weltan-schauung* comprised of knowledge, know-how, promise, faith and hope, but without the religious dimension — on the one hand, and both the so-called secular institutions, together with any religious institutions that may be operative in the secular state, on the other. In general it is probably uncontroversial to claim that both faiths and institutionalized embodiments of these are equally human products in the manner and substance of their expression and formulation. And both are therefore subject in their emergence and continuance to the age-old and apparently everlasting temptation to original sin. Both can be turned by their creators and maintainers into a possession that is theirs and to their advantage alone, or at least predominantly so. And both can feed, rather than neutralize the tendency to aggrandize oneself at the expense of others. Unless of course the others submit or join in, and pay tribute in money or in kind, and usually in both. But in both cases the institutionalized structures, secular or sacred, are by nature more conservative, not to say reactionary, to the necessary change which life itself entails at all levels and in every species of human society. They embody naturally and well-nigh inevitably what Marx called the *vis inertiae* of history. One can see this in our present war-infested world, whether one looks to Christian countries, Muslim countries, or atheistic communist countries.

In the case of Christianity then the words of Bishop Berkeley (if they were his) come true, in that it is clearly possible to be a disciple of Jesus of Nazareth, to follow in the faith he taught and lived, and not be a member, or cease to be a member of any of the institutional churches into which the Christian religion has differentiated and thereby simultaneously enriched and impoverished itself over the course of two millennia. For the faith that Christians trace back to Jesus, thus giving the reason for proclaiming themselves his followers, is a faith that he himself identified as a creation faith. This possibility of avoiding ecclesiastical allegiance is widely verified in practice today, in the widespread practice of people leaving the institutional churches of Christianity, usually because they experience teachings imposed upon them, and especially moral teachings that they know to be false and alien to the spirit of Jesus. They can come upon such conclusions in one of two ways. Either by their own efforts to study their faith in its origins in Jesus and the rNT — in the course of this study alone many distortions by the institutionalized religion called Christianity of the faith that emerges from the teaching and life of Jesus are noted — or through their own experience of living in and with God's good creation, together with their sound common moral and spiritual sense of the truth that is thereby conveyed. And in either case, although some of them still stay in their churches, usually only to see themselves derided as a la carte Christians, most leave, not to return, but to bring with them into the wider world the faith in a good God and in God's good world, and to continue to live as good a life as they can.

But what of those who leave their religious institutions and, as so many also do, say that they leave behind also their faith in the Creator, or indeed in any god in any name, shape or form? What if they leave in order to join the ranks of the atheistic or secular humanists, or indeed no ranks at all, other than the natural societies of family or nation state to which as social animals they already belong, and whose institutional governments they can change when they think it necessary to do so in the interests of truth, justice and progress toward an ever better life? These too can (continue to) be inspired with gratitude, and enlightened for living by this good world and by whatever powers there are within it that produce the profusion of life, together with all the supports and enhancements of life. And they can sense a promise there and a hope for ever better life, to which they may feel, at times at least, they can set no prior limits. After all, some responsible modern physicists who have no time for gods, talk quite seriously about the possibilities of eternal life for some successors of ours, and possibly through them for us also.

These same people too can learn the hard way both of the ancient temptation and original sin of the race, and of the punishing suffering that, when yielded to and committed, it always brings upon sinners and innocents alike. They can learn too that the reversal of such destruction of life and its promises cannot take the form of returning evil to those who do evil, but only by returning good for evil, just as the good world continues to pour out life in abundance to the good and the bad without discrimination. It is difficult indeed to overestimate the humanist implications of the combined principles "the Sabbath was made for man," and "God will have steadfast love before sacrifice." Especially when these sayings are combined with the biblical advice: it is not those who in confessional mood cry "Lord. Lord," but those who do the will of God, who will see the reign of God in all of its goodness, truth and beauty. Together these sayings point to the fact that the purpose of divine creation is contained within the action of continuous creation itself: it is the provision of life eternal to all. And so, at the point of a human being's best, it is possible to be able to hope for life beyond every kind of death. As Ernst Bloch, the renegade Marxist, did when in his humanist philosophy of hope, *Das Prinzip Hoffnung*, he felt himself able to put a question mark after death's apparent finality. Humanist implications of such depth and extent must then reckon with the belief that any human being who cooperates in this permanent creation of life, and who hopes in the advance of life's forms through the deaths of previous forms, is de facto doing God's will, and is always already judged in the self-same manner as Christians are judged, and will receive the same bounty of eternal life in the end.

So the very last laborers who turn up and work in the Lord's vineyard will receive exactly the same as the ones who turned up first; every man a penny. Even the ones who cannot call on the name of God for the cosmic powers that timelessly provide existence and life. Perhaps because they are put off using that name by religious folk who act as if they had a monopoly of that name, and then, more usually than not, paint a picture of a being unworthy of the name of God. Or it might be because the agnostic humanists insist that they really do not know in any expressible manner what this "God" word connotes. For these last, although they may not know it, simply forefront that great agnostic element that always figures largely in the talk of the most thoughtful of traditional believers.

Finally, what more needs to be said concerning religions, those societal structures that are formed from combinations of institutions in charge of credos, codes, cults and constitutions, and of the people who accept and participate in these, and that are separate from the equivalent institutions that characterize so-called secular, civil and political society? Not very much needs to be added about these to what has already emerged in the analysis of Christianity the religion.

First, perhaps, the point can be made that they are not absolutely necessary at all, in addition, that is to say, to the normal structures and institutions of secular society. For, as the agnostic humanist position illustrates, faiths, rational beliefs about life in this universe, can be lived, formulated, advanced and handed on in the normal and natural course of human beings organizing themselves into societies, and protecting and promoting their lives as integral and interdependent parts of the whole living world. And it should not really matter whether the majority of the people and of the leaders who are the ministers of the institutions of their nation states are humanists of the overt theistic, or of the agnostic or of the atheistic kind, and whether, in consequence of a majority in its favor, the overt language of God and of religious faith forms an integral part of the language and symbolism of public, civic and political discourse. Or whether, where the agnostics or atheists are in the majority, overt religious language may be confined to sub-groupings within civic society, but within such restrictions, with equal right to a public presence and a full part in pubic ethical and political discourse. This is because it is the same natural revelation of the ways of the universe and of the creative powers that operate within it, from which life emerges and by which it is sustained and advanced, that all have their knowledge of all of this, their appreciation of, and fidelity and responsibility to it, and the hopes that need know no prior limitation.

The second thing that needs to be said about an institutional religion, and once again from the Christian point of view, is this. Although institutional religion is not strictly necessary for the emergence, the maintenance or the advance of a living and life-promising faith in the full reality perceivable in our universe, it is something so useful for the survival through the erosions of time of the particularly religious dimensions of the faiths by which all peoples live, that prudent people would always try to provide it. Even in a case where the alleged founder of a faith appears to have done little or nothing about it. The ancient temptation, after all, is always there, the temptation for groups of people, or indeed for the whole race of *homo sapiens,* to think that the whole world existed for their need and benefit, and that they have the whole wisdom to use it as they wish in order to secure for themselves as much and as good a living as possible, at whatever the cost in death-dealing and destruction either to fellow-humans or to other creatures.

Against this most natural and insidious of temptations, the larger and more life-promising wisdom that knows of that same wisdom's divine depths and provenance, forever finds it difficult either to emerge or to survive intact for any length of time over all the earth. It is therefore quite commonplace, and it makes for eminent common sense, that among those who think they witness the emergence or reemergence of a living and life-promoting wisdom and faith, some would feel called to the vocation involved in making special provision for its maintenance and its natural evolution; and would select other appropriate people to minister to that faith and to all people who might then be invited to see it and live it out in their lives also. But these ministers, together with the ministries of the institution of which they are then the officers, must take themselves, as their title implies, to be serving to people what is always already there for these people. Something that comes up from the dark depth of the world, like the wheat that comes from the earth and is processed by human hands, and the wine that God brings burning from the sod and humans crush from the grape and leave to ferment. The grace of life and the light that accompanies it, to reveal dimly its eternal source, and even more dimly still its fullest form. And always in any case the way to live in its warmth and illumination, in interdependence with all other created things, so that its furthest promise may be realized more speedily for all.

The third and final and corresponding thing that must be said, is that institutional religion, and certainly Christianity the religion, is always a human construct. It is itself a work of human hands and manned by ordinary men and women who are no more gifted by the grace of God than the rest of us. Nor are they any more than the rest of us ring-fenced from the incursions of the original temptation and the weakness of the race. Jesus apparently promoted to the leadership of the largely symbolic leadership group of the Twelve the disciple who badly mistook the real truth of what appeared to be his true confession of Jesus, and who, every bit as much as Judas, roundly betrayed and abandoned Jesus when the enemy came to kill. And the institutional churches that splinter in successive attempts to correct Christianity the religion's persistent failures to live the grace and tell the truth that came in its fullness in Jesus the Christ, all in their turn at one time or another, and in one way or another, have distorted that truth and worked against that grace. So that, if Christianity the religion is anything to go by, one must say of religions as has already been said of Christian churches, that there is most probably no one, true religion, but that all exhibit in different measures percentages of truth and diminished truth and downright falsehood, of grace and disgrace.

Therefore, the only right way in which the Christian religion, in any of its versions, can relate to other religions, is this. Christians must recognize the fact that the revelation that is at the heart of Christianity through the mediation of Jesus of Nazareth is a revelation that has been available always through the medium of the creation itself to all. This is the truth of the matter, so clearly expressed in the prologue to John's Gospel, when he said that the Word that was then incarnate in Jesus, was the same Creator Word that enlightens every one who comes into this world. Christians must then recognize the fact that they have regularly distorted the truth of the faith of Jesus, in various ways and to varying degrees over virtually the whole history of their religion. And they must therefore conclude that they are as likely to learn from other religions, if not indeed from agnostic forms of humanism, as they may hope to teach them. That lesson for Christians is illustrated with reasonable clarity in the earliest Christian efforts to give their faith a philosophical form of expression, a theology, when they began and ended up borrowing virtually the whole of that theology from the Greeks. (The same illustration is on offer for a similar lesson that might be learned by the other two religions in this monotheistic family, Judaism and Islam, for they also borrowed the same Greek philosophy when they first theologized their respective faiths.) But it is much more graphically illustrated, and once again from the beginning, when Christianity, especially in the course of its expansion beyond the bounds of the Roman Empire, encountered and encultured itself in religious cultures that had not become Romanized.

Patrick, in his extant *Confession*, makes it very clear, as our politicians are wont to say, what his program was to be when he arrived on Irish shores as a missionary bishop sent to convert that country to Christianity. He writes of the Irish as *barbaras itaque gentes*, a barbarian people that worshiped *idola et immunda*, idols and unclean things. So, in his own mind, he set about supplanting their satanic myths and cults with the one, true religion. But it is perfectly clear from the recorded history of Christianity in Ireland, as this can be seen from early texts written both in Latin and in Irish, the oldest recorded written vernacular still extant in Europe, that this was not at all what happened in the course of ancient Ireland's speedy transition to the Christian faith. What happened instead is that the Christianity that was already thoroughly encultured in Greco-Roman religion, its languages, imagery, ideas, ethos, ritual and institutions, was now thoroughly re-encultured in a country that neither Greece nor Rome had ever conquered. And in the event, a very early and a very striking lesson had already emerged for the manner in which Christians must think about the relationship of Christianity to other religions.

What then did the Irish do on conversion to Christianity? Ignoring, as has been their wont, the views of a poorly educated West Briton, Bishop Patrick, they proceeded to see to it that their traditional divine trinities and some other members of the *Tuatha De*, the extended family of divine personae, played some pivotal roles in their new-found religion. As already noted Brigid (herself a trinity) and Lug, a creator god and goddess, continued to hold on the Christian liturgical calendar their ancient places and roles in the continuous creation of the world. Lug and Brigid were now saints, of course, although Lug also turned up in early Irish Christian religion in the guise of the archangel, Michael, an ancient personification of divinity. So all of that did not involve too much of a demotion. For, as great and mighty saints, these two ranked just beneath the Three Persons of the Christian Trinity and Mary, the Mother of God. And this ranking of these great saints must be assessed in the context in which the Creator God descends *into* what is thereby created by becoming present, sequentially, in Son-Word, in Holy Spirit, in Mary, in angels, in the great saints ... and even in the very elements of the created world, in the forms of water and wind, earth and fire. So that the Irish could invoke any of these, for life, its protection and promotion. For the power and presence of the Creator Spirit constantly comes into the world and operated there through an unbroken channel, as it were, comprised of all of these.

In addition, these new converts brought back in various ways others of their traditional divine personae: Cu Chulainn in his ghostly chariot; Fionn through his prophesying; Ossian, son of Fionn, in the flesh.... Why? So that these should specifically endorse the truth and validity of the incoming faith. But why did the Irish feel that they needed such endorsement from their own divine personae for the religion of Jesus Christ, the son of God? The usual answer to that question is given in the form: the Irish wanted their own Original Testament. In the Bible the Israelite Original Testament is used by Jesus-followers in order to endorse what came to be a new religion in the name of Jesus the Christ. But the Hebrew name of the God of that Original Testament meant nothing to the Irish: he would sound to them like a strange tribal divinity, as the god (of) Jesus sounded to the Athenians at the Areopagus.

These are satisfactory answers as far as they go. But the real light on the problem that concerns us here, the problem of the relationship of Christianity to other religions, shines only when we push a little further the analysis of what is really going on here. And it is this. In having their own divine personae endorse, and then take their place in this newly arrived religion, these early Irish are themselves endorsing the truth and validity of Christianity from all that they already know of God and the world through their own traditional religious faith. They are bearing witness to their new (creation) faith by using as their criterion the truth of their traditional (creation) faith. Of course, in switching over to the new religion they are allowing, implicitly at least, that the new is in some respects an improvement on the old, just as the first followers of Jesus did with respect to their traditional religion. Yet, as we have already seen, the Irish also correct their new religion by reference to elements of their traditional faith. As Columbanus does when he lectures the reigning pope on the terms and conditions of the latter's authority over the church, referring on that occasion to the criterion of the *fir flathemon,* the truth of the prince, the wisdom and righteousness that comes, or is not allowed to come, to the prince from God.

In order to feel the full import of this dual witness, at once to the truth and to some shortcomings of their own religion, and then on the criterion of their traditional faith, to the truth and yet some encroaching shortcomings of the incoming religion, simply think about the alternative. For the alternative is crudely but clearly expressed in Patrick's ignorant prattle about barbarity and idolatry, together with his intention to root out the lot of it. And the implications of this alternative are clear. The one, true God, Father Almighty, creator of heaven and earth had left these Irish people in darkness, in error and evil, without a true testament of any kind. And had revealed the divine life-giving and saving presence and promise, both for this life and the next, to some other people in some other time and place. And then left it to the vagaries of the moods, the fidelities or infidelities of this chosen people to take that testament, that truth and life to other peoples meanwhile abandoned to their satanic prisons on earth. You only have to say it like that in order to realize that no people with any sense of truth and justice in this world would accept as true God a god like that, a god so small and petty-minded and partisan, or would dream of converting to the cause of those who preached such a god. Nor, one could well opine, would that same one, true God be at all pleased to hear some self-appointed missionaries, like Patrick, painting such a distorted picture of the steadfast divine love that is forever made real in act in the continuous creation of all that lives and moves and has its being.

Therefore the early Irish, as we can see from their deeds rather than from their words on the subject — for many converts of Patrick did repeat his regrettable sentiments — did bear witness to the truth of their traditional faith in the true God who was revealed in their own time and place, their own history and culture. And with that as their criterion they were then able to bear witness to the truth of the incoming faith. Just as the Jews did who followed Jesus, just as Paul asked the Athenians to do when he reminded them of the Creator God that their own poets (that is to say, their myth-makers) had so aptly described to them.

The much later and much grander expansion of missionary Christianity to "the new world," and to "the heart of darkest Africa" regressed regrettably to Patrick's destructive formula. In consequence, the damage that was done to religion and religious faith contributed to, and kept pace with the awesome and still unreversed damage to lands and livelihoods, and to the very fabric of society itself, that was done by greedy imperialists whose principal purpose in practice, so poorly disguised under the declared purpose of civilizing savages (the barbarity theme again), was the aggrandizement of themselves at the expense of these unfortunate others.

And yet, over this vast arena also, the indigenous peoples of Latin America kept alive the essence of their ancient faiths in their own distinctive forms of Christianity. Just as Africa is currently experiencing phenomenal growth of indigenous Christian churches, where churches planted by European missionaries are static by comparison, if not in some decline. For the indigenous Christian churches in Africa commonly incorporate significant elements of traditional faiths, and thereby modify both Christianity and the traditional religions in which it is now encultured.

So that the dual witness is heard once more, to the truth of traditional faiths and the truth of the Christian faith. And that witness, on a little reflection, can yield the proposal that perhaps the best outcome for religious faith in the world as a whole would consist in the enculturation of the Christian faith in any or all of the family of world religions, or, alternatively, in the enculturation of any or all of these into Christianity, or in any combination of these options. For all religious faiths in the world are world religions in the dual sense that each is a total *Weltanschauung*, however localized in its incidence it may be, and each is therefore translatable into any other religious culture in the world. For as the faith of Jesus was embodied or encultured in the cultural categories of image and idea, ethos, ritual and institution, first in the ancient land of Israel, and then predominantly in the Roman Empire, so it can be embodied and become a religion in equivalent cultural categories anywhere in the world. Perhaps the best example of this, before the barbarian idolatry syndrome took over once more, was the attempt of some Jesuits in the seventeenth century to enculture their Christianity in the cultural categories of China, an attempt that finally faltered on opposition from Catholic church leaders in the European homeland. The reason for such widespread possibilities of enculturation and re-enculturation of faiths is that all are at bottom creation faiths.

Meanwhile back at the ranch, in Christianity's traditional Mediterranean and European stamping ground, and in yet more recent times, some of the stoutest philosophical critics of Christianity, whether professedly atheistic or agnostic, or downright indifferent to that religion, were nevertheless bearing witness to some of its most distinctive elements. Nietzsche was restoring the true connotation of world creation. As he did so he lampooned the self-styled rationalists of the Age of Reason for their lack of faith; addressing them with incisive irony as "you who are paintings (still life, presumably) of all that ever has been believed." While hinting in his references to the Super-Man that the creator of worlds is no ordinary human being, and not even the whole lot of these ordinary human beings so far put together. Marx quite rightly regarded his native Judaism and his unwillingly acquired Christianity — like all religions, he said — as forces for inertia holding back the advancement of the world. Yet he shaped his philosophy of humanity advancing its extended body by reissuing the fundamental principle of the service of all to all: from each according to her gift, to each according to his needs.

Even Sartre, at least for those who can penetrate his all-but-impenetrable metaphysics, paints a picture of the rather unfortunately named *Pour-soi* or For-itself as a being constituted of consciousness, yet not at all the kind or level of human consciousness to which the awareness of finite things seems constitutive. And since Sartre's description of the relationship between this Absolute, this For-itself, and the material world is so reminiscent of the Absolute in both Eastern and Western philosophical theology, he reminds his readers inevitably of the fact that the accompanying "mysticism" is but a theoretical description of a journey common to East and West. A journey that all must travel on the well-sign-posted "way" through all finite, mortal modes of being to the Source and home of all creation. Indeed, if one put together these defining ingredients of the philosophies of Sartre, Nietzsche and Marx — the Absolute (Consciousness), the evolutionary creation, and the universal ethos of the service of others — one would have in one's hands a tolerable recipe from which to cook a very edible theology of the essence of the Christian faith for today.

Such is the host of witnesses from people of every kind, place and time, to the same Creator Spirit eternally active and revealed in all of creation. And if any one of these witnesses entertains the idea that the same Creator Spirit is active and revealed more fully and clearly in the words and life of Jesus of Nazareth than in any other place or time or person in the history of the world, then such a one must first ascertain that she has the true and uncompromised faith of Jesus adequately in view. She can do this by checking both the biblical source and the history of the religion that professes to embody and express that faith in its purity. When she sees, as she must see in these sources, evidences that corruptions of the faith of Jesus always sit beside, or before and after the truer forms of it, she may feel all the more called to go on a mission to recall religion to the purest form of faith. Her mission must then begin with her own church, and beyond that with the Christian religion itself. She has no business starting with other religions before she has tackled her own. Unless of course she judges that her own Christian religion is so compromised, in her own

Christian church at least, that it is unlikely to be properly reformed and representative of the truth, the way and the life that Jesus lived and died. Then she can go to some other church, or to some other available religion, like Buddhism, for instance, that is brought by its representatives to her native shore.

But whenever a Christian feels called upon to spread the true faith of Jesus to other people, to members of any other religion or of none, she must go in the conviction that the eternal Creator of Life signs the same testament and offers the self-same covenant to the benefit of all creatures, and that any or all are as likely as she to know that. She will take herself and her mission therefore to be, first and foremost, a confirmation of the one and only true faith there is, creation faith, no matter what the manner in which it may be embodied and expressed in the particular creed, code, cult and institution that characterize any other religion. She may find that her witness as a Christian to the creation faith as revealed in Jesus works to the improvement, or even to the correction of some essential elements in some other religion. But she must be equally prepared to discover that the witness to creation faith, as it is embodied and expressed in some other religion, or in some so-called secular philosophy offers an improvement, or even a necessary correction to the Christian religion as she knows and practices it. Only in such clear, if somewhat complicated terms can the role of Christianity among the religions and the religionless of the world be properly understood, and acted out in line with the words, actions and attitudes of the prophet and son of God, Jesus of Nazareth.